30 JAN 2025

WITHDRAWN

SOCIOLOGY OF SPORT: A GLOBAL SUBDISCIPLINE IN REVIEW

RESEARCH IN THE SOCIOLOGY OF SPORT

Series Editor: Kevin Young

Recent Volumes:

RESEARCH IN THE SOCIOLOGY OF SPORT   VOLUME 9

SOCIOLOGY OF SPORT: A GLOBAL SUBDISCIPLINE IN REVIEW

EDITED BY

KEVIN YOUNG

Department of Sociology, University of Calgary, Canada

Emerald

United Kingdom – North America – Japan
India – Malaysia – China

Emerald Group Publishing Limited
Howard House, Wagon Lane, Bingley BD16 1WA, UK

First edition 2017

British Library Cataloguing in Publication Data
A catalogue record for this book is available from the British Library

ISBN: 978-1-78635-050-3
ISSN: 1476-2854 (Series)

Printed and bound by CPI Group (UK) Ltd, Croydon, CR0 4YY

ISOQAR certified
Management System,
awarded to Emerald
for adherence to
Environmental
standard
ISO 14001:2004.

Certificate Number 1985
ISO 14001

INVESTOR IN PEOPLE

For pioneer sociologists of sport everywhere, alive and deceased, who never knew a fiftieth anniversary might ever be celebrated.

CONTENTS

AUSTRALASIA

EUROPE

LIST OF CONTRIBUTORS

Cora Burnett   Department of Sport and Movement
                             Studies, University of Johannesburg,
                             Johannesburg, South Africa

Raúl Cadaa   Cátedra Libre de Sociología del Deporte,
                             Universidad Nacional de La Plata, La
                             Plata, Argentina

Miguel Cornejo   Departamento de Educación Física,
   Amestica   Universidad de Concepción,
                             Concepción, Chile

Tamás Dóczi   Department of Social Sciences, University
                             of Physical Education, Budapest, Hungary

Dong Jinxia   Department of Physical Education, Peking
                             University, Beijing, China

Andrea Gál   Department of Social Sciences, University
                             of Physical Education, Budapest, Hungary

Chris Hallinan   Monash Indigenous Centre, Monash
                             University, Melbourne, Australia

Stéphane Héas   Department of Sport and Physical
                             Activities, University of Rennes,
                             Rennes, France

John Horne   School of Sport and Wellbeing, University
                             of Central Lancashire, Preston, UK

Jorid Hovden   Department of Sociology and Political
                             Science, The Norwegian University of
                             Science and Technology,
                             Trondheim, Norway

Steven Jackson   School of Physical Education, Sport &
                             Exercise Sciences, University of Otago,
                             Dunedin, New Zealand

Annelies Knoppers	Utrecht School of Governance, Utrecht University, Utrecht, The Netherlands
Eunha Koh	Independent Scholar, Seoul, South Korea
Pasi Koski	Department of Teacher Education, University of Turku, Rauma, Finland
Mathangi Krishnamurthy	Department of Humanities and Social Sciences, Indian Institute of Technology Madras, Chennai, India
Markus Lamprecht	Lamprecht & Stamm Sozialforschung und Beratung, Zurich, Switzerland
Liu Lingnan	School of Management, Beijing Sports University, Beijing, China
Dominic Malcolm	School of Sport, Exercise and Health Sciences, Loughborough University, Loughborough, UK
Veena Mani	Department of Humanities and Social Sciences, Indian Institute of Technology Madras, Chennai, India
Wanderley Marchi Júnior	Department of Physical Education, Federal University of Parana, Curitiba, Brazil
Roy McCree	Sir Arthur Lewis Institute of Social and Economic Studies, The University of the West Indies, Trinidad and Tobago
Jeffrey Montez de Oca	Department of Sociology, University of Colorado, Colorado Springs, CO, USA
Siegfried Nagel	Institute of Sport Science, University of Bern, Bern, Switzerland
Chiaki Okada	Graduate School of Human Sciences, Osaka University, Osaka, Japan
Núria Puig	National Institute of Physical Education of Catalonia (INEFC), Barcelona, Spain

Kolbjørn Rafoss   College of Sport Sciences, The Arctic
                     University of Norway, Tromsø, Norway

Patrice Régnier   Department of Sport and Physical
                     Activities, University of Rennes,
                     Rennes, France

Parissa Safai   School of Kinesiology and Health Science,
                     York University, Toronto, Canada

Caterina Satta   Department of Humanities, University of
                     Ferrara, Ferrara, Italy

Irena Slepičková   Faculty of Physical Education and Sport,
                     Charles University in Prague, Prague,
                     Czech Republic

Hanspeter Stamm   Lamprecht & Stamm Sozialforschung und
                     Beratung, Zurich, Switzerland

Marc Theeboom   Department of Sport and Movement
                     Sciences, Vrije Universiteit Brussel,
                     Brussels, Belgium

Jasper Truyens   Department of Sport and Movement
                     Sciences, Vrije Universiteit Brussel,
                     Brussels, Belgium

Kazuo Uchiumi   Department of Economics, Hiroshima
                     University of Economics,
                     Hiroshima, Japan

Anna Vilanova   National Institute of Physical Education of
                     Catalonia (INEFC), Barcelona, Spain

Kevin Young   Department of Sociology, University of
                     Calgary, Calgary, Canada

ACKNOWLEDGEMENTS

I would like to thank Michael Atkinson, Jay Coakley, Chris Hallinan, Steven Jackson, Jim McKay and Emma Stevenson for their help and support with this project.

INTRODUCTION

Kevin Young

OCCASION, OBJECTIVE, OUTCOME

This volume marks not one but two anniversaries. Most importantly, the subdiscipline known usually (but inconsistently) as "sociology of sport" recently celebrated the 50th anniversary of its global body, the International Sociology of Sport Association, and its flagship journal, the *International Review for the Sociology of Sport*. A far more modest, but second, anniversary relates to this book series, *Research in the Sociology of Sport*, as it approaches its 10th volume. This is the ninth volume; Volume 10 will quickly follow. Over the past 14 years, the previous eight volumes have dealt with a cluster of sociological matters: theory, risk/pain/injury, the Olympics, sport subcultures, cultural diversity, qualitative methods, indigeneity, and sport, social development, and peace. Including this volume, nearly 200 authors have contributed their ideas culminating in, at this point, an impressive corpus of research papers and knowledge. It is a genuine pleasure to acknowledge both anniversaries with the publication of "RSS9."

The underpinning objective of this volume is very simple. At a time when an often marginalized subfield reaches a half century anniversary, it seems both fitting and useful to take stock of "what's out there" in as inclusive and global a fashion as possible. Of course, not every country or region is represented, nor could it be for all sorts of logistical reasons. If "sociology of sport" exists at all, it does so in fairly predictable places and for fairly predictable reasons having to do with the development, institutionalization, and political economy of education of those settings. Entire blocks of the world are neither well represented in our discipline nor in this book – Africa being the most glaring example. As one of the American leaders of our field has been arguing for some time, the global distribution of sociology of sport knowledge is fundamentally uneven (Coakley, 2007).

That said, I am confident that this volume represents the most inclusive set of subfield summaries ever collated in one source. As two small comparisons, Part Four of Coakley and Dunning's well known, well cited and well respected compendium, *Handbook of Sport Studies*, published by Sage in 2000 ("Sport and Society Research around the Globe") featured brief articles representing 12 different countries, approximately half as many as this volume. Further, the mammoth special issue of the *IRSS* published in 2015 (Pike, Jackson, & Wenner, 2015) certainly highlighted the work of many international scholars scattered around the world (50 to be exact) and thus many international sport issues and experiences, but its primary focus was substantive research, not state-of-play commentaries on the health of the subfield per se in certain places. In this respect, while there have been several thoughtful historical reviews of the subfield (Ingham & Donnelly, 1997; Jackson, 2015; Malcolm, 2014; Pike et al., 2015), this volume represents perhaps the most ambitious and comprehensive overall review of global sociology of sport undertaken to date.

The sociology of sport has grown impressively since its inception in the 1950s and has become robust and diverse, though again uneven. In addition to countries such as the United States, Canada, and the United Kingdom where it is difficult to imagine a scholarly scene without a sociology of sport presence, many countries now boast strong scholars in the field and fascinating research is being done. For instance, Latin American sociology of sport is expanding quickly, and South Korea and Japan have had organized and vibrant sociology of sport communities for some time. Individual or small groups of scholars interested in sociology of sport have bubbled up in other parts of the globe (such as the Middle East, the Caribbean, and India) where there is relatively little institutional infrastructure or help.

To relative degrees, being a sociologist of sport is no cakewalk and, despite the fact that all disciplines develop differentially in social contexts, there seem to be some common denominator challenges across the globe. As so many of the chapters to follow attest and recount, in departments of physical education, kinesiology, and exercise science, the biomechanists and lab researchers who understand sport as a chilly chi square or a blob in a test tube scoff at the touchy-feely nature of our craft ("What do you mean, *'critical'*?!") and the mere possibility of something like qualitative fieldwork or auto-ethnography being "real" science (Bairner, 2012), while in the parent discipline mainstream sociologists often struggle to see sport as a social entity at all. As many readers of this volume know, this is a long and depressing story, but the fact that so few (actually, *almost no*) introduction-to-sociology textbooks feature a chapter on sport (a social institution that surely shapes human lives in impacting ways) is a testament to the often asociological character of sociology itself. To quote one of my own mainstream sociology colleagues from a department meeting some time ago, "What does sport have to do with work and occupations anyway?" While C. Wright Mills performs crocodile rolls in his grave, the only sensible response is "Et tu, Brute?" Among others, Irena Slepičková (Czech Republic) laments this myopia in chastising the "obliviousness" of scholars professing scholarly imaginations.

These, you will quickly see in the following 23 chapters, are not my experiences alone. Almost all of them, though in different ways and to different extents, speak of disciplinary hegemony and how cannibalistic both sociology and kinesiology can be to their subdisciplinary offspring. Authors speak of incessant battles for recognition, for legitimacy, for funding, and for resources, and every chapter, in its own way, records a story of disciplinary and campus struggle. Many sociology of sport colleagues continue to work in isolation ("isolation" need not necessarily only refer to geographical or institutional isolation but also isolation within departments that simply don't recognize the importance of sport socially or sociologically). For my own part, as one of the very few Canadian sociologists based in a mainstream sociology department (see Chapter 18), I have had to frequently rationalize and explain over the past 30 years of teaching to keep sociology of sport alive in the "curriculum," ironically in the face of some of the largest undergraduate classes taught in my department. Strange how sociologists might at times miss the most obvious social facts – sport is *meaningful*. But, for all of this, if you want to see hope and optimism for our subfield you will find it in the sheer robustness and unshakeable commitment of the chapters that follow, every one of which demonstrate that sport, as Eric Dunning so famously put it, "matters" (1999).

CONTENT, LAYOUT, SEQUENCE

Given the task at hand that celebrates not just parts of the world where the subdiscipline has prospered and the research is strong, but other parts of the world where sociology of sport remains in its infancy or is perhaps in decline, it seemed important to format the book in a fashion that rejects any implication of power relations, geo-political domination, or any other such perception of imperialism or colonization. This is a tougher task than it at first seems. Some, for instance, may question countries or regions considered under the rubric of certain names, and others might not agree with the continent certain countries have been slotted into. However, with advice from a number of colleagues along the way, the 23 chapters simply follow an alphabetical protocol, arranged first by continent and then by country or region within that continent. In keeping with this spirit, I have meant no disrespect in deliberately avoiding the flags of the world's most powerful nations on the book cover.

To assist in the framing of chapters, I provided authors with a suggested skeletal outline. Some authors followed it; others didn't. Readers will notice this as they make their way through the chapters. Interestingly, even where authors did not intentionally follow my skeletal framework they tended to address similar themes and categories anyway.

In the same way, while these national/regional summaries have each been written by recognized and experienced scholars within each setting, this is not to say that the respective settings would necessarily have been perceived, understood, and assessed differently by other authors from that country/region. Many authors appropriately acknowledge this possibility.

For readers wondering why x country was left out or y region wasn't invited, please consider the routine perils of book editing that have to do with issues like withdrawal, non-response, missed deadlines and such. This project was no anomaly in this respect. All of this is to say that a genuine attempt was made to eke out subfield summaries which were viable but, given the vagaries of time, space and human communication sometimes lost in translation, such a task can never be exhaustive or complete.

PUTTING IT TOGETHER

This project contains a sort of double resonance. On the one hand, it is institutionally and organizationally rewarding to see our growing subdiscipline mature. As it emerges out of and inevitably interacts with the particulars of the settings that gave rise to it in the first place, it's obviously developing in a nonuniform and nonlinear fashion (Ingham & Donnelly, 1997; Jackson, 2015). For a subdiscipline that struggled for so long in so many settings to liberate itself from the quicksand of description and structural functionalism and now seemingly headed, again in so many (but not all) settings, toward a physical cultural studies metamorphosis (Andrews, 2008; Atkinson, 2011), the sociological study of sport has, as they say, come a long way. Again, almost every chapter speaks to processes of *dynamic* subdisciplinary development, struggle, and change.

But the project contains strands of personal poignance too. Never initially anticipated, this book at one point or another raised the voices of so many sociology of sport colleagues I have met over the years, from my time as a graduate student, to an ISSA member, to two 4-year terms as ISSA Vice President, to my more removed and less involved current role. ISSA colleagues who have experienced how simultaneously diverse and close our international community of scholars is will quickly relate to this not insignificant angle on "knowing" sociology of sport.

Each reader will have her/his own version of this, no doubt, but for me, pulling these chapters together − from inception to correspondence to submission − was filled with ISSA-related nuance. I do not personally know all the authors, but I've had the pleasure of meeting many of them at international conferences. As I read their chapters submitted from thousands of miles away, I could *hear* their culture-infused voices telling their own sociology of sport story. As was always going to be the case in a project like this, dynamics of language, intonation, and expression inevitably frame what's being said and how. Arguably, this enhances rather than detracts from the sensitivity and authenticity that such a project requires in both production and reception phases. Readers should remember that, for most authors, English is a second or even a third language.

Indeed, while these dynamics certainly made editorial tasks more challenging and time-consuming, they also ultimately promoted a far more personified outcome. Furthermore, as these writers "spoke," I could also hear the voices and see the faces of so many influential ISSA characters from the past, many of whom bravely set a track of opportunity for subsequent generations to follow. Their names appear frequently in these pages, and their pioneer contributions in all cases hover in the background.

I am confident that as they read these chapters, sociologists of sport everywhere, especially those connected to ISSA, will also see the faces and hear the voices of those that went before them and helped make their subdisciplinary careers possible. If there is a better way of celebrating "our" 50th anniversary, I cannot think of it.

Happy Anniversary!

REFERENCES

Andrews, D. L. (2008). Kinesiology's inconvenient truth and the physical cultural studies imperative. *Quest, 60*(1), 45−62.

Atkinson, M. (2011). Physical cultural studies [redux]. *Sociology of Sport Journal,* *28*(1), 135–144.

Bairner, A. (2012). For a sociology of sport. *Sociology of Sport Journal, 29,* 102–117.

Coakley, J. (2007). The global distribution of sociology of sport knowledge: The case for an open access discipline. Paper presented at the annual conference of the International Sociology of Sport Association, Copenhagen, Denmark, August 4.

Coakley, J., & Dunning, E. (Eds.). (2000). *Handbook of sports studies.* London: Sage.

Dunning, E. (1999). *Sport matters: Sociological studies of sport, violence and civilization.* London: Routledge.

Ingham, A. G., & Donnelly, P. (1997). A sociology of North American sociology of sport: Disunity in unity, 1965 to 1996. *Sociology of Sport Journal, 14*(4), 362–418.

Jackson, S. (2015). Sport, knowledge and power: Critical reflections and future prospects for an international sociology of sport. *East Asian Sport Thoughts, 4,* 1–24.

Malcolm, D. (2014). The social construction of the sociology of sport: A professional project. *International Review for the Sociology of Sport, 49*(1), 3–21.

Pike, E., Jackson, S., & Wenner, L. (2015). Assessing the sociology of sport: On the trajectory, challenges, and future of the field. *International Review for the Sociology of Sport, 50*(4–5), 357–362.

AFRICA

CHAPTER 1

SOCIOLOGY OF SPORT: SOUTH AFRICA

Cora Burnett

ABSTRACT

This chapter offers a comparative description of the separatist development of mainstream sociology focusing on sport-related phenomena versus the sociology of sport located within Human Movement or Sport Science departments at public universities in South Africa. Key findings relate to the production of fragmented bodies of knowledge, individual research agendas, and national funding in alignment with national development priorities that guide current neo-colonial knowledge production practices. There is a domination of political themes (pre- and post-apartheid) with more recent foci on nation building and Sport for Development and Peace which only partly respond to the call for indigenous knowledge production and critical scholarly work. The increased publications and mainstream sociological inquiry of the 2010 FIFA World Cup were not maintained as scholars continue to work in isolation. Other main sociological themes for both sectors include gender, with only a few established scholars producing critical work in response to a national call for an 'Africanization', anti-colonial stance in knowledge production. There seems to be an increasing trend to bridge the theory—practice divide and serve the public sphere which further pushes critical sociological work to

Sociology of Sport: A Global Subdiscipline in Review
Research in the Sociology of Sport, Volume 9, 3–19
Copyright © 2017 by Emerald Group Publishing Limited
ISSN: 1476-2854/doi:10.1108/S1476-285420160000009001

the margins of both fields. The chapter provides a comparative analysis and critical overview of the development and current sociology of sport practices at public South African universities. It articulates the most significant discourses with global and local manifestations, and as such communicates key critical findings to guide strategic synergies and future sociological research.

Keywords: Sociology of sport; sociological research; anti-colonialism; South Africa

INTRODUCTION

According to Grant Jarvie, 'It is impossible to fully understand contemporary [South African] society and culture without acknowledging the place of sport' (2006, p. 2). As early as the 1960s, when the first mainstream sociologists produced political texts, a critical paradigm was established and a plethora of anti-apartheid publications chartered a political activist approach. South Africa's isolation from world sport and the political significance of dominant male sports (e.g. rugby and cricket) constructed a discourse framed by controversial public debates. For Desai (2010, p. 1), rugby had become '… the sport that would help to catalyse the building of a "rainbow nation" predicated on a common identity, a common sense of "South Africanness"'.

Since the Mandela era, sport (and rugby in particular) fulfilled this role despite voices of discontent when expected racial transformation did not materialise and the national team, 20 years after the abolishment of apartheid laws, continued to represent the white minority. Football remained a sport attracting predominantly players from the (black) majority and the 2010 FIFA World Cup, being offered in Africa for the first time, represented a coming of age for South Africa and global acknowledgement for the new democracy. Over time, the political agency thus changed dramatically to position sport as a force of reconciliation and nation building. Such a notion has been questioned by critical sociologists and increasingly exposed the sport and development mantra of assumed inherent 'good' of dominant sports and sport events (Sugden, 2015).

Booth (1998, p. 93) warned against the 'speculative proposition' that sport is a social integrating force that could break down racial divides 'which ignore the origins, functions, and practices of racism and fails to explain the precise properties of sport that makes it the medium of integration'. Social stratification and inequalities in society and sport are difficult to dislodge from their ideological and cultural societal entrenchment. Yet, critical academic voices and agency are relatively absent from public debates and have remained relatively fragmented and marginal within South African academia in general and in sociology in particular.

The sociology of sport is still seen in some academic quarters as not serious and political enough. Yet despite its apparent marginality, studying sport sociologically provides a valuable lens in which to consider race, gender and class in South African society (Bolsmann & Burnett, 2015). In 2004, Peter Alexander suggested the sociology of sport remained 'worryingly weak' and this is still the case. He incorrectly predicted that studying sport 'will gain greater prominence with the World Cup coming to South Africa' (Alexander, 2004, p. 321). This has not been the case in South African sociology. Desai (2010, p. 11) succinctly notes that 'in a country that has trumpeted sport as a symbol of redress and nation-building, the lack of critical analysis of sporting activities is startling'. The political agenda thus did not meaningfully translate into a critical academic agenda, yet Coakley and Burnett (2014) note that sports have become a pervasive part of life in contemporary society globally.

This chapter traces the development of the sociology of sport as an academic discipline within the public university system of South Africa, and comments on the diverse and isolated disciplinary homes (e.g. mainstream sociology and the sociology of sport within the departments of Human Movement Studies or Sport Science). Prominent sociologists and academics from multiple disciplines have meaningfully contributed to the existing body of sociological knowledge and will feature in the following discussion. Through the thematic clustering of existing and emerging bodies of knowledge, main disciplinary fields informed research foci and demarcated bodies of knowledge. The chapter concludes with a future perspective on the sociology of sport within the South African academic context.

THE HISTORY OF SOCIOLOGY OF SPORT IN SOUTH AFRICAN HIGHER EDUCATION

The history of the sociology of sport is reflected in diverse paradigms presented by mainstream sociologists who published work around the 1960s, and academics within the Human Movement Studies or Sport Science departments who have published mainly since the 1980s with a degree of overlap due to sociological approaches from sub-disciplines such as sport history and sport psychology.

Earlier institutional arrangements, in the 1920s, in the then departments of physical education, directed research in the quest of validating the pedagogical paradigm supported by bio-medical science in substantiation of health education and an emerging sport science field. In these departments, sub-disciplines emerged during the 1960s in line with global trends. Although physical performance (e.g. sport science and bio-kinetics) and positivistic research within the field of physical education still dominated, new sub-disciplinary research emerged such as sport management and sport history (Van der Merwe, 2010). In the 1970s dance ethnological studies were undertaken by post-graduate students from the University of Stellenbosch and some educational courses included aspects of sociology. Few critical works were produced, and only since the 1980s have scholarly contributions (mostly from international scholars and mainstream sociologists) scrutinised apartheid sport, sport boycotts and the subsequent global isolation of South Africa up to the 1990s.

Following the decline of physical education in the 1980s (physical education as a school subject became absolute in government schools), related research and academic coursework were also cut from Higher Education Instructions' curricula. During the early 1990s, University of Leicester scholar Eric Dunning and his team of sociologists visited South Africa to recruit students from Africa for a master's degree in the sociology and management of sport. Local academics from the then Rand Afrikaans University (RAU) (now the University of Johannesburg) assisted, but due to the cost for students and logistical challenges, the course did not continue. However, it provided the impetus for establishing the sociology of sport as a lectured master's degree in RAU's Centre of Distance Learning with graduates who went into lecturing at RAU and the Cape Town University of Technology (CPUT).

National research funding for indigenous knowledge systems, in search of a new South African non-colonist identity, provided the impetus for 11 of the then 23 public South African Higher Institutions participating in collecting and publishing on indigenous games and traditional physical culture (Burnett & Hollander, 2004). Prominent historians, sociologists and anthropologists (e.g. Bolsmann, Odendaal, Van der Merwe, and Grundling) due to their academic backgrounds, published in both mainstream and applied work, while feminist scholars (Burnett, 2004; Jones, 2001) and since

2003, the Sport for Development and Peace movement (Burnett, 2015; Cronin, 2011), gained ground.

In mainstream sociology departments, academic discourses and research priorities were influenced by professional bodies and were reflective of political agendas which underwent dramatic changes since 1994. In post-apartheid South Africa, the higher education architecture transformed dramatically and departments of sociology and anthropology and/or development studies merged to meet the national development goals. Mainstream sociologists formed a new integrated association in 1993, constituted through a merger of the former Association for Sociologists in Southern Africa (ASSA) and the Suid-Afrikaanse Sosiologie Vereniging (SASOV). The newly established South African Sociological Association set itself three main goals: (i) to promote the discipline and the profession of sociology; (ii) to promote research, teaching and debate about society; and (iii) to provide cooperation at the national, regional and international levels among persons engaged in the study of society (see sasaonline.org.za). Institutional positioning and addressing societal issues such as sport (2010), gender equity (2011) and violence (2015) reflect conference themes since 2015 (see Table 1).

At the South African Sociological Association's (SASA) annual conferences from 2001 to 2009, only three papers on sport were presented with a critical mass of papers around social issues relating to the 2010 FIFA World Cup, which took place in South Africa. The papers represented critical work from sociologists, but nobody from Sport Science departments delivered papers, demonstrating an obvious academic divide. Most of the current 26 public South African universities offer mainstream sociology with none focusing on the sociology of sport as an independent discipline. There is a bias towards universities in the Gauteng province featuring eight of the 20 working groups.

Sport-related debates and discourses are provided for, in addition to Sport for Development and Peace (SDP) initiatives that could link to the working group Development, whereas the role of volunteers, youth coaches and peer educators may also connect with the working group, The Sociology of Youth. Other working groups such as Gender; Lesbian, Gay and Queer Studies; or Race, Ethnicity and Class may equally host sport-related topics. These working groups offer the scope for a more nuanced analysis of sport- and leisure-related phenomena as indicative of the discipline's maturity globally. The 2015 Special Edition of the *South African Sociology Association Journal*, on 'Taking South African Sport Seriously: Studying Sport Sociologically' is the most recent initiative to

Table 1. Past Conferences of SASA.

2005	*The renewal of sociology in South Africa*
	University of Limpopo, Polokwane: 26–29 June 2005
2006	*The quality of social existence in a globalising world*
	SASA hosted the ISA in Durban: 23–28 July 2006
2007	*Sociology and social reconstruction in South Africa*
	North-West University, Potchefstroom: 25–28 June 2007
2008	*Society, power and the environment: Challenges for the twenty-first century*
	Stellenbosch University, Stellenbosch: 7–10 July 2008
2009	*Making sense of borders: Identity, citizenship and power in comparative perspective*
	University of the Witwatersrand, Johannesburg: 28 June–2 July 2009
2010	*Sport, leisure and development in the 21st century: Opportunities and challenges*
	Fort Hare University, East London: 13–16 June 2010
2011	*Gender in question: Rights, representation and substantive freedom*
	University of Pretoria: 10–13 July 2011
2012	*Knowledge, technologies and social change*
	University of Cape Town: 1–4 July 2012
2013	*Doing sociology from the periphery: Place, power and knowledge*
	University of South Africa: July 2013
2014	*The point of critique: Knowledge, society and the state in South Africa after 20 years of democracy*
	Nelson Mandela Metropolitan University: 6–8 July 2014
2015	*Contours of violence: Manifestations, interventions and social justice*
	University of Johannesburg: 28 June–1 July 2015

advocate for academic attention to the sociological study of sport-related issues in society.

Departments of Sport Science formed an institutional landscape to optimally deliver on the demands of elite sport, community sport and recreation, as well as a development agenda set by the National Sport and Recreation Plan. National Sport and Recreation Plan developed under the auspices 'of Sport and Recreation South Africa (Ministry of Sport and Recreation). Only eight of the then 24 public South African universities offered sociology of sport programmes, ranging from limited under-graduate modules (some included in educational courses or integrated with sport history) with only four offering it at a post-graduate level (in the honours or fourth-year programme) (Burnett, 2010).

Due to the multi-disciplinary nature of Human Movement Studies, academics are affiliated with multiple professional bodies in which bio-medical sciences have dominated. The relative marginalisation of the sociology of sport and lack of specialisation, contributed to individual academics affiliating to the International Sociology of Sport Association (ISSA) in search of a disciplinary home. South African academics and universities are incentivised to publish in accredited journals (ISI-listed) or national interdisciplinary accredited journals, such as the *African Journal for Physical, Health Education, Recreation and Dance (AJPHERD)* and the *South African Journal for Research in Sport, Physical Education and Recreation.*

MAIN SOCIOLOGISTS AND THEIR FIELDS OF RESEARCH

In mainstream sociology, a long academic tradition of studying South African sport was evident with some of the earlier works being Leo Kuper's *An African Bourgeoisie: Race, Class, and Politics in South Africa* published in 1965. Kuper drew from Bernard Magubane's University of Natal thesis *Sport and Politics in an Urban African Community* completed in 1963. Internationally, a significant body of academic and popular literature was published by activists and scholars from the early 1960s onwards that critiqued apartheid sport (cf. Archer & Bouillon, 1982; Brickhill, 1976; de Broglio, 1970; Jarvie, 1985; Lapchick, 1975; Ramsamy, 1982; Thompson, 1964). During the 1990s, three important academic books on South African sport were published by historians Grundlingh, Odendaal and Spies (1995), Nauright (1997) and Booth (1998).

After 2000, a number of academic books appeared primarily but not exclusively published by historians (cf. Alegi, 2004; Desai, 2010; Gemmel, 2004; Grundlingh, 2013; Merrett, 2009; Odendaal, 2003). The 2010 FIFA World Cup spurred a number of journal articles, special issues and edited book collections (cf. Alegi & Bolsmann, 2010, 2013; Cottle, 2011; Pillay, Tomlinson, & Bass, 2009). This highlights the salience and relevance to studying South African sport. There is, however, a distinct lack of sociologists in either South Africa or abroad dealing with issues related to South African sport. A cursory overview of the *South African Review of Sociology* and its predecessor *Society in Transition* reveals that between 1997 and 2014 three articles were published related to sport: historian Goolam Vahed's research on South African cricket in 2001, sociologist Cock's (2008) article on golf and sports anthropologist and sociologist Mariann Vaczi's article on Basque football in 2011 (Bolsmann & Burnett, 2015).

While during the FIFA World Cup in 2010, encouragingly, over 30 papers addressed issues related to sport with the World Cup being the primary focus with a corresponding peak of papers delivered at the 2010 SASA conference ('Sport, Leisure and Development in the 21st Century: Opportunities and Challenges'). However, since 2010, five papers in the sociology of sport have been presented to South Africa Sociology Association (SASA) conferences. Moreover, Stewart and Zaaiman's (2014) textbook *Sociology: A South African Introduction* barely mentions sport.

As mentioned, a recent initiative includes the first special edition as an initiative from Chris Bolsmann on the sociological significance of sport as a field of academic inquiry; Bolsmann invited Cora Burnett as co-editor (Bolsmann & Burnett, 2015). For the first time academics from mainstream sociology (Bolsmann) and from the sociology of sport within a department of Human Movement Studies (Burnett) collaborated in this way and reviewed 40 abstracts which resulted in the placement of six articles. Academics across the world submitted papers and the diversity was evident in the published papers which reflected on the most influential debates and discourses in a human justice framework. Social issues of negotiating and crossing borders of 'normality' of gender and ability (e.g. case studies on Caster Semenya and Oscar Pistorius) informed several manuscripts. Sport for Development and Peace academic legitimacy, sport legacy (also associated with the 2010 FIFA World Cup and nation building) and football fandom (identity formation) set a socio-political agenda. Also notable is the textbook of Coakley and Burnett (2014) and Burnett's chapter in Seedat-Khan, Jansen, and Smith's (2016) textbook, *Sociology: A South African Perspective*, based on the original text of Joan Ferrante with the addition of several new chapters (Burnett, 2016).

MAIN AREAS OF RESEARCH

Main sociologists delivering critical work in the field include the early human justice advocates and political activist accounts from scholars like Lapchick (1975), Jarvie (1985) and Kidd and Donnelly (2000). From a socio-historical perspective, John Nauright (1997) and Booth (1998) interrogated rugby as a post-colonial phenomenon with deep roots in Afrikaner nationalist identity formation.

Politics and anti-apartheid literature were produced by International Olympics Committee (IOC) member Ramsamy (1982) and political activist Desai (2010) who took a stance against neo-liberalism and neo-colonialism. In recent years, Desai, Padayachee, Reddy, and Vahed's (2003) critical work focused on exposing the power relations and elements of corruption in cricket in much the same vein as Vahed's (2001) watershed publication on the deconstruction of power relations. Significant and insightful work on the apartheid history and political dynamics of cricket has come from the pen of Odendaal (2003) who is also an ex-national player and academic of stature.

More descriptive works were produced in the field of football with the writing of the history of players of colour (non-white in the apartheid dispensation) in acknowledgement of their contribution to the game and anti-apartheid stance during the latter years of apartheid sport (Alegi, 2004). Alegi and Bolsmann (2010) also captured the earlier 'silent voices' and provide significant political insights by interviewing local people and members from minority groups.

From a figurational perspective, papers on football violence followed the more mainstream work on 'public violence' (e.g. gang formation), whereas other studies relate to dance ethnology and gender and sport (Burnett, 2002, 2006). Burnett (2004) was contracted for a national research project titled *The Status of SA Women in Sport and Recreation 1994–2004*, indicating widespread ideological and systemic barriers for women as a vastly heterogeneous population 10 years into the new political dispensation. In the late 1990s and early 2000s, gender became another socio-political discourse with prominent research produced by Hargreaves (1997) on the marginalisation of women in sport, followed by Jones (2001) reporting on gender inequality. Pelak (2005) reports on the triple bind of class, ethnicity/race and gender in the field of netball (a prominent female sport) and football.

In the field of Sport for Development and Peace (SDP), a critical mass of papers are published based on relatively large-scale national and international impact assessments for institutions like Sport and Recreation South Africa, the Australian Sports Commission and the European Union in support of the GIZ/YDF (human legacy) project (German Development Corporation's Youth Development through Football) that was implemented in 10 African countries (Burnett, 2013). Cornelissen (2011) offered a critique of FIFA's coercive power relations, excessive spending and marginalisation of local communities. Coalter (2013) criticised the social problem approach and produced critical work in this field on South African case studies, while Burnett (2012) captured 45 cases demonstrating the lived-realities of youth in *Stories from the Field*. Theory building and methodological innovation, especially in the field of Sport for Development, became a priority as evidenced in multiple publications and the conceptualisation and application of the Sport for Development Impact Assessment Tool

(S·DIAT) (Cronin, 2011). The latter instrument was validated and refined through several national and international impact assessment studies of institutional sports-based or related programmes.

Sport management research by Goslin and Kluka (2010) translated in publications on sport management systems, structures and practices. These authors focused on producing descriptive and pragmatic work, rather than engaging in theory building or utilising critical and interpretive agendas in interrogating the complexity of social reality (Chalip & Costa, 2012). Keim and de Coning (2014) published on sport-related policies of several African countries and De Coning (2015) produced a publication entitled *The Case for Sport in the Western Cape*. A positivist and functional paradigm frames this type of descriptive research with elements of critical reflection of inter-agency comparisons of policies and implementation practices.

THE ACADEMIC ENVIRONMENT AND BARRIERS TO RESEARCH

The relative marginalisation of the sociology of sport in both academic worlds and prioritisation of addressing broad social injustices (mainstream sociology) and bio-medical science in aid of high-performance sport, negatively impacts academics specialising in the sociology of sport. Most postgraduate work is aligned with these focus areas and candidates who pursue further studies in order to build their careers further channel research away from sociological inquiry.

The national funding agency (National Research Foundation) offers incentive funding for rated researchers, while also funding team and inter-institutional research aligned to national priorities and the development of indigenous knowledge systems. The tension between increasing internationalisation and global networking negatively impacts national-level inter-institutional research — particularly across disciplinary boundaries. This contributed to the fragmentation of knowledge production and perpetuation of parallel universes with little exchange and learning within and between mainstream sociologists and their counterparts in departments of Human Movement Studies or Sport Science.

This divisionary approach contributed to reductionist research paradigms along disciplinary lines such as sport management, sport performance, sport and physical education, recreation, the health paradigm and media studies. Andrews (2015) refers to 'unresolved tussles' (structural functionalism and conflict theoretical approaches), as well as relative isolation of the different disciplinary homes. The latter contributed to the institutional marginality of the field – a position maintained by hyper-individuality, lack of cross- or inter-disciplinary work and increased 'healthification'.

Funding opportunities in alignment with national development priorities may determine the focus of research in aid of more strategic research underpinned by critical pragmatism which compromises highly critical approaches. The pressure for applied and action research may further put pressure on academics to conduct research for the validation of various practices, rather than attempt complex issues and longitudinal studies. This would, however, stimulate the development of a 'public sociology' that would contribute to bridging the theory–practice divide (Bairner, 2009). The pressure to publish and generate an income from accredited publications for universities, departments and for authors, results in many academics co-publishing with post-graduate students with the emphasis on quantity, rather than on theory-generating research. The business model of South African universities promotes contract research practices which further undermine critical sociological work in favour of applied work and strategic translational research (Coakley, 2015).

Contract research, underpinned by neo-liberal paradigms and in the field of SDP, perpetuates the domination of the Global North with local voices filtered by preconceived conceptual frameworks which limits the construction of critical and innovative work (Burnett, 2015). The cost of international travel and limited or focused funding contributes to the isolation of critical scholars in favour of positivist research.

THE FUTURE OF SOCIOLOGY OF SPORT IN SOUTH AFRICA

Existing divisionary structures along the lines of disciplinary practices contribute to the marginalisation of the sociology of sport within mainstream sociology and within sport science communities. It would be inevitable that in both fields there would be an increase in searching for international rather than national, or intra-institutional collaboration. Fragmented knowledge academic practices in support of national development priorities (e.g. worker productivity) and preference for empirical evidence and positivistic paradigms, will not address ideological tensions, nor provide a sociological lens of critical reflexivity (Alvesson & Spicer, 2012; Hovden, 2015). This situation will inevitably enhance existing pockets of excellence within the field such as SDP research and theory building, critical work around mega-sport events and social legacy projects, as well as policy and political discourse development.

There would inevitably remain a gap in the pool of knowledge, generated within the sociology of sport, which is detrimental for challenging social injustices and addressing the rights and sociological issues relating to minority populations such as class and athletes with disabilities. The sensitive political climate would continue to threaten academic agency in addressing issues such as sexual harassment in sport (opposed by male hegemony), positive deviance (e.g. over-training) and equitable management practices or unequal power relations.

The selected sociological themes and modular approach to the sociology of sport within mainstream coursework in South Africa would do little to enhance methodological innovation through post-graduate studies. It would be up to a handful of established researchers to form relationships for high-level collaborative research and bridge the domination of the Global North in knowledge production and perpetuation of cultural (Maguire, 2015) and neo-liberal hegemony (McKay, 2015). The drive towards de-colonialization and 'Africanization' of knowledge across South African universities should search for, or develop, new epistemologies based on grounded theoretical approaches and the fusion of Western and African-inspired ideologies.

Cross-disciplinary enrichment in a research team approach around social issues may deliver meaningful insights that address controversial issues and contribute to current academic discourses in South Africa. Research along the lines of social stratification and disenfranchisement would remain a popular approach in the quest for delivering insights to transform the South African sport fraternity and society into a more equitable, inclusive and just society.

ACKNOWLEDGEMENT

Thanks to Chris Bolsmann for his invitation and contribution to act as guest editor for a special edition for the *South African Review of Sociology*, entitled 'Taking South African Sport Seriously', and co-authoring the introduction.

FIVE KEY READINGS

1. **Coakley, J., & Burnett, C. (2014).** *Sport in society: Issues and controversies in Southern Africa.* **Pretoria: Van Schaik Publishers.**

   This reader is currently the main prescribed text for students in the Sport Science departments at South African universities. The text is a southern African adaptation of Coakley's original text, similarly to what Elizabeth Pike did for the United Kingdom. It provides a meaningful framework and depth of sociological issues, theories, concepts and sport practices in Africa, and particularly South Africa. The text forms the basis of exploring the dynamic relationship between sports, culture and society. It also features new content on sports and development.

2. **Seedat-Khan, M., Jansen, Z. L., & Smith, R. (Eds.). (2016).** *Sociology: A South African perspective.* **Andover, Hampshire: Cengage Learning EMEA.**

   This particular edition retains a large portion of the original text's (the Joan Ferrante's text) integrative approach. It aims to bring a distinctive South African voice to a global resource on sociology. Each of the 23 chapters pairs a sociological topic with a global issue and its impact on South African society. It also presents critical voices from the Global South and showcases sociology's influence to stimulate debate around the most compelling issues of contemporary society. The sociology of sport features for the first time in such a sociological mainstream text.

3. *Voices from the global south on sport for development and peace. African Journal for Physical, Health Education, Recreation & Dance (AJPHERD).* **March 2015 Supplement (Special Edition).**

   This special edition features 21 articles in the field of SDP and includes work from prominent South African and international scholars. It is divided into six main thematic areas which include: (i) Strategy and implementation, relating to managerial research; (ii) Meaning and 'matteredness', about identity construction and survival in impoverished communities; (iii) The human face of agency, about gender, fragmented families and limited agency; (iv) SDP Programme 'uptake' and ownership, about impact assessments; (v) Study fields related to SfD, relating to recreational studies; and (vi) Critical questions and perspectives.

4. **Pike, C. J., Jackson, S. J., & Wenner, L. A. (Eds.). (2015). 50@50: Assessing the trajectory and challenges of the sociology of sport. Special 50th anniversary double issue.** *International Review for the Sociology of Sport 50*(4).

This special edition represents the breadth of 50 years of sociology and bring the perspectives together of 50 key scholars to ensure a diversity of voices and perspectives along the range of themes, theories and methods. The articles address two overarching challenges, namely countering the dominance of English and (neo) colonial knowledge production. The diversity of material also represents the advancement of interdisciplinary work and contribution of scholars beyond the sociology of sport as to broaden the dialogue and influence of the sociological field of scientific inquiry and bridge disciplinary boundaries.

5. **Bolsmann, C., & Burnett, C. (2015). Taking South African sport seriously.** *South African Review of Sociology*, **46**(1), 1−6.

Bolsmann and Burnett acted as guest editors for this special edition of the *South African Review of Sociology* inviting scholars from related fields to publish in this issue to demonstrate why sport is a topic of sociological relevance and inquiry. This introduction provides a historical overview of main scholarly work − pre- and post-apartheid − by showing the change in political priorities and thematic approaches. It also features a collection of articles on diverse sociological topics and demonstrates unique and original insights into political, sport for development, gender, football fandom and human mega-event legacy projects (e.g. 2010 FIFA World Cup), as well as the contested nature of museums and memory.

REFERENCES

Alegi, P. (2004). *Laduma! Soccer. Politics and society in South Africa. University of Kwa-Zulu.* Scotsville: Natal Press.

Alegi, P., & Bolsmann, C. (2010). South Africa and the global game: Introduction. *Soccer & Society, 11*(1−2), 1−11.

Alegi, P., & Bolsmann, C. (2013). *South Africa and the global game: Football, apartheid and beyond.* London: Routledge.

Alexander, P. (2004). The national research foundation and priorities for critical research. *Society in Transition, 35*(2), 319−327.

Alvesson, M., & Spicer, A. (2012). Critical leadership studies: The case for critical performativity. *Human Relations, 65*(3), 367−390.

Andrews, D. L. (2015). Assessing the sociology of sport: On the hopes and fears for the sociology of sport in the US. *International Review for the Sociology of Sport, 50*(4–5), 368–374.

Archer, R., & Bouillon, A. (1982). *The South African game: Sport and racism.* London: Zed Books.

Bairner, A. (2009). Sport, intellectuals and public sociology: Obstacles and opportunities. *International Review for the Sociology of Sport, 44*, 115–130.

Bolsmann, C., & Burnett, C. (2015). Taking South African sport seriously. *South African Review of Sociology, 46*(1), 1–6.

Booth, D. (1998). *The race game: Sport and politics in South Africa.* London: Frank Cass.

Brickhill, J. (1976). *Race against race: South Africa's multinational sports fraud.* London: International Defence and Aid Fund.

Burnett, C. (2002). The 'black cat' of South African soccer and the Chiefs-Pirates conflict. In E. Dunning, P. Murphy, I. Waddington, & A. E. Astrinakis (Eds.), *Fighting fans. Football hooliganism as a world phenomenon* (pp. 174–189). Dublin: University College Dublin Press.

Burnett, C. (2004). *The status of SA women in sport & recreation 1994 to 2004.* Centurion: South African Sports Commission.

Burnett, C. (2006). Building social capital through an Active community club. *International Review for the Sociology of Sport, 41*(3–4), 283–294.

Burnett, C. (2010). *Delivery for the sport industry by South African Universities.* Johannesburg: University of Johannesburg.

Burnett, C. (2012). *Stories from the field: GIZ/YDF Footprint in Africa.* Pretoria: Van Schaik Publishers.

Burnett, C. (2013). GIZ/YDF and Youth as drivers for sport for development in the African context. *Journal of Sport for Development, 1*(1), 1–10.

Burnett, C. (2015). Assessing the sociology of sport: On sport for development and peace. *International Review for the Sociology of Sport, 50*(4–5), 385–390.

Burnett, C. (2016). The significance of sports to sociology. In M. Seedat-Khan, Z. L. Jansen, & R. Smith (Eds.), *Sociology. A South African perspective* (pp. 294–307). Andover, Hampshire: Cengage learning EMEA.

Burnett, C., & Hollander, W. J. (2004). The South African Indigenous games research project of 2001/2002. *S.A. Journal for Research in Sport, Physical Education and Recreation, 26*(1), 9–23.

Chalip, L., & Costa, C. Z. (2012). Clashing worldviews: Sources of disappointment in rural hospitality and tourism development. *Hospitality & Society, 2*(1), 25–47.

Coakley, J. (2015). Assessing the sociology of sport: On cultural sensibilities and the greater sport myth. *International Review for the Sociology of Sport, 50*(4–5), 402–406.

Coakley, J., & Burnett, C. (2014). *Sport in society: Issues and controversies in southern Africa.* Pretoria: Van Schaik Publishers.

Coalter, F. (2013). *Sport for development: What game are we playing?* London: Routledge.

Cock, J. (2008). Caddies and 'cronies': Golf and changing patterns of exclusion and inclusion in post-apartheid South Africa. *South African Review of Sociology, 39*(2), 183–200.

Cornelissen, S. (2011). More than a sporting chance? Appraising the sport for development legacy of the 2010 FIFA World Cup. *Third World Quarterly, 32*(3), 503–529.

Cottle, E. (Ed.). (2011). *South Africa's World Cup: A legacy for whom?* Scottsville: University of KwaZulu-Natal Press.

Cronin, O. (2011). *Comic relief review: Mapping the research on the impact of sport and development interventions.* Manchester: Orla Cronin Research.

De Broglio, C. (1970). *South Africa: Racism in sport.* London: International Defence and Aid Fund.

De Coning, C. (Ed.). (2015). *The case for sport in the Western Cape.* Cape Town: ICESSD & DCAS.

Desai, A. (Ed.). (2010). *The race to transform: Sport in post-apartheid South Africa.* Pretoria: HSRC Press.

Desai, A., Padayachee, V., Reddy, K., & Vahed, G. (2003). *Blacks in whites: A century of black cricket in KwaZulu-Natal.* Pietermaritzburg: University of Natal Press.

Gemmel, J. (2004). *The politics of South African cricket.* London: Routledge.

Goslin, A., & Kluka, D. (2010). Affirmative action as a dimension of diversity management: Perceptions of South African sport federations. *Journal of Global Initiatives: Policy, Pedagogy, Perspective, 1*(2), 4.

Grundlingh, A. (2013). *Potent pastimes: Sport and leisure practices in modern Afrikaner history.* Pretoria: Protea Book House.

Grundlingh, A., Odendaal, A., & Spies, B. (1995). *Beyond the tryline.* Johannesburg: Ravan Press.

Hargreaves, J. (1997). Women's sport, development, and cultural diversity: The South African experience. *Women's Studies International Forum, 20*(2), 191–209.

Hovden, J. (2015). Assessing the sociology of sport: On sport organizations and neoliberal discourses. *International Review for the Sociology of Sport, 50*(4–5), 472–476.

Jarvie, G. (1985). *Class, race and sport in South Africa's political economy.* London: Routledge.

Jarvie, G. (2006). *Sport, culture and society.* Abingdon: Routledge.

Jones, D. E. (2001). In pursuit of empowerment: Sensei Nellie Kleinsmot, race and gender challenges in South Africa. *The International Journal of the History of Sport, 18*(1), 219–236.

Keim, M., & De Coning, C. (Eds.). (2014). *Sport and development policy in Africa.* Stellenbosch: Sun Press.

Kidd, B., & Donnelly, P. (2000). Human rights in sports. *International Review for the Sociology of Sport, 35*(2), 131–148.

Kuper, L. (1965). *An African Bourgeoisie: Race, class and politics in South Africa.* New Haven, CT: Yale University Press.

Lapchick, R. (1975). *The politics of race and international sport: Centre for international race relations.* London: Greenwood Press.

Magubane, B. (1963). *Sports and politics in an urban African community.* Unpublished doctoral dissertation. University of Natal, Durban.

Maguire, J. (2015). Assessing the sociology of sport: On globalization and the diffusion of sport. *International Review for the Sociology of Sport, 50*(4–5), 519–523.

McKay, J. (2015). Assessing the sociology of sport: On revisiting the sociological imagination. *International Review for the Sociology of Sport, 50*(4–5), 547–552.

Merrett, C. (2009). *Sport, space and segregation: Politics and society in Pietermaritzburg.* Durban: University of Kwazulu-Natal Press.

Nauright, J. (1997). *Sport, culture and identities in South Africa.* Cape Town: David Philip.

Odendaal, A. (2003). *The story of an African game.* Cape Town: David Philip.

Pelak, C. F. (2005). Negotiating gender/race/class constraints in the new South Africa: A case study of women's football. *International Review for the Sociology of Sport, 40*(1), 53–70.

Pillay, U., Tomlinson, R., & Bass, O. (2009). *Development and dreams: The urban legacy of the 2010 Football World Cup*. Pretoria: HSRC Press.

Ramsamy, S. (1982). *Apartheid: The real hurdle*. London: International Defence and Aid Fund.

Seedat-Khan, M., Jansen, Z. L., & Smith, R. (Eds.). (2016). *Sociology: A South African Perspective*. Andover, Hampshire: Cengage Learning EMEA.

Stewart, P., & Zaaiman, F. (2014). *Sociology: A South African introduction*. Cape Town: Juta.

Sugden, J. (2015). Assessing the sociology of sport: On the capacities and limits of using sport to promote social change. *International Review for the Sociology of Sport*, *50*(4–5), 606–611.

Thompson, R. (1964). *Race and sport*. London: Oxford.

Vaczi, M. (2011). Subversive pleasures, losing games: Basque soccer madness. *South African Review of Sociology*, *42*(1), 21–36.

Vahed, G. (2001). What do they know of cricket who only cricket know? Transformation in South African Cricket, 1990–2000. *International Review for the Sociology of Sport*, *36*(3), 319–336.

Van Der Merwe, F. J. (2010). Race and South African rugby: A review of the 1919 'all black' tour. *South African Journal for Research in Sport, Physical Education & Recreation (SAJR SPER)*, *32*(2), 161–169.

ASIA

CHAPTER 2

SOCIOLOGY OF SPORT: CHINA

Dong Jinxia and Liu Lingnan

ABSTRACT

Sociology of sport in China has evolved from being an "exotic" subject to a localized subject over the past 35 years. It is closely associated with social changes, sports policy and athletic achievement of China. As a discipline of humanitarian and social sciences of sport, it is taught in virtually all universities with sports majors. There are about 500 scholars specializing in sport sociology in the country. Textbooks written by Chinese and foreign scholars are published. Academic papers on sport sociology are often published in the 15 accredited core sports journals. The most productive authors are from universities and the developed provinces and municipalities. The established research areas of sport sociology are extensive. These include national identity, athlete mobility, Olympic legacy, sport for all, sports industry issues, feminist studies, community sport, sport for the aged and disabled, etc. However, there are few studies with critical analysis and only a few in the areas of sport and religion, sport and race, and deviance in sport in China. Various kinds of financial support at different levels are available in the country. Empirical research is common with literature review, questionnaire, case study, and interview being the most frequently used methods. However, sport sociology is not considered as a major topic but as a research

Sociology of Sport: A Global Subdiscipline in Review
Research in the Sociology of Sport, Volume 9, 23–35
Copyright © 2017 by Emerald Group Publishing Limited
ISSN: 1476-2854/doi:10.1108/S1476-285420160000009002

direction and it is not accepted widely by mainstream sociology. The future of sport sociology is promising, but not without challenges.

Keywords: Sport sociology; China; discipline; publication; research; support

INTRODUCTION: THE EMERGENCE AND EXPANSION OF SPORT SOCIOLOGY IN CHINA

"Sociology of sport" is one of the subdisciplines of humanitarian and social sciences of sport, and is a collective term covering a series of individual sciences such as sport history, sport philosophy, sport journalism, and sport economy in China. It has over three decades of history at this point.

The development of sport sociology in China is shaped by the broad social, political, and economic development in general and sports policy and higher education reform in particular. It should be noted that sociology, the mother discipline of sport sociology, was withdrawn from university curricula in 1952 not long after the "New China" came into being in October 1949. It was resumed in 1980 in the major universities of the nation. Obviously, this is directly related to the changed social and political environment after the economic reform and "opening-up" policy introduced in China in late 1970s. The increased economic power, the less ideological political atmosphere, and improved international relationship provided a congenial climate for the development of sociology, including sport sociology. The branch of Sport Social Science (BSSS) of China Sport Science Society was founded in 1980.

With the growing exchanges between China and the West, the Chinese government began to send scholars to places like Japan, the United States, the former Soviet Union, Canada, Britain, Poland, and Australia to study. The latest developments in sport sociology in the West caught Chinese attention. Western works of sport sociology were first translated by Professor Lin Qiwu who was trained in sociology and physical education in both China and the United States in the 1930s, and then was a teacher at Peking University. The introduction of Western sport sociology first appeared in the *Journal of Beijing Sports Institute* in 1981. Based on this, Lin also wrote a textbook of Sport Sociology in 1982, which provided a framework for the scholars of sport studies to understand sport sociology at the time. Soon, other scholars of sport studies including Cai Junwu, Liu Depei, Niu Xinhua, Wang Ping, Li Shuyi, Ke Ni, Gu Yuanyan began to write articles to either introduce the nature and methodology of sport sociology or examine and explain social issues connected to sport by using the paradigm of sport sociology.[1]

Organization often plays an important part in promoting the development of a subject. In 1983 the Jiangsu Provincial Society of Sports Sociology, the first-ever provincial academic organization in China, was set up. In 1986 the Study Group of Sports Sociology was created within the BSSS of China Sports Science Society (it was later renamed the Committee of Sports Sociology). In the same year, the teaching and research office of sport sociology was created at Shenyang Sports Institute.

In 1987, the State Sports Committee stressed that research on sport sociology should be systematically enhanced in its document "The Decision of Strengthening the Construction of Sports Theory." By the end of the 1980s, the theoretical system of sport sociology was established and studies of sport and social issues had made solid progress. As a result, a number of sports institutes in Beijing, Tianjin, and Shenyang started to provide students with sports sociology courses, and Beijing Sports Institute began to enroll graduates pursuing the subdiscipline.

It should be pointed out that the study of sport sociology in the 1980s was centered on the social functions of sport, sports reform, sport and recreation theory, and the relationship between sports and media, and often adopted a structural functionalist approach to understanding and displaying the values of sport and the role of sport in social reform and development.

Of course, offering such courses requires reference books about sport sociology. The first officially published book *Sociology of Sport* was authored by Liu Depei and published in 1990. This marked the beginning of the independent development of the discipline in the country. Liu later became the first Chinese person to become a member of the Executive Committee of the International Sociology of Sport Association (ISSA) in 1995. In the early 1990s, five more books or textbooks on sport sociology written by Xu Longrui, LV Shuting, Huang Jierong, Lu Yuanzheng, and Mao Xiuzhu were published. Meanwhile, increasing numbers of articles were contributed to sport sociology with broader research areas and depth. They aroused great interest from scholars and practitioners and helped promote sports reform and social development.[2] In this situation a special committee of sport sociology was established by the China

Sociology Society in 1994. To some extent this reflects the growing recognition of sport sociology by mainstream disciplines in China.

In the early 1990s, a type of market-oriented reform and fast urbanization took place in China. This led to fundamental changes in Chinese society and sport in particular. Sports reform was introduced in 1992 in 10 areas including the administrative system, the competition system, sports associations, and sports training. Further, a Sports Law and National Fitness Program was introduced in 1995, which resulted in the rise of sports participation. Hand in hand with these changes were the social issues and problems that caught great attention from both the public and scholars in China. Topics such as the sports industry, elite sport and athlete social mobility, urban community sport, and sport for all became the heated topics of sociological debate in the 1990s. After Tiyu Xue (in the discipline of Physical Education and Sport) was awarded in July 1996 the status of a first level discipline (i.e., the same as Mathematics, Sociology, and many others), sport sociology, the basic subject of sports social science, accelerated in its development.

Since the beginning of the 21st century, China's rise has been witnessed in many aspects – economic, political, military, art, and sport. The successful Olympic bid and admission to the World Trade Organization in 2001 unleashed the process. The Beijing Olympics was an important social, political, and sporting event for the Chinese. In 2004 the idea to further develop philosophy and social science by the Central Committee of Communist Party of China was publicized. Accordingly, the State Administration of Sport issued a similar document to promote the development of sports social science.[3] Guided by these two documents, sport sociology entered a golden development period in China. A glance at Chinese sports journals provides ample evidence of the expansion of sport sociology in the country. In 1997 there were only about 20 papers on sport sociology; by 2013 the number had reached over 100.

A seminar on sport sociology was held in 1987, 1989, and 1992 by the China Sports Science Society to discuss the construction of the subject, research methods, and talent cultivation of the discipline. Since then, a conference on sport sociology has been organized annually in different cities of the country with over 300 participants each time. In line with the increased integration of China with the world, Chinese scholars of sport sociology have also been visible internationally. In 1997 the Asian Sports Sociology Congress was held in Beijing. Five Chinese participated in the 1998 World Sociology Congress and Sports Sociology Conference held in Montreal, Canada. After that, more and more Chinese presented at the ISSA conferences. Professor Dong Jinxia from Peking University became a member of the Extended Executive Board of ISSA in 2013. She was responsible for staging the 2014 ISSA World Congress in Beijing on the campus of Peking University. This event attracted over 300 participants from home and abroad and gained ISSA 60 more members from China. Needless to say, it surely promoted the development of the sociology of sport in the country and provided a platform for academic exchange between Chinese and foreign scholars.

The 2008 Beijing Olympics was an important social, political, and sporting event for Chinese. The Olympics was one of the first hot topics for the study of sport sociology. Additionally, peasant and rural sport, public service of sport, talent cultivation for elite sport, the social problems of match fixing and corruption in football, and lifestyle and sports participation were other areas for sociological studies between 2001 and 2011.[4]

THE PRESENT: PEOPLE, POLICY, AND PRACTICE OF CHINESE SPORT SOCIOLOGY

Sport sociology has become an established subject in China. It is a compulsory course for students from sports universities, colleges, and departments of physical education. Some universities offer sport sociology to MA and PhD students. Arguably, the development of sport sociology is influenced by sports development and policy in China. Sport has been utilized as an effective tool to modernize China and obtain world recognition after the People's Republic of China (PRC) was created in 1949. In the early 1950s national and provincial sports teams, administration and competition systems, and educational institutions for sports talents were put in place. Sports studies and publications were stressed as early as in the late 1950s. However, due to the domestic and international politics Chinese athletes did not show their full force in international competitions until the 1970s. The first Olympic victory in Los Angeles in 1984 convinced the Chinese of the contemporary global significance of the Olympic Games. To become an Olympic power has been the persistent and ultimate dream of China since the mid-1980s when the Olympic Strategy was introduced. From that point, a winning-oriented sports policy has dominated the sports community of China, and Olympic sports have been the focus of elite sport. Indeed, China progressed in the ranking of Olympic medals and became second at the medal count in 2008 and 2012. The extraordinary performances sparked considerable interest at home and abroad. In step with these changes, sports studies, including sport sociology, has boomed since the mid-1980s.

In China, 64 universities offer a program in the humanitarian and social science of sport (HSSS). They are divided into four different levels according to performance. The programs in Beijing Sports University, Chengdu Sports Institute, and Shanghai Sports Institute ranked in the top three of the 64 programs nationally. Virtually all the colleges and universities teach courses in sociology of sport. Unexpectedly, the book *Sport in Society: Issues and Controversies* written by Jay Coakley and published in 1998 was translated into Chinese and published by Tsinghua University Press in 2003. It turned out to be the most-wanted textbook for sport sociology in many universities. At that time, Coakley thus became the most famous scholar of sport sociology in China.

It is estimated that there are about 500 scholars in the field of sport sociology in China. They are located in universities and research institutes across the whole country. Additionally, a few scholars from sociology and other areas of sport studies also undertake research on sociology of sport. According to Lei Wenxiu, those who authored six or more papers between 2001 and 2010 reached 21 in number, including Qiu Jun from Tsinghua University, Tian Yupu from Nanjing Normal University, Lv Shuting and Pei Lixin from Guangzhou Sports University, Lu Yuanzheng from South China Normal University, Ren Hai from Beijing Sports University, Dong Jinxia from Peking University, and Li Xiangru and Luo Bingquan from Capital Sports University, as well as many more. It is noticeable that most of the authors are from sports universities and colleges, and especially from Beijing, Shanghai, Guangdong, Zhejiang and Shandong, Jiangsu – the most developed provinces and municipalities in the country.

In 2010 some 173 Chinese universities had tiyu-majored[5] programs including the eight majors – physical education, sports coaching, national traditional sports, social sport, leisure sport, kinesiology, sports physiotherapy and health, and sports industry management. Over 20 universities have sport-related PhD programs.

From 1995 papers published in the 13 core sports journals and the 202 projects supported by the National Social Science Fund between 2001 and 2010, it is obvious that the major research topics include hosting the Olympic Games and its impact, the theory and practice of implementing the National Fitness Program, the sustainable development of sport, the sports industry, the centralized sports system, the sports service system, globalization and sports development, Chinese elite sport in the transformational period to a market-oriented system, the construction of sport sociology as a subject, modern sports development and urbanization, professional sport, rural sport and facilities and stadiums for mega-sports events and reform of sports associations in China, regional development of sport, sports and leisure studies, allocation of sports resources and social justice, and the standardization of sports and sports media.[6]

We calculated the publications of sport sociology at the 15 accredited sport-oriented key journals between 2011 and 2015 and found that sociology of sport in China and other countries, Olympic studies, women's sport and/or bodies, football, and athletes were the major topics of sports sociological inquiry.

Research funding is crucial for the development of any discipline. In China, there is national, provincial, and university support for the studies of social phenomena in sport. The top level funding is the National Social Science Fund, whose financial volume has increased from 5 million yuan at its creation in 1991 to 600 million yuan in 2010. Within this fund, Tiyu Xue is one of the 23 academic subjects that have their own review group. Between 1997 and 2013 some 190 projects financed by the National Social Science Fund used a sport sociology approach, higher than other sports subjects. It should be noted that the number of winning projects increased over time, from 27 in 1997 to 125 in 2013. This shows that sport has become a more acceptable subject in China.[7]

In addition to the Fund, the Project of Philosophy and Social Science run by the State Sports Administration, the Project of Humanitarian and Social Science by the Ministry of Education, and other provincial- or municipal-level projects and universities that have humanitarian and social science subjects all provide funding for sports sociology research. About 44 percent of the papers published in the 13 key sports journals between 2001 and 2010 acquired various kinds of funds from the national to the university levels.[8]

Structural functionalism is the most employed theory in the sociological study into sport in China. Other theories are seldom used. The work of French sociologist Pierre Bourdieu has been influential in China since the mid-1990s in sociology and then sport sociology. In recent years concepts such as field, capital, habitus, and symbolic violence have been used as theoretical tools by scholars and students to understand the nature and purpose of sport, leisure, physical education, and human movement within the wider society.

A wide range of methodological and theoretical paradigms, such as qualitative and quantitative methods, as well as critical, figurational, feminist, interpretive, and historical paradigms are used by Chinese scholars.

Literature review, questionnaire, and interview are popular methods. Some even utilize quantitative analysis combined with computer technology, focus survey, case study, and field survey to examine the social issues in sport. An interpretational approach was adopted at the early stage of sociology of sport in China. Now, positivism and interpretivism mutually infiltrate and converge.[9] The published papers of sociology of sport in the core journals before 2000 used equally empirical and theoretical approaches, but after 2000 empirical research tends to have surpassed theoretical research.[10]

So far, 15 sports-related journals (such as *Sports Science, Sport and Science,* and *Sports Culture Guide*) are accredited core journals in China. They are either affiliated with state or provincial sports administrations or with universities such as Beijing Sports University. In the past decade, the *Sports Journal* run by the South China Normal University located in Guangzhou published the most articles (160) on sport sociology, followed by *Sport Culture Guide* and *Sports Science* (69 and 32 respectively), both affiliated with the State Sports Administration.

Liu Depei, Lv Shuting, Lu Yuanzheng, and Qiu Jun made contributions to the construction of sociology of sport as an academic subject in the country by writing monographs in this area. Ren Hai is a recognized scholar of Olympic studies. He coauthored a number of quality papers on sports reform and development with Yang Hua and Wang Kaizhen, such as "Transforming the mode of sports development: From the mode of catching up to that of sustainable development," "Study of the 2008 Beijing Games' impact on lifting China's international status and reputation," and "Chinese sports reform in the context of socio-economic transformation." Wang Kaizhen and Huang Yalin wrote their doctoral dissertations on community sport and sports associations in China respectively and published books and papers in these areas. Dong Jinxia and Xiong Huan both received PhD education in Britain, focusing more on women and sport and published books and papers in both English and Chinese (e.g., *Women, Sport and Society in Modern China* by Dong Jinxia (2002), and *Urbanization and Transformation of Chinese Women's Sport Since 1980: Reconstruction, Stratification and Emancipation* by Xiong (2009)). Zhong Bingshu's (1998) book *Performance Capital and Status Acquirement: Study of the social mobility of elite athletes in China* and Qiu Jun's (2002) book *Theoretic Exploration and Empirical Research on Sports Population in China* are also worth mentioning.

In spite of the above progress of sport sociology in China, there are some challenges and problems. First, as the organization of sports sociology in China is under the supervision of the mother discipline of sociology and Tiyu Xue, there is the matter of the lack of autonomy. Sport sociology is under the major of sports humanitarian and social science in most Chinese universities and colleges. Because of such structure, more and more sports scholars have employed the theories and methodologies of sports sociology to explore sports phenomena and more interdisciplinary findings have been produced. It seems that sport sociological studies in China now pay great attention to people in sport and sports reform and development. In spite of a varied focus over time, research on sport populations, sociological study of different sports, and community sports in cities are currently the most studied areas. However, there is little study of sport and religion, sport and race, and deviance in sport in the country. Most studies are experience-based application studies and there is a shortage of quality theory-based studies.

THE FUTURE: CERTAINTY AND UNCERTAINTY OF CHINESE SPORT SOCIOLOGY

In China, after over three decades, sociology of sport has transformed greatly in many aspects, reflected in the number of researchers and their training, the methodology and approach of study, and the content of teaching. Its status as a discipline has been consolidated and it is taught as an optional course in virtually all sports universities and colleges and departments of physical education and sport within comprehensive or normal universities. No doubt, sport sociology will become an ever-more influential subject in the country.

First, in the context of China's integration into the world and close exchange between China and foreign countries, increasing numbers of researchers of sport sociology have the opportunity to go abroad to study and visit. They thus become more international. With the increase of research findings Chinese scholars begin to export their studies to other countries and communities and integrate with the world.

Second, in the era of new media, ordinary people without training in sport sociology can also have their voices expressed in various social media. They again thus help push the development of sport sociology in China.

Third, the involvement of sociology-trained young scholars in sport sociology[11] will bring about changes in sociological theories, paradigms, and methodology. This can already be seen. For example, He Ke employed the method of typological comparison to investigate the respective part of the social elite, public organizations, and government and their interactions in running sports for all at three different grassroots communities in Hu Nan province[12] Although they are only a tiny part of the research community, young scholars with sociology knowledge will further generate changes in the contents, approaches, and quality of sociological research in sport.

Fourth, the rapid development of the Internet and Wi-Fi in China will also have an impact on the study of sport sociology. Now, a number of scholars in sport sociology have begun to use computer software-aided data statistics and analysis and Internet-based databases to search documents and information.

Fifth, governmental policy on sport is beneficial for the development of sport sociology. In 2015 the Chinese government endorsed the fast development of the sports industry and regarded national fitness as a state strategy.[13] Immediately an unprecedented wave of sports participation and investment in the sports industry was witnessed across the whole country. Due to the increasing concern about individual interests and demands in society, studies on the aged and disabled and their sports participation are also increasing.

Last but not least, Beijing and Zhang Jiakou's successful bid for the 2022 Winter Olympic Games will provide plenty of research topics for sport sociologists as the mega event will bring about great changes in infrastructure, regional and national economies, education, media, and personal lives. It is expected that empirical sociological studies in association with the event will emerge. There are promising signs that sociocultural aspects of the sports industry and sports events will continue to grow as a fertile field of study.

Sport sociology in China has experienced the transformation of localization after it was imported to China in early 1980s by exploring the specific issues and problems facing China and trying to create its own theories. This process continues in the 21st century. In terms of its development towards maturity, sport sociology in China can best be described as a young adult. It has not been fully accepted within sociology as it is hardly seen as part of the curriculum of sociology. It needs to be more clearly grounded in social theory in order to upgrade its quality of research in the field of sport sociology.

It is predicted that the future role for sport sociology in China is to interpret the reciprocal influences of sport in society and society in sport. It will move towards the combined direction of diversification, scientification, and glocalization.

NOTES

1. Lu and Lin (2008).
2. Shen and Su (2009).
3. Shen and Su (2009).
4. Ji and Jin (2012).
5. Tiyu is a collective term for physical education, sport and exercise in China.
6. Lei (2012).
7. Cong (2014).
8. Lei (2012).
9. Qiu (2006).
10. Shen and Su (op. cit.).
11. It is found that more than 100 out of the 667 authors of the publications of sport sociology in the 10 core sports journals between 2009 and 2013 were lecturers or below. See Shen and Su (2009).
12. He (2012).
13. The State Council (2014).

FIVE KEY READINGS

1. **Lu, Y., & Lin, W. (2008). Zhongguo tiyu shehui xue san shi nian [The development of sports sociology in the past thirty years in China].** *Jilin Sports College Journal, 24(5), 1−5.*

This paper reviews the historic process of sport sociology in China between 1981 and 2008. It claims that, in spite of its short history, sport sociology has established itself as an academic subject by broadening its research range, employing the concepts of sociology to analyze sports phenomena, and forming its own theory about sports reform.

2. **Qiu, J. (2006). 20 shiji 80 niandai yilai zhongguo tiyu shehui xue de fazhan [The development of sports sociology in China since 1980s].** *Sports Science, 2, 57−63.*

Based on a brief review of its development in the country, Qiu's paper argues that sport sociology in China has established its own theory system by paying attention to standardization and academic research, combining research methods of different disciplines, keeping an eye on social issues of sports development in the country, and expanding the study field. It discusses the process of glocalization with attention on both academic and realistic needs.

3. **Lei, W. (2012).** *Dui 2001–2010 nian zhongwen tiyu hexin qikan tiyu she-hui xue zaiwen fenxi [Statistic analysis of the publication of papers from 2001–2010 Chinese Core Sports Periodicals].* **Dissertation of Beijing Sports University.**

Lei's dissertation examined the 1995 sport sociology papers published in the 13 Chinese core sports journals between 2001 and 2010 in terms of the publication time and type of titles, authors' institutions and locations, financial support, and the group of authors who have produced the largest number of sports sociology papers in the country. It provided a valuable reference for understanding the current state of sport sociology in China.

4. **Ji, M., & Jin, Y. (2012). Jin 10 nian woguo tiyu shehui xue yanjiu shu ping [Reviews on the Study of Sports Society in China in the Last 10 Years].** *Guangzhou Sports Institute Journal, 32*(6), 13–18.

This paper searched not only the number of publications in China's major sports journals but also the number of projects that were awarded funding from the National Social Science Fund and the Philosophy and Social Science Project of State Sports Administration between 2001 and 2011. It found that there was a rise in terms of publications and projects with research funding for sport sociology; the focus of theoretic debate and exploration were on the nature of the discipline and research para-digm and methodology and the application studies centered on peasants and rural sport, sports public service, the Beijing Olympics, and talent cultivation for elite sport and post-athletic career. It argues that sport sociology in China has preferred macro- rather than microstudies, and has gradually formed a clear disciplinary field but is lacking in critical analysis and is heavily influenced by state policies.

5. **Shen, G., & Li, S. (2009). Jin 10 nian woguo tiyu shehui xue yanjiu redian yu fangfa [Hot Research Issues and methods in the past 10 years].** *33*(3), 33–36.

Shen's paper analyzed sport sociology-related articles published in the nine core sports periodicals between 1997 and 2006. It found that publi-cation of sports sociology has increased significantly since 2002 and the interest research topics at the turn of the century were sociological ana-lysis of sport for all, elite sport and school sport, community or urban sport, countryside or village sport, as well as sports sociology develop-ment in other countries. It also pointed out that male researchers were dominant in the community of sports sociology in China.

REFERENCES

Cong, M. (2014). 1997–2013 nian guojia sheke jijin tiyu xue lixiang fenxi [Analysis of the projects of PE and sport that won national social science fund between 1997 and 2013]. *Sports Culture Guide, 6*, 23–26.

Dong, J. (2002). *Women, sport and society in modern China: Holding up more than half the sky.* London: Routledge.

He, K. (2012). *shehui jingyin, minjian zuzhi, zhengfu zhi yu qunzhong tiyu yunxing yanjiu [Study of social elite, public organization and government's role in managing mass sport].* Doctorate dissertation of Shang Sports Institute.

Ji, M., & Jin, Y. (2012). Jin 10 nian woguo tiyu shehui xue yanjiu shu ping [Research review of sports sociology in China]. *Guangzhou Sports Institute Journal, 32*(6), 13–18.

Lei, W. (2012). *Dui 2001–2010 nian zhongwen tiyu hexin qikan tiyu shehui xue zaiwen fenxi [Analysis of the sports sociology papers at the sports core journals between 2001 and 2010].* Dissertation of Beijing Sports University.

Lin, Q. (1982). *Tiyu yundong shehui xue [Sports Sociology].* Unpublished handout.

Liu, D. (1990). *Tiyu shehui xue [Sociology of Sport].* People's Sports Press.

Lu, Y., & Lin, W. (2008). Zhongguo tiyu shehui xue san shi nian [Development of sports sociology in the past thirty years in China]. *Jilin Sports College Journal, 24*(5), 1–5.

Qiu, J. (2002). *zhongguo tiyu renkou de lilun tansu yu shizheng yanjiu [Theoretic exploration and empirical research on sports population in China].* Beijing: Beijing Sports University Press.

Qiu, J. (2006). 20 shiji 80 niandai yilai zhongguo tiyu shehui xue de fazhan [The development of sports sociology in China since 1980s]. *Sports Science, 2*, 57–63.

Shen, G., & Su, L. (2009). Jin 10 nian woguo tiyu shehui xue yanjiu redian yu fangfa [Hot research issues and methods in the past 10 years], *Shanghai Sports Institute Journal, 33*(3), 33–36.

The State Council. (2014). Guo wu yuan guanyu jiakuai fazhan tiyu chanye cujin tiyu xiaofei de ruogan yijian [Several opinions of the State Council on speeding up sports industry and enhancing sports consumption]. *Zhong hua renmin gong he guo guo wu yuan gongbao [The Bulletin of the State Council of PRC], 30*, 5–10.

Xiong, H. (2009). *Urbanisation and transformation of Chinese women's sport since 1980: Reconstruction, stratification and emancipation.* London: VDM Verlag Publisher.

Zhong, B. (1998). *Chengji ziben yu diwei huode: woguo youxiu yundong yuan qunti shehui liudong fenxi [Performance capital and status acquirement: Study of the social mobility of elite athletes in China].* Beijing: Beijing Sports University Press.

CHAPTER 3

SOCIOLOGY OF SPORT: INDIA

Veena Mani and Mathangi Krishnamurthy

ABSTRACT

This chapter is a collation and review of literature that can be considered to form the terrain of sports studies in India. It attempts two broad tasks: firstly, to aggregate these studies, and secondly, to predict the very possibility of a sociology of sport in India. To this end, this chapter is classified into three separate yet intertwined themes: modernity and nationalism; sub-nationalisms or regional nationalisms; and gender, masculinities, and culture. The first section looks at questions of modernity and nationalism within the Indian context through a close reading of studies on sports like field hockey and cricket. The second section is a critical look at the role of sub-nationalisms in complicating the notion of a singular nationalism, as played out in the domain of football in India. Lastly, the chapter examines questions of gender, especially masculinities, as a consistent yet plural presence in all of these literatures. These themes are neither exclusive nor all encompassing, and the chapter produces them in continuity as well as in rupture with one another. It concludes by speculating upon the possibilities and

Sociology of Sport: A Global Subdiscipline in Review
Research in the Sociology of Sport, Volume 9, 37–57
Copyright © 2017 by Emerald Group Publishing Limited
All rights of reproduction in any form reserved
ISSN: 1476-2854/doi:10.1108/S1476-285420160000009003

challenges for a sociology of sport in India, with suggestions for possible methodological interventions.

Keywords: Sociology of sport; post-coloniality; nationalism; gender; masculinities

INTRODUCTION

The idea of the study of sport as a unique and consolidated phenomenon is a relatively recent development in India. While the sociology of sport can be traced across discipline-specific research work on varied sports such as cricket, football, wrestling, and hockey, attempts to study them together or to understand sport as deserving of its own registers of analyses are nascent, but on the rise. In writing this chapter, we considered our task to be twofold — firstly, to locate the research concerns that are common to these studies of sport, and secondly, to review these to understand the possibility of a sociology of sport in India. To this end, our chapter has been classified into three separate, yet intertwined themes, namely modernity and nationalism; sub-nationalisms or regional nationalisms; and gender, masculinities, and culture.

Our choice of these themes has been determined by a review of existing literature. The specificity of analysis lies in the way in which each theme is shaped and enunciated by the particularities through which the sport is played. Nationalism, for example, is a common yet heterogeneous trend. The concept of nationalism, closely tied to the ethos of time and space, seems to underlie these studies on sport, wherein each sport is understood in terms of its ability to sufficiently or insufficiently illuminate the nationalist agenda. Our second theme, however, led from the ways in which regional specificity and its relation to nationalism was emphasized in certain literatures. These we understand to be sub-nationalisms, that is, those enunciations of spatial and cultural identity, based on regions and/or religions that may or may not dialogue with the dominant nationalism of the nation-state. These literatures allowed us to further explore the relationship between regions, religions, and bodily culture. Lastly, one of the most dominant and charged discussions within these studies of sport were related to questions of body and gender, which were both ubiquitous and contested.

Even as we have divided our review into these sections, they are by no means exhaustive. Our purpose in this chapter is to produce the terrain within which a sociology of sport is made possible. To this end, we conclude by talking about possible ways to expand the understanding of sport in India, and speculate on its location within Indian academia.

MODERNITY AND NATIONALISM

Our conception of nationalism in the Indian context specifically locates itself in postcoloniality. In conversation with nationalist literature, which argues that India, like other postcolonial nations, defines itself and its claim to modernity in conflict and cohort with its colonial past (Chatterjee, 1993), we locate the study of sport as part and parcel of this nationalist project. In this section, we focus specifically on cricket and field hockey as vehicles par excellence to understand the ways in which the nation-state and sport became inextricably entangled, and why, we argue, it remains so to this day.

Field Hockey

Field hockey is a sport introduced to India by the British as part of the colonial civilizing process. Scholars of postcolonial studies have commented widely on the civilizing process as inherent to the discourse and justification of "empire" (Elias & Dunning, 1986). To this extent, field hockey served as a means to introduce discipline, ritual, and motivation to a set of imagined barbarians (Dunning, 1999), and it was men in the army and railways who were primarily inducted into the sport.

Majumdar (2008) takes us through the history of field hockey in India, offering a special emphasis on the Indian team's performances in various international competitions. Between 1928 and 1956, India won six consecutive Olympic gold medals in 24 matches (*ibid.*, p. 1594). In addition, India won gold in 1964 and 1980, respectively. Even as the team upheld colonial victory until Indian independence in 1947, their continuing dominance posed a challenge to their erstwhile rulers after this period, thus disturbing many colonial narratives on the supremacy of the West, and contributing to emerging nationalist assertions in India. When the English field hockey team withdrew from the Amsterdam Olympics in 1928, the event triggered rumors that Britain was scared of defeat against its colony (*ibid.*, p. 1598). In this analysis, field hockey thus becomes a site to understand colonial tensions, racial anxieties, and nationalist competitions, particularly during inter-war periods. In 1948, the Indian team went on to beat the British field hockey team with a score of 4-0, and the ensuing jubilations were said to reflect upon the newly independent state of India (*ibid.*). It was field hockey that placed India on the world sporting map through exceptional and continuous domination. The fact that India had its own national team, even before its independence, tells us something about the domain of sport acting as an alternate political battleground. An imagination of the nation was embodied through India's national field hockey team even before India established itself as an independent nation. Majumdar (2008) and Sen (2015) explain how hockey became a national game after the Indian national team's victories on the world stage, including six consecutive Olympic gold medals.

Cricket

Cricket was the subject of most of the early writings in English on sport in India. A large part of this consists of the narratives of renowned Indian cricket players such as Ranjitsinhji (1901), and Mohammed Mansoor Ali Khan, the Nawab of Pataudi (1969). Scholarly works, however, have overwhelmingly focused on the colonial origins of cricket, and its adaptation and popularity in the Indian context.

Bose (2006) and Guha and Vaidyanathan (1994), for example, explain how cricket was a colonial product, participated in by Indians, thereby constructing an identity in line with colonial expectations, but steeped in nationalist values. Nandy (2015) quixotically remarks: "Cricket is an Indian game accidentally discovered by the English" (p. 1). He argues how values inherent to cricket such as fate, the idea of the opponent as a worthy other, and a sense of ahistoricity were easily adaptable to the Indian context, and paved the way for it to become an Indian national game. Cashman (1980) has argued that it was primarily patronage that shaped Indian cricket. He narrates how British and Indian princes were the largest number of patrons in the early phase of cricket in India. He also explains the political intent behind patronizing cricket, which was to introduce Indians to a new set of cultural values, even as the sport allowed the maintenance of separate colonial identities. Like polo (McDevitt, 2003), cricket was the business of the elite. Using a historical and psychoanalytical lens, Nandy (2015) reads cricket in India as developing and contributing to a conception of Indian nationalism. He describes how in the process of playing cricket, Indians negotiated their identities both with, and against, the British. He grounds his analysis in the contrary lives of two cricketing icons, Ranjitsinhji and Dinkar Deodhar.

Nandy (2015) narrates the life of Ranjitsinhji to explain the latter's process of identification with the British Empire, even as he engages with the figure of Dinkar Deodhar to disturb this seemingly uncritical reception of English values through cricket. Ranjitsinhji and Deodhar, in his analysis, represent the loyalists and the nationalists respectively. Ranjitsinhji was an Indian prince who played for the English clubs between the 1890s and 1920s, and was celebrated as "the Indian ... as the supreme exponent of the Englishman's game" (Gardiner, as quoted in Nandy, 2015, p. 67). On the other hand, Ranjitsinhji himself identified as an English cricketer (*ibid.*, p. 69). In Nandy's understanding, his identification with the English alone, however, does not make him a non-nationalist. Nandy argues that Ranjitsinhji's concept of nationalism was inextricably linked with that of English nationalism, which demanded unconditional loyalty to the crown. Ranjitsinhji, in Nandy's analysis, represented the Indian elite who wished to identify themselves with the British middle class, even as they desired to distinguish themselves from the natives. Cricket was a perfect medium for this Indian elite to solidify their identification with the British. Thus cricket helped produce Indian nationalism as a mirror to English nationalism. In contrast, Dinkar Deodhar, Nandy argues, can be read as representing middle-class Indians who participated in cricket. Nandy notes how "his orientation to cricket therefore provides crucial clues to the way the game grew out of its aristocratic, upper-class, western connection and became the national game of India" (*ibid.*, p. 79). Deodhar was a player who had primarily trained and established himself within India, and his cricketing spaces were schools and college teams in India from the 1910s to the 1930s. Nandy further elaborates on what he reads to be Deodhar's critiques of the colonial situation in cricket. He writes, "the first of these was the dominance of the princes in cricket, their close links with the colonial regime, and their obvious contempt for common Indians" (*ibid.*, p. 82), and adds that the second related to "the mindless manner in which Indian cricket followed English practices" (*ibid.*, p. 79). Nandy explains how Deodhar felt that Indians should devise their own ways of playing cricket in light of the country's climactic conditions, as well as other variations from England (*ibid.*, p. 80). In Nandy's analysis, Deodhar represented a form of cricket nationalism, which consciously tried to move away from the English nationalism of Ranjitsinhji. For Deodhar, cricket, as well as nationalism, ought to have been played in a way not only distinct from that of the English, but also from the Indian elite who did not identify with the masses.

Appadurai (1998) takes a slightly contrary view to Nandy's arguments in arguing for cricket to be a "hard" cultural form, which resists any reinterpretation, as the values ingrained in the sport are puritan in their orientation. Paying specific heed to processes of decolonization, he argues that Indian cricket only became Indian through a long set of multiply located processes. He explains the relationship between the process of decolonization, emergent nationalism, and cricket in two ways. Firstly, he argues that Indian nationalism emerged as a by-product of a colonial enterprise, which needed an oppositional Indian team to play against the English team. Appadurai (ibid.), and Guha (2002) describe how early cricket clubs in India were mostly segregated among communal lines. Parsees were the first among Indians to play cricket and were also pioneers in cricket writing (Mukherjee, 1976). An Indian team was constructed out of these varied communal teams so as to serve as worthy opponents for the British colonial team. The consolidated Indian cricket team, and the subsequent nationalist feelings it inspired, were the by-products of English cricket nationalism. A nation was imagined simultaneously with that of a cricket team. Here, Appadurai (ibid.) seems to suggest through cricket in India that colonial and decolonizing aspirations overlap, reproduce, and co-constitute one another.

Secondly, in Appadurai's argument, decolonization in cricket took place through what he understands to be the vernacularization of the sport (Appadurai, 1998, p. 33). He puts forward an argument that emphasizes the role of vernacular language and media in the 1960s, in indigenizing the game. Majumdar (2002) also explains how vernacular literature on cricket in Bengal allowed for the reception and dissemination of the sport among the masses. In other words, the form and vocabulary of cricket had to be "linguistically domesticated" (Appadurai, 1998, p. 34) in order for it to be popularized. A large vernacular literature and commentary explained cricket to an audience, which readily translated its "lived experience of bodily competence" (ibid., p. 45) into everyday lives. These cricket writings also acclimated the people to the English language by transcribing English names and technical terms in the vernacular. Cricket in India was thus indigenized through a massive textualization. In this set of arguments, the reception of cricket constructed a certain type of "subjectivity and agency in the process of decolonization" (ibid., p. 38). By this, Appadurai means that the masses were not passive recipients of cricket as an English form but instead, literate participants who understood the culture of this sport through its vernacularization, and therefore, as a native form. Cricket, in these analyses, while being a colonial product, served as the medium for decolonization, and in later years as a site of intense nationalist expression.

In contemporary times, Nandy (2015), Appadurai (1998), and Guha (2002), among others (Beech, Rigby, Talbot, & Thandi, 2005; Dasgupta, 2004; Nair, 2011), explain how cricket has become a medium for many Indians both inside and outside the country, to identify with the idea of the nation. Cricket further became a new domain for the creation of national heroes (Dasgupta, 2004). After many impressive victories on the international stage, and especially since 1983, when India won the Cricket World Cup, identification with the national team, and by extension the nation, became easy and enriching for many Indians. The nation-state of India, like many other post-colonial nations, continues to be a contested terrain (Aloysius, 1998). In this scenario, the performance of the Indian national team on the global stage came as a relief for those who confronted post-colonial anxieties, and identity and power politics in a globalized and diasporic world.

The diaspora is a particularly important site of analysis for these arguments. Majumdar (2007) argues for cricket as a tool for identification with the homeland for non-resident Indians. In the way that discourses around football in the United Kingdom, at one point in time, attempted to solidify the identity of the British (Carrington, 1998), cricket similarly became a site of cultural nationalism even outside the geographical boundaries of the nation. Majumdar (2007) is rather optimistic when he argues that cricket provides "a space where all differences are overcome" (p. 89). However, he does have a point in that the Indian diaspora imagine and continue to take pride in the identity of the homeland through cricket victories on the world stage. He seems to suggest that cricket unifies people and levels differences, albeit provisionally, therefore constructing and abetting the illusion of a homogeneous Indian culture.

These studies on cricket in India seem to suggest the prominent role of the sport in defining and holding in place the tense and never-resolved relationship between modernity, decolonization, and nationalism, throughout the long and short history of the Indian nation. Through various negotiations with the values attached to cricket, analyses read the game as a palimpsest to inscribe, erase, and re-inscribe changing post-colonial enunciations of identity and nationalism. However, as we argue in the subsequent sections of this chapter, these are neither unitary nor uncontested, and in all cases, can be critiqued for their particular, gendered, and exclusive understanding of identity and nation.

REGIONAL AND SUB-NATIONALISMS

Sub-nationalism is a useful concept to question the homogeneity ascribed to the concept of nation, and also to disconnect nationalism from an imagined and unitary national history. Sub-nationalisms acknowledge the role of regions, religions, and races in the process of identity formation (Gellner & Breuilly, 2008). In this section, we focus on regional enunciations of the game of football, in order to read these burgeoning forms of what we understand to be sub-nationalism or regional nationalism. The specific regions we explore are Bengal, Kashmir, Hyderabad, and Goa.

Football

The status of football in India has always remained lower on the hierarchy than cricket, and it has not succeeded in speaking to a pan-Indian imagination. Analyzing various international performances of the Indian football team, Dimeo (2001a) argues that Indian football began on a promising note and then underwent a prolonged period of depression. He speculates on the Indian national team's withdrawal from the 1950 World Cup in Brazil given that many suspected a set of critical state, infrastructural, and bureaucratic hurdles. However, performances in the Olympics in 1948, 1952, 1956, and 1960 in London, Helsinki, Melbourne, and Rome, respectively, speak of a robust history of participation by Indian football players. Many consider the Melbourne Olympics stint to be the most memorable; India finished fourth, and Neville D'Souza became a national hero after scoring three goals against Australia. Indian football could not retain this glory in successive years (*ibid.*). Football, however, continues to be a highly popular sport in the states of West Bengal, Goa, Manipur, and Kerala, and is noteworthy in its presence in studies on sport.

The Bengal Chapter
West Bengal in India is an erstwhile presidency of the British Empire situated on the coast of the Bay of Bengal, sharing borders with Bangladesh, Nepal, and Bhutan. Paul Dimeo, in his article "Football and Politics in Bengal: Colonialism, Nationalism, Communalism" (2001b), shows how football reflected and reproduced various tensions such as racial segregation, caste discrimination, regional enmities, and communal disharmony in Bengali society in the early twentieth century. Played since the 1870s by

Europeans in Bengal, who also introduced the sport to the region, football was a marker of the modern "civilized" subject as originating in English public schools. Dimeo narrates how the sport was popularized by the army, merchants, civil servants, and missionaries, and explains how it "reflected the social structures of European society in Bengal, which was far from a homogeneous unit, fissured as it was by class, profession and geography" (Dimeo, 2001b, p. 59). He also points out that football clubs were initially segregated along racial lines; Calcutta Football Club and Dalhousie Club, among other clubs, for example, disallowed Indians from membership, this being congruent with the everyday state of affairs after the 1857 mutiny[1] when cultural interactions between the natives and the colonial rulers were severely and forcefully limited. The author speaks of how despite this norm, many Europeans introduced the game to the natives. For colonial subjects, football then went on to become a site to negotiate and contest the British assumption of Bengali men as effeminate, and intellectually superior, but physically weak (Dimeo, 2002). Thus every win against the colonizer's team by the natives was read as a challenge to the alleged racial and masculine superiority of the colonizers. It was also in the context of the partition of Bengal[2] that the Indian Football Association (IFA) shield victory of Mohun Bagan A.C.[3] against the East Yorkshire Regiment in 1911 was celebrated by Indian newspapers like *Amrita Bazar Patrika* as an assertion not only of nationhood, but also of masculinity by the Bengalis.

Post-independence football narratives, however, speak of a fractured nationalism, in that rivalries attest to communal and sub-regional turns in the history of football in Bengal (Bandyopadhyay, 2011). Dimeo (2003) expands upon the relationship between football and communalism by way of a history of the Mohammedan Sporting Club[4] in Bengal. He explains how anxieties regarding the partition of India and the formation of Pakistan were reflected in the promotion, as well as hostile reception to the clubs' activities by various stakeholders. He argues that the prominent political party, the Muslim League[5] used the spaces opened by the Mohammedan Sporting Club to mobilize Muslims, and to assert the religious identity of their nationalist project. However, he does not analyze the role of other clubs, and places the burden of participating in the politics of communalism entirely on the shoulders of a single football club. Bandyopadhyay (2009) argues that it would be misleading and over-determined to argue for the communal roots of the Mohammedan Sporting Club in its inception. Instead, he discusses the ways in which many considered the success of the club to be as much about victory over the British, even though it also signified conflict between Muslims and Hindus. However, Bandyopadhyay (*ibid.*) clearly states that the Mohammedan Sporting Club's five straight Calcutta Football League titles between 1934 and 1938 were not celebrated as nationalist triumph, in comparison with the Mohun Bagan Club's victory against the East Yorkshire Regiment in the IFA Shield final in 1911. It seems that the football grounds in Bengal deeply reflected the anxieties, uncertainties, and aspirations of various communal identities in the process of nation-state formation. In addition to that, the history of football in Bengal speaks specifically of a certain mode of Bengali/East Bengali nationalism and/or Hindu/Muslim nationalism, given its tense, and communal, colonial and post-colonial history.

In his article, "The Nation and its Fragments: Football and Community in India" (2008), Bandyopadhyay further discusses communal nuances within the Bengali community in relation to football. Bringing in a wider array of stakeholders, he portrays the rivalries of Mohun Bagan A.C., Mohammedan Sporting Club, and the East Bengal Football Club as signifying emerging religious anxieties, migrant despair, and troubled masculinities. Engaging with the ways in which the partition of Bengal in post-independence India, into West Bengal and East Pakistan (currently Bangladesh), brought communal and sub-regional nuances into the already fraught domain of football rivalries, he discusses the complex relationship between Hindus from West Bengal, and Hindus who migrated from East Bengal (*ibid.*). The unwelcoming and patronizing attitude of the natives toward the migrant population created a chasm between the people belonging to the same religion, and this was played out not only on the football fields but also in the spectator galleries. Men from West Bengal and East Bengal supported Mohun Bagan and East Bengal teams respectively, and spectator violence became a part of football reception in the region. Mukherjee (2013) also talks about sub-nationalist tones during the victory of Mohun Bagan against the East Yorkshire Regiment in the IFA Shield in 1911, and the subsequent communal and regional tensions in matches between Mohun Bagan and East Bengal, that persist in contemporary times. A noteworthy aspect of these narrations is their emphasis on the identity of the region as asserting itself over an identity based on religion. This does not mean that there was no communal sub-text, but these arguments compel us to examine the complex ways in which migration affected the lives of a fledgling nation-state, as reflected in the fan base of both the Mohun Bagan and East Bengal football teams.

The Hyderabad Chapter

Hyderabad was a princely state in the south of India. Contrary to the common assumption that only cricket received royal patronage in colonial India, the history of football in Hyderabad tells us a different story. Kapadia (2001) argues that the reigning royal families of the time, the Nizams of Hyderabad, encouraged the sport as early as the 1920s. In the pre- and post-colonial period, football clubs in Hyderabad, however, were perceived in opposition to the Bengal clubs. Speaking about the Hyderabad City Police Club, for example, Kapadia (2001) writes:

> Playing with exemplary manners and receiving few rewards for their performances, the club was popular all over India and came to be identified as the team of the common man, in opposition to the elite clubs of Calcutta. In the period just after Independence, Hyderabad City Police came to symbolize the ethos and spirit of the age, the will to sacrifice, overcome odds and work for great ideals, and their popularity transcended regional and religious identities. (p. 20)

Here, it is interesting to note how patronage worked differently for cricket and football. Royal patronage in football produced an identification with the masses, distinguishing the Hyderabad players from the elite and exclusive status ascribed to the Bengal clubs. Moreover, the mis-identification of the Hyderabad club with the Bengal clubs as well as Bengal sub-nationalism is pronounced. As we notice in Kapadia's narration (*ibid.*), there is a clear attempt to disconnect the Hyderabad City Police Club from any region or religion. The question of nationalism and sub-nationalism is doubly complex in the case of Hyderabad as it was one of the princely states, which resisted union with India (Sherman, 2007). Hence, the idea of nationalism in this context could not be easily translated into that of Indian nationalism. A similar yet different example can be found in the princely state of Kashmir, which also demonstrated resistance to the idea of Indian nationalism at the time of independence from the British in 1947.

The Kashmir Chapter

Football in Kashmir was introduced by missionaries, like in other parts of the country, through their schools. Sport was used to inculcate values like "energy," "courage," and "willpower" (Bourdieu, 1999, p. 431) in the students to make them conform to the norms of a muscular Christianity. Muscular Christianity symbolizes a particular muscular body, and also refers to the highest form of physical health, one that is capable of performing piety (MacAloon, 2006). At the same time, it also serves to attack and intervene within ideas of otherness and backwardness as defined by and against missionary values. Mangan (2001) talks about how a church missionary named Cecil Earle Tyndale-Biscoe introduced football in a school in Kashmir to disturb notions of traditional caste as attached to the body of Brahmin boys. The opposition between the Brahmin male body, and its notions of purity in relation to touch and the preservation of caste, as against the modern sport of football, with its attendant connotations of mixing and corruption, are emphasized in this narrative.

In current-day India, football has grown into a popular sport in Kashmir amid painful histories of conflict, and state-imposed curfews. Football therefore also functions as an important analytical tool to look into questions of boundaries, citizenship, and migration in places like Kashmir. A documentary titled *Inshallah, Football*[6] narrates the story of a young Kashmiri football player who finds it difficult to pursue a football career in Brazil because of the denial of his passport application by the Indian state. This story of the son of an ex-militant had to undergo a long tussle with the Central Board of Film Certification because it engaged with questions of war and militarization, and the violence embedded in the making of the Indian nation-state.

The Goa Chapter

Goa, an erstwhile Portuguese territory situated along the southeastern coast of India, is unique in its football narratives. Dimeo (2001a) sees Goan football as highly professionalized owing to the involvement of rich, local, industrial club owners such as Salgoacar, Dempo, and the Churchill brothers. Mills (2001) brilliantly locates football in Goa in specific relation to the culture and politics of the region. Discussing the history of football in Goa, he explains how studying football in the Goan context makes us confront the role of the church, questions of migration, industrialization, decolonization, and the fight for independent territory within an independent India. He speaks of how football emerged as an expression of a distinct Goan identity at times of crucial political transformation during and after Goa's transition to independence from the Portuguese. He discusses how football in Goa disseminated through the villages and was absorbed into the everyday by the majority of the population. Therefore, football came to play an important part in people's understanding of a Goan identity. He further shows how Goan workers in Bombay formed communities held together by football. Most importantly, he argues that during the process of decolonization, football became the site of contestation for numerous political groups to capture power in the newly freed territory of Goa, even as Goa was integrated into the Indian Union after Portuguese rule ended in 1961 (Rao, 1963).

These narratives of regional football show how the sport in many parts in India was closely linked with the history, political conflict, and identity of the region, and helped highlight the distinctness of the region in opposition to other regions, or in opposition to the idea of an uncontested and monolithic Indian nation.

GENDER, MASCULINITIES, AND CULTURE

Our third area of focus for this chapter is in relation to a thread that runs across all discussions of sport, either as sub-text, or overt area of focus. That sport is a gendered arena is almost a truism (Connell, 2005; Kidd, 2013), but what we seek to outline in this section, are the ways in which gender figures as a mode of analysis in the sociology of sport in India. The two ways in which we understand gender for the purpose of this discussion are, first, as the stated statistical inadequacy of literature on women's participation in sport, and second, as the ways in which sport creates particular understandings of gendered subjectivity.

There is very little mention of women players or women's clubs in historical and sociological research on sport in India. In one of the few works referencing women's participation in sport, Majumdar (2003) argues that the condition of women's football in India is merely an extension of and a comment on contemporary India, where a large section of women are discriminated against in their everyday lives. He expands upon this observation to show how even in its scant evidence of participation, football remains an arena for women from the lower classes, owing to the cultural stigma attached to women in public space in general, and women in sports in particular. While the history of football in India is dominated by masculine narratives from Bengal and Goa, Majumdar (*ibid.*) highlights the role of other states like Manipur and Kerala in the growth of Indian women's football. He explains how Manipur has had a strong Women's Football Federation since 1975, and how it has helped Manipur retain its primacy in national women's tournaments.

While the role of women in sport is accorded very little space in scholarly work on sport in India, the question of gendered subjectivities and culture, however, is a dominant and widely discussed question. The history of football, in West Bengal, for example, has been discussed not only in its nationalist fervor, but also in regard to masculine assertion. Dimeo (2002) states that given how the British considered Bengali men to be intellectually superior but physically weak and effeminate in nature, the oft-quoted IFA shield victory of Mohan Bagan against the East Yorkshire Regiment in 1911 was celebrated as evidence of Bengalis as proper masculine subjects. The narratives of the match celebrated Mohun Bagan's victory through a curious valorization of a casteist notion of masculinity wherein customs such as child marriage were legitimized (Bandyopadhyay & Mallick, 2013, p. 57). These reports explained how most of the Bagan players were children born out of what the British considered to be the barbaric custom of child marriages. The football victory of children born out of these seemingly uncivilized and anti-modern arrangements was used to articulate and justify a certain caste-bound way of life. These notions of caste and class as enunciated through ideals of masculinity were evident not only in the sphere of football but also in Indian cricket.

Cricket functioned in the colonies as a medium to transfer a repertoire of metropolitan values, many linked to Victorian notions of upper-class masculinity (Appadurai, 1998). Values such as fair play, stoicism, and respect toward the opponents, and physical symbols such as toned but non-muscular bodies, and clean, white clothes were markers of a certain dominant masculinity prevalent in England. Even as colonialism has been theorized through gendered categories where the colonizer is termed masculine while the colonized is the feminine (Nagel, 1998), discussions highlight how the world of cricket allowed for the blurring of these boundaries, in allowing for the colonized to occupy the role of the masculine. Nandy (2015), for example, uses the work of T. G. Vaidyanathan to argue for the understanding of the batsman and the bowler in terms of the masculine and feminine respectively (p. 128). He explains how the masculine form of batting is affected by the feminine bowling, and how cricket transcends any strictly gendered distinctions. This can be read along with his thesis on the intimate enemy, in which one mirrors the enemy and often finds oneself conflicted on having to confront those hated qualities within oneself (Nandy, 1989). By this argument, we do not wish to solidify the binary between masculine and feminine but to take seriously the masculine imagination in relation to colonialism and sport.

Another sport that has produced writings demonstrating this tense and conflictual relationship is that of wrestling, which promotes a masculine subject distinct from the modern colonial notion of masculinity. If, as Connell (2005) argues, masculinities are not unified and homogeneous, but contain internal hierarchies based on class, race, age, sexuality, and other social categories, they can also be reconfigured to serve purposes of differentiation, and exclusion, especially from other masculine populations. Joseph Alter's seminal work on the Hindu wrestler (1992), for example, distinguishes itself from other masculinities of consumption and secularism, by promoting abstinence and discipline, as clearly circumscribed within a particular Hindu ethos. The politics of masculinities, in this case, become linked with the politics of religion, caste, body, and the nation. Wrestling in India, Alter argues (*ibid.*), is a sport where the participant's body is marked by cultural nationalism, a nationalism deeply embedded in a dominant Hindu way of life. An Indian wrestler in Alter's understanding is a cultural hero and his sporting practices do not separate him from domestic life, economy, politics, and religion. In another discussion, Gupta (2012) engages with the figure of the wrestler Gobor Guha[7] to explain the nexus of body culture, nationalism, and masculine crisis in the context of Bengal. Both Alter (1992) and Gupta (2012) argue the centrality of body in building a discourse on particular forms of nationalism, and reiterate that the nation is imagined in continuity with a specific, nurtured, masculine self.

McDonald (2003) argues, however, that this imagination of the nation through body does not always produce the same cultural formation, and offers the contrary examples of training undertaken by the Hindu right-wing cultural organization, the Rashtriya Swayamsevak Sangh (RSS), as against the martial art of Kalaripayattu,[8] to instantiate his argument. While for the RSS, "shakha training" (*ibid.*, p. 1564), namely a set of "Western-style military drill and indigenous games and exercises" (*ibid.*), functions as the necessary condition to the healthy body of the nation, Kalaripayattu is almost meditative, seeking unity of body and mind, and an immersive consciousness. McDonald (2007) traces the history and the cultural gravity of Kalaripayattu in the globalized spaces of Kerala, and discusses the ways in which it disturbs the easy differences between categories such as competitive sport, dance, and theater. Thus, these two forms of practice, "embedded in their respective globalizing cultural socioscapes, yet offering a contrasting set of cultural meanings and political possibilities" (McDonald, 2003, p. 1564) function as evidence of diverse masculine possibilities. The training offered by the RSS is stated to be a process toward remasculinizing Hindu subjects, emasculated through colonial occupation, in order to build a competitive, and culturally located, strong nation. On the other hand, McDonald (2003) argues that Kalaripayattu makes no such claims to any nationalist masculinity but imagines a masculinity steeped in spectacle, for a global audience. Kalaripayattu focuses on a masculine yet melodramatic performance to effectively produce exotic regional culture. Even as these two masculinities share features of performance, exhibitionism, and spectacle, they are nevertheless distinct in the ways in which they interpellate the national subject in relation to the world.

In these examinations of the relationship between sport and masculinity, one can read Judith Butler's arguments on performativity, gender, and identity (Butler, 1999) to argue for the performance of masculinity as the very edifice that produces the sporting arena. It is not surprising that gender forms one of the core areas of analysis in studies of sport in India, given the ways in which it produces the subject and the nation-state in the same breath, albeit on a wide variety of registers.

CONCLUSION

McDonald (2000) argues that studies on sport in India constitute a young and unexplored territory that has, over the last decade and a half, shown slow signs of an upsurge. In an article titled "Sports History in India: Prospects and Problems" (2005), Bandyopadhyay explores the challenges in writing any histories of sport in India. He argues that conventional disciplines in India still find sport a subject unworthy of serious academic attention; work on sport therefore remains the realm of journalism and practitioners themselves. While his arguments are well taken, what might help produce a more robust sociology of sport in India is a turn toward unconventional sources and archives. In a post-colonial country like India, where historians struggle to find "authentic" sources, it is all the more important to explore the subject of sport through an interdisciplinary archive and methodology. Along with a reading of official documents, pamphlets, and architectures, it is also necessary to look at sport through oral histories, ethnographic research, and participant observation. A notable step toward a better sports studies environment has been the formation of an ad hoc group in 2015 by the Indian Sociological Society, in order to discuss and encourage sports research in India. This is a welcoming and heartening development, which will help build networks, foster shared resources, and allow for diverse and interdisciplinary discussions.

We would like to conclude by pointing to one of the major lacunae in existing studies on sport in India. In our review, the category of sport seems to be limited to professional and organized modern sports. There are many active and traditional sports, which are immensely popular in many parts of India. Jallikattu, a form of bull-fighting, for example, is a sport conducted in relation to many temple festivals in the southern parts of Tamil Nadu. This sport, closely related to the lives of agricultural communities, draws thousands of spectators, but did not find mention in our survey of literature on sport in English. Other sports that have not found a place yet in sports studies in India include Dahi Handi,[9] which is popular in Maharashtra, and the annual boat race conducted in Alappuzha, Kerala. Scholars of sport need to reflect on the category of sport itself so that the domain of sports studies can be inclusive, diverse, and vibrant. In sport studies, as Dunning (1999) has pointed out, there is always a tension in regard to the definition of sport even as it encourages us to reflect upon what is stake in the search for a sociology of sport.

NOTES

1. The Sepoy Mutiny of 1857 is considered to be the first war of independence against the British in India. For more information, please see Chattopadhyaya (1957).
2. The British Viceroy of India partitioned Bengal in 1905. In the face of prolonged local protest, these divided areas of West Bengal and East Bengal were later reunited in 1911, and subsequently separated along linguistic lines. For further reading, see Eustis and Zaidi (1964).
3. Mohun Bagan Athletic Club is a Calcutta based football club formed in 1889.
4. Mohammedan Sporting Club was founded in Calcutta in 1891.
5. The Muslim League was formed in 1906 by Agha Khan III to safeguard the political rights of Muslims in the Indian subcontinent.
6. *Inshallah, Football* is a 2010 documentary directed by Ashvin Kumar and produced by Javed Jaffrey. To view the trailer, please see https://www.youtube.com/watch?v=6_zBZ5gz7eY. Accessed on March 20, 2016.
7. Gobor Guha was a wrestler from colonial Bengal who won a world heavyweight title in 1921.
8. Kalaripayattu is an indigenous martial art that originated in Kerala, India.
9. A pot filled with curd, hung high on a bar, is broken by forming a human pyramid, wherein one person climbs to the top to access and break the pot.

FIVE KEY READINGS

1. **Alter, J. S. (1992). *The wrestler's body: Identity and ideology in North India*. Berkeley, CA: University of California Press.**

Alter's ethnographic work brilliantly lays out the relationship between body, physical training, and cultural nationalism in the context of India.

He narrates how everyday practices shape identity and ideology within the domain of wrestling.

2. **Bandyopadhyay, K. (2011).** *Scoring off the field: Football culture in Bengal,* **1911–1980. New Delhi: Routledge.**

This work explains the history and sociology of football in Bengal over a period of seven decades. The book discusses themes such as nationalism, regionalism, communalism, and casteism in relation to football and shows us how history of the sport in Bengal is intertwined with social forces in the region.

3. **Sen, R. (2015).** *Nation at play: A history of sport in India.* **Gurgaon: Penguin India.**

Sen's book attempts to give a comprehensive account of the history of sport in India. The book deals with many sports such as cricket, football, and hockey during the times of monarchy, anti-colonial struggle and independent India, and it gives us an insight into the evolution and gravity of these sports within the diverse socio-cultural fabric of India.

4. **McDonald, I. (2003). Hindu nationalism, cultural spaces, and bodily practices in India.** *American Behavioral Scientist, 46*(11), 1563–1576.

McDonald's work deals with physical practices at the fringes of Indian society. He deals with the physical training sessions of the Rashtriya Swayamsevak Sangh, a Hindu organization, and also that of Kalaripayattu, which is a martial art form practiced in parts of Kerala. He tries to understand the particularities of these practices in order to further an understanding of nationalism and masculinities.

5. **Mangan, J. A. (2001). Soccer as moral training: Missionary intentions and imperial legacies.** *Soccer and Society, 2*(2), 41–56.

Mangan's article carefully examines the workings of the colonial machinery and missionaries in promoting football in India. The article is also important in that it discusses football in the context of the Kashmir and Afghan frontiers, producing a different narrative than that of Bengal or Goa because of geographical, political, and cultural specificities.

REFERENCES

Aloysius, G. (1998). *Nationalism without a nation in India.* New Delhi: Oxford University Press.

Alter, J. S. (1992). *The wrestler's body: Identity and ideology in North India.* Berkeley, CA: University of California Press.

Appadurai, A. (1998). Playing with modernity: The decolonization of Indian cricket. In C. Breckenridge (Ed.), *Consuming modernity: Public culture in a South Asian world* (pp. 23−48). Minneapolis, MN: University of Minnesota Press.

Bandyopadhyay, K. (2005). Sports history in India: Prospects and problems. *The International Journal of the History of Sport, 22*(4), 708−721.

Bandyopadhyay, K. (2008). 'The nation and its fragments': Football and community in India. *Soccer & Society, 9*(3), 377−393.

Bandyopadhyay, K. (2009). In search of an identity: The Muslims and football in colonial India. *Soccer & Society, 10*(6), 843−865.

Bandyopadhyay, K. (2011). *Scoring off the field: Football culture in Bengal* (pp. 1911−1980). New Delhi: Routledge.

Bandyopadhyay, K., & Mallick, S. (2013). *Fringe nations in world soccer.* London: Routledge.

Beech, J., Rigby, A., Talbot, I., & Thandi, S. (2005). Sport tourism as a means of reconciliation? The case of India-Pakistan cricket. *Tourism Recreation Research, 30*(1), 83−91.

Bose, M. (2006). *A maidan view: The magic of Indian cricket.* New Delhi: Penguin India.

Bourdieu, P. (1999). How can one be a sports fan? In S. During (Ed.), *The cultural studies reader* (pp. 427−478). London: Routledge.

Butler, J. (1999). *Gender trouble: Feminism and the subversion of identity.* New York, NY: Routledge.

Carrington, B. (1998). 'Football's coming home' but whose home? And do we want it?: Nation, football and the politics of exclusion. In A. Brown (Ed.), *Fanatics: Power, identity and fandom in football* (pp. 101−123). London: Routledge.

Cashman, R. (1980). *Patrons, players and the crowd: The phenomenon of Indian cricket.* New Delhi: Orient Longman.

Chatterjee, P. (1993). *The nation and its fragments: Colonial and postcolonial histories.* Princeton, NJ: Princeton University Press.

Chattopadhyaya, H. (1957). *The Sepoy Mutiny, 1857: A social study and analysis.* Calcutta: Bookland.

Connell, R. W. (2005). *Masculinities.* Berkeley, CA: University of California Press.

Dasgupta, J. (2004). Manufacturing unison: Muslims, Hindus and Indians during the India-Pakistan match. *The International Journal of the History of Sport, 21*(3−4), 573−584.

Dimeo, P. (2001a). Contemporary developments in Indian football. *Contemporary South Asia, 10*(2), 251−264.

Dimeo, P. (2001b). Football and politics in Bengal: Colonialism, nationalism, communalism. *Soccer & Society, 2*(2), 57−74.

Dimeo, P. (2002). Colonial bodies, colonial sport: 'Martial' Punjabis, 'Effeminate' Bengalis and the development of Indian football. *The International Journal of the History of Sport, 19*(1), 72−90.

Dimeo, P. (2003). 'With political Pakistan in the offing …': Football and communal politics in South Asia, 1887−1947. *Journal of Contemporary History, 38*(3), 377−394.

Dunning, E. (1999). *Sport matters: Sociological studies of sport, violence, and civilization.* London: Routledge.

Elias, N., & Dunning, E. (1986). *Quest for excitement: Sport and leisure in the civilizing process.* Oxford: Basil Blackwell.

Eustis, F. A., & Zaidi, Z. H. (1964). King, viceroy and cabinet: The modification of the partition of Bengal, 1911. *History, 49*(166), 171–184.

Gellner, E., & Breuilly, J. (2008). *Nations and nationalism.* New York, NY: Cornell University Press.

Guha, R. (2002). *A corner of a foreign field.* London: Picador.

Guha, R., & Vaidyanathan, T. G. (Eds.). (1994). *An Indian cricket omnibus.* Delhi, Oxford: Oxford University Press.

Gupta, A. (2012). Cultures of the body in colonial Bengal: The career of Gobor Guha. *The International Journal of the History of Sport, 29*(12), 1687–1700.

Kapadia, N. (2001). Triumphs and disasters: The story of Indian football, 1889–2000. *Soccer and Society, 2*(2), 17–40.

Kidd, B. (2013). Sports and masculinity. *Sport in Society, 16*(4), 553–564.

MacAloon, J. J. (2006). Introduction: Muscular Christianity after 150 years. *The International Journal of the History of Sport, 23*(5), 687–700.

Majumdar, B. (2002). The vernacular in sports history. *Economic and Political Weekly, 37*(29), 3069–3075.

Majumdar, B. (2003). Forwards and backwards: Women's soccer in twentieth-century India. *Soccer and Society, 4*(2–3), 80–94.

Majumdar, B. (2007). Nationalist romance to postcolonial sport: Cricket in 2006 India. *Sport in Society, 10*(1), 88–100.

Majumdar, B. (2008). The golden years of Indian hockey: 'We Climb the Victory Stand'. *The International Journal of the History of Sport, 25*(12), 1592–1611.

Mangan, J. A. (2001). Soccer as moral training: Missionary intentions and imperial legacies. *Soccer and Society, 2*(2), 41–56.

McDevitt, P. (2003). The king of sports: Polo in late Victorian and Edwardian India. *The International Journal of the History of Sport, 20*(1), 1–27.

McDonald, I. (2000). India. In J. Coakley & E. Dunning (Eds.), *Handbook of sports studies* (p. 540). London: Sage.

McDonald, I. (2003). Hindu nationalism, cultural spaces, and bodily practices in India. *American Behavioral Scientist, 46*(11), 1563–1576.

McDonald, I. (2007). Bodily practice, performance art, competitive sport: A critique of kalaripayattu, the martial art of Kerala. *Contributions to Indian Sociology, 41*(2), 143–168.

Mills, J. (2001). Football in Goa: Sport, politics and the Portuguese in India. *Soccer and Society, 2*(2), 75–88.

Mukherjee, M. (2013). The otherness of self: Football, fandom and fragmented (sub)nationalism in Bengal. *Soccer & Society, 14*(5), 652–669.

Mukherjee, S. (1976). *Between Indian wickets.* New Delhi: Orient Paperbacks.

Nagel, J. (1998). Masculinity and nationalism: Gender and sexuality in the making of nations. *Ethnic and Racial Studies, 21*(2), 242–269.

Nair, N. (2011). Cricket obsession in India: Through the lens of identity theory. *Sport in Society, 14*(5), 569–580.

Nandy, A. (1989). *Intimate enemy.* Oxford: Oxford University Press.

Nandy, A. (2015). *A very popular exile* (3rd ed.). New Delhi: Oxford University Press.

Pataudi, M. A. K. (1969). *Tiger's tale: The story of the Nawab of Pataudi.* Delhi: Hind Pocket Books (P) Ltd.

Ranjitsinhji, K. S. (1901). *The jubilee book of cricket.* Edinburgh, London: William Blackwood & Sons.

Rao, R. P. (1963). *Portuguese rule in Goa: 1510–1961.* Bombay: Asia Publishing House.

Sen, R. (2015). *Nation at play: A history of sport in India.* Gurgaon: Penguin India.

Sherman, T. C. (2007). The integration of the princely state of Hyderabad and the making of the postcolonial state in India, 1948–56. *Indian Economic & Social History Review, 44*(4), 489–516.

CHAPTER 4

SOCIOLOGY OF SPORT: JAPAN

Chiaki Okada and Kazuo Uchiumi

ABSTRACT

This chapter introduces the development of sport sociology in Japan especially focusing on the activities of the Japanese Society of Sport Sociology (JSSS) and research by members of the society. Following a brief history, we discuss some notable and influential research in Japanese sport sociology. Then we pick up the two areas of Olympic Studies and Sport for Development and Peace to show the current situation of sport sociology in Japan. In Japan, the development of sport sociology and sport itself are tightly linked with the development of the society as a whole, especially influenced by economic factors. In regards to the future of sport sociology as well as sport, we believe that this will depend on the economic situation, although sport-related persons (except for sociologists) tend to expect much of the governmental body. Because the volume of Olympic Studies and Sport for Development and Peace research is increasing, sport sociology will achieve a certain amount of success by the 2020 Tokyo Olympics/Paralympics. However, we need to seek a way to maintain the momentum of sport sociology in Japan after the year 2020.

Keywords: Japan Society of Sport Sociology (JSSS); Olympic studies; sport for development and peace; Tokyo 2020 Olympics/Paralympics

---

Sociology of Sport: A Global Subdiscipline in Review
Research in the Sociology of Sport, Volume 9, 59–74
Copyright © 2017 by Emerald Group Publishing Limited
ISSN: 1476-2854/doi:10.1108/S1476-285420160000009004

INTRODUCTION

In this chapter we address the brief history and recent situation of sport sociology in Japan. We mainly verify the situation by referring to the achievements of the Japanese Society of Sport Sociology (JSSS) established in 1991 and the Japan Journal of Sport Sociology (JJSS) published twice a year as one of the activities of JSSS. Although there are several notable researchers of sport sociology in Japan, it is not possible in this chapter to acknowledge every Japanese sport sociologist. There are some researchers who have only published in Japanese and, of course, translations of some works from Japanese into English accurately are quite difficult for the authors. The book titles and formal articles translated in this chapter represent approximate translations from Japanese only. However, in this chapter, we attempt to display the academic contributions of Japanese sport sociologists as concretely as possible, and try to highlight the characteristics of sport sociology in Japan.

BRIEF HISTORY OF SPORT SOCIOLOGY IN JAPAN

The development of sport sociology, and sport itself, in Japan is closely linked to the political and economic situation in each decade. Kiku (2000) noted that the term "sport sociology" was used in Japan as early as 1932, but genuine systematic study did not begin until the establishment of the Japanese Society of Physical Education (JSPE) in 1950 (Kiku, 2000, p. 542). Although sport sociology is an academic area based on people's sport participation in general, in pre-war Japan sport could be enjoyed only by students who were from the elite level of society. Actually the Japanese words for "society" and "sociology" had been prohibited by the militarization of Japanese society until the end of World War II because those words were thought to be related to socialism.

After the war, Japanese education introduced sports to schools as teaching materials of physical education and as extra-curricular school activities (Bukatsu[1]), which aimed to foster not only physical strength but also democratic human relations. While passing through the high economic growth of 1960s–1970s and the Tokyo Olympic Games in 1964, demands for sports not only in schools but also in communities rose gradually. Although "sport for all" policies in the welfare states of Europe were partially introduced to Japan, by the time of the oil crisis in 1973, the welfare policies including sport had not existed in Japan. However, sport had been enjoyed by students in schools and in major companies as welfare programs for employees and as private activities for a long time.

Kiku indicated that "during the 1970s attention was given to a wider range of systematic studies of sports participation. Research investigated the relationship between individuals and sports by levels of consciousness, attitude and personality from the social psychological viewpoint" (2000, p. 542). However, the differentiation between sport as a popular rural community activity and sport sociology as an academic area was not realized until around the turn of the century.

The European Sport for All Charter (Council of Europe, 1978) and International Charter of Physical Education and Sport (UNESCO, 1978) were adopted, and in Japan "the right to sport" became popular in sport sociology and among sport law researchers in the late 1970s. The introduction of European and American sport sociology and the exchange of researchers also prospered gradually during this time.

As noted above, sport sociology in Japan developed from the sociology of physical education, and was affected by American structural functionalism. The International Committee for the Sociology of Sport (ICSS) founded in 1964,[2] and its journal *International Review for the Sociology of Sport* had a certain influence on Japanese sport sociology. Japanese sport sociology in the early 1970s had also been influenced by British sport sociology such as cultural studies and figurational sociology. Research programs unique to Japan had not then been formed because of an ambiguity in research methodology that existed during that time. Under the fascism of the pre-war period, repressive politics and ideologies suppressed the freedom of speech and thought. In post-war Japan, the American occupation policy brought a change from liberalism to anti-communism to Japan, enforcing the "red purge" in response to the Chinese Revolution and the Korean War. After that, reformist thought including Marxism and liberalism were severely suppressed and excluded from the academic community. Such a background forced researchers to avoid expressing their research methodologies clearly in research arenas. The inactivity of both the ideological factor and people's sport participation made the development of sport sociology original to Japan difficult.

THE JAPAN SOCIETY OF SPORT SOCIOLOGY (JSSS)

The Japan Society of Sport Sociology (JSSS) was established in 1991, and has a close relationship with the International Sociology of Sport

Association (ISSA) and the North American Society for the Sociology of Sport (NASSS). There were over 400 members in 2015, and the President of JSSS in 2015–16 is Dr. Koichi Kiku. In the 25 years since the establishment of the JSSS, Dr. Kiku has become the first president with a background in physical education/sport sciences. Before this, sociologists had taken this position. Although almost all the contents of this chapter are based on JSSS's academic activities, there are many related areas as shown in Table 1.

Table 1 shows the member associations of the Japan Academic Alliance for Sport, Physical Education, and Health Sciences (JAASPEHS), which took over the role from the Science Council of Japan (SCJ). As SCJ had the function of accepting registration from academic associations and of giving them authorization under the umbrella of the Ministry of Education, Culture, Sport, Science and Technology (MEXT), JAASPEHS member associations are to be regarded as having a certain level of academic importance.

The Japan Society of Physical Education, Health and Sport Sciences (JSPEHSS) was the first sport-related association was established in 1950, and became incorporated in 2002. The association has over 6,000 members

Table 1. Surrounding Areas of Sport Sociology in Japan by the Establishment of the Academic Societies.

1950	Japan Society of Physical Education, Health and Sport Sciences
1954	The Japanese Association of School Health
1973	Japanese Society of Sport Psychology
1978	Japan Society for the Philosophy of Sport and Physical Education
1981	Japanese Society of Sport Education
1984	Japanese Society of Management for Physical Education and Sports
1986	The Japan Society of Sport History
1991	Japan Society of Sport Sociology
1995	Japan Society for the Pedagogy of Physical Education
1997	Japan Outdoor Education Society
	Japanese Society for Adapted Physical Education and Exercises
1998	Japan Society of Physical Exercise and Sport Sciences
	Japan Society of Sport Anthropology
1999	Japanese Society of Lifelong Sports
	Japanese Society of Policy for Physical Education and Sport
2002	Japan Society for Sport and Gender Studies
2008	Japan Academic Alliance for Sport, Physical Education, and Health Sciences

from science/art areas related to physical education and sport sciences, with 18 geographic branches and 15 specialized committees of philosophy, history, sociology, psychology, biomechanics, management, growth and development, testing and measurement, coaching and training, health promotion and aging, pedagogy, cultural anthropology, adapted sport, nursing, and welfare and health promotion. Fifty-eight members in JSPEHSS organized a specialized committee for sociology in 1962, and some original members tried to open up the area to pure sociologists in the 1980s. Their challenge succeeded to some extent and some notable sociologists participated in the establishment of JSSS in 1991. Although their ideal to create a new arena of sport sociology with pure sociologists seems to have made the association solid, by the fact of establishing the JAASPEHS, more collaboration with the other related areas has been recently in demand.

There are some notable researchers/works that take the role of the driving force of Japanese sport sociology. These include: Ikei's "Art and Technique in Sports Instruction: Some Brief Thoughts on Training and Learning" (2006) and *Sociology of Human "Body"* with Kiku (2008), Inoue's "The Possibility of Sport Sociology" (1993) and *Sociology of Sport and Art* (2000), Ito's "We, Japanese, Gotta Have WA?[3]: 'Collectivism' in Japanese Sport Culture" (2009) and *Body, Sexuality, Sports* with Inoue (2010), Kameyama's "What is the Concept of 'Ikiru Chikara'?[4]: An Interpretation from the Socio-anthropological Perspective" (2009) and "Children's 'World-Making' and Tuning of the World: An Approach in Terms of Body-in-Becoming" (2013a), Kiku's "A Problem in the Recognition of Body Theory in Sport Sociology: To Seek the Potential for Physics Approach" (2008) and "The Possibilities for Historical Sociology in Sport Sociology" (2011), Matsuda's "How We Should Perceive the 'Body': The 'Living Organism' Point of View" (2003) and "What in the World are 'Children's Sports'?: Thinking About 'New Public Commons' in Sports" (2011), Morikawa's "The Ideological Genealogy of 'Sports as a National Policy' and Problems of 'Reinforced Plan of Top Athletes' and Its Future Problems" (2010), and "'New Public Commons' and Sport: Who Supports Children's Sport?" (2011), and Saeki's "A Consideration on the Future of Physical Power and Technology: Focusing on the Metamorphosis of Sporting Body" (2009), and "The Tokyo 2020 Olympic Games: 'Fact and Fiction' of Their Legacy Strategy" (2015).

In the glocalized society, international exchange and its local influence will be indispensable. Especially, English communication ability has become almost indispensable in Japan. Traditionally, knowledge of Western countries was all that was required. However, the present globalization makes direct communication necessary. There were some Japanese researchers who wrote in *IRSS*, such as Thompson's "Assessing the Sociology of Sport: On Western Hegemony and Alternative Discourses" (2015), Kobayashi's "Football 'Wantok': Sport and Social Capital in Vanuatu" with Nicholson and Hoye (2013), Kobayashi's "Globalization, Corporate Nationalism and Japanese Cultural Intermediaries: Representation of Bukatsu through Nike Advertising at the Global–Local Nexus" (2012), Okada's "Sport and Social Development: Promise and Caution from an Incipient Cambodian Football League" with Young (2011), Okayasu's "The Relationship between Community Sport Clubs and Social Capital in Japan: A Comparative Study between the Comprehensive Community Sport Clubs and the Traditional Community Sports Clubs" with Kawahara and Nogawa (2010).

EXAMPLES OF JAPANESE SPORT SOCIOLOGY

Olympic Studies

The Beijing Summer Olympics/Paralympics was held in 2008, and the 2016 Summer Olympics/Paralympics will be held in Rio de Janeiro; the 2018 Winter Olympics/Paralympics in Pyeong Chang, the 2020 Summer Olympics/Paralympics in Tokyo; and the 2022 Winter Olympics/ Paralympics in Beijing. It seems that the Olympics/Paralympics have been leaving the Western countries.

However, Olympic research is centralized in the West. In Japan, although many introductory books on the Olympics have been published, Olympic researchers and research books are still only few in number. Some reasons for this are the far geographical distance from Europe, English language barriers, and the magnitude of the Olympics/Paralympics themselves. Under these circumstances, Olympic research (history, sociology) in Japan is still at the stage of "catching up with the West." Olympic research has been advancing little by little during recent years, accelerated by the bidding movement for the 2016 and 2020 Summer Olympics/Paralympics. Historical research on the Olympics increased after the Athens Olympics/ Paralympics in 2004. Kusumi's *Ancient Olympics in Greece* (2004) and Sakurai et al.'s *Ancient Olympics* (2004) studied the ancient Olympics. Yuki's *Olympic Story: From Ancient to Modern* (2004) overviewed the Olympic history from the ancient to the modern times. Hirohata's *From Athens to Athens* (2004) looked at the 110 years of the modern Olympics.

Before the Beijing Olympics/Paralympics few books on the Olympics/Paralympics had been published in Japan. But around the time of Tokyo's bidding for 2016 and 2020, more Olympic-related books were published. These included Sakaue et al.'s *No-realized 1940 Tokyo Olympics and That Age: Sport, City, Body in the War Time* (2009), Katagi's *Olympic City Tokyo 1940–1964* (2010), Ishizaka et al.'s *Sociology of "Legacy of the Olympics": Nagano Winter Olympics and Its Following Ten Years* (2013), and Ishizaka et al.'s *Nationalism by the Olympics: From the Aspect of Sporting Nationalism* (2015). More research papers were published – for example, Sanada published a book on the Zappas Olympics in Greece preceding the first Athens Olympics, *Olympia Game Festival of the 19th Century* (2011), and Uchiumi's *Olympic Games and Peace: Research Problems and Methodology* (2012).

As previously mentioned, in the bidding process for the Olympic Games 2016 and 2020, the Sport Promotion Law, which was enacted in 1961 in preparation for the Tokyo Olympics in 1964, was revised, and the new Basic Law of Sport was enacted in 2011. Under this new law, the people's "the right to sport" was clarified for the first time in the history of sport policy of Japan.

On the other hand, participation in sport in Japan has been declining. However, sport sociology and sport policy study did not comment on the trend. Neither the central government nor local governments have sufficient management in sport facilities. Consequently these have been decreasing by about 1,000 per year. To face the actual situation of people's participation in sport should be a foundation of sport sociology and of Olympic research. However, in Olympic research, sport sociology will play an important role for studying the Olympic legacies.

Sport for Development and Peace

Sport has been regarded as one of the effective tools for the development or peace building in the developing fields which have severe global issues such as extreme poverty, armed conflicts, HIV/AIDS, violation of human rights and more. The area of International Development through Sport (IDS) or Sport for Development and Peace (SDP) is new in the international academic society, and is very new in sport sociology, especially in Japan.

Although in Japan SDP has not been recognized as a core area of sport sciences, some field activities have been implemented for a number of years by several governmental/private organizations. The budgetary scale for SDP work was not huge compared to that of other countries; however, as for the dispatch of human resources as governmental volunteers, the Japan International Cooperation Agency (JICA) operates the large-scale Japan Overseas Cooperation Volunteers (JOCV). The total number of JOCVs related to sport and physical education, as of October 2015, was 3,200 out of 41,000 volunteers, about 7.8%.[5] Over 3,000 Japanese young people in total had worked as sport coaches, teachers, administrators, or organizers in over 70 developing countries by the year 2015.

The Japanese Prime Minister, Shinzo Abe, in his concluding speech for the Tokyo 2020 Summer Olympics/Paralympics candidacy, outlined the Sport for Tomorrow (SFT) program: "Under our new plan, Sport for Tomorrow, young Japanese will go out into the world in even larger numbers. They will help build schools, bring in equipment, and create sport education programs. And by the time the Olympic torch reaches Tokyo in 2020, they will bring the joy of sports directly to 10 million people in over one hundred countries."[6] The SFT is a plan comprised of three pillars: (1) international cooperation and exchange through sports, (2) Academy for Tomorrow's Leaders in Sport, and (3) PLAY TRUE 2020, which aims to develop sport integrity through strengthening global anti-doping activities.

SFT has been launched as a policy-based endeavor, and the alumni of sport-related JOCVs have a network called the Association of Ex-Physical Education and Sports JICA Volunteers. Almost all core members in this association are university researchers, and they have established a research group, International Health and Sport, in the Japanese Society of Physical Exercise and Sport Sciences (JSPESS). Although the members were the first generation for SDP research, it seems the academic trend did not allow them to make themselves part of the area of sport sociology. Therefore, although their themes contain sociological perspectives in many cases, they were actually members of other associations in other areas such as sport management, comparative education, sport psychology, and sport anthropology. Around the same time as the research group's establishment, some SDP researchers started publishing, including Kobayashi's "A New Perspective on Sport as a Development Strategy: The Issue of 'Authenticity' in Sport" (2000) and "International Development and Sport for Development: Is Sport a Cost-Effective Solution for Development?" (2014), Saito's *Sport and International Cooperation* (2015), Suzuki's "FIFA World Cup 2010 and Its Legacy on 'Sport and Development' Practices in South African Cities" (2014) and "Towards an Ecological Understanding of 'Sport and Development' Movement Using an Organizational

Database" with Kurosu (2012), and Okada's "Sport, Social Development and Peace: Acknowledging Potential, Respecting Balance" with Young (2014) and *One Ball Can Change the World* (2015).

THEORY, FIELD, AND ACTION RESEARCH

In this section, we try to capture the recent scene of sport sociology in Japan from the viewpoint of three dimensions: theory, field research, and action research.

Theory

In 2009 Uchiumi pointed out the lack of philosophical framework in Japanese sport sociology research:

> In the UK, philosophical frames such as Marxism, the work of Weber and Mead, Figuration theory, Functionalism, Cultural Studies and Gender Studies were set as an introduction, and then, academic disciplines followed. Finally, the various issues are discussed based on these generally. However, in Japan, there has been no such introduction for almost all of the researches. There are many works focusing only on 'issues' in sport sciences with academic disciplines. That tendency was relatively common in many researches. (Uchiumi, 2009, p. 35)

Uchiumi analyzed this by understanding the circumstances surrounding Japanese researchers in sport sociology, and clarified some reasons such as the lack of academic training in their undergraduate courses, time restrictions, difficulty to attain their positions according to certain ideologies, and so on. In addition to these reasons, it seems that many Japanese researchers do not have a clear understanding about the differences between the philosophical frame and theoretical frame. When we talk about "theory," it contains both, and rigorous distinctions are usually not required.

Field Research

Kawanishi (2002) studied the keywords of the presentations in the academic conference of the Japan Society of Physical Education, Health and Sport Sciences (JSPEHSS) from 1950 to 2000. There were 1,746 presentations total in sport sociology, which was about 6.7% of the total number of

Table 2.   20 Most-Common Keywords in JSPEHSS, 1950–2000.

Keyword	Total
Sport	121
Physical Education	109
Sport Behavior	99
Recreation	98
Sport Education in Community	98
Community	98
School Athletic Club	80
Students	74
Sport Participation	6
Life Style	57
Sport Group	56
University	55
School Extension	54
Socialization	50
Sport Club	50
Rural Area	50
Participation	49
Women Sport	43
Community Sport	40
Play Group	40

Source: Translated and adapted from Kawanishi (2002, p. 46).

the presentations in JSPEHSS. Table 2 shows the keywords in the 1,746 presentations to observe the sequence of the research.

Kameyama (2013b) reviewed 150 peer-reviewed theses in the *Japan Journal of Sport Sociology* (*JJSS*), dated from 1993 to 2010, and found 33 theses that had the word "body" in their titles or keywords. He pointed out two dimensions of body theory: (1) based on the physical experience (physics approach), and (2) based on the system and function (functional approach). Kiku (2008) explained these dimensions in the following way: "The sociology and theory of physical education has presumed an educated human body as the perspective, and that sociology in itself has expected the body as humanism to oppose structuralism and functionalism and sought the body to take the place of the mind" (Kiku, 2008, p. 72). Although we may not always be able to connect the body theory, which is based on physical experience, to humanism, Kameyama expected the possibility of the academic contribution of sport sociology on sociology in

Happy to see you making use
of the 9k :3 ♡

-07956 39 6266

general by focusing on the physics approach. However, the number of research ventures with the physics approach is decreasing in sport sociology in Japan. Although he avoided jumping to conclusions, Kameyama suggested that it would be a disappointment if this trend shows a conservative swing of sport sociology in Japan.

Action Research

Chalip (2015) argued that "a 1989 call for the development of an applied sociology of sport by Yiannakis was not well-received by the sociology of sport scholarly community" (Chalip, 2015, p. 397). The situation was similar in Japan, and the expansion of applied sport sociology has been limited. One of the pioneer researchers of sport sociology in Japan, Ikeda and Morino (1998) pointed out that "to what and to whom the research impacts of sport sociology can contribute, and how we can reduce the acquired knowledges to the real societies and individuals have not been enough discussed in the past" (p. 226). Although the significance of applied sociology in the sporting field was shown in 1999, even after 15 years, we cannot see many concrete contributions to the fields by researchers, except at the policy level.

Action research was proposed by Lewin[7] as a practical method in the field of group dynamics in the 1940s. Although several definitions and the merits/demerits of the method have been discussed, the core target of the discussion is how sociologists can contribute to the real society. Although, in Japan, the amount of action research is limited, the thesis *Action Research of Community Development by the Sport Tourism: Aiming to Make Nago City, Okinawa a Sport Tourist Town* by Park et al. (2011) and research projects *The Impact Analysis and Action Research on Social Benefits of Masters Sport Promotion Projects* by Chogahara and Ishizawa in 2009–2011[8] are good examples of existing literature.

Saeki (2013)[9] asserted the importance of critics to the real sport scene in society as one of the missions of sport sociologists, referring to Boulder's belief that "sport sociology is despised by academics, at the same time, treated as a nuisance by the practical fields." Action research is at the center of this discussion, and some researchers have been in a dilemma with regard to the principles of being there, doing something, and making a concrete contribution as a researcher, which is a thorny path when seeking a healthy balance of observation and intervention.

CONCLUSION

As we mentioned previously, sport development should be considered along with social development. In the developing countries, sport cannot become a target of development but is positioned as a means or an instrument for development. Both in developed and developing countries, the relations of sport and human rights/welfare/peace are becoming very important issues respectively. How can sport sociology contribute to them? In recent years, sport sociology has been expanding its range in Japan. For example, a body theory and an event theory have been emerging, and systematization of the academic field is also occurring. The most strongly required task for the development of sport sociology in Japan is to further clarify its research methodologies and try to capture the figure and significances of sport in the dynamics of social changes — to seek for the core value of sport in society.

ACKNOWLEDGMENT

We would like to thank the editor, Professor Kevin Young, for his help with previous drafts of this chapter.

NOTES

1. Bukatsu is a sport club at schools in Japan. Kobayashi (2012) explained "Bukatsu is a primary site for Japanese youth to participate in sport and can be considered as a 'glocalized' form of modern sport because sport came to serve as a cultural signifier of Japanese traditional values, virtues and morals including bushido (way of the samurai)" (Kobayashi, 2012, p. 7).

2. The name was changed in 1995 to ISSA (International Sociology of Sport Association).

3. The meaning of WA was explained by Ito in the abstract of the paper. The spirit of WA is collective-oriented attitudes, which were mentioned in Robert Whiting's book *You Gotta Have WA* published in 1989.

4. Ikiru Chikara was explained in Kameyama's abstract; "Ikiru Chikara," which literally means "power to live," has also been translated as "zest for living" by the Japanese Ministry of Education, Culture, Sport, Science and Technology (MEXT).

5. The number of the volunteers are shown in statistical form on the webpage of JICA http://www.jica.go.jp/volunteer/outline/publication/results/jocv.html#r03. Accessed December 23, 2015.

6. Part of Shinzo Abe's concluding speech for Tokyo's candidacy to be the host city of the 2020 summer Olympic/Paralympic Games can be viewed at https://www.youtube.com/watch?v=zf90ImlFDuU. Accessed April 2, 2016.

7. Lewin (1946)

8. Japanese Research Grant-in-Aid "KAKEN" No. 21500593. Retrieved from https://kaken.nii.ac.jp/d/p/21500593.en.html. Accessed March 3, 2016.

9. In the award lecture of the 14th Chichibu Memorial Sports Medicine and Science Prize, "The philosophy and practice in sports culture." The whole presentation is in *The Japan Society of Sport Sociology* (2013, pp. 254−261).

FIVE KEY READINGS

1. **Inoue, S., & Ito, K. (2010).** *Bodies, sexualities and sport.* **Tokyo: Sekaishisosha.**

This series introduces notable books in several branch areas of sociology, with 10 complete volumes and a supplement. The editors selected over 270 books and introduce them in three sections: (1) brief abstract of the book, (2) sketch of the authors' personal histories, and (3) theoretical backgrounds and academic significances/contributions.

2. **Kameyama, Y. (2012).** *Sociology of becoming in the body: Sport performance, flow experience, rhythm.* **Tokyo: Sekaishisosha.**

The author investigates some cases of dialogues/episodes in the Japanese sport scene based on the physics approach, an opposite concept to the structural approach. Pursuing the significances of physics approach in sport sociology shows the advantages and potentials of the area itself, which has particular influences on other researches.

3. **The Japan Society of Sport Sociology. (2013).** *The sociology of sport in the twenty-first century.* **Tokyo: Soubunkikaku.**

This book explores how sport sociology in the twenty-first century should be, what it should aim at and how it should contribute to the real society. It consists of three chapters: (1) play and sport in the modern society, (2) issues in public policy and development, and (3) cultural politics around the body, and includes two appendices.

4. **Matsumura, K., Ishioka, T., & Murata, S. (2014).** *The sociology of 'development and sport'.* **Tokyo: Nansosha.**

Matsumura has continuously concentrated on development, especially in the contexts of rural development. This book consists of 15 chapters in three sections: (1) transformation of sport space in Asian countries, (2) environmental conservation and regional transformation from the viewpoint of sport, and (3) perspective toward a new era of development and sport.

5. **Uchiumi, K. (2015).** *Sport, human rights and welfare.* **Tokyo: Soubunkikaku.**

This work is based on the concept that sport is one of the human rights and an element of welfare. The ownership of sport and the role of national and local authorities are discussed with historical and theoretical backgrounds to achieve sport for all. Although sport in Japan tends to be treated in isolation, the visions of simultaneous and mutually reinforcing pursuit of sport are required.

REFERENCES

Chalip, L. (2015). Assessing the sociology of sport: On theory relevance and action research. *International Review for the Sociology of Sport, 50*(4–5), 397–401.

Council of Europe. (1978). *European sport for all charter.* Retrieved from http://www.coe.int/t/dg4/sport/Resources/texts/spchart2_en.asp. Accessed on 02 April, 2016.

Hirohata, S. (2004). *From Athens to Athens.* Tokyo: Hon no Izumi-sha.

Ikeda, M., & Morino, S. (1998). *Modern society and sport: The sociology of sport.* Tokyo: Kyorinshoin.

Ikei, N. (2006). Art and technique in sports instruction: Some brief thoughts on training and learning. *Japan Journal of Sport Sociology, 14,* 3–8.

Ikei, N., & Kiku, K. (2008). *Sociology of human 'body'.* Tokyo: Sekaishisosha.

Inoue, S. (1993). The possibility of sport sociology. *Japan Journal of Sport Sociology, 1,* 35–39.

Inoue, S. (2000). *The sociology of sport and art.* Tokyo: Sekaishisosha.

Inoue, S., & Ito, K. (2010). *Body, sexuality, sports.* Tokyo: Sekaishisosha.

Ishizaka, Y., & Matsubayashi, H. (2013). *Sociology of 'legacy of the olympics': Nagano winter olympics and its following ten years.* Tokyo: Seikyusha.

Ishizaka, Y., & Ozawa, T. (2015). *Nationalism by the olympics: From the aspect of sporting nationalism.* Kyoto: Kamogawa-Shuppan.

Ito, K. (2009). We, Japanese, gotta have WA?: "Collectivism" in Japanese sport culture. *Japan Journal of Sport Sociology, 17*(1), 3–12.

Kameyama, Y. (2009). What is the concept of 'Ikiru Chikara'?: An interpretation from the socio-anthropological perspective. *Japan Journal of Sport Sociology, 17*(1), 59–71.

Kameyama, Y. (2013a). Children's 'world-making' and tuning of the world: An approach in terms of body-in-becoming. *Japan Journal of Sport Sociology, 21*(1), 3–20.

Kameyama, Y. (2013b). *Sociology of becoming in the body: Sport performance, flow experience, rhythm.* Tokyo: Sekaishisosha.

Katagi, A. (2010). Olympic city Tokyo 1940–1964. Tokyo: Kawade Books.

Kawanishi, M. (2002). The trend of life-long sport research in the area of physical education and sport sociology. In M. Ikeda (Ed.), *The socioeconomics of life-long sport* (pp. 43–53). Tokyo: Kyorinshoin.

Kiku, K. (2000). Japan. In J. Coakley & E. Dunning (Eds.), *The handbook of sports studies* (pp. 542–544). London: Sage.

Kiku, K. (2008). A problem in the recognition of body theory in sport sociology: To seek the potential for physics' approach. *Japan Journal of Sport Sociology, 16*, 71–86.

Kiku, K. (2011). The possibilities for historical sociology in sport sociology. *Japan Journal of Sport Sociology, 19*(1), 21–38.

Kobayashi, K. (2012). Globalization, corporate nationalism and Japanese cultural intermediaries: Representation of Bukatsu through Nike advertising at the global-local Nexus. *International Review for the Sociology of Sport, 47*(6), 724–742.

Kobayashi, T. (2000). A new perspective on sport as a development strategy: The issue of 'authenticity' in sport. *Japan Journal of Physical Education, Health and Sport Sciences, 45*, 707–718.

Kobayashi, T. (2014). International development and sport for development: Is sport a cost-effective solution for development? *Japan Journal of Sport Sociology, 22*(1), 61–78.

Kobayashi, T., Nicholson, M., & Hoye, R. (2013). Football 'Wantok': Sport and social capital in Vanuatu. *International Review for the Sociology of Sport, 48*, 38–53.

Kusumi, C. (2004). *Ancient olympics in Greece*. Tokyo: Kodansha.

Lewin, K. (1946). Action research and minority problems. *Journal of Social Issues, 2*(4), 34–46.

Matsuda, K. (2003). How we should perceive the 'body': The 'living organism' point of view. *Japan Journal of Sport Sociology, 11*, 13–21.

Matsuda, K. (2011). What in the world are 'children's sports'?: Thinking about 'new public commons' in sports. *Japan Journal of Sport Sociology, 19*(2), 5–18.

Morikawa, S. (2010). The ideological genealogy of "sports as a national policy" and problems of "reinforced plan of top athletes" and its future problems. *Japan Journal of Sport Sociology, 18*(1), 27–42.

Morikawa, S. (2011). 'New public commons' and sport: Who supports children's sport? *Japan Journal of Sport Sociology, 19*(2), 19–32.

Okada, C., & Young, K. (2011). Sport and social development: Promise and caution from an incipient Cambodian football league. *International Review for the Sociology of Sport, 47*(1), 5–26.

Okayasu, I., Kawahara, Y., & Nogawa, H. (2010). The relationship between community sport clubs and social capital in Japan: A comparative study between the comprehensive community sport clubs and the traditional community sports clubs. *International Review for the Sociology of Sport, 45*, 163–186.

Park, Y., Akiyoshi, R., Inaba, S., Yamaguchi, S., & Yamaguchi, Y. (2011). Action research of community development by the sport tourism: Aiming to make Nago city, Okinawa a sport tourist town. *SSF Journal of Sport for Everyone, 1*(1), 150–159.

Saeki, T. (2009). A consideration on the future of physical power and technology: Focusing on the metamorphosis of sporting body. *Japan Journal of Sport Sociology, 17*(1), 45–57.

Saeki, T. (2013). Ideology and practice of sport culture. In The Japan Society of Sport Sociology (Ed.), *The sociology of sport in the twenty-first century* (pp. 254–261). Tokyo: Soubunkikaku.

Saeki, T. (2015). The Tokyo 2020 Olympic games: 'Fact and fiction' of their legacy strategy. *Japan Journal of Sport Sociology, 23*(2), 25–44.

Saito, K. (2015). *Sport and international cooperation*. Tokyo: Taishukan.

Sakaue, Y., & Takaoka, H. (2009). *No-realised 1940 Tokyo olympics and that age: Sport, city, body in the war time.* Tokyo: Seikyusha.

Sakurai, M., & Hashiba, Y. (2004). *Ancient olympics.* Tokyo: Iwanami-shoten.

Sanada, H. (2011). *Olympia games festival of the 19th century.* Tokyo: Meiwa-shuppan.

Suzuki, N. (2014). The FIFA world cup 2010 and its legacy on "sport and development" practices in South African cities. In K. Young & C. Okada (Eds.), *Sport, social development and peace* (pp. 127–145). Bingley, UK: Emerald Group Publishing Limited.

Suzuki, N., & Kurosu, A. (2012). *Towards an ecological understanding of 'sport and development' movement using an organizational database.* ISSA World Congress of Sociology of Sport 2012.

The Japan Society of Sport Sociology. (2013). *The sociology of sport in the twenty-first century.* Tokyo: Soubunkikaku.

Thompson, L. (2015). Assessing the sociology of sport: On Western Hegemony and alternative discourses. *International Review for the Sociology of Sport, 50,* 617–622.

Uchiumi, K. (2009). *The research of sport sciences.* Tokyo: Soubunkikaku.

Uchiumi, K. (2012). *Olympic games and peace: Research problems and methodology.* Tokyo: Fumaido-shuppan.

UNESCO. (1978). *International charter of physical education and sport.* UNESCO the General Conference at its twentieth session, Paris. Retrieved from http://assets.sportanddev.org/downloads/17__intl_charter_of_pe_and_sport.pdf. Accessed on 02 April, 2016.

Whiting, R. (1989). *You gotta have WA.* London: Macmillan Pub Co.

Young, K., & Okada, C. (2014). Sport, social development and peace: Acknowledging potential, respecting balance. In K. Young & C. Okada (Eds.), *Sport, social development and peace* (pp. ix–xxix). Bingley, UK: Emerald Group Publishing Limited.

Yuki, W. (2004). *Olympic story: From ancient to modern.* Tokyo: Chuko-Shinsho.

CHAPTER 5

SOCIOLOGY OF SPORT: SOUTH KOREA

Eunha Koh

ABSTRACT

Although Korean sociology of sport is relatively unknown to the international community of scholars, it is a mature field in Korea. Sociology of sport was first introduced in Korea in the mid-1960s when the field first evolved in North America and Europe. However, the development of the field shows different aspects from its Western counterpart due to unique cultural and environmental factors both in academia and in society. There are three major research trends that form Korean sociology of sport. First, there is the research focus on the benefit of sport and physical activity by examining empirical data using quantitative methodologies. The second group of researchers pays attention to individual experience in diverse sport fields and utilize qualitative methodologies to investigate empirical or secondary data. The third and most recent trend is a critical approach that theoretically analyzes ideologies, power relations, and identity politics in sport and society. When looking at the future, there are problems and limitations within the field in Korea. These include lack of continuity in terms of conference sub-themes, over-production of doctoral degree graduates, conservatism rooted in the field, and a danger of regarding sport policy research as an exit for

Sociology of Sport: A Global Subdiscipline in Review
Research in the Sociology of Sport, Volume 9, 75—91
Copyright © 2017 by Emerald Group Publishing Limited
ISSN: 1476-2854/doi:10.1108/S1476-285420160000009005

sport sociologists. However, there are also possibilities and reasons for optimism. The biggest possibility for Korean sociology of sport is globalization of the field. Another significant possibility is the need for sport sociologists in planning, developing, and evaluating sport policy. Finally, diversification of the field gives ample opportunities for future research.

Keywords: Sociology of Sport; Korea; social theory; sport policy; globalization

INTRODUCTION: HISTORY OF SOCIOLOGY OF SPORT IN KOREA

Although Korean sociology of sport is relatively unknown to the international community of scholars, it is a mature field in Korea. Sociology of sport was first introduced in Korea in the mid-1960s when the field first evolved in North America and Europe. However, the development of the field shows different aspects from its Western counterpart.

"Sociology of sport" was first introduced as a sub-discipline of sport studies[1] in *"Introduction to Sport Studies"* (Jang, 1963) and articles on sport, leisure and recreation, and sport for all are first appeared in the journal of KAHPERD.[2] The first "sociology of sport" document published in book form was "Sociology of Sport" by the Ministry of Culture and Education (1973), followed by translation and publication of several Japanese books (Cho, 1976; Cho & Han, 1981; Han, 1979; Lee, 1975). Although these early publications were based on Japanese books on sociology of sport rather than English books, which was the general trend in the 1960s, Japanese sociology of sport had little influence on the development of Korean sociology of sport as an academic field.

Instead, Korean sociology of sport has been greatly influenced by North American sociology of sport. This can be shown easily by the effort of Professor Burn Jang Lim, who in many ways laid a foundation for the development of Korean sociology of sport. He obtained his BA and MA degrees from Seoul National University and went to George Williams College located in Illinois, United States for another MA degree (Lee, 2010a, 2010b). The first "sociology of sport" course was offered as an undergraduate course in the Department of Physical Education at Seoul

National University (SNU) in the fall semester of 1976 by Professor Burn Jang Lim; by the 1980s, most universities with sport-related departments were offering the course. The first graduate course on sociology of sport was offered in the MA program offered by the Department of Physical Education at SNU in the spring semester of 1978, followed by another class in the doctoral program in the spring of 1982, both of which were taught by Burn Jang Lim (Lee, 2010a). Most of the research conducted at this time was simple survey rather than delving into sociological theories and methodologies.

With growing interest in the field of sport and its impact on society, the necessity of sociology of sport as an academic field and professional research was discussed in the early 1980s. The year 1984 marked the unofficial beginning of the Korean Society for the Sociology of Sport (KSSS) when a sociology of sport study group was formed at SNU and Professor John Loy was invited in the same year for the first invited lecture by a foreign scholar. Beginning in 1984, Lim held weekly seminars with graduate students at SNU, and later graduate students from Ewha Women's University joined. *Sport and Social Order* (Ball & Loy, 1975), *Sport & Social Systems* (Loy, McPherson, & Kenyon, 1978), *Social Significance of Sport* (McPherson, Curtis, & Loy, 1989), and *Sport in Social Development* (Ingham & Loy, 1993) were the major textbooks used for the seminar along with other books and articles published in *International Review for the Sociology of Sport* (*IRSS*) and *Sociology of Sport Journal* (*SSJ*) (Lee, 2010a, 2010b). The seminar members became the second generation of scholars of the Korean sociology of sport.

These collective efforts bore fruit in 1990 when the Korean Society for the Sociology of Sport (KSSS) was formally founded and became the center of the field in Korea. The first president of KSSS was Burn Jang Lim (1991−1997) who also served as an executive board member (1990−1991), vice president (1992−1997), and bulletin editor (1992−1997) of the International Sociology of Sport Association (ISSA). KSSS has been the only national academic organization in the field of sociology of sport in Korea. Throughout its 26-year history, a number of national conferences, seminars, workshops, and meetings have been held. The number and season of each event has changed over time. In its initial stage, there were monthly seminars held at SNU whose purpose was for scholars and graduate students to gather and study as a group. During the 1990s, summer and winter workshops were held mainly for graduate students and many lectures on research methodology were offered. Seasonal seminars during the summer and winter vacations were also held.

As sociology of sport became established as a strong sub-discipline of sport studies and KSSS welcomed more members across the country, the number of seminars and workshops were reduced while more seminars were held as a session of KAHPERD conferences on different occasions. As of 2016, there are the following regular national conferences, seminars, and workshops held according to annual plans: the annual general meeting is held in late November along with an annual conference; three more conferences held in association with KAHPERD – International Sport Science Conference, and Pre-National Games Scientific Congress, and Sport Scientists Conference; there are two annual seminars held by KSSS (the summer seminar and special seminar, of which the latter deals with pressing social issues in Korean sport and society. The winter workshop is held during the winter vacation and covers a wide range of topics. From its early stage, KSSS has invited one to three foreign scholars every year for seminars and additional invited lectures at member universities and given opportunities to members to share knowledge of recognized international scholars. Recently, one to two foreign scholars have been invited to the International Sport Science Conference held in August.

APPROXIMATE NUMBERS OF SCHOLARS AND WHERE THEY ARE LOCATED

There are approximately 200 sport sociologists and graduate students actively participating in research and affiliated with KSSS across the country. As of December 2015, there are 166 individual members registered as members of KSSS, while 2,074 cumulative members and 28 institutional members are registered as members on the KSSS webpage (Korean Society for the Sociology of Sport [KSSS], 2015). The 28 institutional members are the ones whose libraries subscribe to KSSS journals. There are a number of universities with established graduate programs in sociology of sport while most universities and colleges with sport-related departments offer sociology of sport and related courses in undergraduate programs on a regular basis.

There are more than 20 universities that have MA and PhD degrees in sociology of sport scattered around the Korean peninsula. They include all kinds of institutions from national to private: Catholic Kwandong University, Chonnam National University, Chungnam National University, Dankook University, Dong-A University, Dong-Eui University, Hanyang

University, Hoseo University, Incheon National University, Inha University, Seoul National University, Konkuk University, Kookmin University, Korea National Sport University, Kyonggi University, Kyunghee University, Kyungpook National University, Pusan National University, Seowon University, Silla University, Sungkyunkwan University, Yeungnam University, Yonsei University, and University of Suwon.[3]

Scholars are scattered across the institutions mentioned above and work cooperatively according to their theoretical and methodological orientations. Most recognized programs are found at SNU, Yonsei University, Korea and National Sport University (located in Seoul), Kyungpook National University (located in Daegu), and Pusan National University (located in Pusan). These programs are listed here based on the following standards: long history of sociology of sport program, constant number of master and doctoral students in the school, the production of academic articles on a regular basis, and production of faculty members at university level.

THE ACADEMIC ENVIRONMENT AND BARRIERS TO RESEARCH

With a Confucian tradition that emphasizes the role of scholars and degrades the use of bodily skills deeply rooted in Korean society, sport and physical activities have been historically regarded as not as important as so-called core subjects such as literature, mathematics, and science. However, the benefits of sport on health and wellbeing have been emphasized and the roles of national sport teams and professional athletes have been praised since the 1970s, especially after the holding of 1988 Seoul Olympic Games. The public started enjoying sport and physical activity and the media competed to deliver various sport events to the public. National interest in sport can be identified in well-established sport promotion systems that will be explained below.

The sport governance system in Korea can be summarized as a *triangle* system of Ministry of Culture, Sport and Tourism (MCST), Korean Olympic Committee (KOC) and Korea Sports Promotion Foundation (KSPO). MCST prepares sport policies and funds and supervises sport organizations to manage diverse policies and practices. KSC/KOC implements various sport promotion policies and manages national sport federations and trains national athletes and enters them into international competitions. KOC recently integrated the National Council of Sport for All (NACOSA) in March 2016 and became the only umbrella organization in sport. KSPO raises sport promotion funds mainly through a sport lottery as well as motorboat racing, bicycle racing, and other sources, distributes them to related organizations, and evaluates the use of funds in different sectors of sports. Another notable organization is the Korean Institute of Sport Science (KISS), a KSPO-affiliated organization. KISS conducts research, support, and education for national sport promotion in the areas of sport policy, sport science, and sport industry. KISS recently integrated the Next Generation Sport Talent Foundation (NEST) in 2015 and expanded its business to sport talent development and education. These sport governance structures are the combination of the state-leading model (e.g., China), sport council-leading model (e.g., United Kingdom and Australia), and National Olympic Committee (NOC)-leading model (e.g., United States) that still emphasizes the role of the state but at the same time allows sport organizations to play diverse roles.

The national efforts for sport promotion explained above coupled with public interest in sport and people's daily lives led to the development of research in the field of sport studies both from a social science and a sport science point of view. All national universities and most private universities have undergraduate programs under the name of sport studies, sport science, physical education, kinesiology, sport for all, or related names on either the department or college levels, which seems to be due to the constant increase in related jobs in sport and the fitness industry, both in number and variety.

In particular, it is notable that the number of sociology of sport programs at the university level has increased gradually, especially at the graduate level. This is in contrast to a recent decrease of sociology of sport programs in some countries. Two universities opened sociology of sport doctoral programs recently. Sociology of sport has been regarded as one of the core curriculum sub-disciplines to be taught as a required subject in sport-related departments and the major derived class subjects such as "sport in society," "sport and media," "sport for all," "leisure studies." Another notable feature of Korean sociology of sport is that researchers have been involved in numerous sport policy research projects since 1980s, as well as worked on various committees of government and sport organizations both at the national and regional levels. KSSS and its mother organization, the Korean Sport Promotion Foundation, have been playing an important role in the close link between academia and the Ministry of Culture, Sport and Tourism by offering research grants, inviting researchers to meetings and supporting academic conferences.

Although there are a number of sport sociologists actively participating in research and education nationwide as well as the programs offered at university level, there are barriers to further development of Korean sociology of sport. It seems sociology of sport graduate programs may have reached a saturation point now and some of them may soon close. A decline in the school-age population and saturation of faculty positions of the major seem to be main reasons. Recent emphasis on more "practical" disciplines like sport management is another barrier to further development of Korean sociology of sport. Lastly, over-emphasis on quantitative research achievement in the academic field has prevented researchers from creatively seeking new research agendas.

MAIN AREAS OF RESEARCH STRENGTH

There are different opinions when it comes to identifying the main areas of research strength in Korean sociology of sport. The research areas identified below are based on the analysis of *Korean Journal of Sociology of Sport* (*KJSS*), the official journal of KSSS. Although there are other nationally published journals in which sociology of sport articles are published, the analysis in this chapter is made on the basis of *KJSS* because it represents the only major sociology of sport journal, not to mention the higher quality of the articles compared to those in other journals. Consequently, the main research areas of Korean sociology of sport can be divided into roughly three categories.

First, there are researchers who focus on the benefit of sport and physical activities by examining empirical data using quantitative methodologies. This approach marked the first generation of Korean sport sociology and has formed a major research trend so far. The second group of researchers pays attention to individual experience in diverse sport fields and utilizes qualitative methodologies to investigate empirical or secondary data. The third and most recent trend is a more critical approach that theoretically analyzes ideologies, power relations, and identity politics in sport and society. These research trends mark different periods of time and form three major research groups.

The major trend in the 1990s when *KJSS* was first published was research that dealt with social psychological variables such as life satisfaction, self-efficacy, and self-respect to quantitatively examine the positive effects of sport participation in people's daily lives. Another approach from the functionalist perspective was research on the sport socialization process and its effects on general participants of diverse age groups as well as athletes. At this stage, a number of leisure studies articles using similar research frames appeared in *KJSS*, which seems to have resulted from the fact that at that time, academic differentiation in the social science of sport was yet to be completed, and there was no professional organization or journal for leisure studies. The same reason can be applied to those articles with sport management topics such as leadership, collective cohesiveness, organization effectiveness, and job attitudes. On the other hand, a national effort for sport promotion after the 1988 Seoul Olympic Games led to academic research on various elements of sport for all such as facilities, programs, personnel, and regulations, which was later extended to sport policy research in the new millennium.

While the majority of research in the 1990s through the early 2000s was conducted in the above areas using quantitative research methods, some research asserting the necessity of a more critical approach and feminist perspective and introducing related theories arose (Ahn, 1997, 2000; Ahn & Goo, 1996; Cho, 1994; Andrews & Koh, 2002). Despite the conservative tradition of Korean sociology of sport, a critical approach to diverse topics in sport and society slowly became popular in the early 2000s. Qualitative research delving into individual experience in sport and physical activity appeared at the end of the 1990s and slowly increased with more diverse topics being examined.

With the rapidly growing number of articles, *KJSS* became triannual in 2004 and became quarterly in 2008.[4] With the quantitative research approach already having gained a strong foothold (Kim, 2008, 2009, 2010), a critical approach started gaining popularity among the younger generation of researchers during the mid-2000s. Cultural studies had a great influence on the scholars who would critically explore topics such as nationalism, consumerism, power relations, body, and celebrity, among other matters, utilizing diverse theories and methodologies (Chung, 2008; Han, 2010; Kim, 2003; Koh & Lee, 2004; Kwon, 2006; Lee, 2010a, 2010b; Lee & Lee, 2007; Nam & Lee, 2005; Park, 2006; Seo, 2004). International journals such as *IRSS* and *SSJ* played an important role in this new trend, and their articles were eagerly devoured by young Korean researchers who studied abroad or at home. Media studies became popular and touched on issues related to gender and nationalism utilizing multiple sources such as newspapers, broadcasting, documentaries, and film (Chang, Lee, & Lee, 2010;

Cho, 2007; Kim, 2005, 2007). On the other hand, an interpretive approach to exploring the sporting experience of both athletes and the general public became popular too. Various topics such as gender, doping, subculture and labor migration were discussed mostly using in-depth interview (Chung, Chang, & Lee, 2005; Kwon, Song, & Park, 2007; Lee, Song, & Lim, 2006; Yang & Won, 2007).

The diversification of research topics, theories, and methodologies has accelerated over the last decade across the aforementioned three major research groups. Critical research rapidly increased during the last few years, heavily influenced by the Western cultural studies trend (Chang, 2015; Chung & Kim, 2013; Han, 2013; Jang & Lee, 2014; Nam & Koh, 2011, 2014; Park, 2010). The first special issue of *KJSS* was published in 2014 on the topic of "celebrity," which shows the recent popularity of the topic. On the other hand, the functionalist approach showed rapid decline while interpretive research has maintained its foothold (Kim & Kwon, 2013; Kwon & Lee, 2015; Kwon & Lim, 2012; Lee, 2015; Lee & Kwon, 2013; Lee & Lee, 2015; Lim & Lee, 2014). Critical and interpretive analyses of media texts are gaining popularity, too (Hwang, 2013; Jang & Lee, 2013; Kim, Na, Kim, Nam, & Kim, 2013).

KEY CONTRIBUTORS AND KEY PUBLICATIONS

The increase of departments dedicated to sport studies and/or sport science at universities nationwide and the growing interest in various sports in Korean society guaranteed the rapid growth of the sociological study of sport, which led to a number of books and articles, as well as frequent contributions to newspapers and magazines.

There is a wealth of publications in the research areas described in the previous section. First, there are publications dedicated to the study of the benefits of sport participation and that analyze the impact of various factors using empirical data. The second area of publication focuses on individual experience in sport and physical activity and takes an interpretive approach to explore the meanings of sport. The third major research area is a critical approach to theoretically investigating ideologies, identities, and power relations in diverse sport scenes and practices. Although these areas have equal importance in terms of numbers of articles and contribution to Korean sociology of sport, this chapter lists a limited amount of research and number of publications due to issues of space. When it comes to identifying key publications, the emphasis was put on the impact of the study on the further development of Korean sociology of sport and the motivation for follow-up research.

There are few books dedicated to specific sport topics or edited books with multiple authors that contain chapters on Korean sociology of sport. A notable publication is *Sport and Social Theory* (KSSS, 2012), which introduces diverse social theory applied to research in sociology of sport. The book is composed of an introductory chapter and 12 chapters dedicated to different social theories and their application to sociology of sport.

On the other hand, there have been quite a number of textbooks published. This can be explained historically when many universities competed to open classes and courses on sociology of sport during the 1980s and 1990s and desperately needed textbooks written in Korean. The first textbook that gained wide recognition was *Introduction to Sociology of Sport* (Lim, 1994). The book enjoyed nationwide readership until the mid-2000s and published its third edition in 2010. Another notable textbook is *Sociology of Sport* (Lee & Nam, 2013), which was first published in 2009 and published its third edition in 2013 with consistent readership. Additionally, Jay Coakley's well-known *Sport in Society* was translated into Korean and chosen by many readers (Goo & Kwon, 2011).

Korean academics have produced some significant work as noted above but most of it is published in Korean and thus only read by Korean readers. For many academics whose first language is not English, it has not been easy to publish internationally. However, as a growing number of students study abroad for their MA or PhD degree, more articles are being published in well-known international journals like *IRSS* and *SSJ*. Another important motivation was the changing criteria both for the selection of new faculty members and for the evaluation of research achievements of the existing members, emphasizing the importance of publication in international journals listed on Science Citation Index (SCI)/Social Sciences Citation Index (SSCI).

FUTURE PROBLEMS AND PROSPECTS

As witnessed in many countries where sociology of sport "has been introduced" from the West rather than "developed" within, Korean sociology of sport has followed the footsteps of, for example, North American and British sociology of sport. However, the direction and speed of development of different research areas vary due to unique historical and cultural backgrounds. Unlike the dominance of the critical approach in many regions, especially in North America, there are at least three major research approaches looking at contemporary sport and society from different angles. This can be considered a strength of Korean sociology of sport despite its relatively short history and small number of scholars.

However, there are problems and limitations within the field. First is the lack of continuity in terms of conference design. When we look at recent conferences and seminars, there is a tendency that the presentations are "allocated" to specific themes chosen for the event, while there were few papers presented in "free topics" sessions. Leading scholars present papers on the given topic rather than leading sessions dedicated to long-term research interests. This tends to hinder the formation of critical masses. Second, there is the over-production of doctoral degree graduates. With the rapid growth of the field, many universities have competed to build doctoral programs. However, a decline in the school-age population coupled with saturation of faculty positions in the sociology of sport field has resulted in the unemployment of graduates with doctoral degrees. It seems inevitable that some programs will close and the number of scholars may decrease. Third, there is the conservatism that seems rooted in the field. While the field is open to new research areas and topics, it is still conservative to "critical" scholars. Feminism and neo-liberalism are regarded as "theories" to be taken for research rather than "attitudes" of scholars. The necessity of feminism was raised by male scholars in the mid-1990s, who came back from the United States with doctoral degrees (Ahn, 1997; Cho, 1994); the female scholars remained relatively silent until the late 1990s. Last but not least, there is a danger of regarding sport policy research as an exit for sport sociologists. Despite the increasing need for sport policy research from national/regional government and sport organizations, jumping on the bandwagon with no background or preparation can result in side effects such as lack of professional knowledge in both the field and loss of scholastic identity and achievement.

Some of the problems above can be overcome by the academic efforts of individual researchers while others need institutional and cultural change in the field of sociology of sport. In either case, the future seems to hold more possibilities than limitations. From one point of view, some problems are just another face of opportunity.

The biggest possibility is *globalization* of the field. It has become easier to find any international publication at home. More and more scholars are producing publications internationally (Chung, 2003; Koh, 2009;

Koh, Andrews, & White, 2006) while others register as members of international organizations like ISSA and NASSS and attend international conferences on a regular basis. Attendance at international conferences provides good opportunities, especially for students, to witness international research trends. On the other hand, with increasing similarities shown among articles in the sociology of sport field at large, the Korean context can be a unique research environment that allows originality of academic work.

Another significant possibility is the need for sport sociologists in planning, developing, and evaluating *sport policy*. According to Park (2009), the contribution of sociology of sport on sport policy research can be found in three ways: studying sub-themes of sport policy through sport sociology and developing sport policy; dealing with taken-for-granted premises in sport policy (e.g., gaining medals is the top priority in elite sport); and finally, investigating the impact of sport policy on society. While there have been a number of sport policy projects by sport sociologists, most of them have dealt with the first topic, with some researchers challenging the taken-for-granted premise in sport policy. On the other hand, policy evaluation has been limited to the evaluation of policy outcome rather than long-term effects, which demands more attention from sport sociologists both on research and consultation.

Finally, *diversification* of themes is a challenge and at the same time a possibility for Korean sport sociologists. We should note that there is always a danger to either ignorantly reject new themes and approaches or accept them without further examination. In other words, we need to beware of rash adoption of themes or theories without thoroughly studying them. For example, some recent publications try to apply specific social theory to the interpretation of interview data, but make the mistake of putting all the results into the theoretical model, like solving jigsaw puzzles.

NOTES

1. "Sport studies (체육학; 體育學)" in Korea is an extensive term encompassing all sport-related research areas, including sport studies in a more specific sense and sport science.

2. The Korean Alliance for Health, Physical Education, Recreation and Dance (KAHPERD) was established in 1953 and the first KAHPERD journal was published in 1955.

3. In alphabetical order.

4. The *KJSS* was first published in 1993, became biannual in 1996, triannual in 2004, and finally quarterly in 2008.

FIVE KEY READINGS

1. **Lim, B. J. (1994).** *Introduction to sociology of sport* **(1st ed.). Seoul: Donghwa Munhwasa.**

Lim's book is the first single-authored textbook of sociology of sport that gives a detailed account of research areas in the sociology of sport. The chapters include concepts and theories in sociology of sport, sport and social institutions (politics, economy, education, religion, and media), sport and social process (socialization, class), and sport and social problems (gender, deviation, collective behaviors, and future society).

2. **Korean Society for the Sociology of Sport. (2012).** *Sport and social theory.* **Seoul: Rainbow Books.**

This book is the first and only attempt in Korea to introduce diverse social theory applied to the sociology of sport. Each chapter provides an overview of the theory, main concepts and/or history, and application in sociology of sport; the book concludes with future prospects. The chapter titles and authors are as follows: Sport and social theory (Jong-Young Lee), Structural functionalism and sport (Jung-Woo Lee), Conflict theory and sport (Geun-Mo Lee), Symbolic interactionism and sport (Min-Hyuk Kwon), Critical theory and sport (Seong-Sik Cho), Exchange theory and sport (Su-Won Lim), Feminism and sport (Young-Shin Won), Cultural studies and sport (Eunha Koh), Figurational sociology and sport (Hee-Jin Seo), Foucault's sociology and sport (So-Ye Yang), Bourdieu's sociology and sport (Sang-Woo Nam), Social network theory and sport (Woo-Sung Kim), and Globalization theory and sport (Sun-Yong Kwon).

3. **Andrews, D., & Koh, E. (2002). Mapping cultural studies within sporting analysis: Toward critical, contextual sensibilities.** *Korean Journal of Sociology of Sport,* **15(2), 499–520.**

This article introduces the history and theoretical background of British cultural studies based on the notions of Stuart Hall's "Marxism without guarantees" and Lawrence Grossberg's "radical contextualism" and lists some key readings published in the sociology of sport. With the theoretical and methodological premise discussed in the previous sections, this article presents an ideal approach for sporting analysis in Korea and suggests possible research topics based on an understanding of its unique cultural background.

4. **Koh, E. (2011). Affective body, nationalism and consumer capitalism: Consumption and reproduction of celebrated bodies through media.** *Korean Journal of Sociology of Sport, 24*(1), 63–78.

This study pays attention to the mediated body of sport celebrity as an exemplary case of "affective body" (Featherstone, 2010) that constructs the charisma of sport celebrity and provides intense emotion to the consumer. It investigates the condition and context in which famous sport celebrity Yuna Kim's affective body is globalized, consumed, and ideologically employed through production, reproduction, modification, and consumption of various media content. The discussion on the way in which Yuna Kim's body is globalized by "banal cosmopolitanism" (Beck, 2002) and then returned to the nation by "rooted cosmopolitanism" (Molz, 2006) while inevitably connected to corporate nationalism is a unique approach to contextualizing sport celebrity, body, and ideology.

5. **Chung, H. J. (2001). What defines sport hero: Reading ideological conditions through its emergence and demise.** *Korean Journal of Sociology of Sport, 14*(1), 257–272.

This study is an early effort to analyze the ways in which the sport hero, now called sport celebrity, is defined in relation to ideologies using a cultural studies approach. Three sport heroes are chosen for investigation: Bum-Geun Cha, aka Cha Boom, who played an active role in the Bundesliga in the 1980s; Chan-Ho Park, who is the first Major League Baseball player from Korea; and Seri Pak, who is the first Korean golfer who won a major tournament and made an entry to the Ladies Professional Golf Association (LPGA) Hall of Fame. This article is one of the earliest studies employing critical theory and is referenced by many follow-up studies.

REFERENCES

Ahn, M. S. (1997). Masculinity in Korean traditional sport culture. *Korean Journal of Sociology of Sport, 8*, 177–184.

Ahn, M. S. (2000). Hegemony theory as an integrated theory. *Korean Journal of Sociology of Sport, 13*(2), 427–442.

Ahn, M. S., & Goo, C. M. (1996). Sport discourse through cultural studies. *Korean Journal of Sociology of Sport, 6*, 51–70.

Andrews, D., & Koh, E. (2002). Mapping cultural studies within sporting analysis: Toward critical, contextual sensibilities. *Korean Journal of Sociology of Sport, 15*(2), 499–520.

Ball, D. W., & Loy, J. W. (1975). *Sport and social order: Contributions to the sociology of sport.* Reading, MA: Addison Wesley.

Beck, U. (1992). *Risk society.* London: Sage.

Chang, I. Y. (2015). Exploring the possibility of leisure sports as a consideration in the process of lifestyle migration decision making: A case of South Korean immigrants in New Zealand. *Korean Journal of Sociology of Sport, 28*(1), 89–107.

Chang, S. H., Lee, N. M., & Lee, G. M. (2010). A semiotical approach to represented masculinity of Mixed Martial Arts. *Korean Journal of Sociology of Sport, 23*(4), 129–144.

Cho, M. R. (1976). *Sociology of physical education.* Seoul: Hyungseol Publications.

Cho, M. R., & Han, S. I. (1981). *Sociology of physical education.*

Cho, S. S. (1994). Sport as the site for production and reproduction of gender inequalities. *Korean Journal of Sociology of Sport, 2*, 63–74.

Cho, S. S. (2007). Constructive characteristics and ideological discourses of TV sports cartoon. *Korean Journal of Sociology of Sport, 20*(2), 233–247.

Chung, H. J. (2003). Sport star vs. rock star in globalizing popular culture: Similarities, difference and paradox in discussion of celebrities. *International Review for the Sociology of Sport, 38*(1), 99–108.

Chung, H. J. (2008). Sport mega-events and economic impacts: Reconstruction of 'invented truth'. *Korean Journal of Sociology of Sport, 21*(1), 229–251.

Chung, H. J., Chang, I. Y., & Lee, J. Y. (2005). Winter making of ski-club members: An ethnographic study on the socialization process of new members. *Korean Journal of Sociology of Sport, 18*(2), 211–228.

Chung, H. J., & Kim, M. J. (2013). Sport and online communities: Probing of its possibilities for public sphere. *Korean Journal of Sociology of Sport, 26*(3), 127–147.

Featherstone, M. (2010). Body, image and affect in consumer culture. *Body and Society, 16*(1), 193–221.

Goo, C. M., & Kwon, S. Y. (2011). *Contemporary sociology of sport.* (J. Coakley, Trans., Sport in Society, 10th ed.). Daehan Media.

Han, S. B. (2010). The dynamics of local politics and civil society in the bidding process for hosting Pyeongchang Winter Olympic Games. *Korean Journal of Sociology of Sport, 23*(1), 121–138.

Han, S. B. (2013). The social production and extinction of tennis court in urban space: The case of private and apartment complex tennis court in Seoul. *Korean Journal of Sociology of Sport, 26*(1), 125–149.

Han, S. I. (1979). *Sociology of physical education.*

Hwang, M. K. (2013). An analysis of racial discourses on foreign players in Korean professional sports league. *Korean Journal of Sociology of Sport, 26*(1), 151–166.

Ingham, A. G., & Loy, J. W. (1993). *Sport in social development: Traditions, transitions, and transformations*. Champaign, IL: Human Kinetics.

Jang, S. H., & Lee, G. M. (2013). The realistic consideration of Korean elite sports in the movie 'Lifting King Kong'. *Korean Journal of Sociology of Sport, 26*(1), 23–43.

Jang, S. H., & Lee, G. M. (2014). The production of fitness club's space: The practice, representation, appropriation of space. *Korean Journal of Sociology of Sport, 27*(1), 51–78.

Jang, Y. H. (1963). *Introduction to sport studies*.

Kim, H. B., & Kwon, S. Y. (2013). Exploring the meanings of injury experiences among college soccer players. *Korean Journal of Sociology of Sport, 26*(1), 107–124.

Kim, H. J. (2005). A study on TV news framing of FIFA World Cup. *Korean Journal of Sociology of Sport, 18*(2), 229–244.

Kim, H. J. (2007). Representation of post-world Cup documentary. *Korean Journal of Sociology of Sport, 20*(2), 249–268.

Kim, I. H. (2008). Analysis of relationship among of enjoyment factors, flow experience and addiction among the dance sport manias. *Korean Journal of Sociology of Sport, 21*(1), 129–149.

Kim, K. S. (2009). Structural equation modeling analysis of the negotiation process of leisure constraints among leisure and sports participants. *Korean Journal of Sociology of Sport, 22*(1), 61–76.

Kim, K. S. (2010). Power structure and inequality of resource exchange in network of badminton club members: Embedded effect of centrality and peripherality. *Korean Journal of Sociology of Sport, 23*(2), 19–39.

Kim, M. C. (2003). A study on compressed modernity of Korean sport. *Korean Journal of Sociology of Sport, 16*(1), 111–123.

Kim, Y. E., Na, D. K., Kim, J. H., Nam, M. K., & Kim, B. S. (2013). A study on represented image of sport movie 'As one'. *Korean Journal of Sociology of Sport, 26*(1), 167–184.

Koh, E. (2009). Heroes, sisters and beauties: Korean printed media's representation of sport women in 2004 Olympics. In P. Markula, T. Bruce, & J. Hovden (Eds.), *Olympic women and the media: International perspectives*. London: Palgrave Macmillan.

Koh, E., Andrews, D. L., & White, R. (2006). Beyond the stadium, and into the street: Sport and anti-Americanism in South Korea. In S. Wagg & D. Andrews (Eds.), *East Plays West: Essays on Sport and the Cold War*. London: Routledge.

Koh, E., & Lee, W. Y. (2004). The conditions of Korean sport celebrity: Seri Pak and corporate nationalism. *Korean Journal of Sociology of Sport, 17*(1), 121–137.

Korean Society for the Sociology of Sport. (Ed.). (2012). *Sport and social theory*. Seoul: Rainbow books.

Korean Society for the Sociology of Sport. (2015). *KSSS Annual Meetings*. Unpublished document.

Kwon, H. S., & Lee, J. Y. (2015). A study on internationalization process for members' organizational culture in sport clubs: Focusing on Schein's organizational cultural theory. *Korean Journal of Sociology of Sport, 28*(2), 1–26.

Kwon, K. N., Song, E. J., & Park, C. B. (2007). The understanding of drug choice mechanism of the men male high school bodybuilders. *Korean Journal of Sociology of Sport, 20*(2), 301–313.

Kwon, S. Y. (2006). Seri Pak, golf and nationalism: Unnatural articulation in the context of IMF. *Korean Journal of Sociology of Sport, 19*(1), 101–116.

Kwon, S. Y., & Lim, S. W. (2012). Docility aspect of elite female college football players. *Korean Journal of Sociology of Sport, 25*(4), 109–125.

Lee, C. S., & Nam, S. W. (2013). *Sociology of sport* (3rd ed.). Daejun: Gung Media.

Lee, H. K., Song, E. J., & Lim, S. W. (2006). The characteristics and functions of the sub-culture of married woman soccer club members. *Korean Journal of Sociology of Sport*, *19*(1), 85−100.

Lee, H. S. (2015). Competition between nationalism and transnationalism in the discourse on a naturalized sport celebrity, Vitore Ahn. *Korean Journal of Sociology of Sport*, *28*(1), 153−182.

Lee, J. G. (1975). *Sociology of Physical Education.*

Lee, J. R., & Kwon, K. N. (2013). A grounded theory approach toward female bodybuilders' occupational identity conflicts. *Korean Journal of Sociology of Sport*, *26*(3), 79−100.

Lee, J. Y. (2010a). *Past, present and future of Korean sociology of sport*. In *Past, present and future of Korean sociology of sport*. The 20th Anniversary Seminar of KSSS (pp. 49−72). Seoul: Seoul National University.

Lee, N. M. (2010b). The phenomenon of sport migration and manifestation of flexible citizenship in Korea. *Korean Journal of Sociology of Sport*, *23*(3), 155−178.

Lee, N. M., & Lee, G. M. (2007). The discourses of nationalism and multiculturalism through mass media news of Hines Ward. *Korean Journal of Sociology of Sport*, *20*(1), 107−125.

Lee, W. M., & Lee, J. Y. (2015). Habitus of exercise choice barriers in women's body shaping. *Korean Journal of Sociology of Sport*, *28*(1), 19−40.

Lim, B. J. (1994). *Introduction to sociology of sport* (1st ed.). Seoul: Donghwa Munhwasa.

Lim, S. M., & Lee, G. M. (2014). The sub-cultural characteristics of professor tennis clubs. *Korean Journal of Sociology of Sport*, *27*(4), 1−26.

Loy, J. W., McPherson, B., & Kenyon, G. (1978). *Sport and social system: Reader on the sociology of sport*. Reading, MA: Addison Wesley.

McPherson, B., Curtis, J., & Loy, J. (1989). *Social significance of sport*. Champaign, IL: Human Kinetics.

Ministry of Culture and Education. (1973). *Sociology of sport*. Ministry of Culture and Education.

Molz. (2006). Cosmopolitan bodies: Fit to travel, traveling to fit. *Body & Society*, *12*(3), 1−21.

Nam, S. W., & Koh, E. (2011). Emergence of diet heroes: Obesity discourse and cultural significance of reality show. *Korean Journal of Sociology of Sport*, *24*(2), 69−97.

Nam, S. W., & Koh, E. (2014). National hero Park Chan Ho vs. cosmopolitan Ryu Hyun-Jin: Globalization, nationalism and the meaning of sport star. *Korean Journal of Sociology of Sport*, *27*(4), 243−259.

Nam, S. W., & Lee, C. S. (2005). Mechanisms of surveilance, disciplinary power, and making weight: A Foucauldian perspective. *Korean Journal of Sociology of Sport*, *18*(2), 287−309.

Park, B. H. (2006). The lost gold medal: Media text analysis of bad call made at the Athens Olympics. *Korean Journal of Sociology of Sport*, *19*(1), 117−131.

Park, B. H. (2010). The privatization of street cheering space by a capital: A case study of "Hyundai Fan Park 2010". *Korean Journal of Sociology of Sport*, *23*(4), 29−43.

Park, Y. O. (2009). *Sport sociological approach to sport policy*. In *Sport sociological approach to sport policy: 2009 KSSS Annual Conference* (pp. 127−136). Seoul: Seoul National University.

Seo, H. J. (2004). A reading of sociocultural code reflected in mixed martial arts. *Korean Journal of Sociology of Sport*, *17*(1), 61–71.

Yang, S. Y., & Won, Y. S. (2007). Labor migration and adjustment experience of foreign players in Korean professional Basketball League. *Korean Journal of Sociology of Sport*, *20*(3), 537−554.

AUSTRALASIA

CHAPTER 6

SOCIOLOGY OF SPORT: AOTEAROA/NEW ZEALAND AND AUSTRALIA

Chris Hallinan and Steven Jackson

ABSTRACT

This chapter adopts a reflective approach exploring and setting out the contrasting factors that led to the establishment of the subdiscipline in both countries. The factors included the role of key individuals and their respective academic backgrounds and specialisations within each country's higher education system. Furthermore, attention is given to the particular circumstances in a case analysis comparison of the oldest programs in Aotearoa/New Zealand and Australia. This sheds light upon the factors linked to the disproportionate success profile for the sociology of sport in Aotearoa/New Zealand. An analysis of scholars and programs within each country reveals important differences aligned with the politics of funding and the variety and extent of systematic structures. Additionally, scholars' specialisations and preferences reveal a broad offering but are primarily linked to globalisation, gender relations, indigeneity and race relations, social policy, and media studies. This work has been undertaken variously via the critical tradition including Birmingham School cultural studies, ethnographic and qualitative approaches and,

Sociology of Sport: A Global Subdiscipline in Review
Research in the Sociology of Sport, Volume 9, 95–110
ISSN: 1476-2854/doi:10.1108/S1476-285420160000009009

more recently by some, a postmodern poststructuralist trend. Lastly, along with a brief discussion of current issues, future challenges are set out.

Keywords: Aotearoa/New Zealand; Australia; sociology of sport; programs; scholars

INTRODUCTION: THE HISTORY OF SOCIOLOGY OF SPORT IN AOTEAROA/NEW ZEALAND AND AUSTRALIA

The emergence and growth of sociology of sport as a subdiscipline in Aotearoa/New Zealand and Australia was brought about by several key factors: the (re)structuring of physical education curriculum developments in major university programs so as to require the inclusion of sociology as a core subject, the influence of scholars in sociology departments, and the regular intercontinental exchanges and migrations of numerous key scholars.

Perhaps ironically, the establishment of sociology of sport in Australian universities can be attributed to the scientising and expansion of the heretofore physical education (for school teaching) only curriculum (McKay, Gore, & Kirk, 1990). Under the initial oversight of Professor John Bloomfield (the first-ever professor of sports science in an Australian university) from the University of Western Australia (UWA), at least 12 universities over time established programs derived from the UWA model. Bloomfield's model was driven by the goal of aiding the development of high-performance sports in Australia via the research resources of universities as well as the newly established Australian Institute of Sport. Through this reconstitution of the curriculum, the general model adopted for the newly formed human movement degree programs was multidisciplinary. For example, the University of Wollongong model set up under Bloomfield's direction required students to study physiology, anatomy, psychology, motor learning, sociology and recreation. It is likely that the inclusion of sociology was assumed to be descriptive and celebratory rather than the critical studies model that mostly ensued. For a long period, there was considerable resistance to the critical study of sport. As noted by leading sport historians at the time, 'one of the things that emerges clearly is the egalitarian nature of sport in Australia, something which is contrary to what the sociologists like to tell us … (unlike sociologists) we tried to put forward the positive sides of sport' (McKay, 1991, p. 2). Such a disposition towards writing was an outgrowth of a legacy of the commemorative literature about sport that had been the standard offering well before the advent of academic sports studies. Among the streams available to human movement/physical education/sports science students in Australia, sociology of sport is usually, but not always, a complementary/supportive unit of study within a student's undergraduate degree requirement.

Broadly speaking the establishment of sociological analysis of sport in Aoteoroa/New Zealand can be traced to a range of scholars and writers (see Thomson & Jackson, 2016) including Richard Thompson, even though 'the significance of Thompson's contribution to New Zealand sociology via his continuing study of race, politics and sport has yet to be appreciated' (Pearson & McKay, 1981, p. 71). Thompson's *Race and Sport* (1964) examined the role of sport in South Africa under apartheid and the issue of sporting boycotts of South Africa with particular regard to New Zealand's relationships to that country in both rugby and cricket (Thomson & Jackson, 2016). This was an early contribution to the subdiscipline which was at that time being established on the international scene, but Thompson's work has been largely overlooked in many 'state of the field' discussions (Malcolm, 2014). Thompson's work aside, the formal institutionalisation of sociology of sport in New Zealand was initiated in 1976 when the Director of the School of Physical Education at the University of Otago, English historian, sociologist and philosopher Peter McIntosh, hired former student Rex Thomson to develop the programme which he did over the next 26 years. Otago has remained a key centre for teaching and research in the sociology of sport at the undergraduate and postgraduate level demonstrated by the long list of former students who have now established themselves in the field, including Michael Silk, Toni Bruce, Jay Scherer, Brendan Hokowhitu, Richard Pringle, Lisette Burrows, Farah Rangikoepa Palmer, Sarah Gee and Holly Thorpe among others.

Most of the scholars in each country regularly attend and present papers at established and long-running conferences. The principal conferences are International Sociology of Sport Association (ISSA), The Australian Sociology Association (TASA), North American Society for the Sociology of Sport (NASSS) and the Australian and New Zealand Association for Leisure Studies (ANZALS), and these routinely draw regulars, especially those who are also members. ISSA is the most popular site for academics from both countries. Steve Jackson served as president of ISSA, and

Chris Hallinan was one of the longest serving executive board members, while Brent McDonald (Australia) and Michael Sam (Aotearoa/New Zealand) currently serve as executive board members. A number of other Australian and New Zealand scholars have also held key organisational positions including Jim McKay (editor of the *International Review for the Sociology of Sport* and Toni Bruce, president of NASSS. The TASA Sport Working Group, based upon the British Sociological Association (BSA) model, is convened by Ramon Spaaij and Brent McDonald, and allows for members to meet annually within Australia and forgo the substantial cost of international air fares as most members' conference budget allocations are now modest.

SCHOLARS AND LOCALITIES

In Australia the academic study of sport has primarily been based within schools/departments of human movement/physical education/sport studies. Likewise, the majority of research output and teaching of sociology of sport are similarly located. As such, there are some established clusters within each country for the research and teaching of the sociology of sport. The distances and cost of travel within both countries make contact relatively limited, but new technologies facilitate better communication, and several places such as University of Otago, University of Waikato, University of Auckland, University of Queensland, University of Western Sydney, Victoria University and Monash University maintain several scholars in each location. In Aotearoa/New Zealand there are scholars who identify as sport sociologists at seven of the nation's eight universities, with some having clusters of five or more.

THE ACADEMIC ENVIRONMENT AND BARRIERS TO RESEARCH

In both countries sport is at the forefront of national everyday discourse and identity. It may surprise international readers that neither Australia nor Aotearoa/New Zealand have taken up the decision to sever ties with the English monarchy as head of state. Yet, the prominence of national sports teams clad in green and gold colours and with nicknames such as Kangaroos, Wallabies, Socceroos, Opals, etc., serves as a faux and determined nationalism in Australia. A similar pattern occurs in New Zealand where the silver fern adorns black and white uniforms for teams including the All Blacks, Black Ferns, Black Caps, All Whites, Tall Blacks and even Ice Blacks. With respect to Australia, national attention and devotion is so complete that sports and sports organisations are a subject for business interests and sport serves a mostly uncritical cultural function/institutional support and infrastructure. Although now well established in Australia, the threats continue from multiple sources. One of the main reasons that sociology of sport became primarily housed in physical education/sport science/human movement departments was because the study of sport was generally shunned by sociology departments.

There are over 50 public universities in Australia compared to only 8 in Aotearoa/New Zealand. Yet, Aotearoa/New Zealand has decidedly more organised programs and scholars in the sociology of sport subdiscipline. Two brief case examples may help illustrate the differences between the two countries and explain how and why. The two longest-established programs in each country are housed at Victoria University (VU) and the University of Otago. Although the Sports Studies programme ranks at or near the top of departments at Victoria University, the university has long languished well behind most other universities for overall research output and grant success. As such, incoming federal government funding has been relatively limited especially compared to the major universities in Victoria — Melbourne and Monash. Consequently, academics at VU must deal with higher teaching loads and restricted research resources and opportunities. Thus, despite having the longest-existing sociology of sport programme, the programme commenced outside the national university system within Footscray Institute of Technology (FIT). While the federal government supported the expansion of the national university system when institutions such as FIT amalgamated with similar institutions to form VU in 1992, the hollowing out of federal funds within a decade of such has disaffected lower-ranking universities such as VU. As several have noted, Australian programmes are decidedly scientised in that they are heavily tilted towards bioscience or essentialist teacher preparation degrees (Kirk, 1990; McKay et al., 1990).

In Aotearoa/New Zealand, sociology of sport has been a core or required course at the University of Otago since the 1970s including a period from the early 1990s to the early 2000s where the annual intake was 200 students per year for a 4-year degree. This, combined with the fact that Otago has had a strong core of sociocultural scholars for over a quarter of a century, helped establish a strong pedagogical platform and research culture which has directly or indirectly influenced programmes at other universities, including Waikato, Auckland, Canterbury, Massey and Lincoln. Notably, sociology of sport has not only survived but thrived despite a lack of research funding which tends to be allocated to those whose scholarship is perceived to support elite, high-performance sport.

MAIN AREAS OF RESEARCH STRENGTH

There are a variety of research specialisations across both countries resulting in a rich tapestry of teaching and research interests. Nevertheless, many scholars have established international reputations for specific areas that have had a sustained focus throughout. The principal general areas of research in Australia have resided within media studies, gender and race relations/ethnic studies. The pattern in New Zealand is similar with a focus on globalisation, national identity, media, gender and race/ethnicity/ Indigenous studies. A notable, if not distinguishing, feature of the subdiscipline in both countries rests with its international connections and layers. A considerable number of scholars relocated from other countries (see Thomson & Jackson, 2016 for an overview of the strong national and international collaborations established by New Zealand scholars). Both authors are, in fact, dual nationals. Hallinan is a citizen of both Australia and the United States and was educated and later worked at several universities in both countries. Jackson, born in Canada, received his PhD from University of Illinois (United States) before moving to New Zealand. Indeed, there have been several University of Illinois graduates who have moved to and taken up key leadership positions in New Zealand including Toni Bruce, Jim Denison, Pirrko Markula, Steve Jackson and Bob Rinehart. To add further to the connection, John Loy, who was one of the founders of the subdiscipline, left Illinois to take up the position of chair at the University of Otago in the early 1990s. The international migration of academic labour has included David Rowe, Chris Hallinan, Peter Mewett, Catherine Palmer, John Hughson, Mark Falcous, Josh Newman, Belinda Wheaton, Fiona McLachlan, Jim McKay, Camilla Obel, Michael Sam, Sarah Gee and Koji Kobayashi.

MAIN APPROACHES TAKEN

Acknowledging a few exceptions, it is fair to say that the sociology of sport research tradition within both countries has been 'critical' − challenging the status quo within academia and seeking to expose how sport reproduces a wide range of social inequalities. Through the 1980s and 1990s there was a strong Birmingham cultural studies influence apparent in the work of Jim McKay, David Rowe, Steve Jackson and others. At the same time there was a strong tradition of qualitative and ethnographic work being undertaken by Hallinan, Obel and others. The late 1990s and early 2000s witnessed the emergence of a postmodern/poststructural trend as highlighted in the work of Burrows at Otago and Markula and Denison at Waikato.

Arguably, both Australian and New Zealand early sociology of sport scholars were fortunate to be working within contexts where critical analysis was at least tolerated, if not actually valued. And, while critical approaches continue to dominate within both countries, increasing state and institutional pressures to secure research funding aligned with particular priorities and to meet specific publication targets are slowly having an impact. Nevertheless, there is a steady body of quality work emerging out of both countries. In Australia we note Hallinan and Judd's work on Indigenous sport in Australia, Rowe's research on media and citizenship, Palmer's work on sport and alcohol as well as the experience of Muslim women in sport, and McDonald's analysis of Japanese sporting culture and Pacific Island athletic labour migration. In New Zealand, there has been considerable work done on sport, globalisation and nationalism (Jackson, Kobayashi, Obel), identity politics (Bruce, Falcous, Hokowhitu, Jackson, Markula, Newman, Pringle), lifestyle and extreme sport (Booth, Crocket, Rinehart, Thorpe, Wheaton) and social policy (Gee, Jackson, Sam). What tends to be missing in both countries are large-scale analyses of sport participation patterns as related to health although the discourse of the obesity epidemic is likely to offer some opportunities for those scholars wishing to undertake specific forms of 'evidence-based' research. Overall, it is highly likely that the research traditions in both nations will continue though they will no doubt respond and adapt to shifts in paradigms and public policy.

KEY CONTRIBUTORS AND KEY PUBLICATIONS

There have been innumerable key publications throughout the lifespan of Australian sociology of sport. These publications have emanated from three groups of scholars: (1) those influential sociologists who limited their work in sport to one or two papers, (2) emerging scholars who are beginning to establish a track record in sport and (3) key contributors who, through a combination of international recognition, well-established specialisations and track records, have provided leadership in the subdiscipline.

It is admittedly a contentious endeavour to credit the emergence of sociology of sport to a limited number of individuals, let alone one. Even though both countries now have well-established and independent (from each others') systems and structures, it transpires that a New Zealander who was mostly based in Australia may need prime credit. Ken Pearson was born in Christchurch and received bachelor's and master's degrees from University of Canterbury. He then moved to University of New England and later to University of Queensland. He remained a frequent guest presenter at conferences in Aotearoa/New Zealand and did so with considerable accolade and impact (Thomson & Jackson, 2016). Likewise, his output in Australia was considerable and roundly lauded. Before his tragic and sudden death at age 39, he produced a considerable body of work (e.g., Pearson, 1979) which had an enduring impact on the sociology of sport. Pearson had commenced working with Jim McKay who subsequently emerged as the leading scholar and mentor for sociology of sport in Australia.

McKay was undoubtedly the most influential and well-known scholar in the field. His book *No Pain No Gain* was a breakthrough volume but was exceeded in impact by the groundbreaking volume *Managing Gender: Affirmative Action and Organisational Power in Australian, Canadian, and New Zealand Sport* which drew unprecedented attention for an Australian sociology of sport volume. Additionally, McKay published a multitude of articles primarily on masculinities and gender relations and identity politics (e.g., see McKay, 1991, 1994, 1997, 2013; McKay & Miller, 1991; McKay, Messner, & Sabo, 2000; McKay & Roderick, 2010). McKay served as editor of the *International Review for the Sociology of Sport* through an important transformation period. Lois Bryson was best known and acknowledged for her publications regarding social policy, gender, welfare state and women's health. Thus, she was an example of that group of sociologists whose primary focus was outside of sports studies. However, she entered the discussion on the prevailing subject at the time, women in sport, with several key publications that grounded male privilege in both hegemony and late capitalism (Bryson, 1983, 1990).

With Jim McKay in transition to retirement from full-time university employment, David Rowe has clearly emerged as the most prominent scholar in Australia with continuing high volume of research articles and chapters. Rowe, along with Chris Hallinan, McKay and Catherine Palmer was selected as one of the 50 notable scholars worldwide in the sociology of sport by the International Sociology of Sport Association. David Rowe is a much sought-after media commentator, and has achieved considerable success with securing external funding from the Australian Research Council. His principal research focus is with media culture as it relates to sport, journalism and music (e.g., see Hutchins & Rowe, 2014; Rowe, 1995, 2004, 2007, 2008, 2011; Rowe & McKay, 1987).

Chris Hallinan's principal area of focus rested with race and race relations and later more specifically with Australian Indigenous studies especially after he joined the Centre for Australian Indigenous Studies at Monash University in 2009. Hallinan also teamed up with other scholars including Steven Jackson to produce two editions of the *Sports in Society* books which were suitably adapted for Australia and New Zealand. But the core of the output was in the key research domain of Australian Indigenous studies and race relations in Australian sports. Most of that research output occurred with Indigenous scholar Barry Judd. (e.g., see Hallinan & Judd, 2007, 2010a, 2010b, 2012a, 2012b, 2012c, 2014). Catherine Palmer's research subject matter includes sport and alcohol, social inequalities and sport, sport for development and peace, risk and lifestyle sport, as well as major sporting events such as the Tour de France (e.g., see Palmer, 2001, 2005, 2009, 2010, 2011, 2013).

Another key sociologist from Australia is John Hughson who worked initially at University of Western Sydney and the University of New England before departing for overseas universities. Hughson's PhD thesis *A Feel for the Game: An Ethnographic Study of Soccer Support and Ethnic Identity* (Hughson, 1996) achieved rare acclamation in Australian sociology. John Hughson published numerous articles from that thesis as well as several on the politics of identity in Australia (e.g., see Hughson, 1997, 1998a, 1998b, 1999, 2000). He spent several years in New Zealand at the University of Otago, as well as at Wolverhampton and Durham, and currently works at the University of Central Lancashire in the United Kingdom. Beyond those key contributors, several other scholars including Karen Farquarson, Brett Hutchins, Ruth Jeanes, Brent McDonald, Tim Marjoribanks, Toby Miller, Ramon Spaiij and Jan Wright have been significant contributors as both authors and for the securing of external research funding in publications of significance to Australian sociology of sport.

Within Aotearoa/New Zealand, Rex Thomson's early work had an immediate impact. He published two papers in the *International Review of Sport Sociology* (1977, 1978), the first by a New Zealander in this journal. Thomson's work has focussed largely on the subculture of rugby, along with issues of gender, ethnicity and youth sport (Thomson, 2000;

Thomson & Sim, 2007). Jackson's early research focused on sport and Canadian identity (Jackson, 1998a, 1998b, 1998c, 2004) but this quickly expanded to a focus on sport and globalisation, corporate nationalism, media and promotional culture (Collins & Jackson, 2007; Jackson & Andrews, 1999, 2005; Jackson & Haigh, 2008; Jackson & Hokowhitu, 2002; Scherer & Jackson, 2010, 2013; Wenner & Jackson, 2009). Another Otago scholar, Falcous, has focused on media and national identity as well as race/ ethnicity (Falcous, 2007, 2014, Falcous & Newman, 2016) while Michael Sam has been at the forefront of linking sociology of sport and sport policy research (Sam, 2003, 2005; Sam & Macris, 2014). Toni Bruce has an established research record in the area of gender and media (Bruce, 2013, 2015; Wensing & Bruce, 2003) while her colleague Richard Pringle has developed strengths in the areas of Foucault and masculinity (Markula & Pringle, 2006; Pringle, 2009). The sociology of sport scholars now located at Waikato including Rinehart (2008), Rinehart and Sydnor (2003), Thorpe (2012), Thorpe and Ahmad (2013), Wheaton (2015) and Crocket (2015) are slowly developing a niche area related to lifestyle sport. Camilla Obel at Canterbury has studied rugby and national identity along with body culture (Obel, 1996, 2004), Sarah Gee at Massey University is quickly establishing a solid line of research related to sport and alcohol (2014; Gee & Jackson, 2012; Gee, Jackson, & Sam, 2016) and at Lincoln University Roslyn Kerr has studied science and technology particularly in relation to gymnastics (Kerr, 2012, 2014) while her colleague Kobayashi (2012a, 2012b) focuses on globalisation and corporate nationalism. Without doubt there are other scholars in both Australia and New Zealand who have made, and are making, valuable contributions to the field and we apologise for anyone we have overlooked.

THE FUTURE

One of the founders of the subdiscipline (John Loy) also played a key role in the continuing development in Aotearoa/New Zealand sociology of sport. It is perhaps fitting to draw upon some of his recent writing regarding the future of the subdiscipline when framing our views. Mindful of John Loy's comment that the future of the subdiscipline "will largely depend upon the personal choices sport sociologists make in terms of vocation and method" (Loy, 2015, p. 515), it can be mostly concluded that the establishment and maintenance of the subdiscipline in Australia has more to do with personal choices of key individuals rather than any institutional commitment. Indeed, David Rowe made a similar reflective comment when observing that his entry into a career as sport sociologist was a matter of "happenstance" (Rowe, 2015, p. 576).

Overall, the challenges facing sociology of sport in Aotearoa/New Zealand and Australia are generally similar to those facing the subdiscipline (and parent discipline and arguably social sciences more generally). Perhaps the biggest threat is the impending and potential impact of neoliberalism on the education sector. While signs of what Jackson (2015) has referred to as the 'neoliberal academic performance measurement imperative' are already at play, particularly through state-governed initiatives such as New Zealand's Performance Based Research Funding (PBRF), the long-term threat is the complete commodification of knowledge and the demise of academic freedom within completely corporatised universities. As such the challenge for sociology of sport is to remain relevant through collaborative efforts that, in the spirit of C. Wright Mills, connect *private experience* with wider *social structures*, *personal problems* with *public issues* and *scientific analysis* with *political awareness*.

FIVE KEY READINGS

1. **Coakley, J., Hallinan, C., Jackson, S., & Mewett, P. (2009).** *Sports in society: Issues and controversies in Australia and New Zealand.* **Sydney: McGraw-Hill Australia**.

   Drawn from the popular North American text, this volume constructs content and examples specifically for students in Aotearoa/New Zealand and Australia.

2. **Collins, C., & Jackson, S. (2007).** *Sport in Aotearoa/New Zealand Society.* **Melbourne: Thomson-Nelson.**

   This is the first dedicated Aotearoa/New Zealand collection of sport sociology research drawing upon the nation's leading scholars.

3. **Hallinan, C., & Judd, B. (Eds.) (2014).** *Indigenous people, race relations and Australian sport.* **London: Routledge.**

   A groundbreaking volume that assembled key researchers who had a direct connection to Australian Indigenous studies units in various universities across the country.

4. **McKay, J. (1997).** *Managing gender: Affirmative action and organisational power in Australian, Canadian, and New Zealand sport.* **Albany, NY: SUNY Press.**

This volume is drawn from a comprehensive study of sports organisations in each country. It elicits both quantitative and qualitative data to investigate the general pattern of men in control and women in support within sports organisations regarding gender.

5. **Thompson, S. M. (1999).** *Mother's taxi: Sport and women's labor.* **Albany, NY: State University of New York Press.**

This book offers a detailed analysis of how 'women facilitate and service the sport played by others'.

REFERENCES

Bruce, T. (2013). Communication and sport: Reflections on women and femininities. *Communication and Sport, 1*, 125–137.

Bruce, T. (2015). Assessing the sociology of sport: On media and representations of sportswomen. *International Review for the Sociology of Sport, 50*(4–5), 380–384.

Bryson, L. (1983). Sport and the oppression of women. *Journal of Sociology, 19*(3), 413–426.

Bryson, L. (1990). Challenges to male hegemony in sport. In D. Sabo & M. Messner (Eds.), *Sport, men and the gender order: Critical feminist perspectives* (pp. 173–184). Champaign, IL: Human Kinetics.

Collins, C., & Jackson, S. (Eds.). (2007). *Sport in Aotearoa/New Zealand society.* Melbourne: Thomson-Nelson.

Crocket, H. (2015). Foucault, flying discs and calling fouls: Ascetic practices of the self in ultimate frisbee. *Sociology of Sport Journal, 32*(1), 89–105.

Falcous, M. (2007). The decolonising national imaginary: Promotional media constructions during the 2005 lions tour of aotearoa New Zealand. *Journal of Sport and Social Issues, 41*(3), 374–393.

Falcous, M. (2014). White is the new black? Football, media and the New Zealand imagination. *Soccer & Society, 16*(4), 555–572.

Falcous, M., & Newman, J. I. (2016). Sporting mythscapes, neoliberal histories, and postcolonial amnesia in Aotearoa/New Zealand. *International Review for the Sociology of Sport, 51*(1), 61–77.

Gee, S. (2014). Sport and alcohol consumption as a neoteric moral panic in New Zealand: Context, voices and control. *Journal of Policy Research in Tourism, Leisure and Events, 6*(2), 153–171.

Gee, S., & Jackson, S. J. (2012). Leisure corporations, beer brand culture, and the crisis of masculinity: The Speight's "Southern Man" advertising campaign. *Leisure Studies, 31*(1), 83–102.

Gee, S., Jackson, S. J., & Sam, M. P. (2016). Carnivalesque culture and alcohol promotion and consumption at an annual international sports event in New Zealand. *International Review for the Sociology of Sport, 51*, 265–283.

Hallinan, C., & Judd, B. (2007). 'Blackfellas' basketball: Aboriginal identity and Anglo-Australian race relations in provincial basketball. *Sociology of Sport Journal, 24*, 421–436.

Hallinan, C., & Judd, B. (2010a). Race relations, indigenous Australia and the social impact of professional Australian football. In R. Spaaj (Ed.), *Social impact of sport.* London: Routledge.

Hallinan, C., & Judd, B. (2010b). From exclusion to enlightenment: Changes in the assumptions about Australian indigenous footballers. *International Journal of the History of Sport, 26*(16), 2358–2375.

Hallinan, C., & Judd, B. (2012a). Indigenous studies and race relations in Australian sports. *Sport in Society: Cultures, Commerce, Media, Politics, 15*(7), 915–921.

Hallinan, C., & Judd, B. (2012b). Duelling paradigms: Australian aborigines, marn-grook and football histories. *Sport in Society: Cultures, Commerce, Media, Politics, 15*(7), 975–986.

Hallinan, C., & Judd, B. (2012c). Producing benevolence and expertise: Whitestreaming marn-grook & the other constraints of Australian Football. *Journal of Australian Indigenous Studies, 15*(2), 5–13.

Hallinan, C., & Judd, B. (Eds.). (2014). *Indigenous people, race relations and Australian sport.* London: Routledge.

Hughson, J. (1996). *A feel for the game: An ethnographic study of soccer support and ethnic identity.* Unpublished PhD Thesis, University of New South Wales.

Hughson, J. (1997). Football, folk dancing and fascism: Diversity and difference in multicultural Australia. *Journal of Sport and Social Issues, 33*(2), 167–186.

Hughson, J. (1998a). Among the thugs: The 'new ethnographies' of football supporting subcultures. *International Review for the Sociology of Sport, 33*, 43–57.

Hughson, J. (1998b). Soccer support and social identity. *International Review for the Sociology of Sport, 33*, 403–409.

Hughson, J. (1999). A tale of two tribes: Expressive fandom in Australia's a-league. *Sport in Society, 2*(3), 10–30.

Hughson, J. (2000). The boys are back in town: Soccer support and the social production of masculinity. *Journal of Sport and Social Issues, 24*(1), 8–23.

Hutchins, B., & Rowe, D. (2014). *Sport beyond television: The internet, digital media, and the rise of networked media sport.* New York, NY: Routledge.

Jackson, S., & Andrews, D. (Eds.). (2005). *Sport, culture and advertising: Identities, commodities and the politics of representation.* London: Routledge.

Jackson, S., & Hokowhitu, B. (2002). Sport, tribes and technology: The New Zealand all blacks *haka* and the politics of identity. *Journal of Sport and Social Issues, 26*(1), 125–139.

Jackson, S. J. (1998a). A twist of race: Ben Johnson & the Canadian crisis of racial and national identity. *Sociology of Sport Journal, 15*, 21–40.

Jackson, S. J. (1998b). Life in the (mediated) faust lane: Ben Johnson, national affect and the 1988 crisis of Canadian identity. *International Review for the Sociology of Sport, 33*(3), 227–238.

Jackson, S. J. (1998c). The 49th paradox: The 1988 calgary winter Olympic games and Canadian identity as contested terrain. In M. Duncan, G. Chick, & A. Aycock (Eds.), *Diversions and divergences in the fields of play* (pp. 191–208). Greenwich, CT: Ablex Publishing.

Jackson, S. J. (2004). Exorcising the ghost: Donovan Bailey, Ben Johnson and the politics of Canadian identity. *Media, Culture and Society, 26*(1), 121–141.

Jackson, S. J. (2015). Future challenges and opportunities for the sociology of sport. Plenary Panel Presentation, World Congress of Sociology of Sport – 50th Anniversary, June, Paris, France.

Jackson, S. J., & Andrews, D. L. (1999). Between and beyond the global and the local: American popular sporting culture in New Zealand. *International Review for the Sociology of Sport, 34*(1), 31–42.

Jackson, S. J., & Haigh, S. (2008). Between and beyond politics: Sport and foreign policy in a globalising world. *Special Issue of* Sport in Society, *11*(4), 349–358.

Kerr, R. (2012). Integrating scientists into the sports environment: A case study of gymnastics in New Zealand. *Journal of Sport and Social Issues, 36*(1), 3–24.

Kerr, R. (2014). From foucault to latour: Gymnastics training as a socio-technical network. *Sociology of Sport Journal, 31*(1), 85–101.

Kirk, D. (1990). Knowledge, science and the rise and rise of human movement studies. *ACHPER National Journal, 127*, 25–27.

Kobayashi, K. (2012a). Globalization, corporate nationalism and Japanese cultural intermediaries: Representation of bukatsu through Nike advertising at the global-local nexus. *International Review for the Sociology of Sport, 47*(6), 724–742.

Kobayashi, K. (2012b). Corporate nationalism and glocalization of Nike advertising in "Asia": Production and representation practices of cultural intermediaries. *Sociology of Sport Journal, 29*(1), 42–61.

Loy, J. L. (2015). Assessing the sociology of sport: On theory and method. *International Review for the Sociology of Sport, 50*, 512–518.

Malcolm, D. (2014). The social construction of the sociology of sport: A professional project. *International Review for the Sociology of Sport, 49*(1), 3–21.

Markula, P., & Pringle, R. (2006). *Foucault, sport and exercise: Power, knowledge, and transforming the self.* London: Routledge.

McKay, J. (1991). *No pain, no gain? Sport and Australian culture.* Sydney: Prentice Hall.

McKay, J. (1994). Masculine hegemony, the state and the incorporation of gender equity discourse: The case of Australian sport. *Australian Journal of Political Science, 29*, 82–95.

McKay, J. (1997). *Managing gender: Affirmative action and organisational power in Australian, Canadian, and New Zealand sport.* Albany, NY: SUNY Press.

McKay, J. (2013). 'We didn't want to do a dial-a-haka': Performing New Zealand nationhood in Turkey. *Journal of Sport and Tourism, 8*(2), 117–135.

McKay, J., Gore, J., & Kirk, D. (1990). Beyond the limits of technocratic physical education. *Quest, 41*(1), 52–76.

McKay, J., Messner, M., & Sabo, D. (Eds.) (2000). *Masculinities, gender relations, and sport.* Thousand Oaks, CA: Sage.

McKay, J., & Miller, T. (1991). From old boys to men and women of the corporation: The Americanization and corporatization of Australian sport. *Sociology of Sport Journal, 3*(1), 86–94.

McKay, J., & Roderick, M. (2010). 'Lay down sally': Media narratives of failure in Australian sport. *Journal of Australian Studies, 34*(3), 295–315.

Obel, C. (1996). Collapsing gender in competitive bodybuilding: Researching contradiction and ambiguity in sport. *International Review for the Sociology of Sport, 31*(2), 185–203.

Obel, C. (2004). Researching rugby in New Zealand: Reflections on writing the self and the research problem. *Sociology of Sport Journal, 21*(4), 418–434.

Palmer, C. (2001). Outside the imagined community: Basque terrorism, political activism and the Tour de France. *Sociology of Sport Journal, 18*(2), 143–161.

Palmer, C. (2005). A world of fine difference: Sport and identity among young refugee women. *Journal of Interdisciplinary Gender Studies, 6*(2), 11–20.

Palmer, C. (2009). Soccer and the politics of identity for young Muslim refugee women in South Australia. *Soccer and Society, 10*(1), 27–38.

Palmer, C. (2010). Everyday risks and professional dilemmas: Fieldwork with alcohol-based (sporting) subcultures. *Qualitative Research, 10*(4), 1–20.

Palmer, C. (2011). Key themes and research agendas in the sport-alcohol nexus. *Journal of Sport and Social Issues, 35*(2), 168–185.

Palmer, C. (2013). Sport and alcohol – Who's missing? New directions for a sociology of sport-related drinking. *International Review for the Sociology of Sport, 49*(3–4), 263–277.

Pearson, K. (1979). *Surfing subcultures of Australia and New Zealand.* St. Lucia: University of Queensland Press.

Pearson, K., & McKay, J. (1981). Sociology of Australian and New Zealand sport: State of the field overview. *Australian & New Zealand Journal of Sociology, 17*(2), 66–75.

Pringle, R. (2009). Defamiliarizing heavy-contact Sports: A critical examination of rugby, discipline, and pleasure. *Sociology of Sport Journal, 26*(2), 211–234.

Rinehart, R. E. (2008). ESPN's X games: Contests of opposition, resistance, co-option, and negotiation. In K. Young (Ed.), *Tribal play: Sport subcultures and counterculture. Research in the sociology of sport* (Vol. 4). London: Emerald.

Rinehart, R. E., & Sydnor, S. S. (Eds.). (2003). *To the extreme: Alternative sports, inside and out.* Albany, NY: State University of New York Press.

Rowe. (2015). Assessing the sociology of sport: On media and power. *International Review for the Sociology of Sport, 50*, 576.

Rowe, D. (1995). *Popular cultures: Rock music, sport and the politics of pleasure.* London: Sage.

Rowe, D. (2004). *Sport, culture, and the media: The unruly trinity* (2nd ed.). Maidenhead: Open University Press.

Rowe, D. (2007). Sports journalism: Still the "toy department" of the news media? *Journalism, 8*(4), 385–405.

Rowe, D. (2008). Culture, sport and the night-time economy. *The International Journal of Cultural Policy, 14*(4), 399–415.

Rowe, D. (2011). *Global media sport: Flows, forms and futures.* London: Bloomsbury Academic.

Rowe, D., & McKay, J. (1987). Ideology, the media, and Australian sport. *Sociology of Sport Journal, 4*(3), 258–278.

Sam, M. P. (2003). What's the big idea? Reading the rhetoric of a national sport policy process. *Sociology of Sport Journal, 20*(3), 189–213.

Sam, M. P. (2005). The makers of sport policy: A task(force) to be reckoned with. *Sociology of Sport Journal, 21*, 78–99.

Sam, M. P., & Macris, L. I. (2014). Performance regimes in sport policy: Exploring con-
    sequences, vulnerabilities and politics. *International Journal of Sport Policy and Politics,*
    6(3), 513–532.
Scherer, J., & Jackson, S. J. (2010). *Globalization, sport and corporate nationalism: The newcul-*
    tural economy of the New Zealand all blacks. Oxford: Peter Lang Publishers.
Scherer, J., & Jackson, S. J. (2013). *The contested terrain of the New Zealand all blacks: Rugby,*
    commerce, and cultural politics in the age of globalisation. Oxford: Peter Lang
    Publishers.
Thompson, R. (1964). *Race and sport.* London: Oxford University Press.
Thomson, R. W. (1977). Participant observation in the sociological analysis of sport.
    International Review of Sport Sociology, 12(4), 99–109.
Thomson, R. W. (1978). Sport and ideology in contemporary society. *International Review of*
    Sport Sociology, 13(2), 81–94.
Thomson, R. W. (2000). Globalization and national differences: The changing face of youth
    sport. *New Zealand Sociology, 15*(1), 30–45.
Thomson, R. W., & Jackson, S. J. (2016). History and development of the sociology of sport
    in Aotearoa-New Zealand. *New Zealand Sociology, 31*(3), 78–110.
Thomson, R. W., & Sim, J. (2007). Sport and culture: Passion and paradox. In C. Collins &
    S. Jackson (Eds.), *Sport in aotearoa/New Zealand society* (2nd ed., pp. 113–129).
    Australia: Thomson.
Thorpe, H. (2012). Sex, drugs and snowboarding: (Il)legitimate definitions of taste and lifestyle
    in a physical youth culture. *Leisure Studies, 31*(1), 35–51.
Thorpe, H., & Ahmad, N. (2013). Youth, action sports and political agency in the Middle
    East: Lessons from a grassroots parkour group in Gaza. *International Review for the*
    Sociology of Sport, 50(6), 678–704.
Wenner, L., & Jackson, S. J. (2009). *Sport, beer, and gender: Promotional culture and contem-*
    porary social life. Zurich: Peter Lang Publishers.
Wensing, E. H., & Bruce, T. (2003). Bending the rules: Media representations of gender during
    an international sporting event. *International Review for the Sociology of Sport,*
    38(4), 387–396.
Wheaton, B. (2015). Assessing the sociology of sport: On action sport and the politics of iden-
    tity. *International Review for the Sociology of Sport, 50*(4–5), 634–639.

EUROPE

CHAPTER 7

SOCIOLOGY OF SPORT: CZECH REPUBLIC

Irena Slepičková

ABSTRACT

The purpose of this chapter is to provide an overview of the development of Czech sociology of sport with respect to socio-political changes over the last 50 years. A comparative sociological approach was used to analyze books, articles, and other types of research productivity. The analysis shows that Czech sociology of sport has developed in three different periods: first, linked to the development of mainstream sociology; second, as a body of socially oriented sport research; and third, as an educational sub-discipline increasingly located in university sport faculties. However, the interest of the State in sociology has significantly decreased since 1990, which has created its own Czech-specific issues. The chapter is based on the method of literature review and, because of the author's professional activities in sport organizations as well university research, also on a type of "auto-ethnography."

Keywords: Socio-political changes; university education; research topics; sport sociology

Sociology of Sport: A Global Subdiscipline in Review
Research in the Sociology of Sport, Volume 9, 113–131
Copyright © 2017 by Emerald Group Publishing Limited
ISSN: 1476-2854/doi:10.1108/S1476-285420160000009011

INTRODUCTION

As a special issue within their series of publications focused on sociology and published since 2006, Czech scholar Jiří Šubrt and his colleagues prepared the monograph *Current Sociology VI: Fields of Interest and Specializations* (Šubrt et al., 2014). Sociology of sport was acknowledged in this publication (Slepičková, 2014) and considered one of the discipline's important sub-specializations along with other areas such as the sociology of the family and the sociology of leisure. This provided us with an opportunity to remind the Czech sociological community that sport is an integral part of people's lives, and that sociology not only helps explain the phenomenon as such, but that it also contributes to studying and understanding social reality in general. The study argued that an evaluation of Czech sociology of sport was needed. Hence, the volume that this contribution is a part of can be considered a significant challenge and simultaneously a commitment to present a complete (as far as possible) and objective overview of the origins, development, position, and problems of the sociology of sport in the Czech Republic.

THE HISTORY OF SOCIOLOGY OF SPORT IN THE CZECH (OSLOVAK) REPUBLIC

The Stage of Partnership of Sociology and Sociology of Sport

In the Czech territory, sociology of sport, as one of the sub-specializations of mainstream sociology, began to emerge at the time of the revival of Czechoslovak sociology in the 1980s, although papers of a sociological nature focused on sports had already existed since the 1960s. As already mentioned, general sociology did not have an easy position in the Czech or Czechoslovak environment, and it could not develop in the same way as occurred in the West. To explain this situation it is necessary first to describe the history of Czech sociology in the former Czechoslovakia.

The essential reason for fragmentation in the development of Czech sociology can be found in the geographic position of the Czech territory that used to be the area affected by different (and often conflicting) political, cultural, and economic influences. The Czech territory lies on the border of West and East Europe (i.e., in Central Europe). Different authors in different historical periods have understood this geographical circumstance in various ways. Based on the notion of "mental maps," Havelka (2010; cited in Janák et al., 2014) shows differences in the Hungarian, Polish, and Czech interpretations and characteristics of Central Europe. According to this position, the Polish interpretation accents the so-called "intermarium"; the Hungarian one the "Carpathian Arc" as a notion in political science; and the Czech one the belt of small nations between Germany and Russia, continuously endangered by power and politics. Next to geographical and political circumstances, culture is also important; increasingly so since the 1980s. This approach working with so-called heartlands (Poland, Hungary, Czechoslovakia) strengthened after the collapse of the communist bloc at the beginning of the 1990s. As part of the so-called "Visegrad" group of four states (after the division of Czechoslovakia into two states), the Czech Republic and the Slovak Republic in 1993 was established. Common activities included not only political or economic matters but also scholarly collaborations including sociology of sport (Fölesiné & Dóczi, 2011). The long-time "isolation" of Central Europe also affected the position of sociology (of sport) in the society involved. Hence, there were national sociologies concentrated on "their own society" and representing themselves above all in national languages (Janák et al., 2011).

Since sociology of sport began to establish itself in the world in the 1960s and 1970s, I will not describe the very beginnings of Czech or Czechoslovak sociology. It is worth mentioning that sociology as a free science was developing in 1919–1948. Nešpor (2014) speak about two sociological schools – the Prague school and the Brno school – which developed a kind of rivalry. The rivalry developed on the basis of their members' institutional affiliation with Prague or Brno universities, and above all on different conceptions of sociological work conducted there (Brno preferred philosophical foundations, functionalism, and qualitative methods; while Prague preferred more empirical research and quantitative methods without the general sociological theory). Sociological work at the time was concerned, for example, with social community problems, the family, education, politics, and bureaucracy. However, sport was not one of the topics studied widely at the time.

With the change in political system in 1948, a complicated period started in the development of Czech sociology. It found itself under the influence of a version of Marxism replete with ideology. Academic sociology at the time was abandoned as "bourgeois" and antagonistic to historical materialism. However, Marxists slowly began to look for a way to enrich the evidential basis of society, how to strengthen the experience utilizing the knowledge in practice, and how to create sociology comparable to the contemporary Western sociology. Around 1965 (Marxist) sociology became an independent scientific discipline integrated in the centrally controlled system of science and research in university programs. It became a part of the newly established (after a Soviet pattern) Czechoslovak Academy of Sciences (ČSAV) and a study field at higher education institutions (Nešpor, 2014, p. 299). Research in ČSAV was focused on general sociological theory, sociological methodology, sociology of working groups, sociology of leisure, and theory and sociology of religion. In 1967, the Institute for Public Opinion Research was established to carry out public opinion research. I mention the general topics of Czechoslovak sociology of that time because many researchers that took part in them later participated in sociology of sport or sociology of physical culture, either in the form of theoretical and methodological inspiration, or their own empirical activity. In 1965, *Sociologický Časopis* (*Sociological Journal*) was launched, which has been the main periodical of the field until today. Within the reform process in the 1960s, there was an overall political relaxation in Czechoslovakia, which also made possible a blossoming of sociology and emergence of sociology as individual fields. Thanks to a kind of liberal situation, the sixties enabled the first works of a sociological character in the field of sports in the Czech environment, around the same time that sociology of sport was forming its own identity on the global stage.

After the reform movement defeat at the end of summer 1968, a return to the central directive control of the whole society and to the Marxism—Leninism ideology as the basic doctrine took place. This change significantly limited the development of sociology as a discipline. Some experts were forced to stop their professional career in the field, and also the choice of topics sociology was allowed to deal with became limited. Despite this weakening, official sociological research remained funded by the government.

In the 1970s, the number of non-academic establishments and research institutes (e.g., of work, agricultural economy) grew, and many sociologists found jobs there. Academics were forced to leave universities or the Academy of Sciences for political reasons, and sociological studies became used in human activities off campus (Voříšek & Nešpor, 2014). Among these institutes, there was also Sportpropag, an establishment of the Czechoslovak Union of Physical Education (ČSTV), more precisely of its Department of Complex Prognostic Modelling. An institutional interconnection between sport and sociology took place that initiated interest in the application of a sociological approach to sport on the one hand, and provided a peaceful environment for work for sociologists (and economists) outside the mainstream of science and research on the other hand. This establishment was initially abundantly funded and employed professionals of various expertise to write studies. This workplace used to be a scene of regular professional discussions, seminars, and conferences throughout the 1970s until its liquidation in 1984. Sociologist Jiří Kábele, who was employed there for some time, spoke about Sportpropag in his commemorative paper as of "an unlikely place for studying the society" (Kábele, 2011, p. 1). Many experts had a chance to meet there; many of them won recognition in professional or even political spheres after the political and economic changes at the turn of the 1980s and 1990s. The department was headed by economist Miloš Zeman;[1] Pavel Machonin, an expert on social stratification in Czech society and lifestyle; and Martin Potůček, who studied public politics and health politics. Importantly, the environment at the time was inspiring from the point of view of empirical survey methodology and publications focused on physical culture.

Above all in the 1980s there was a collaboration between sport specialists from the Research Institute of Physical Education (a part of the Fakulta tělesné výchovy a sportu UK, or FTVS UK) and sociologists dealing with research on public opinion and leisure. The ČSTV had its Department of Scientific Methodology collaborating with the above-mentioned Department of Prognostic Modelling, and the Scientific Council of the ČSTV publishing *Proceedings of the Scientific Council of the Central Committee of ČSTV* from 1965 to 1990. Research results concerning the importance of physical culture as a part of leisure, the socialist way of life, and citizen standpoint and involvement in sport were published there. It should be mentioned that the Ninth International Symposium of Sociology of Sport on the topic Physical Culture and Sports in the Way of Life of the Young Generation took place in Prague in 1984. Thanks to the involvement of general sociologists in the field of sport, both through their employment and expert activities, one issue of *Sociologický Časopis* was focused entirely on sport (1985).

Czech Sociology of Sport Under New Social Conditions

Unfortunately, the changes in Czech society after 1989 did not lead to an institutional and research relationship between sociology and sociology of sport; indeed, they almost completely separated. Sociologists returned to universities where departments often disposed of Marxist ideology. Many sociologists also left for the private sector, where there were newly established for-profit organizations concentrating their activities on various surveys, such as public opinion surveys, frequently working for interest groups composed of current or former politicians. The main sociological centers have concentrated once again in Prague and Brno, and also on some newly established public universities, notably Olomouc and Ostrava.

In the changing Czech society that chose the way of a free, politically pluralist, liberal and free-market development, new problems began to appear connected with growing social differences between people, increased incidence of pathological social phenomena, and forms of consumerism that constituted rich matter for both general sociology and the development of its individual sub-specializations. Many new institutions appeared but, with some exceptions, they rarely studied sport and its sociological context.

Thus, sociology of sport began to look for its own way forward, more or less without connection to the rest of the sociological community. The re-establishment of Czech sociology of sport has taken place mainly at universities, above all by faculties of sport, stemming from the professional interest and involvement of certain individuals. The possibility of participation at international and European sociological conferences, contacts with foreign universities, and international collaboration in research made the entry to the field of sociology of sport easier. In 1999 the Czech Society of Kinanthropology (ČKS) was founded to cover the field of sport and physical education. ČKS is a member of the Council of Scientific Societies of the Czech Republic. Initiated by scholars from the FTVS UK in Prague (led by this author), the Section of Sociology of Sport was initiated in 2006. Approximately every 18 months they organize meetings in Prague focused on various topics (see Table 1). It is interesting primarily for the sociology of sport, but often the subjects exist on the border of sociology, social psychology, and political science. Reviewed thematic proceedings have been published from these small one-day conferences. The conferences have a rather intimate character with 25–50 participants, mainly from sport and pedagogic faculties of public universities both from the Czech Republic and from neighboring Slovakia, and on average 10–15 contributions. Among the participants there are also representatives of the sport movement, regional and local public administration, and other organizations; sometimes also foreign guests during their exchange program at the FTVS UK. The conference is financed by research funds from FTVS UK.

Conference themes try to react to topical problems of sport in the Czech environment. The first conference aspired to find a follow-up to Czech sociology (of sport) of the 1980s and to draw attention to its position in

Table 1. List of Conferences of Sociology of Sport and Their Main Topics.

No.	Year Published	Title	Number of Contributions	Proceedings	Form
I.	2006	Limits of (Czech) sociology of sport	7	–	–
II.	2007	Topical questions of sociology of sport	15	Reviewed	CD ROM
III.	2008	Media, sport and their role in active lifestyle	17	Reviewed	CD ROM
IV.	2009	Social role of sport	13	Reviewed	CD ROM
V.	2010	Sport and politics	15	Reviewed	Book
VI.	2011	Sport and social stratification	10	Reviewed	Book
VII.	2013	Socio-economic conditions of sport for children and youth – prospects and obstacles	11	Reviewed	CD ROM
VIII.	2016	Problems of doping in children and youth sport	11	Reviewed	Book

current research. Among the participants there were some actors from the 1980s that were either employed in the environment of sport and/or sport organizations, or concentrated directly on sport topics in their activities at that time. The second conference, next to open topics, concentrated on sport spectatorship. The following conference focused on media (this attracted the interest of sport managers and sport journalists). Thanks to its broad theme, the 2009 conference provided free space for presenting diverse issues concerning the place of sport in society. The conference in the next year responded to issues of sport politics from institutional, organizational, and financial perspectives and from the point of view of sport governance and other specific problems. Changes in the political and socio-economic structures of Czech society have also projected to the active and passive participation in sport, which was the theme of the 2011 and 2013 conferences. The last conference focused on the issue of doping in youth, also in connection to a World Anti-Doping Agency (WADA) project based at FTVS UK.

SCHOLARS AND INSTITUTIONS

Before 1989 there were two university departments dealing with physical education and sport in Czechoslovakia – the FTVS UK in Prague, and the

Faculty of Physical Education and Sport of Comenius University in Bratislava. Research institutes of physical education were affiliated to each of them, but both liquidated after 1990. Sociology of sport was not taught as a special course per se. Some traces of a sociological approach could be seen in the so-called theory of physical culture that officially had to present the ideology of that time. Nevertheless, some empirical surveys and professional publications, linked through their authors with the sociological community of that time, presented topical sociological issues currently studied in sociology of sport abroad (Čechák & Linhart, 1986).

At present there are three faculties of sport at public universities in the Czech Republic – the FTVS UK in Prague, the Faculty of Sport Studies of Masaryk University in Brno, and the Faculty of Physical Culture of Palacký University in Olomouc. Sociology of sport does not have an independent department at any of these universities. In all cases it belongs, with a minimum of people, to departments covering social sciences or humanities. General sociology is usually taught as a part of program foundations, and then (as a separate course) sociology of sport or its application to specialized topics (e.g., sport and leisure, sport organizations, or sociology of sport) as a part of sociology. However, it should be stressed that topics of sociology of sport (doping, spectatorship, etc.) are taught also within social psychology at FTVS UK. I should also mention that there are other establishments where we can meet specialists interested in sociology of sport, either at universities (Faculty of Social Sciences of Charles University, Faculty of Social Studies of Masaryk University), or in certain research organizations.

Trying to summarize how many people are regularly or often involved in sociology of sport, about 3–4 scholars have graduated in sport, and 3–4 scholars have graduated in sociology. We can add those who have carried out some research in topics typical for sociology of sport, although being oriented to other fields in their professional life (i.e., about 5–10 persons in the country at present). Hence, we can see that the family of sociology of sport is very small and fragmented, comprising only between 10 and 20 persons.

THE CZECH ACADEMIC ENVIRONMENT AND BARRIERS TO RESEARCH

As mentioned above, sociology of sport, either as a part of student education or a research activity, does not have an independent position in the organizational scheme of universities in the Czech Republic. Rather, it is a part of departments covering social sciences. As compared with the period before 1990, sociology of sport or its applications have been fully established in the study programs, mostly in the form of one-semester obligatory courses.

The advantage of the current research situation is the freedom in academia and the possibility to select one's own research agenda. According to the Higher Education Act, research is part of a teacher's duties; hence, they should devote themselves to it. At the university level there are several sources of research funding. Most often these include the funds of the faculty or university; subsidies from ministries such as the Ministry of Education, Youth and Sport; and/or support from the Czech Science Foundation (GA ČR). Funding is not automatic − individual universities, faculties, scholars, and research teams have to compete for it. However, in the case of funding from extramural sources, there is a huge competition, and not only from the academic sphere. This system gives everybody a chance. However, in the competition between specialized sociological establishments consisting of more specialists and support staff, it is very challenging for sociology of sport, which builds on a small group of scholars dispersed in the whole country. Financial support can be obtained also from various international organizations (e.g., the European Commission, WADA, etc.), again in grant competitions, where Czech sport sociologists usually take part within international teams.

Listing the fundamental problems of sociological research in sport, we can name a small number of sociologists or similarly oriented scholars that are not concentrated in one workplace, on the one hand, and the competition of sociologists of other specializations that does not always consider sport to be a significant social issue on the other hand. Also worth mentioning is the "solidarity" (or lack of solidarity) of the general sociological community (its members are simultaneously reviewers of the projects) and its occasional obliviousness to sport as an important phenomenon, which can play a role in decisions about the allocation of research funds.

Recently, the government, through the Ministry of Education, Youth and Sport, has not opened invitations to bids of sociological topics in the field of sport governance, which it used to do almost regularly until 2000. However, local public authorities will place orders for drafting documents for local sport governance, where approaches of sociology of sport may apply.

MAIN AREAS OF RESEARCH STRENGTH

As with other countries, recent topics of research interest for the sociology of sport reflect new problems in Czech society. These often shift depending upon the position of sport governance in the society. It is possible to identify four main fields of research interest that Czech sociology of sport concentrates on. These include both topics of relevance from the earlier period as well as new social issues.

Sport as a Social Phenomenon

Sport has been always presented as a social phenomenon, but the specific way it has been presented has depended on the ideological orientation of the day. In the 1960s, initial works describing the importance of sport appeared, similar to Western countries. Later on, sport was presented as a development tool of the (communist) society. At present, liberalism and the market economy govern the Czech environment, bringing problems that we have not experienced previously. Thus, sport is studied as a possible tool of prevention or solution in terms of these new problems. How sport is perceived also by citizens, and what importance they attach to it, is the subject of public opinion investigations, related usually to monitoring participation levels in sport. Such surveys had been conducted relatively frequently from the 1980s until the turn of the century, when they were financially supported by the government. Recently, data of this type became a part of the so-called Eurobarometer funded and organized by the EU, which provides information about all member countries. The Eurobarometer monitors participation in sport as an aspect of leisure, and is particularly focused on sport features such as participation, opinion, and accessibility, etc. Data are often collected by private agencies, and the research is quantitative and descriptive without any interpretation of the results from a sociological point of view. Obviously, some research is organized also at university faculties, often focused on specific population groups (such as children, youth, or seniors). Finally, changes in interest in traditional or new sports and their governance are also studied.

Social Stratification and Social Justice

Due to changes in the social structure of Czech society, the connection between the life of individuals or social groups and socio-economic status is studied in Czech sociology of sport. The continuous increase in economic

(way of life and lifestyle) are quite often confused. This causes misunderstandings in general sociology and in sport sociology, too. Works of internationally recognized sport sociologists addressing this problem are reviewed.

4. **Slepička, P., Slepičková, I., Kotlík, K., & Landa, P. (2010).** *Divácká reflexe sportu.* **Praha: Karolinum.**

The book sums up the results of a survey of sport spectators in the six most popular team sports in the Czech Republic. Using quantitative and qualitative methods, the survey was particularly oriented towards the investigation of spectators' motivation to attend matches, their reactions in stadiums, and their value orientations. The interpretation of results also reflected the social structure of spectators and showed differences compared to similar research undertaken 25 years ago.

5. **Numerato, D. (2010). Czech sport governance culture and plurality of social capitals: Politicking zone, movement and community. In M. Groeneveld, B. Houlihan & F. Ohl (Eds.),** *Social capital and sport governance in Europe* **(pp. 41−62). New York, NY: Routledge.**

Over the last 25 years, Czech society has dramatically changed. This has left a mark on the sport field, sport values, sport governance, etc. Based on Bourdieu's theory, the author analyzed three sports differing in their social capital. He showed how the social capital impacts on the position of each of these sports in sport governance and sport promotion. The research was conducted within the framework of an EU project.

REFERENCES

Adamec, Č., & Teplý, Z. (1989). *Výzkum veřejného mínění na téma Sport pro všechny: Závěrečná zpráva.* Praha: Sport.

Čechák, V., & Linhart, J. (1986). *Sociologie sportu.* Praha: Olympia.

Choutka, M. (1978). *Sport a společnost.* Praha: Olympia.

Fölesiné, S. G., & Dóczi, T. (Eds.). (2011). *The interaction of sport and society in the V4 countries.* Budapest: Hungarian Society of Sport Science.

Havelka, M. (2010). *Ideje, dějiny, společnost: studie k historické sociologii věděn.* Brno: CDK.

Janák, D., Berešová, A., Mašata, J., Klobucký, R., Bezsényi, T., Halász, I., Kubíková, A., et al. (2014). *Počátky sociologie ve střední Evropě. Studie o formování sociologie jako vědy v Polsku, českých zemích, na Slovensku a v Maďarsku.* Praha: Sociologické nakladatelství.

Kábele, J. (2011). Sportpropag − Nepravděpodobné místo pro studium společnosti: Osobní pohled. *Sociální Studia, 1,* 17−32.

Kotlík, K. (2006). *Psychosociální determinanty chování fotbalových diváků*. PhD thesis, FTVS UK, Praha.

Kožíšek, V., Bárta, M., Holda, D., & Nekola, J. (1989). *Tělesná kultura v životě naší společnosti. Fakta-teorie-problémy-výhledy*. Praha: Olympia.

Landa, P. (2009). *Hodnotové orientace sportovních diváků*. PhD thesis, FTVS UK, Praha.

Machonin, P. (1967). *Sociální struktura socialistické společnosti: (sociologické problémy soudobé československé společnosti)*. Praha: Svoboda.

Machonin, P., & Tuček, M. (Eds.). (1996). *Česká společnost v transformaci. K proměnám sociální struktury*. Praha: Sociologické nakladatelství.

Nešpor, Z. (Ed.). (2014). *Dějiny české sociologie*. Praha: Academia.

Nešpor, Z., & Kopecká, A. (2011). *Kdo je kdo v české sociologii a příbuzných oborech*. Praha: Sociologické nakladatelství.

Numerato, D. (2010). Czech sport governance culture and plurality of social capitals: Politicking zone, movement and community. In M. Groeneveld, B. Houlihan, & F. Ohl (Eds.), *Social capital and sport governance in Europe* (pp. 41–62). New York, NY: Routledge.

Petrák, B. (1967). *Sociologie a tělesná kultura: Úvod do sociologie tělesné kultury*. Praha: Státní pedagogické nakladatelství.

Popelka, J. (2014). *Sport jako veřejná služba: Sociálnisí spravedlnost a efektivnost sportovních zařízení v obcích*. PhD thesis, FTVS UK, Praha.

Rychtecký, A. (2006). *Monitorování účasti mládeže ve sportu a pohybové aktivitě v České republice*. Praha: Univerzita Karlova v Praze, Fakulta tělesné výchovy a sportu.

Sekot, A. (2006). *Sociologie sportu*. Brno: Masarykova univerzita a Paido.

Slepička, P. (1991). *Spectator reflection on sports performance*. Praha: Univerzita Karlova.

Slepička, P. (2002). Bohemian rhapsody: Football supporters in Czech Republic. In E. E. Dunning (Ed.), *Fighting fans. Football hooliganism as a world phenomenon* (pp. 49–62). Dublin: University College Dublin Press.

Slepička, P. (Ed.). (2009). *Sport and life style*. Praha: Karolinum.

Slepička, P., Jansa, P., Rychtecký, A., & Slepičková, I. (2001). *Společenská reflexe sportu*. Praha: FTVS UK.

Slepička, P., Mudrák, J., & Slepičková, I. (2015). *Sport a pohyb v životě seniorů*. Praha: Karolinum.

Slepička, P., Slepičková, I., Kotlík, K., & Landa, P. (2010). *Divácká reflexe sportu*. Praha: Karolinum.

Slepičková, I. (2007). From centralized to democratic sport governance and organization. *Transition, 47*(1), 95–106.

Slepičková, I. (2011). New space for a new face of sport in central and Eastern European countries. In S. G. Fölesiné & T. Dóczi (Eds.), *The interaction of sport and society in the v4 countries* (pp. 35–48). Budapest: Hungarian Society of Sport Science.

Slepičková, I. (2014). Sociologie sportu – Význam, přístupy a témata studia sportu v sociologickém pohledu. In J. Šubrt, S. Ferenčuhová, D. Hamplová, F. Kalvas, S. Kreisslová, J. Váně, et al. (Eds.), *Soudobá sociologie VI (oblasti a specializace)* (pp. 245–273). Praha: Karolinum.

Sociologický časopis. (1985). *Sociologický časopis, 21*(3).

Špaček, O. (2011). Sport pro všechny? Sociální nerovnosti a sportovní aktivity. *Sociální Studia, 8*(2), 53–78.

Špaček, O., & Šafr, J. (2010). Volný čas, sport a kulturní vkus: rozdíly podle společenského postavení. In H. Maříková, H. Kostelecký, T. Lebeda, & M. Škodová (Eds.), *Jaká je naše společnost? Otázky, které si často klademe* (pp. 81–99). Praha: Sociologické nakladatelství.

Šubrt, J., Ferenčuhová, S., Hamplová, D., Kalvas, F., Kreisslová, S., Váně, J., et al. (2014). *Soudobá sociologie VI Oblasti a specializace.* Praha: Karolinum.

Svoboda, A. (2015). *Vrcholový sport a autenticita: sportovní hvězdy mimo zájem médií.* PhD thesis, Fakulta sportovních studií MUNI, Brno.

Teplý, Z. (1990). *Pohybový režim dospělých: základní poznatky o současném pohybovém režimu 18–59 letých občanů ČSR.* Praha: Univerzita Karlova.

Teplý, Z., & Adamec, Č. (1990). Pohyb v životě dospělých občanů ČSR. *Sborník vědecké rady ČSTV, 21,* 28–43.

Teplý, Z., & Rejšek, R. (1976). Účast pracujících na některých sezónních pohybově rekreačních aktivitách. *Teor. A Praxe těl. Vých, 24*(5), 268–272.

Voříšek, M., & Nešpor, Z. R. (2014). Organizační zázemí akademického života. In Z. Nešpor (Ed.), *Dějiny české sociologie* (pp. 306–321). Praha: Academia.

Zeman, M. (1980). Prognostika a plánování rozvoje ČSTV. Teor. a Praxe těl. *Vých., 1980, 28*(1), 5–9.

CHAPTER 8

SOCIOLOGY OF SPORT: FINLAND

Pasi Koski

ABSTRACT

Compared with the history of many other countries, sport has had an exceptional role in the Finnish transformation from a young to a mature nation. Finland has a relatively long tradition in the sociology of sport. The interest has been focused on a wide range of physical activities. At the same time, the parent discipline of sociology has been a "mother" science in the field; as such the more representative term in Finland for this area is the "social science of sport and physical activity." Finnish sociology of sport is strongly concentrated in Jyväskylä and most of the scholars in the field have been educated at the University of Jyväskylä. Recently the research in the field has spread to other universities and new perspectives have enriched the research. The critical mass of Finnish sociology of sport is not very big. Approximately 400 students have graduated in the field during its history and approximately 60 have worked in the field as professional researchers. Most of the publications in the field are for a domestic audience. The group of internationally active scholars is relative small. The variety of research themes is nevertheless wide. However, interest has continued in a few of them, and has focused on several researchers. In this respect, the most central themes have included changes in sports culture, socialization into sport and physical activities,

Sociology of Sport: A Global Subdiscipline in Review
Research in the Sociology of Sport, Volume 9, 133−151
ISSN: 1476-2854/doi:10.1108/S1476-285420160000009012

gender and physical activities, the social significance of sport and physical activity, and organized sport movements.

Keywords: Physical culture; social sciences of sport; physical activity; branch of science; research; education

INTRODUCTION

The development of modern sport with its different phases coheres to the trajectory of Finnish national history. Partly due to this, sport has been a specific and significant factor for the population of such a small country (at present 5.5 million). Finland was a part of the Swedish kingdom for approximately 700 years and, subsequently, a Grand Duchy of Russia from 1809 to 1917, when Finland gained full independence. As recently as 100 years ago, Finland was a poor, remote corner of the world. The nation searched for its identity and place in the sun. Independent Finland has transformed from a poor, agriculture-dependent peripheral country into an affluent Nordic social welfare nation with a high standard of living supported by strong education and technology. (Koski & Lämsä, 2015, p. 422). Compared with the history of many other countries sport has had an exceptional role in this Finnish transformation from a young to a mature nation. Early success in the international sporting arena and the emergence of national sport heroes strengthened national pride. This was evident especially during the process of independence and after the birth as an independent nation. Sport had an important role in the pursuit of fostering national identity, national self-consciousness, patriotism, and world recognition. Sport served not only the unification process of the nation but it also had a role in the process of political polarization of the young nation. After the Civil War in 1918, because of the political cleavage between the political left and right, the Finnish sport movement was separated in two camps (Heinilä, 1987). Consequently, the relationship between sport and society was noticed relatively early in Finland. This background may be one of the explanations as to why the sociology of sport developed early in the country. Social questions have been present in Finnish sport from the beginning.

The purpose of this chapter is to describe the history and current status of Finnish sociology of sport as a scientific and educational field. First, it is necessary to provide some information about the conceptual diversity in the field.

CONCEPTUAL DIVERSITY: FROM SPORT TO PHYSICAL ACTIVITY AND FROM SOCIOLOGY TO SOCIAL SCIENCES

When the trajectory of Finnish sociology of sport is analyzed, the researcher will soon encounter the problem of conceptual diversity. This concerns both parts of the phrase: the first part, sociology, and the last part, sport.

The hegemony of competitive sport was evident during the first part of the 20th century. Consequently, the thinking and discussions in the field percolated through the spirit of competitive sport for a long time. This ethos was strong until the 1980s. A unique Finnish term – liikunta – started to become more common, especially since the 1960s. During the national seminar for sport and physical activities arranged in 1967, a statement was made whereby the culture of physical activity was defined to consist of three sectors: competitive and elite sport, sport for all, and physical education. The general concept which combines all these aspects was liikunta. Subsequently, political parties started to create political programs for liikunta. The status of the term was strengthened in societal discussions and it became more frequent in the 1970s. The insight of the concept, with its breadth and a sort of critical view of the narrowness of top sport, fits the spirit of the times and the phase of the creation of the welfare state (Kokkonen, 2013, pp. 11–19). Liikunta has been a more usable and more contemporary generic term since the 1980s, when the interests and needs for physical activity started to increase in the process of diversification of physical culture.

The sociological approach that analyzes physical culture, the sociology of sport, has focused in Finland on the whole range of the described liikunta scale. That is, the research in the field has been interested in competitive and top sport, sport for all, as well as physical education. Additionally, during the past few years, the whole field of sport sciences has focused on sedentary lifestyles and everyday activities. These are topics that have found their route as well to the tables of sport sociologists. In their evaluation of Nordic sport sciences, Haskell et al. note that there has been a paradigm shift from performance to health and wellbeing. This shift is also evident in the social and behavioral sciences at least in Nordic countries such as Finland (Haskell et al., 2012, p. 51).

In Finland, sociology can be understood as a parent of academic research, which has tried to increase our understanding about social issues of sport and physical activity. But the dependency on sociology is not always orthodox. Therefore "the social sciences of sport" have become a more common expression about the academic work conducted than the sociology of sport per se. In the international setting, due to the utilitarian and economic perspectives in politics, the social sciences of sport have differentiated and institutionalized into smaller subfields (such as sport management, sport development, and sport economics) (Koski, 2015). The critical mass in the different subfields is not large in Finland and the process has not happened at the national level. The borderlines and boundaries of the discipline are tattered and the core is leaking (Koski, 2015). The process whereby the sociology of sport transformed into the social sciences of sport best describes the situation. In these circumstances, the last mentioned term could be the correct one for academic research done in the field. The broad perspective of physical activity themes such as health, wellbeing, and healthy lifestyle policy and politics are not very far from the focus of researchers. The evaluation group of Nordic sport sciences describe the situation as a conceptual crisis in research regarding the concept of sport (Haskell et al., 2012, p. 51).

When reading this chapter, the reader should keep in mind the above-described conceptual variety, which concerns both sport and sociology. For the author of this chapter, it meant that a not-very-strict definition could be applied. On the other hand, the broad nature of both concepts has given a relatively fruitful basis for research, especially in our time when the demand for and development of multidisciplinary research are evident.

HISTORY OF THE SOCIOLOGY OF SPORT IN FINLAND

According to the evaluation report of the Nordic sport sciences, "Finland has a long and successful history in the sport and exercise sciences, and in particular in sports pedagogy/sociology" (Haskell et al., 2012, p. 53). The history of Finnish sociology of sport is indeed comparatively long. This can be explained by the fact that one of the forefathers and pioneers of the field, Kalevi Heinilä, is Finnish. Heinilä educated himself first as a physical education teacher and later as a sociologist. His doctoral dissertation was approved at the University of Helsinki in 1959. The topic was leisure and sport. His friend and colleague, internationally renowned sport sociologist Seppänen (1998, p. 14), characterized the dissertation as follows: "Although the work itself is a rather conventional type of study, it is, however, one of the first modern pieces of empirical research in sociology of sport in Finland. Undoubtedly, it is, also a work which gave rise to a wider and more profound discussion of the role of social sciences and their application in the sport life on the country." During his career, Heinilä had an important role when the basis of the education of Finnish sport sciences had been created and, in many respects, this is true as far as the research is concerned, especially the social research on sport and physical activity. An indicator of his initiative and his international significance is the fact that he was a member of a small group of scholars who founded the International Committee for Sociology of Sport (currently the International Sociology of Sport Association (ISSA)) in 1965.

Before Heinilä's time, there had been in Finland some sociological inquiries that bore sport sociological elements. For instance, research on youth leisure where physical activity had an essential role had been done already (e.g., Allardt, Jartti, Jyrkilä, & Littunen, 1958; Helanko, 1957). Heinilä's dissertation was not the first doctoral thesis in Finland in the field. However, it was the first *Finnish* one. Before it, in 1954, Maximilian Stejskall published his doctoral dissertation at the Åbo Akademi University in Swedish with the title *Folklig Idrott* (*Folk Sport*). It has been described as an ethno-sociological analysis of traditional folk sports in the region of Swedish-speaking people in Finland (Heinilä, 1987, p. 5; Roiko-Jokela, 2012, p. 169). It took some time after these initial forays into the field before the discipline started to become established and institutionalized.

The process of institutionalization was supported when the faculty of sport sciences was founded in the University of Jyväskylä in 1968. In Finland there is only one university that has a governmental mandate to focus on sport sciences. The scientific and academic education of sport sciences in Finland has been centralized to the Faculty of Sport Sciences at the University of Jyväskylä. In 1971, the Department of Sport Planning was founded. This name was changed to the Department of Social Sciences of Sport at the end of the 1980s. Some years ago, because of the administrative intensification process, the department became a part of the Department of Sport Sciences.

The first and still only professorship of sociology of sport in Finland was founded in 1972. When the foundation of the professorship was prepared, it was stated that there was a strong societal demand for the discipline and its development. At that time, generalized social planning and the increased problems of leisure time created a need for leisure studies and applied studies. The first purpose was to create a professorship for the sociology of sport and leisure. The themes of special interest were voluntary sport and association activities, public sport policy, collective behavior in sports, and leisure activity. Eventually, the professorship was named as the professorship of sport sociology and Kalevi Heinilä was offered the position. After Heinilä's retirement in 1987, the chair was taken by Pauli Vuolle in 1988 and in 2004 by current incumbent Hannu Itkonen. (Roiko-Jokela, 2012, pp. 82, 169–170).

Narrowly defined, Finnish sociology of sport has still only one chair. However, referring to the broad definition of the field it is worth mentioning one more professorship. In the same department, there is a chair for sport planning. In the beginning, from 1974 to 1998, it was a readership. Then it was changed to a professorship. The main theme has been sport policy as a part of social policy and sport planning as a part of community planning. The first office-holder was Pauli Vuolle from 1974 to 1988, and the second was Kalevi Olin from 1989 to 2005. Thereafter the professorship has been held by Kimmo Suomi.

When academic education in the field was started in the 1970s, the Nordic welfare state was under construction. At that time, the development of public administration provided the academic development of sport administration and sport management as well. Due to this, sport administration was created as a field of study for students. This decision meant that sport administration and sport management were defined as important themes for education and research. In this respect it could be said that Finland was interested relatively early not only in the sociology of sport but also in the academic development of sport management and sport administration. The sociology of sport was harnessed as a mother discipline for sport administration and it was the main subject for students. This perspective was supported by the view of community planning, which was based on the optimism of planning and was so typical for the 1970s. Because of this background it is not surprising that perspectives of management, administration, and planning have had a relatively strong role in our sport studies tradition. (Koski, 1999).

NUMBER OF SCHOLARS, GEOGRAPHY, AND ACADEMIC ENVIRONMENT FOR THE SOCIAL SCIENCES OF SPORT IN FINLAND

In the past, the annual number of new students in the field of the social sciences of sport at the University of Jyväskylä was as low as 10. However, in the 2000s the number has been between 12 and 14 depending on how two study places for disabled students are filled. Currently the amount of new students per year is on average 16 or 17. During the whole history of Finnish sport study about 450 students have studied in the field. About 400 of them have already graduated. Where MAs are concerned, at the time of writing, 180 students have graduated in the sociology of sport, 127 in the social sciences of sport, and 105 in sport planning and administration (personal communiqué by Minna Kettunen and Päivi Saari, January 2016). When interpreting these figures, it is worth recalling the vagueness of the definition of the fields.

By 2012, as many as 11 doctoral dissertations in the field of the sociology of sport had been published in the Faculty of Sport Sciences at the University of Jyväskylä (Kiviaho, Vuolle, Olin, Laakso, Koski, Juppi, Ilmanen, Viita, Feng, Heinonen, and Kokkonen), although at least three or four of those could be classified as sport history (cf., Roiko-Jokela, 2012, pp. 62, 294–295). Also, five dissertations were approved in sport planning and administration (Suomi, Karimäki, Gretschel, Salmikangas, and Rajaniemi) and four in the field of the social sciences of sport (Huovinen, Vehmas, Laine, and Pavelka). We should also note the five dissertations in the social sciences of sport (Simula, Borgogni, Kauravaara, Ojala, and Takalo) that were published after 2011 in the Faculty of Sport Sciences and more than 10 doctoral dissertations approved during the history in some other faculty or university (e.g., Heinilä, Itkonen, Markula, Kosonen, Heikkala, Veijola, Puronaho, Tiihonen, Berg, Parviainen, Sironen, Pirinen, Lehmuskallio, Zacheus, Turtiainen, and Laakso). All in all, depending on how one does the counting, about 30–40 doctoral theses have been published in the field in Finland or by a Finnish scholar.

According to data from the turn of the millennium, we can estimate that about 15% of graduated sport sociology students will work in the field of research after graduation (see Koski, 1999, p. 181). From 400 graduated students, this means about 60 researchers. Of course, it should be remembered that one can end up in research work in the field from other routes as well as from the faculty of sport sciences.

The Finnish Society of Sport Sciences (previously known as the Finnish Society for Research in Sport Science and Physical Education) maintains a register of Finnish sport scientists. Currently, it consists of about 900 names of experts and/or scholars. Retrieval from the register by the social sciences of sport (defined to include the sociology of sport, sport philosophy, sport history, sport communication, and sport tourism) provides 60 names. This is surprisingly exactly the same number as above. It is clear that over the years there have been scholars who are not presented in the system and, as well, the register has not necessarily caught all from the target group. It can be concluded that in Finland, depending on the definitions used, there have been about 50–100 researchers who have been interested in social issues of sport and physical activity.

When the geography of the field is analyzed, it is unsurprising that the University of Jyväskylä is the only academic institute for sport sciences. Jyväskylä is an important town in this sense, but not only because of the university. Additionally, there are two nationally important research institutes for sport sciences. LIKES (Foundation for Sport and Health Sciences) and KIHU (Research Institute for Olympic Sports) are both institutes where research in the social sciences of sport is undertaken. LIKES conducts and develops multidisciplinary and applied research on physical activity. It was founded in 1970. At the moment, it employs 30 people in research. Five of them work in the field of social sciences. KIHU was founded in 1991. Its mission is to promote Finnish top-level sport through advanced, innovative, and ethically responsible applied research. The research institute employs altogether 35 experts, researchers, and members of technical staff, representing various fields of biological, behavioral, and social sciences. At the moment, five of them are working in the social sciences of sport.

Outside of Jyväskylä, the research in the field has been rather unestablished and has been dependent on the interest of individual researchers or research groups. Consequently, the work they have done on the social science of sport has been sporadic. The University of Helsinki and the University of Joensuu have been institutions where historically oriented research on the social aspects of sport have done (e.g., Hentilä, 1982; Itkonen, 1996). Research undertaken at the University of Tampere in the field could be characterized as philosophical (e.g., Parviainen, 1998) or administrative scientific (e.g., Heikkala, 1998) (see Roiko-Jokela, 2012, p. 171).

Outside the Faculty of Sport Sciences at the University of Jyväskylä, the University of Turku could be named as an active institute in the field. Research applying sociological approaches to sport and physical activity has been done there for about 20 years (see Viljanen, Matilainen,

Perko, & Sinkkonen, 1994; Zacheus, Tähtinen, Rinne, Koski, & Heinonen, 2003). In the background of this initiative in the first place was the interest of the city of Turku to develop its operations based on scientific information. Consequently, the Paavo Nurmi Center started to collect basic information about the physical activities of the citizens. Most of the research projects have been multidisciplinary. However, the majority of research in the field has been done in the Faculty of Education. The research group in the University of Turku has consisted over the years of more than 10 different researchers. Outside the discussed four universities, the social study of sport and physical activity has not operated within the typical interest of scholars in the other Finnish universities. However, some individuals who are attracted to the field could be identified (e.g., the University of Lapland, the University of Oulu).

The UKK Institute and the National Institute of Health and Welfare (THL) are research centers where research on public administration is carried out. The focus of both is the study of health-enhancing physical activities. THL is a research and development institute under the Finnish Ministry of Social Affairs and Health. It seeks to serve the broader society in addition to the scientific community, actors in the field, and decision-makers in central government and municipalities. The aim is to promote health and welfare in Finland. The research at the UKK Institute in Tampere is multidisciplinary and pragmatic. The perspective of the social sciences is included in these institutes, especially in multidisciplinary projects.

During the past 15 years the Finnish Youth Research Society and the Finnish Youth Research Network (FYRN) have become more interested in the field of sport and physical activity, and sociological questions are being asked. This has strengthened the focus of young age groups. Their coming to the field is also fresh and fruitful because they are not usually coming from the perspective of sport and sport sciences.

Finnish sport sociology, or even the social sciences of sport in Finland, do not have their own professional associations. Some Finnish scholars have been actively involved in international co-operation, especially in ISSA and the European Association for the Sociology of Sport (EASS). The important association for Finnish sport sciences is the already mentioned Finnish Society of Sport Sciences (LTS), which works as a node of the Finnish network and discussions about sport sciences. The society was founded in 1933 and not only organizes seminars and education but also maintains and activates societal and critical discussions. Since 1963, it has published a journal called *Liikunta & Tiede* (*Sport & Science*; the name was

Stadion in the years 1963—1979). Sociological and social scientific perspectives are relatively well represented in it. LTS organizes national seminars about sport policy and social issues about every second year.

CHARACTERISTICS OF FINNISH RESEARCH

Criteria such as international publishing, impact factors, number of publications, etc., which new public management systems have brought to the academic world, have not been very favorable for the tradition and customs of Finnish sociology of sport. For example, international perspectives and international publishing have not been typical in Finland. Most of the publications in the field are for domestic audiences. A relatively large proportion of all publications take the form of monographs and research reports. Authors have been active not only in scientific writing but many of them are used to publish popular texts too. Publishing in international peer-reviewed journals has been relatively infrequent. In preparation for or this chapter I examined the lists of publications for the institutes and researchers in the field who are at the active phase of their career. The overall volume of publications was about 700 in the sample. Only about 20% of the publications were published in a language other than Finnish. In this non-Finnish part, English was of course the most used language. All in all, more than 10 different languages were used. The most common languages after English were Swedish and Russian. About 5% of the sample was classified as research articles in English peer-reviewed journals. Of course, these figures do not cover the whole history and picture of Finnish sociology of sport, but they do describe the trends in Finnish publishing activities in the field.

The critical mass of researchers has been relatively small overall and it has been typical that researchers have worked on their own projects. During the last two decades, working in larger research groups became more common. This is partly because of the increased number of multidisciplinary projects.

Conventions of the field are not the only factors that explain the emphasis of publishing activities. Issues of resource also contribute to publishing trends. Several researchers have to rely on allocated resources. Quite often it is a question of strictly limited work that serves public administration when the focus is not on scientific and theoretical approach or the development of science. Thus articles published in the international science journals are quite rare. If a researcher is interested and willing to write one, in many cases he or she has to do it on their own time. Before the ideas of new public management the first generation of Finnish sport sociologists could focus on the themes and questions they saw as worthy of analysis. The situation for the current scholars is somewhat different. The evaluation group (Haskell et al., 2012, p. 51) wrote that researchers face a double output pressure: "On the one hand, international peer-reviewed publications are required. On the other hand, local and national reports, policy documents and national-language publications are demanded. Researchers experience this double pressure as both difficult and frustrating. They feel pushed or punished in one or the other direction."

One of the consequences when trying to serve public administrations is the rather thin theoretical orientation of the research. The use of sociological theories in particular is relatively unusual. However, over time the theoretical influence on Finnish sociology of sport has found versatility from the trends of general sociology. Heinilä studied in the United States as a student of Herbert Blumer. The influence of the Chicago school and symbolic interactionism is thus visible in Heinilä's and his students' work. However, the versatile use of theoretical ideas by a limited group of researchers has meant that the cumulative nature of the theoretical perspectives has been relatively thin, and it is hard to find common or agreed-upon theoretical schools in the field in Finland. To cut to the chase, the application of theoretical backgrounds has been in many cases subordinate to the purposes of the research. The ideas of the important European sociologists (such as Bourdieu, Lévi-Strauss, or Weber) can be found as well as combinations of such theorists. In some cases, Anglo-American influences are clearer. For instance, organizational and sport management studies have taken their theoretical bases mostly from the Anglo-American traditions. Heikkala's (1998) work leaning on Luhmann's ideas is a refreshing exception.

Quantitative methods have been most applied especially during the first few decades of Finnish sport studies when the lack of basic information was evident. Gradually, the methodological range adopted has become more diverse and today almost all kinds of known methods can be found in the field. Even seldom applied ethnographical and narrative methods have recently started to be used.

MAIN AREAS OF FINNISH RESEARCH

The first generation of Finnish sport sociologists (including Allardt, Heinilä, Seppänen, and Sänkiaho) were educated as sociologists, but they were all obviously intrigued by sport. From that group, only Heinilä was educated in physical education. After the foundation of the Faculty of Sport Sciences, the group of scholars without a background in general sociology started to grow. Pekka Kiviaho studied sport associations and their regional and political structures. The theme was especially current and meaningful at that time. Kiviaho was also a central figure in the METELI project, which in a multidisciplinary way analyzed the association of physical activities, health, and environment among the staff of one factory. Pauli Vuolle was involved in the International Committee for Sociology of Sport (ICSS) project about the careers of the top athletes. In addition he is known inter alia for his research on physical activities at the national level and nature as an environment for physical activity. Kalevi Olin was especially interested in sport policy, and especially the decision-making process in sports policy. After Kiviaho's untimely death, Paavo Seppänen was inspired to study the organized sport movement and its membership structures. In addition Seppänen explored international sport. He is probably best known because of his analyses on the connections between international elite sport and value orientations of different nations (e.g., Seppänen, 1981).

Heinilä's diverse range of research contributions is not easy to summarize. His scientific interests focused on issues of sport and physical activity and their role in society, at both the national and international levels. Among other matters, he has explored domestic ideology in sports, fair play, policy and planning in sports and physical education, sport for all, sport and politics, values and value orientations of sport, socialization into sports, the role of mass media of sport, spectator sport, sport and mutual understanding, sport and ethics, the role of women in sport, sport as a peace movement, sport organizations and sport management, and the problems of international sport. Internationally, he is probably best known for his idea of the totalization process in international sport (see Heinilä, 1984). Professor Heinilä has continued to write more than three decades after his retirement (e.g., Heinilä, 2010).

Research on many of the themes that Heinilä initiated has continued with contemporary generations. During the past 20 years central topics in the Finnish social sciences of sport have been the social significance of sport and physical activities, the national sport system and its organizations, civil activity in sport and physical activities, the local role and meaning of physical activities, the meanings of sport and physical activities during the lifespan, socialization into sport and physical activities, and gender and physical activities.

Along the process of diversification, the social political emphasis of sport in Finland has moved first from the building of national identity and a tool of education to part of leisure policy and thereafter to the instrument for welfare and health policy (Koski, 2008, p. 160). Finnish government officials have been interested in the versatile role of physical activity and the target group is no longer just youth but the whole life span. The Ministry of Education (currently the Ministry of Education and Culture) was the initiator for the analysis of the social significance of sport and physical activities that was enforced in the 1990s. The role of social scientists was central in the analysis. (e.g., LIKES, 1994; Mertaniemi & Miettinen, 1999).

Kiviaho's, Seppänen's, and Heinilä's studies on Finnish sport organizations and membership structures have inspired researchers of organized sports movement (e.g., Heikkala, 1998; Itkonen, 1996; Koski, 2012; Olin & Ranto, 1986). This theme, which has been one of the most popular in the field, has a natural link to sport administration and the educational task of the department of social sciences of sport. Civil activity in sport has been approached from different perspectives. Roughly, these perspectives could be classified in three ways. Population level analyses were among the first. Thereafter, analyses applying organizational perspectives became popular. Finally, the third perspective utilized historical-sociological perspectives trying to understand changes and progressions of sport systems (Koski, 2009; pp. 6–8). Introduced around the turn of the millennium, an important project in this theme was called Civil Activity in Sports. The project applied a sociological frame of reference to the aforementioned three perspectives. It especially deepened the understanding about sports clubs and their contexts (e.g., Itkonen, Heikkala, Ilmanen, & Koski, 2000).

The analysis of social change and especially of the cultural changes in sports and through sports has been one of the aims of the research (e.g., Itkonen, 1996; Koski & Lämsä, 2015; Zacheus, 2008). Hannu Itkonen's research, often with Kalervo Ilmanen, has focused on civil activities in sports as well as physical activities and physical culture as a local phenomenon. They have been interested in local histories of sport. A similar approach has been applied by Itkonen's post-graduates (such as Kokkonen and Viita). In addition, Itkonen has been interested in the role of physicality in youth culture.

The increase in sedentary lifestyle as well as the competition of different lifestyles are reasons why the socialization into sports is so important and interested theme. In Finland, for the promotion of active lifestyles and physical education, new approaches in addition to skill and motivation-oriented perspectives have been sought. The concept and approach of the physical activity relationship (PAR) has been created for these purposes. Sport and physical activities are understood as a sort of language that consists of meanings. The main concept is meaning, which has two essential aspects. First, it refers to what something means and, second, it refers to a sort of scale of importance, or *meaningfulness*. Cultures that guide lifestyle choices in everyday life are understood as a web of meanings (Koski, 2008, 2013, p. 99). The research of PAR and the studies that apply this approach have appeared during the past 10 years. PAR has been so far used when analyzing children's and youth sport (e.g., Koski & Tähtinen, 2005; Lehmuskallio, 2007), mothers' physical activity (e.g., Rovio, Saaranen-Kauppinen, Pirkkalainen, & Lautamatti, 2013; Saaranen-Kauppinen, Rovio, & Parikka, 2013), acculturation of immigrants (e.g., Zacheus, Koski, Rinne, & Tähtinen, 2012), Finnish generations (e.g., Zacheus, 2008), physical activity during the life span (Koski & Zacheus, 2012), and among class teacher students (Kari, 2016). Still, the work is in its initial phases of development.

Gender has been one of the important themes in the Finnish social sciences of sport (e.g., Heinilä, 1987, p. 17). Even early on, Finnish researchers were interested in questions of equality. The international congress on Movement and Sport in Women's Life was arranged in Jyväskylä, Finland in 1987. It was the first on such a theme. Heinilä's studies on women's sport and the LIIkunta and NAinen (LIINA) project that was inspired from it were in the background of the congress. The leading scholar of the project was Arja Laitinen. Much gender-oriented research has been done since then. Internationally, the best-known name in gender studies and probably of all Finnish sport sociologists at the moment is Pirkko Markula (University of Alberta, Canada). Markula has focused on the women's movement, dance, and sport. She describes herself as a post-structural feminist (personal communiqué with Pirkko Markula, January 2016). Markula applies qualitative methods such as ethnography and especially auto-ethnography and performance ethnography to represent her research. Other names that should be mentioned here are Jaana Parviainen, Päivi Berg, Riitta Pirinen, and Ulla Kosonen, all of whom have explored physical culture from a feminist perspective. Arto Tiihonen has done corresponding work from a "masculine" point of view.

Like gender, the sport career (e.g., Salasuo, Piispa, & Huhta, 2015; Vuolle, 1977) as well as doping (Hemanus, 1997; Salasuo & Piispa, 2012) are topics that have intrigued different Finnish researchers across the decades. Of course, social development has inevitably raised new targets for researchers in the field. Themes such as sport tourism (Vehmas, 2010) and sedentary lifestyle (Kauravaara, 2013) are current examples of such work.

THE FUTURE OF SOCIOLOGY OF SPORT IN FINLAND

As one small area of science, the status of sociology of sport is not very strong in Finland. Science policy in general and governmental decisions as far as the academic world is concerned have not been particularly favorable for small sub-communities like the sociology of sport. Finnish universities and research institutions are expected to largely self-fund or find money to fund. Thus small disciplines struggle to be and stay among the main areas. No doubt, the current political environment is a threat to the discipline. In Finland, the status of the social science of sport in the one and only university for sport sciences is likely not under threat, whereas other promising activity that has recently arisen in different parts of the country may have more problems.

The sociology of sport has not been able to capitalize on its potential. This is true not only in Finland but at the international level as well. The researchers in the field should in concert grab the questions big enough from the perspective of social significance. In the other words, we should use sport as a subject to help understand larger societal questions (Koski, 2015). This could improve the status and the role of the sub-discipline moving forward.

ACKNOWLEDGMENT

I would like to thank the editor, Professor Kevin Young, for his help with previous drafts of this paper.

FIVE KEY READINGS

1. **Vuolle, P. (Ed.) (1998).** *Sport in social context by Kalevi Heinilä.* **University of Jyväskylä, Jyväskylä.**

   The book is a collection of papers written by Kalevi Heinilä. It covers some parts of his valuable contribution to the sociology of sport. The topics include sport in society, sociology of sport, ethics of sport, sport and international understanding, meaning content of sport, and key roles in sport.

2. **Itkonen, H., Heikkala, J., Ilmanen, K., & Koski, P. (Eds.) (2000).** *Liikunnan kansalaistoiminta – muutokset, merkitykset ja reunaehdot. [Civil activity in sports – Changes, meanings and preconditions.]* **Helsinki: Liikuntatieteellinen Seura.**

The publication is the final report of the Civil Activity in Sports research program. It focuses on the changes of Finnish civil activity in sports, the relationships between sports clubs, sports organizations and public administration, as well as local characteristics of sport culture and the cultural meanings of the activity.

3. **LIKES (1994).** *Liikunnan yhteiskunnallinen perustelu: tieteellinen katsaus. [Social significance of sport: A scientific review.]* **Jyväskylä: Liikunnan ja kansanterveyden edistämissäätiö.**

The social significance of sport and physical activities is analyzed from different perspectives by the leading scholars of Finland. The book is the first collection and it was updated in 2000.

4. **Koski, P. (2008). Physical activity relationship (PAR).** *International Review for the Sociology of Sport,* **43**(2), 151–163.

The article explains the basic ideas of the new approach by which the socialization process into sport and physical culture is analyzed in Finland in recent years.

5. **Markula, P., & Pringle, R. (2006).** *Foucault, sport and exercise: Power, knowledge and transforming the self.* **London: Routledge.**

This book explores how Foucauldian theory can inform our understanding of the body, domination, identity, and freedom as experienced through sport and exercise. It considers exercise and fitness cultures, coaching, and health promotion, and suggests innovative ways of understanding the body in action.

REFERENCES

Allardt, E., Jartti, P., Jyrkilä, F., & Littunen, Y. (1958). On the cumulative nature of leisure activities. *Acta Sociologica, 3*(1), 165–172.
Haskell, W. L., Bärtsch, P., Biddle, P., Esser, K., Hargreaves, J., Maughan, R., & Vanreusel, B. (2012). *Sport sciences in Nordic countries. Evaluation report.* Helsinki: Academy of Finland.

Sociology of Sport: Finland   149

Heikkala, J. (1998). *Ajolähtö turvattomiin kotipesiin. Liikuntajärjestökentän muutos* 1990-luvun Suomessa. [Finnish sport federations and associations in transition.] Acta Universitatis Temperensis 641. Tampere: Tampereen yliopisto.

Heinilä, K. (1984). The totalization process in international sport. In M. Ilmarinen (Ed.), *Sport and international understanding* (pp. 20–30). Proceeding of the Congress held in Helsinki, Finland, July, 7–10, 1982. Berlin: Springer.

Heinilä, K. (1987). Social research on sports in Finland. *International Review for Sociology of Sports*, *22*(1), 3–24.

Heinilä, K. (2010). *Liikunta- ja urheilukulttuurimme. Eilen – tänään – huomenna. [Finnish sports culture. Yesterday – today – tomorrow.]* Helsinki: Kalevi Heinilä.

Helanko, R. (1957). Sports and socialization. *Acta Sociologica*, *2*(1), 229–240.

Hemánus, P. (1997). *Doping, hyvä vihollinen. [Doping, a good enemy.]* Jyväskylä: University Library Publications.

Hentilä, S. (1982). *Suomen työläisurheilun historia I. Työväen Urheiluliitto 1919–1944. [History of workers' sport in Finland I. Workers' sports federation 1919–1944.]* Hämeenlinna: Karisto.

Itkonen, H. (1996). *Kenttien kutsu. Tutkimus liikuntakulttuurin muutoksesta. [The call of fields. The study about the change in sport culture.]* Tampere: Gaudeamus.

Itkonen, H., Heikkala, J., Ilmanen, K., & Koski, P. (2000). *Liikunnan kansalaistoiminta – muutokset, merkitykset ja reunaehdot. [Civil activity in sports – Changes, meanings and preconditions.]* Helsinki: Liikuntatieteellinen Seura.

Kari, J. (2016). *Hyvä opettaja. Luokanopettajaopiskelijat liikuntakokemuksensa ja opettajuutensa tulkitsijoina. [A good teacher: Class teacher students' interpretations of their exercise history and teacher identity.]* Jyväskylä: Jyväskylän yliopisto.

Kauravaara, K. (2013). *Mitä sitten, jos ei liikuta? Etnografinen tutkimus nuorista miehistä. [If we don't move at all, then what? – Ethnographic study of young men.]* Liikunnan ja kansanterveystieteen julkaisuja 276.

Kokkonen, J. (2013). *Liikuntaa hyvinvointivaltiossa. Suomalaisen liikuntakulttuurin lähihistoria. [Sport in welfare state. Recent history of Finnish sport culture.]* Keruu: Suomen Urheilumuseo.

Koski, P. (1999). Liikuntahallinnon koulutus ja sen muuttuvat haasteet. *[Education of sport administration and its changing challenges.]* Teoksessa K. Suomi (toim.) *Vaajan virran vuolteesta – kirjoituksia liikunnasta ja yhteiskunnasta* (pp. 173–189). Jyväskylä: Liikunnan kehittämiskeskus.

Koski, P. (2008). Physical activity relationship (PAR). *International Review for the Sociology of Sport*, *43*(2), 151–163.

Koski, P. (2009). *Liikunta- ja urheiluseurat muutoksessa. [Sports clubs in change.]* Helsinki: SLU.

Koski, P. (2012). Finnish sports club as a mirror of society. *International Journal of Sport Policy and Politics*, *4*(2), 257–275.

Koski, P. (2013). Liikuntasuhde ja liikuntakasvatus. [Physical activity relationship (PAR) and physical education.] In T. Jaakkola, J. Liukkonen, & A. Sääkslahti (Eds.), *Liikuntapedagogiikka* (pp. 96–124). Jyväskylä: PS-kustannus.

Koski, P. (2015). Assessing the sociology of sport: On N + 1 and the cultural approach. *International Review for the Sociology of Sport*, *50*(4–5), 502–506.

Koski, P., & Lämsä, J. (2015). Finland as a small sports nation: Socio-historical perspectives on the development of national sport policy. *International Journal of Sport Policy and Politics*, *7*(3), 421–441.

Koski, P., & Tähtinen, J. (2005). Liikunnan merkitykset nuoruudessa. [The meanings of sport and physical activities in youth.] *Nuorisotutkimus, 23*(1), 3–21.

Koski, P., & Zacheus, T. (2012). Physical activity relationship during the lifespan. In J. Kivirauma, A. Jauhiainen, P. Seppänen, & T. Kaunisto (Eds.), *Koulutuksen yhteiskunnallinen ymmärrys. Social Perspectives on Education.* Suomen kasvatustieteellinen seura, kasvatusalan tutkimuksia 59. Jyväskylä: Jyväskylän yliopistopaino.

Lehmuskallio, M. (2007). *Liikuntakulutus ja kaupunkilaislasten ja -nuorten liikuntasuhde. [Consumption of sport in urban children's and adolescents' physical activity relationship.]* Turku: Turun yliopisto.

LIKES (1994). *Liikunnan yhteiskunnallinen perustelu: tieteellinen katsaus. [Social significance of sport: A scientific review.]* Jyväskylä: Liikunnan ja kansanterveyden edistämissäätiö.

Mertaniemi, M., & Miettinen, M. (Eds.). (1999). *Towards well-being – How do physical activity and sport help?* Reports on Physical Culture and Health 120. Jyväskylä: LIKES – Foundation for sport and health sciences.

Olin, K., & Ranto, E. (1986). *Urheilujärjestöt suomalaisessa yhteiskunnassa.* [Sport organizations in finnish society.] Jyväskylä: Jyväskylän yliopisto.

Parviainen, J. (1998). *Bodies moving and moved. A phenomenological analysis of the dancing subject and the cognitive and ethical values of dance art.* Tampere: Tampere University Press.

Roiko-Jokela, H. (2012). *Näkökulmia liikuntatieteiden kehittymiseen 1960-luvulta 2010-luvulle – hallinto, toimijat, tutkimus ja tiedonvälitys. [Perspectives to the development of sport sciences from 1960s to 2010s – administration, actors, research and communication.]* Helsinki: Liikuntatieteellinen Seura.

Rovio, E., Saaranen-Kauppinen, A., Pirkkalainen, M., & Lautamatti, L. (2013). Mikä sienirihmasto siellä alla piileekään? Toimintatutkimukseen osallistuneen perheenäidin liikuntasuhde osana identiteettiä. [What lies beneath a fungal thread? An identity construction of a mother who participated in an action research.] *Liikunta & Tiede, 50*(1), 67–74.

Saaranen-Kauppinen, A., Rovio, E., & Parikka, L. (2013). "Mähän ajattelin, että lapsen voi viedä vauvaparkkiin" – Perheenäitien arjen jännitteet liikuntasuhdetta rakentamassa. ["I thought I could just take the child to the baby park" – Mothers' everyday life tensions and physical activity relationship.] *Liikunta & Tiede, 50*(6), 40–46.

Salasuo, M., & Piispa, M. (2012). *Perspectives to doping substance use outside elite sports in Finland.* Helsinki: Finnish Youth Research Network and Finnish Youth Research Society.

Salasuo, M., Piispa, M., & Huhta, H. (2015). *Huippu-urheilijan elämänkulku. Tutkimus urheilijoista 2000-luvun Suomessa.* Helsinki: Nuorisotutkimusseura.

Seppänen, P. (1981). Olympic success. A crossnational perspective. In G. R. F. Lüschen & G. H. Sage (Eds.), *Handbook of social sciences of sport* (pp. 93–116). Champaign, IL: Stipes Publishing.

Seppänen, P. (1998). Kalevi Heinilä – A scholar and fighter by Paavo Seppänen. In P. Vuolle (Ed.), *Sport in social context by Kalevi Heinilä* (pp. 13–17). Jyväskylä: University of Jyväskylä.

Vehmas, H. (2010). *Liikuntamatkalla Suomessa – vapaa-ajan valintoja jälkimodernissa yhteiskunnassa. [Sport tourism in Finland – Leisure choices in post-modern society.]* Jyväskylä: Jyväskylän yliopisto.

Viljanen, T., Matilainen, P., Perko, P., & Sinkkonen, A. (1994). *Näin Turku liikkuu. [Turku moves in this way.]* Turku: Turun kaupungin liikuntavirasto & Paavo Nurmi -keskus.

Vuolle, P. (1977). *Urheilu elämänsisältönä. Menestyneiden urheilijoiden elämänura kilpailuvuosina.* *[Top sport as content of life.]* Jyväskylä: University of Jyväskylä.

Zacheus, T. (2008). *Luonnonmukaisesta arkiliikunnasta liikunnan eriytymiseen. Suomalaiset liikuntasukupolvet ja liikuntakulttuurin muutos.* *[From natural everyday exercise to a personalized exercise experience. Finnish physical generations and the changes in physical culture.]* Turku: University of Turku.

Zacheus, T., Koski, P., Rinne, R., & Tähtinen, J. (2012). *Maahanmuuttajat ja liikunta. Liikuntasuhteen merkitys kotoutumiseen Suomessa. [Immigrants and physical activities. The role of PAR in the process of acculturation.]* Turku: Turun yliopisto.

Zacheus, T., Tähtinen, J., Rinne, R., Koski, P., & Heinonen, O. J. (2003). *Kaupunkilaisten liikunta ikäpolvittain. Turkulaisten liikuntatottumukset 2000-luvun alussa. [Physical activities of townspeople according to the age groups.]* Turku: Turun yliopisto. Kasvatustieteiden laitoksen julkaisut A:201.

CHAPTER 9

SOCIOLOGY OF SPORT: FLANDERS

Jasper Truyens and Marc Theeboom

ABSTRACT

In 2008, Paul De Knop (Vrije Universiteit Brussels) stated that "in spite of the social value of sport and its role as a policy tool, human sport sciences still lack a fulfilling position in the academic world." In Belgium and in Flanders (the northern and Dutch-speaking part of the country), the sociology of sport is still a small field of research among the sport sciences. The discipline is institutionalized within the institutes of physical education of the three universities (University of Ghent; Katholieke Universiteit Leuven; Vrije Universiteit Brussels). The scarcity of academic funding streams resulted in a focus on more applied, policy-based research in Flanders. Additionally, all institutes emphasize increasingly an interdisciplinary cooperation to connect with stronger research fields (e.g., health sciences, social studies, or international studies on sport participation). Even though each university has its own research tradition, the universities and the government cooperate in a longitudinal study on sport participation in Flanders. De Knop, who became rector of the Vrije Universiteit Brussels (VUB) in 2008, was the first lecturer of the course sociology of sport at his university. He graduated in 1975 as licentiate in physical education and his career at the university converged with the development of the discipline. Together with Roland Renson and

Sociology of Sport: A Global Subdiscipline in Review
Research in the Sociology of Sport, Volume 9, 153–167
ISSN: 1476-2854/doi:10.1108/S1476-285420160000009013

Bart Vanreusel (KU Leuven), he was one of the academic pioneers for the sociology of sport in Flanders.

Keywords: Institutes of physical education; interdisciplinary approach; participation surveys; sport light; social exclusion

INTRODUCTION: A HISTORY OF SOCIOLOGY OF SPORT IN FLANDERS

Belgium's greatest impact on the organization of sport during the last few decades can probably be attributed to Jean-Marc Bosman and Jacques Rogge. Jean-Marc Bosman and especially the Bosman ruling (1996) had a major effect on how football (soccer) has developed into the major money-spinning sport it is today. The case determined the legality of the system of transfers for football players and the existence of so-called "quota systems," whereby only a limited number of foreign players were allowed to play in a club match. Jacques Rogge was the president of the International Olympic Committee (IOC) between 2002 and 2014. He provided steadiness and reliability to the Olympic family after the bribery scandal at the Salt Lake Games, even though he was also criticized for remaining under tutelage about human rights at the 2008 Beijing Games and the 2014 Sochi Games. Jacques Rogge, a former Olympic sailor, is an alumnus of the University of Ghent, the university that founded the first academic institution for physical education in the world in 1908.

A history of the sociology of sport in Belgium is a difficult task. Sport participation data covering Belgium is lacking (Scheerder & Vos, 2013). Starting in 1970, Belgium evolved from a unitary state to a federal state with communities, regions, and language areas due to different state reforms. As a result of the first (1970) and second (1980) state reform, cultural communities were established with a strong cultural autonomy including health, youth, and sport. Due to the divided sport policy system in Belgium, there is no national research tradition in sport or the sociology of sport. Flanders, the Dutch-speaking northern part of Belgium, has a strong civic involvement in sport (Scheerder & Vos, 2013). Since the 1960s Flanders was, together with the Nordic countries, one of the pioneering regions in Europe to launch large-scale "sport for all" campaigns (Vanreusel, Taks, & Renson, 2002).

Likewise, the first sport participation surveys were conducted by researchers from the institutes of physical education of the three Flemish universities. Historically, the core of sport science research is based at these universities (the University of Ghent; Katholieke Universiteit Leuven (KUL); and Vrije Universiteit Brussels) and their institutes for physical education in particular. Before student protests in 1968, these universities were bilingual. Afterwards, these universities split and new French-speaking universities emerged. These cultural and organizational changes are interwoven into the development of physical education and the sociology of sport.

In the first part of this chapter, the development of different research institutes for physical education is discussed. This overview is presented largely based on two articles, published in 1986 and 1989 in the journal *Sport* of the Ministry of the Flemish Community. In 1989, the journal dedicated a full edition to the three universities in Flanders and their role in the development of physical education. Next, the first sociological studies on sport and leisure are discussed, followed by the main approaches taken at the three universities in Flanders. In the end, attention is drawn toward the contribution of the major founding fathers and their sport institutes for the sociology of sport in Flanders, along with the (im)balance between policy-based and academic research, including the academic position of the sociology of sport.

THE INSTITUTIONALIZATION OF PHYSICAL EDUCATION

In 1908, the first academic institution for physical education in the world was established in Ghent (Flanders). The Institut Supérieur d'Education Physique (ISEP or HILO) was established by Director General of Higher Education Cyriel Van Overbergh (1866–1959). At that time, the official language at the university was French. The institute was affiliated with the Faculty of Medicine and Health Sciences and predominantly focused on Swedish gymnastics and medical sciences. In 1923, the ISEP turned Flemish even though the first teachers at the institute were opposed to the language shift. As a result, a French-speaking higher institute for physical education was established in Liège in 1930. Both students of the Flemish University of Ghent and the University of Liège had to hold a candidate degree in health sciences or natural sciences as a prerequisite for the one-year course in physical education. This had a baleful influence on the number of students.

This situation changed when the University of Leuven (Katholieke Universiteit Leuven or KU Leuven) introduced an Institute of Physical Education in 1942. Since then, students in Ghent and Liège had the opportunity to obtain a two-year candidate and two-year licentiate degree in physical education (Renson, 1989). After the introduction of a special chair on physical education in 1937, KU Leuven established a licentiate and doctorate degree in physical education in 1942. Only candidate degrees in health sciences could participate in these courses. Pierre-Paul De Nayer, who had been working, literally, with frogs in the physiological institute of the university became responsible for the development of the sport and research institute for physical education (ILO). In 1961–1962, a candidate and licentiate structure was established. While the physical education (PE) courses for girls were previously organized in Elsene, both men and women could enter the candidate and licentiate degree in Leuven in 1976. One year later, French-speaking students left the institute, as an independent Flemish- and French-speaking university was established in 1968 (e.g., the French-speaking University of Louvain-La-Neuve) (Renson, 1989). Only in 1993, would the sport institute be recognized as a faculty of the KU Leuven (Faber, 2016).

Immediately after World War II, the Université Libre de Bruxelles founded an Institute of Physical Education (HILOK), allied to the Faculty of Health Sciences and including a two-year candidate degree, a two-year licentiate degree, and a doctoral degree. At that moment in time, all Belgian universities provided a degree in physical education. At the foundation of the institute, students and staff were recruited from their own university, but also from the institute in Ghent. Comparable to the situation in Ghent and Leuven, Flemish students insisted on an independent Flemish university. This idea was also supported by Professor Frank Mathijs, who was also adjunct secretary-general of the National Institute for Physical Education and Sport (NILOS, which was the precursor of Bevordering van de Lichamelijke Ontwikkeling, de Sport en de Openluchtrecreatie (BLOSO) and Sport Vlaanderen). In 1968, the Flemish Vrije Universiteit Brussels became independent. Two years later, the HILOK developed a special licentiate for applied leisure studies. Finally, in 1978, the Institute for Physical Education took up new residence at the Etterbeek campus (Renson, 1989).

It can be stated that the historical and contemporary field of the sociology of sport in Flanders is dominated by researchers from these three universities. Besides their academic contribution, the sport institutes of these universities also cooperated in a more pragmatic (e.g., policy-based research) approach in the late 1970s and the early 2000s to strengthen sport science research.

In 1975, Roland Renson (KU Leuven) was entitled by the national sport agency BLOSO to develop a national information center (centre de relais) on sport sciences in Belgium. Originally, representatives from all five Belgian universities and the respective sport institutes were involved (e.g., the three Flemish universities: Ghent University, KU Leuven, Free University of Brussels, and three Wallonian universities: University of Liege, Université Libre de Bruxelles, and the Université Catholique de Louvain). The original purpose of the national information center was to collect questionnaires, develop factsheets for research projects, and collect data on conferences, seminars, etc. (Renson, 1978). Between 1978 and 1980, different inventories were published regarding the current state of sport research in Flanders (e.g., structure of universities, the topics of research, libraries and journals, PhDs and theses). Between 2002 and 2015, the Flemish government invested in a Flemish policy research center on sport. This research center was a cooperation between the three universities, supported and financed by the Flemish government. The organization of this research center can be subdivided among three different generations: (1) nine sport projects between 2002 and 2006; (2) six sport-for-all and six elite sport projects between 2007 and 2011; and (3) 17 sport research projects between 2012 and 2015. The last two generations of the research center included a general participation survey on sport (e.g., PaS09 and PaS14). All these research projects provided the Institutes for Physical Education of all three universities financial opportunities to appoint PhD researchers on a full-time basis. Due to public savings from the Flemish government, the research center was discontinued in 2016. Future projects funded by the Flemish government will be more pragmatic and ad hoc, rather than taking a four-year period to develop specific policy recommendations. As a result, the different research institutes of these universities lost important financial opportunities to invest in academic research. The new and more pragmatic sport research projects will be coordinated by KICS, the knowledge and information center on sport of the Flemish government. KICS was founded in October 2014. KICS wants to become the Flemish digital database on sport research and will support cooperation between different partners in sport (e.g., the universities, the national governing bodies for sport, the Paralympic sport federation, and the knowledge organizations on local sport policy and development). Annually, KICS organizes a national sport innovation conference and a one-day seminar to propagate current knowledge on sport to all relevant organizations.

THE DEVELOPMENT OF SPORT SCIENCE RESEARCH AND THE SOCIOLOGY OF SPORT

The introduction of the eight-hour working day in Belgium in 1921 and the concern of the different socio-political groups as to whether or not workers could deal with the extra spare time gave occasion to different educational programs and the first (nonacademic) research programs on leisure time and sport. Especially the Catholic labor organizations applied a normative approach toward the leisure time of families and youngsters to discourage participation in commercialized leisure activities. The first academics who studied leisure time and sport in Flanders were Urbain Claeys and Frans Van Mechelen. They worked at the Sociological Research Institute (SOI), founded in 1955 at KU Leuven. Van Mechelen dominated the cultural development in Flanders both from a research as well as a policy perspective. In 1964 he was the first to publish on leisure time and sport in Flanders, while he was a representative in the Parliament and became Minister of Flemish Culture in 1968 (Corijn in De Knop, 2000). Their publication on leisure time and sport was the first of multiple surveys on sport between 1964 and 1981 in Flanders. In this period, the first sport sociologist at the three different universities published on sport participation figures. Even though these studies used various sample sizes and definitions of sport, they indicated comparable trends with regard to sport participation – namely, the gender difference between men and women has decreased over time, sport participation has extended to older age categories, and the negative impact of lower socioeconomic status on sport participation.

MAIN APPROACHES TAKEN

KU Leuven is probably the university with the strongest tradition in research on the sociology of sport and sport participation in particular in Flanders. The first studies on leisure were executed by the Research Institute of Social Sciences (currently ISPO). In 1964, Frans Van Mechelen and his colleagues published the first study on leisure time in Flanders in which attention was drawn to playing music, reading, radio and television, movies and drama, folklore, and finally sport and physical games (Van Mechelen, 1964). According to this study, sport participation figures in this period were very low. Participation in sport was dominated by men and focused especially on football (soccer) and swimming. Both among men and women, playing cards was referred to as the most popular sport. The Institute for Physical Education at KU Leuven started a tradition in large-scale survey research in 1969. At the Research Institute for Physical Education, Roland Renson and Bart Vanreusel have been the most influential sport sociologists. Roland Renson obtained his PhD in 1973 on the sociocultural determinants of the sports behavior of 13-year-old boys. He taught courses on the history of physical education, sociology of sport, and comparative physical education and sport. He began research projects on the Flemish Games File in 1973 and archives of modern sports in 1980. As a result, the Flemish Folk Games Center (1980) and the Sports Museum Flanders (1983) were founded. These temporary expeditions amalgamated into the Sportimonium in 2004 of which Roland Renson is still chairperson. Bart Vanreusel focused his research on the sociocultural studies of physical activity. His PhD provided a trend analysis of sport participation styles. He is a member of the advisory board for sport of the Flemish government and was previously secretary of the International Sociology for Sport Association (ISSA). At present, Jeroen Scheerder (KU Leuven) is the most active sport sociologist in Flanders. Scheerder has continued the tradition of sport participation research at KU Leuven since the early 2000s. He teaches the sociology of sport at KU Leuven, but he also has been guest lecturer at the University of Ghent. Together with Koen Breedveld and Remco Hoekman of the Mulier Institute (NED), Jeroen Scheerder founded the international MEASURE Network in 2010. This initiative was launched to create a better understanding of differences in sports participation in Europe. Since 2014, Scheerder has been president of the European Association for the Sociology of Sport (EASS). As a researcher and supervisor of different PhD studies, he has extended the scope from general sport participation studies to specific organizational contexts like the commercial (Vos et al., 2012), light communities (Borgers, Vanreusel, Vos, Forsberg, & Scheerder, 2016), and social exclusion and poverty (cf. Vandermeerschen, Vos, & Scheerder, 2016).

Ever since the foundation of HILO at Ghent University, the institute has had a strong biomedical focus, completed with input from other research perspectives like sociology, psychology, economy, and movement sciences. Given the fact that HILO always has been a part of the Faculty of Medicine and Health Sciences, most researchers at the institute had a medical background (e.g., exercise physiology, biometrics, and movement sciences). Due to a strong focus on the educational tasks at the university, the number of research staff has always been limited, leading to a smaller scientific output compared to the other institutes in Flanders. At the

Department of Movement and Sport Sciences, research on the sociology of sport and sport management research are strongly allied. Sport ethics and the effectiveness of sport organizations are recurring topics in peer-reviewed publications. Recent PhD studies at the University of Ghent have focused on the intersectoral partnership in sport (Marlier, 2016), physical activity (D'Haese, 2016), and fair play in sport organizations (De Waegeneer, 2015). Marc Maes has been the most influential academic in sport management in the department. He earned his master's degree in physical education in 1969. After 10 years at the university, he joined the Belgian Olympic and Interfederal Committee (BOIC) where he explored Olympic values and ethical aspects of sports. In the early 2000s, the Department of Movement and Sport Sciences developed into a full-fledged department. Marc Maes was one of the supervisors of the first doctoral dissertation in sports management at Ghent University in 2009 ("In Memoriam," 2011).

De Vrije Universiteit Brussels, which is the youngest university in Flanders to provide physical education as a university degree, always tried to be innovative in the education programs they provided. In 1970, the university launched a course titled "Leisure Time Issues," culminating in the degree of applied leisure-time studies (Renson, 1989). In 1975, Livin Bollaert started a sociological research department, using a more pragmatic approach than the other universities. Starting from a more general perspective on sport participation, the focus shifted toward a more applied, policy preparatory research perspective, including contract research (Corijn et al., 2000). Under the leadership of De Knop, research focuses more on youth sport, quality management, and social exclusion. De Knop, licentiate of physical activity and applied leisure studies, started his career in 1978 at the Vrije Universiteit Brussels. His main interest can be found in youth sport, quality management, and the sociology of sport. He was the first author to publish on the potential value of sport as a means for social integration in 1993. In 2004, he became dean of his faculty and since 2008, he is rector of the university. He also had an active role in the development of (elite) sport policy in Flanders as chairman of the national sport organization and as private secretary at the Ministry of Sport between 1999 and 2004. Currently, he is also the chairman of the Fund for Scientific Research (FWO). Both Paul De Knop and Marc Theeboom initiated a critical perspective on the value of sport for socially vulnerable groups, and especially youth, within themes like social capital, sport+, and community sport development. Additionally, both academics emphasized the importance of a strong cooperation with civil society during the analysis of the value of sport. Under their supervision, both elite (De Bosscher, De Knop, van Bottenburg, Shibli, & Bingham, 2009; Truyens, De Bosscher, Sotiriadou, Heyndels, & Westerbeek, 2016) and community sport research traditions (Haudenhuyse, Theeboom, Nols, & Coussee, 2014) were developed. In 2015, Theeboom, Haudenhuyse, and Vertonghen (2015) edited a book on sport and social innovation including different chapters on empowerment, poverty, sport and imprisonment, football and corporate social responsibility (CSR), and community sport development.

SPORT PARTICIPATION IN FLANDERS

In 1969, researchers at KU Leuven started a time-trend analysis on sport participation. The time series includes five different waves (1969−2009), executed once every 10 years. The first studies (1969 and 1979) were part of a larger growth study on youth development (Ostyn, Simons, Beunen, Renson, & Van Gerven, 1980; Simons et al., 1990). The sport-related part of the study focused either on the physical fitness of boys (1969) or girls (1979) and girls' parents (1979). Later on, two major cross-sectional sport studies were conducted in 1989 (Taks, Renson, & Vanreusel, 1991) and 1999 (Scheerder, Taks, Vanreusel, & Renson, 2002). These studies focused on the sport participation of primary and secondary school boys, girls, and their parents.

The most recent study was conducted in 2009 (Scheerder & Vos, 2011), focusing on sport participation and sport consumption. These five studies allow a time-trend analysis of active sport involvement over a period of 40 years. These large-scale surveys represent the longest time series on sport participation and changing trends in sport participation in Flanders. In these studies, a broad definition of sport participation is used. Sport is defined as a physical activity that requires a sufficient rate of exertion that takes place in a sportive context. It refers to nonprofessional participation in leisure-time sport, over a one-year period prior to the investigation. Organized and nonorganized physical sport activities as well as recreational and competitive physical sport activities are included. Neither the level, frequency, context, nor the location of the sport involvement is decisive to be considered as a sport participant (Scheerder & Vos, 2013).

Based on these studies between 1969 and 2009, executed by KU Leuven, it can be stated that sport participation has become a leisure-time physical activity in which 64% of all adults actively are involved. In 1969, only 21%

of all adults were physically active. Between 1969 and 2009, two "sport waves" were identified, representing a strong increase of sport participation. The first wave occurred during the 1970s, a period representing strong sport policy incentives to stimulate the population to be active in leisure-time sport activities. During this wave, there has been an increase of both nonorganized sport participants as sport club participants. Between the end of the 1980s and 2009, a second wave was identified, representing a strong increase of nonorganized sport participants and a stagnation of sport club participants. This implies that the rise of sport participation in Flanders can be mainly attributed to nonorganized sport participants. These so-called light sporting communities and commercial sport providers arose apart from the traditional sport clubs (Borgers et al., 2016; Scheerder & Vos, 2011). Additionally, 89% of all children between 6 and 12 years of age and 86% of all youngsters 13−18 years old are sport active in 2009.

The most recent participation figures for Flanders are available for 2014, based on the general participation survey (PaS14), executed by the Flemish Policy Research Center on Sport. In the PaS surveys, the same definition of sport participation is applied as in the studies conducted by KU Leuven, so results can easily be compared among 15−86-year-old people in Flanders. The increase of sport participation levels identified in the 40 years before 2009 stagnated between 2009 and 2014. Just like in 2009, 63% of the population in this survey participates in sports during their leisure time.

THE POSITION OF SOCIOLOGY OF SPORT IN FLANDERS

At various moments in time, scientists drew a state of affairs in the development of sport sciences in Flanders. In 1986, Renson, Borms, Vrijens, and Van der Aerschot described three different inventories of the sport science projects and theses executed at the three major universities. The analysis was repeated in 1989 in a study reported by Van der Aerschot (1989), including a time-frame from 1965 until 1987. During that period, the sociology of sport (as part of socio-cultural kinanthropology) had witnessed a decrease according to the number of research projects, but an increase related to master theses. Together with sports medicine, the sociology of sport was one of the smallest disciplines among the sport sciences. Renson et al. (1986) and Van der Aerschot (1989) concluded that even though physiology and biomechanics were still the major sport research disciplines, the sport sciences became more diversified, including an inter-disciplinary and transdisciplinary approach in which the sociology of sport had grown (Renson et al., 1986). In 2002, De Knop made a state of affairs on the sociology of sport in the first chapter of the most popular handbook on the sociology of sport. His evaluation of the sociology of sport included nine different arguments (De Knop, 2002):

• The number of studies in this discipline is smaller than in any other disci-pline within sport sciences.
• Sport is increasingly the subject of sociological research. There should be a stronger cooperation between different disciplines to revalue the sociol-ogy of sport.
• The sociology of sport and sport management are strong allies.
• The sociology of sport in both Flanders and the Netherlands is a rhap-sody of multiple research disciplines.
• The sociology of sport receives little or no attention in the curriculum of physical education at the different universities. Within the sport sciences, the human sciences are undervalued.
• There is a lack of theoretical foundation in most sociological research in sport.
• Most research projects are government funded.
• Current research has a strong tradition regarding sport participation, social stratification, and the social meaning of sport in society. It is, how-ever, less clear how the socialization process takes place through sport.
• There is a need for more fundamental research.

Six years later, De Knop repeated most of these reasons at the end of a special chair on the societal, political, and didactical aspects of sport and physical education in the Netherlands: "In spite of the social value of sport and its role as a policy tool, human sport sciences still lack a ful-filling position in the academic world" (De Knop, 2008, p. 3). These arguments also stand for Flanders. The sociology of sport has to deal with different thresholds to develop as a research discipline, even though it is recognized as a valuable practice in our society. The lack of funda-mental funding, the "publish or perish" principle, the second-class role of human sciences in sport science research, and the level of specialization in research obstruct researchers and institutes from growing and flourish-ing. As a result, the universities in Flanders seek new ways of funding and academic cooperation to extend their knowledge and preserve their research tradition.

FIVE KEY READINGS

1. **De Knop, P., Scheerder, J., & Vanreusel, B. (2006).** *Sportsociologie: Het spel en de spelers [The sociology of sport: The game and the players].* **Maarssen: Elsevier.**

This book is the general handbook for the sociology of sport at the three Flemish universities. It includes an introduction to the sociology of sport, different sociological issues (e.g., sport and society, elite sport and mass participation, sport participation and social inclusion) and multiple sociological cases (sport and identity, sport and racism, volunteers in sport).

2. **Lievens, J., Siongers, J., & Waege H. (2015).** *Participatie in Vlaanderen [Participation in Flanders].* **Leuven: Acco.**

This is the most recent publication on the leisure activities of Flemish inhabitants. The third participation survey (PaS14) of a longitudinal study financed by the Flemish government was conducted in 2014, which questioned 9,958 inhabitants on their participation in youth, culture, sport, or media activities. Researchers at the three major universities in Flanders cooperated in the development of the survey for sport. The most important conclusion of this study is that, for the first time, the general sport participation level stagnated. After a first wave in the 1970s and a second wave at the end of the 1990s and the early 2000s, the number of people doing sports or being physical active during leisure time remained stationary.

3. **Scheerder, J., Vandermeerschen, H., Borgers, J., Thibault, E., & Vos, S. (2013).** *Vlaanderen sport! [Flanders sports!].* **Ghent: Academia Press.**

During the last decade, Professor Jeroen Scheerder has been the most active Belgian author on the sociology of sport. This book provides an overview of four decades of sport participation (research) in Flanders. Different meanings (e.g., the social, organizational, and the economical) and issues (e.g., the role of the sport club, current participation trends, sport light) are discussed. Following this publication, *Vlaanderen Loopt! (Flanders Runs!)* and *Vlaanderen Fietst! (Flanders Cycles!)* were published.

4. **Haudenhuyse, P.R., Theeboom, M., & Coalter, F. (2012). The potential of sports-based social interventions for vulnerable youth: Implications for sport coaches and youth workers. *Journal of Youth Studies*, *15*(4), 437–454. doi:10.1080/13676261.2012.663895**

The social value of sport, social exclusion, and vulnerable youth always have been major research topics in the sociology of sport at Vrije Universiteit Brussels. This article explored how sports are delivered to and experienced by youth who could be considered as socially vulnerable. As sport is viewed as an opportunity to actively engage young people in a leisure context, there are some indications that when working towards broader outcomes with socially vulnerable youth a specific methodology is required. The article provides an understanding of how organized sports, as a series of social relationships and processes, can contribute in making socially vulnerable youth less vulnerable.

5. **De Bosscher, V., Sotiriadou, P., & van Bottenburg, M. (2013). Scrutinizing the sport pyramid metaphor: An examination of the relationship between elite success and mass participation in Flanders. *International Journal of Sport Policy and Politics*, *5*(3), 319–339. doi:10.1080/19406940.2013.806340**

De Bosscher is the founder and coordinator of the Sports Policy Factors Leading to International Sporting Success (SPLISS) network, a research cooperation that shares expertise on high-performance sport policy research, including different international benchmark studies. This article questions the influence of elite sport success on mass participation (the trickle-down effect) in Flanders. The results show that positive correlations between membership levels and international sporting success were notable in Flanders in four of the eight sports in which elite Flemish competitors achieved significant international successes during the study period (athletics, gymnastics, judo, and tennis).

REFERENCES

Borgers, J., Vanreusel, B., Vos, S., Forsberg, P., & Scheerder, J. (2016). Do light sport facilities foster sports participation? A case study on the use of bark running tracks. *International Journal of Sport Policy*, *8*(2), 287–304.

Corijn, E., Stoffen, M., Neefs, H., Matthijs, K., De Knop, P., & Theeboom, M. (2000). Vrijetijd, onderzoek en beleid. In P. De Knop (Ed.), *Veertig jaar sport en vrijetijdsbeleid in Vlaanderen* (pp. 15−31). Brussel: VUBPRESS.

De Bosscher, V., De Knop, P., van Bottenburg, M., Shibli, S., & Bingham, J. (2009). Explaining international sporting success. An international comparison of elite sport systems and policies in six nations. *Sport Management Review, 12*, 113−136.

De Bosscher, V., Sotiriadou, P., & van Bottenburg, M. (2013). Scrutinizing the sport pyramid metaphor: An examination of the relationship between elite success and mass participation in Flanders. *International Journal of Sport Policy and Politics, 5*(3), 319−339. doi:10.1080/19406940.2013.806340

De Knop, P. (2000). *Veertig jaar sport- en vrijetijdsbeleid in Vlaanderen*. Brussel: VUB Press.

De Knop, P. (2002). Conceptverduidelijking en begrippenrapport. In P. De Knop, J. Scheerder, & B. Vanreusel (Eds.), *Sportsociologie: Het spel en de spelers* (pp. 15−33). Maarssen: Elsevier.

De Knop, P. (2008). *De humane sportwetenschappen nog steeds op de reservebank?* [*Human sport sciences still on the bench?*]. Niewegein: Arko Sports Media.

De Knop, P., Scheerder, J., & Vanreusel, B. (2006). *Sportsociologie: Het spel en de spelers* [*The sociology of sport: The game and the players*]. Maarssen: Elsevier.

De Waegeneer, E. (2015). *Fair play in sports organizations: Effectiveness of ethical codes.* Unpublished doctoral dissertation, Ghent University, Ghent.

D'Haese, S. (2016). *Insights into individual and environmental correlates of physical activity among youth*, Unpublished doctoral thesis, Ghent University, Ghent.

Faber. (2016, April 14). *Historiek* [*History*]. Retrieved from https://faber.kuleuven.be/nl/over-ons/historiek

Haudenhuyse, P. R., Theeboom, M., & Coalter, F. (2012). The potential of sports-based social interventions for vulnerable youth: Implications for sport coaches and youth workers. *Journal of Youth Studies, 15*(4), 437−454.

Haudenhuyse, R., Theeboom, M., Nols, Z., & Coussee, F. (2014). Socially vulnerable young people in Flemish sports clubs: Investigating youth experiences. *European Physical Education Review, 20*(2), 179−198.

In Memoriam Prof. Dr. Marc Maes °8-7-1946−†14-8-2010 (Ghent, Belgium). (2011). *European Sport Management Quarterly, 11*(3), 325.

Lievens, J., Siongers, J., & Waege, H. (2015). *Participatie in vlaanderen [Participation in Flanders]*. Leuven: Acco.

Marlier, M. (2016). *The value of intersectoral partnership in sport − Promoting sport participation, physical activity, social capital and mental health through a sport development program in disadvantaged communities.* Unpublished doctoral dissertation, Ghent University, Ghent.

Ostyn, M., Simons, J., Beunen, G., Renson, R., & Van Gerven, D. (Eds.). (1980). *Somatic and motor development of Belgian secondary schoolboys. Norms and standards.* Leuven: Leuven University Press.

Renson, R. (1978). *Sportwetenschappelijk onderzoek in Vlaanderen. Structuur en thematiek.* Leuven: Katholieke Universiteit Leuven.

Renson, R. (1989). Een kwestie van lichaam en geest: De universitaire instituten Voor L.O. in Vlaanderen. *Sport, 1*, 6−15.

Renson, R., Borms, J., Vrijens, J., & Van der Aerschot, H. (1986). Sportwetenschappelijk onderzoek in Vlaanderen [Sport science research in Flanders]. *Sport, 3*, 55−59.

Scheerder, J., Taks, M., Vanreusel, B., & Renson, R. (2002). *30 jaar breedtesport in Vlaanderen: participatie en beleid. Trends 1969–1999 (sport & maatschappij 1)*. Gent: Publicatiefonds voor Lichamelijke Opvoeding.

Scheerder, J., Vandermeerschen, H., Borgers, J., Thibaut, E., & Vos, S. (2013). *Vlaanderen sport!* Leuven: Academia Press.

Scheerder, J., & Vos, S. (2011). Social stratification in adults' sports participation from a time-trend perspective. Results from a 40-year household study. *European Journal for Sport and Society, 8*(1–2), 31–44.

Scheerder, J., & Vos, S. (2013). Belgium: Flanders. In K. Hallmann & K. Petry (Eds.), *Comparative sport development: Systems, participation and public policy* (pp. 7–21). New York, NY: Springer.

Simons, J., Beunen, G., Renson, R., Claessens, A., Vanreusel, B., & Lefevre, J. (Eds.). (1990). *Growth and fitness of Flemish girls: The Leuven growth study (HKP sport science monograph 3)*. Champaign, IL: Human Kinetics.

Taks, M., Renson, R., & Vanreusel, B. (1991). *Hoe sportief is de Vlaming? Een terugblik op 20 jaar sportbeoefening 1969–1989*. Leuven: Katholieke Universiteit Leuven.

Theeboom, M., Haudenhuyse, R., & Vertonghen, J. (2015). *Sport en sociale innovatie [Sport and social innovation]*. Brussels: VUBPress.

Truyens, J., De Bosscher, V., Sotiriadou, P., Heyndels, B., & Westerbeek, H. (2016). A method to evaluate countries' organisational capacity: A four country comparison in athletics. *Sport Management Review, 19*(3), 279–292. doi:10.1016/j.smr.2015.05.002

Van der Aerschot, H. (1989). Trends in het sportwetenschappelijk onderzoek in Vlaanderen [Trends in sport science research in Flanders]. *Sport, 1*, 17–22.

Vandermeerschen, H., Vos, S., & Scheerder, J. (2016). Towards level playing fields? A time trend analysis of young people's participation in club-organised sports. *International Review for the Sociology of Sport, 51*(4), 468–484. doi:10.1177/1012690214532450

Van Mechelen, F. (1964). *Vrijetijdsbesteding in Vlaanderen [Leisure time activities in Flanders]*. Antwerp: S.M. Ontwikkeling.

Vanreusel, B., Taks, M., & Renson, R. (2002). Belgium-Flanders: Origins, developments and trends of sport for all. In L. P. Dacosta & A. Miragaya (Eds.), *Worldwide experiences and tends in sport for all* (pp. 397–400). Oxford: Meyer & Meyer Sport.

Vos, S., Breesch, D., Késenne, S., Lagae, W., Van Hoecke, J., Vanreusel, B., & Scheerder, J. (2012). The value of value of human resources in non-public sports providers: The importance of volunteers in non-profit sports clubs versus professionals in for-profit fitness and health clubs. *International Journal of Sport Management and Marketing, 11*(1–2), 3–25.

CHAPTER 10

SOCIOLOGY OF SPORT: FRANCE

Stéphane Héas and Patrice Régnier

ABSTRACT

Nowadays, several processes help organize scholarly work about sport and physical activities in France. These include professional development activities of sport and leisure organizations; cultural innovations within sports and physical activities, which involve new spaces with new technologies; questions of public health; and questions of inclusion for marginal groups such as handicapped persons. Questions of power are important to understand each sport situation and each sport sociocultural, economic, and ecologic system. Behind the political and institutional instrumentalization of sport, the reality of social and cultural changes is rarely clear. Strong social, cultural, and economic forces continue to govern sports and seem to be more and more prominent. When sport scandals emerge, the media reveal the case, notably but not exclusively in the context of commercial interests. The possibility for a caring and respectful physical education experience and to improve inclusion for all (Gardou, C. (2012). La société inclusive, parlons-en! Toulouse: Erès) seems like an uphill battle.

Keywords: Sports; power; inequality; cheating; innovation; social and sport participation

Sociology of Sport: A Global Subdiscipline in Review
Research in the Sociology of Sport, Volume 9, 169–185
Copyright © 2017 by Emerald Group Publishing Limited
ISSN: 1476-2854/doi:10.1108/S1476-285420160000009014

HISTORY OF SOCIOLOGY OF SPORT IN FRANCE: A MATURE FIELD OR A NEW FIELD?

In France, the sociology of sport and physical activity is not really a new field. The humanities and social sciences have dealt with the field in several ways. A radical approach has underlined the iatrogeny of competitive and professional sports for several decades. Another has been to analyze the surveillance of the human body by national institutions like schools, sporting and military organizations, and even jails. Other approaches have announced the rise of leisure activities. Underlining the last scientific approaches to a very positive vision of sport has been developed and supported by several institutions and individuals – ministries, sporting associations, politicians, medias, etc. The oscillation between objective approaches and more invested approaches seems to have been constant for several decades.

Some French pioneers wrote articles or books about games and sports but also leisure activities. For example, we can cite Vial (1952), Caillois (1958), and Clouscard (1963). Games and sports appear to be very important and even essential to understanding individual and collective human relations in France. Magnane (1964) may be the first author in France specifically questioning sociology and sport in a book, after a short paper with a number of heuristic ideas such as sport as "total social fact" (Dumazedier, 1959). Surprisingly, Magnane was not a scientist, not even a sociologist, but a writer and sports enthusiast. He was associated with the newspaper *L'Humanité* (linked to the French Communist Party) and wrote sports reports during the London Olympics in 1948. But this pursuit was rapidly aborted. A few years later he published with Baquet et Dumazedier – *Regards Neufs sur les Jeux Olympiques* (1952). Magnane was especially interested in the research of a work group on the recreation of French people – the work of Friedman at the National Center for Scientific Research (CNRS) with Dumazedier (Attali, 2015). It was then that a new research field emerged, with a clear sociological leaning. With a paper in the same year (1959) and then a famous book, *Vers une Civilisation des Loisirs*, Dumazedier (1962) also offered a macrosocial point of view about leisure activities and, consequently, about physical activities in France and in Western Europe and the world.

Gradually, sport as an object of inquiry became more legitimate in France and focus was placed on such matters as social, cultural, and economic transformation, and the role of identification and integration for young people, especially those with popular social status (Attali, 2015). The philosopher Bouet underlined the multiple *Significations du Sport* (1968),[1] in a phenomenological essay that underlined variety and importance of this "major feature of the twentieth century" (p. 8). This book, however, also pointed to the weak advances in the social science of sport at that time, in favor of biological and other hard science approaches. Bouet, Magnane, and Dumazedier all recognized the weakness and unsystematic research on physical education and sport in the 1960s.

An important influence during the 1970s could be found in the work of Pierre Bourdieu, even if this author wrote little about physical activity per se, and also little about sport in a specific sense. For instance, *La Distinction* (1979) offered a large and systematic analysis of social, economic, domestic, and leisure activities and social judgments. This theoretical frame helped to organize Pociello's work in the 1980s (Pociello, 1981), which analyzed sport as a sociocultural practice, and specifically analyzed the division of labor in rugby (1983). Later, Pociello theorized on the "space of sports" and "sport cultures" (1995), which had a strong impact on sociology of sport in France until recently. Among his arguments, each social class has valorized and developed a type of physical culture related to socio-economic background and social uses and habits. This theoretical frame focuses on the conflict between social classes to impose legitimate physical habits and techniques.

These permanent oppositions contributed to promote new physical activities and sports, and helped us to understand the hierarchization of sports. Other researchers such as Clément (1981, 1985), Faure (1987), Michon (1993), and Defrance (1995, 2011) were also interested in the status and roles of physical education and sport. Davisse and Louveau (1991, 1998) analyzed gender socialization and hierarchization in physical education and sports. Masculine identity was a focus as was the feminization of physical activities (Duret, 1999; Mennesson, 2005; Saouter, 2000). A special place has to be given to Thomas, a former shotput athlete (with several records and gold medals in national competitions) who wrote at length but in a popular way about different sports and social and human sciences: the history of sport (Thomas, 1991), psychology of sport (Thomas, 1998), and sociology of sport (Thomas, 1993). A unifying theme for many of these authors is that they were former athletes with a strong physical education and competencies.

However, Brohm (1976, 1981), Brohm and Caillat (1984) and other authors such as Baillette (1985, 1987) also played a role in making this field of research stronger. Their works represented a critical approach to sport and its practice. For such authors, competitive sport was seen as a "total institution" that generates the domination and exploitation of humans. Nationalism, racism, (hetero)sexism, homophobia, etc., were thus seen as the logical consequences of competitive sport. The globalization and commercialization of sport tends to confirm this exploitation of people, with many sportsmen and sportswomen being paid and traded as economic commodities. Gradually, the body started to take a more central place (Berthelot, 1982, 1983; Boltanski, 1971; Vigarello, 1978, 1988, 2002). Some authors like Le Breton (1985, 1990), Duret (1993, 1999) and Duret and Roussel (2003), with different theoretical perspectives, developed arguments about constraints, interactions, and actions that can be observed in sport and physical activities, especially for young people.

A Question of Definition and Categorization

To define sport was, and is, always very difficult. The contradictions within sports are numerous and contain many social, political, economic functions. Some of these functions are manifest (e.g., to give or receive pleasure, pain, enthusiasm, violence, etc.) and others more latent (e.g., functions that support and even promote dominant power) (Brohm, 1976; Jeu, 1973).

Since the very beginning, the study of the categorization of games and sports has always been strong in France (Caillois, 1958). Caillois proposed certain distinctions between aspects of play and games: mimicry (parody, travesty), agon (competition), alea (chance), and ilinx (vertigo). These four suggestions were only four poles "to better reflect their fundamental kinship." Bouet (1968) differentiated between hyper-competitive sport and other forms of sport, which he termed "desport" (such as leisure physical activities).

Studying sport also involves comparing contemporary and modern sports with traditional, local, or historical games. Parlebas specified distinctions between competitive sports and other games (Parlebas, 1984). He examined sport using a synthetic definition: "Sport represents the playful and competitive motor approved by the sport institution" (1986, p. 26). Indeed, he suggested some specific categories like "*quasi sport*" (Parlebas, 1984) (physical activities with "only" a local or even a national influence like "*longue paume*" in a few regions of France, or like Scottish games) and "quasi sporting games" (*quasi jeux sportifs* in French) such as jogging, skiing, kayaking, cycling, swimming for leisure; the "sporting traditional games" (*jeux sportifs traditionnels* in French) such as skipping rope, marbles, war games, playing Mummies and Daddies (Dugas, 2002; Parlebas, 1999). The reduction of the number and legitimacy of traditional games seems to be inevitable, but another view is that the perpetuation of traditional games in some areas is combined with a permanent creation and modification of games (Adamkiewicz, 1988; Allain, 2010; Ballin, 1996; Lebreton, 2010). With the input of some pioneers, some of these areas try to become new sports disciplines or have succeeded to become new recognized sports: freeride style on motorcycles, roller skating, IOC snowboard (slopestyle, halfpipe) or BMX, new types of "descent" like the snowboardcross, downhill mountain biking, etc. (Heimbourger, 2006). Some traditional techniques like regional wrestling (the Breton wrestling called *Gouren*, with more and more interceltic wrestling tournaments) tend to adopt rules from other sports, standardized configurations, rational physical preparation, and so on (Czornyj, 2012; Epron, 2008). Different socio-analysts consider the complex sportification of some specific physical exercises (Delalandre & Collinet, 2013; Lebreton, 2010). These approaches highlight a continuum between legitimate sport (such as the Olympics Games and the major international sports) and less legitimated pursuits (Régnier, 2014, 2016).

What Prompted the Field to Grow?

The strong mobilization of sport and physical activity teachers (EPS teachers in French) enhanced the study of physical activities, first for young people (in primary and secondary schools) and secondly for postgraduate schools and university students. Other organizations have emerged such as the National Institute of Sport and Education (INSEP, created in 1975, became the Sport Performance and Valuation National Institute in 1979). Also, postgraduate education on sport and physical education has contributed to the recognition of sport research at the college level (with the highest degree in sport and physical education teaching called *agrégation* in France, and the development of academic departments called UER EPS, then UFR STAPS).

The final phase of recognition of the specific field of research in the sciences of sports, and specifically sociology of sport, was reached with the creation of the 74th section of the French National Council of Universities (http://www.cpcnu.fr/web/section-74) called STAPS, (Sciences and Techniques in Sports and Physical Activities, or *Sciences et Techniques des Activités Physiques et Sportives* in French). Nowadays, this section validates new academic teachers and researchers in sport at a high level of education (so, access is possible only with a PhD and qualifications at the university level. Then, one prepares the national competitive examination). In this national public frame, between 2012 and 2015, 627 candidates tried to become researcher-teacher (assistant professor) in sports universities, and 335 were admitted and considered to have the scientific and pedagogic abilities. The entire field of the social and human sciences involves 42% of cases (255 cases handled). Not surprisingly, the fields of physiology (22%), neuroscience (19%), and sociology (19%) account alone for 60% of the files assessed[2]. Relative to the status of senior professor, of the 189 files reviewed by the CNU, 61 were qualified (32.27%); between 2012 and 2015, five sociologists were qualified to apply for a job of senior professor.

However, the STAPS field is not the only one in France that has an interest in research on sport and physical activity. For example, we have made a non-exhaustive test for this issue. On the website http://www.theses.fr, one can find all the theses (finished and ongoing) written since 1985 in France. We looked at four themes: sociology + leisure, sociology + physical activities, sociology + body, and sociology + sport. We focused our attention on two main fields of research: sociology/anthropology and STAPS.

For the "sociology + physical activities" research, we found 104 theses about sport, physical activities, or EPS in human sciences. Of these theses, 68 were STAPS theses and 57 researched "sociology + sport," 29 were in the sociology field, and 16 of them researched "sociology + sport." Three of them were also themed in "sociology + body", only one also concentrated on "sociology + leisure."

For the "sociology + leisure" research, there were 46 theses with a subject related to sport or physical activities. Five of them were STAPS theses and also had a sports theme, and 37 were sociological theses with only 5 of them considering a sports theme. One of them was also concerned with "sociology + physical activity," and another with "sociology + body." When we looked at "sociology + body" research, we found 56 theses. Thirty-nine of them were sociological/anthropological theses with 13 of them having a sports theme, and 14 STAPS theses with 7 showing a sports theme. As noted above, four of them were concerned with leisure or physical activity.

With the keywords "sociology + sport", we found 283 theses. In this pool, 88 theses are STAPS, and 134 were sociological or anthropological. Of course, this list included several theses marked as sport themes in other lists. The most interesting thing to consider is, first, that STAPS theses are not only focused on sport or physical activities, as 7 of them, in our research, only talked about the body.

Such quantitative research allows us to consider several points about sport research in France. First, we cannot consider "sport" as the only subject of research. Indeed, physical activities in which sport is included represent a larger subject area in France. It is very important to understand this situation in France to truly embrace all of the categories in which sport and physical activities can be observed and studied. It also appears that the subjects of sport and physical activity are very dynamic fields in France. Indeed, we only report here sociology and STAPS theses. There are also plenty of fields discussing sport and physical activities (geography, economy, history, linguistic, education sciences, movement sciences, etc.) that are not the subject of this chapter.

The STAPS field is growing in an important way. We must note that the STAPS thesis can be used in a number of disciplines — history, psychology, social psychology, etc. Each research field is concerned with its own studies. For this chapter, we only checked sociological topics. We also observe that sociology is still very interested in sport and physical activities, with a larger result for the thesis with the "sociology + sport" keywords research (134 in sociology, 88 in STAPS). Further, for the "sociology + physical activity" keywords results, we obtained 11 STAPS and 13 sociology, for "sociology + body" 26 sociology and 7 STAPS, and for "sociology + leisure" 30 sociology and 0 STAPS. Of course, for this last research we only noted theses concerning sport or physical activities. It shows the multiplicity of research based on sport and physical activities, even if the theses concerned do not mention these themes.

Are There Any Established Sociology of Sport Organizations or Associations in France?

There are many research associations and organizations in France and/or in the French language about sport and physical activities all over the world. The merging and development of this theme of research is not yet established. There is sometimes competition and conflict regarding scientific and academic legitimacy concerning several of these associations and organizations.

We can distinguish between several organizations, sometimes strongly autonomous and sometimes with close relations between them. The radical criticism of sport and sport spectacles has strong support in several reviews like *Quel Corps?* (1975–1997, which was the year of its dissolution), or *Prétentaine* (since 1994). This kind of radical sociology is always active with *Quel Sport?* papers (directed by P. Vassort, then by F. Ollier). While speaking about education and school, there are some professional reviews like *Contre Pied, EPS, Sports Cultures*. Each of these underlines the possibility to experience sport in ways other than as competition – such as to have fun and pleasure. Brohm, Vassort, Perelman, and/or Ollier have published several books over the last few years and continue to write radical reviews. There is one specific French-speaking organization entitled Sociology of Sports called 3SLF (http://3slf.fr/, Société de Sociologie du Sport de Langue Française or Sociology of Sport in French Language Society, since 2007). 3SLF regularly organizes congresses and publishes with the French Society of Sports History (*Société Française d'Histoire du Sport*, SFHS) a common review, *Sciences Sociales et Sport*.

There are other sport and physical activity research organizations such as *Association des Chercheurs en Activités Physiques et Sportives* (ACAPS, or Researchers in Sports and Physical Activities Association) (http://www.acaps.asso.fr/) and *Association Francophone de Recherche Sur les Activités Physiques et Sportives* (AFRAPS, or Research on Sports and Physical Activities in French Language Association) (http://afraps.org/). AFRAPS edits the review *STAPS* (since 1980). The *Association Française de Sociologie* (AFS or French Sociology Association) (http://www.test-afs-socio.fr/) and *Association Internationale des Sociologues de Langue Française* (AISLF or International Sociologists in French Language Association) (http://www.aislf.org/) have their own workshops dedicated to sports and physical activities.

Regular Conferences/Workshops/Seminars?

Every single research laboratory in France is encouraged to regularly organize seminars (often every month). Regarding national or international congresses, AFS meets every two years, and the AISLF every four years. In each of them, workshops are organized around sports and physical activities.

There are two specific congresses regularly organized in France by French research associations around sport and physical activities research (not only with sociological approaches). Since 1985, ACAPS has net every two years. Here, all sciences of sport are included but mostly biologically and biomechanically oriented. For instance, in 2013, ACAPS's congress saw a predominance of biological and biomechanical disciplines. Of the 216 oral communications presented, more than 20 were sociological (about

10%). In the ACAPS congress of 2015, of the 251 oral communications, only 9% were sociological (versus 17% psychological).

Since 1980, AFRAPS has gathered mostly, but not exclusively, human and social sciences communications. At the 2012 AFRAPS congress, which was organized by and for humanities and social scientists within a multidisciplinary approach, there were 68 oral papers, more than 11 of which were strictly sociological (16%); if we add anthropological and psychosociological communications, the proportion is nearly 25%, and even higher if we include psychological research. At the 2014 AFRAPS congress, which was a little smaller, about 45% of oral communications were developing a sociological topic.

When we focus on the specific French-speaking association of sport sociology (3SLF), the two last 3SLF congresses (2013 and 2015) contained dozens of scientific communications. It is sometimes difficult to distinguish sociological communications from other disciplines. Nevertheless, in 2013, 134 oral papers were presented and selected from an original collection of 352. Some themes have increased in popularity such as sport, work, and profession. Others seem to decrease such as gender, colonization, or sociology of sciences and technics of physical and sport activities. In 2015, of 114 oral communications, 53 were specifically sociological, 23 developed a more specific management and economical approach, and 17 communications involved an historical approach.

Around these scientific associations, there are also some parallel initiatives, often aligned with political parties or political movements. Regularly they invite sociologists or other humanities scientists to collaborate with them. Yet other associations sometimes have sociologists in their ranks, like *Femixsports* (2000−) whose objective is to promote male/female integration into sports (http://www.femixsports.fr/, women, mixing, sports). Femix Sports is an association that is working to promote equal access to sport and exercise in schools and elsewhere. We can cite, for instance, ARIS (*Association pour la Recherche sur l'Intervention en Sport*), an Association for Research on Sport Intervention since 1999, or the Thinktank "*Sport et Citoyenneté*" (sport and citizenship, http://sportetcitoyennete.com/). There are different trade unions concerning higher education and research institutions. Each of them promotes and supports physical activities and sports for students, researchers, and administrative personnel working in public or private higher education institutions. Some other associations like *Le Trimaran* use theatrical improvisations to make young people aware of discrimination in the sphere of sport.

Several private and professional initiatives exist in France to take care of vulnerable sport participants. Such interventions are not strictly sociological, but also psychological or in terms of public health – to prevent addictions or disease, etc. (Ferez & Thomas, 2012; Quin & Bohuon, 2015) with sport, or to fight against sexism, racism, homotransphobia, etc. Different evolutions in academic formation tend to gather small teams of social scientists. Often, there are more than two sociologists in each sport university in France. With methods similar to researchers of management, economic and gestion of sports ones, it appears that 5 or 10 researchers can work together in these universities.

What Are the Most Recognized Sport Science Programs in France?

It is difficult to identify the most recognized sport science programs in France because it depends on the criteria used. There is some financial support for regional research, even national and international dissemination. This is the case with respect to research about the River Seine and leisure activities organized around it (Sirost, Evrard, & Féménias, 2011), for research about violent supporters (Nuytens, 2011), youth cultures (Gibout & Lebreton, 2013), and research on outdoor and risky pastimes in mountainous regions (Corneloup, 2010; Corneloup, & Bourdeau, 2004). Such collaboration with international institutions (AMAWADA, FIFA, etc.) or, for instance, the Council of Europe offered to some researchers the opportunity to be more visible outside of France with specific analysis of violence in sport (Bodin, Robène, & Héas, 2004), discrimination in sports (Gasparini & Talleu, 2010; Héas, 2010), and the practice and organization of sports in European prisons (Sempé, 2016).

Substantively, What Is Popular to Study and What Is Left Out?

The research we did on the French Internet site theses.fr gives us an accurate look into the kind of studies realized over recent decades. Social phenomena linked to sport or physical activities such as integration and inclusion, and sport as a social issue or a social tool to integrate vulnerable people (in France but also in other countries like Algeria, Tunisia, Benin, Madagascar, etc.) are popular topics. When we examine themes found with "sociology + sport" keywords, we find that studies are devoted to sport and physical activities in foreign countries. These countries are, on the whole part, former colonies of France, such as Benin (1990, STAPS PhD), Togo (2010, STAPS PhD) or Cameroon (1997, STAPS PhD).

The matter of sport in human evolution is still a subject of interest to French researchers. Haridas (2011, STAPS PhD) questioned human potential through sport. Lucq (2007, STAPS) questioned the place of sport values in social regulation. Verschave (2012, STAPS PhD) examined collective sports and their role in socialization. The professional worlds of sport are also a popular subject for French sociology of sport. For example, Jelen (2009, STAPS PhD) speaks about the social construction of sport teachers, Negro (2008 Sociology PhD) and Javerlhiac (2010, STAPS PhD) questioned the reconversion of high-level sportsmen, while Bujon (2002, Sociology and Anthropology PhD) talked about the sporting hero. Sekulovic (2013, STAPS PhD) opens a new field when he questions the place of the sport agent as a professional.

There is a last important subject that is questioned by French sociology of sport — health. The fact that society is getting older seems to emphasize the importance of physical activities in self-maintenance. Let's take three examples: Nache (2004, STAPS PhD) worked on the link between physical activities and alcohol for young people. Henaff-Pineau (2008, STAPS PhD), after Feillet (2000), focused her interest on physical activity for older people. Tchirkov (2012, STAPS PhD) questioned the place of the handicapped in New Guinea.

CONCLUSION

These following analyses are significative theoretical and methodological discussions and innovations that underline the robustness of sociology of sports in France.

Le Sport et ses Affaires (Duret & Trabal, 2000) analyzes underground businesses in sport (such as doping and other cheating like undeclared money and corruption) with a pragmatic approach of empirical sociology. The aim is to take account of the sense of justice and of critics of all these participants. Each experience is analyzed towards *les économies de la grandeur* from Boltanski and Thévenot (1987). The "scandal" of evaluations, decisions, and notations by a referee, for instance, becomes, in the area of sport, similar to a tribunal, which is very often managed internally rather than externally. When the scandal is taken outside the area of sport, it becomes an "affair" that can reaffirm solidarity and fraternity inside sports spheres, which tend to have an orientation towards group protection. When an "affair" appears in media supports, each implicated person tends to justify his position, and tries to negotiate with other actors of this phenomenon. These negotiations try to preserve personal interests of course, but also to reinforce the ethic of sport, to balance justice and injustice, and to preserve the dynamic of sport as an important sector of contemporary societies.

Two different theoretical approaches to the sport of boxing seem to reinvigorate sociology and ethnology (Wacquant, 2002; Beauchez, 2014). The first has used the theory of Pierre Bourdieu combined with an intersectional approach: in Wacquant's gym, black boxers who trained and succeeded did not belong to the lower class; they accepted the white investigator even if he was not yet a boxer, even if he was a stranger. Results indicated that in order to become a boxer, one needed strong discipline, to make regular efforts, to optimize free time, etc., all things inherited by social habits and by parents and neighborhood education. Then, the work of boxing reinforces this rigorous self-restraint. Even if the research of Wacquant was not on French territory, it has had a strong impact on sociology in general and sociology of sport in particular.

Beauchez used a comprehensive approach, focusing on everyday life interactions. Contrary to the body-object analyzed by Wacquant where the whole body engaged in "the inculcation of a pugilistic habitus" (p. 117), Beauchez highlights how, by becoming a boxer, the person learns to resist, to feint, to adapt to the constraints to better combat, to develop winning strategies. He understood boxing as a great and a subtle experience to learn to fight against sociocultural domination (inside and outside the boxing ring), to build pride and again strong discipline. Boxing becomes a tool to resist, outside, against social and economic constraints (unemployment, racism, social segregation, etc.). These two inquiries have underlined the capabilities learned by boxers to become a "real" and significant boxer, a man proud of himself because of this strong experience of the boxing fight. They also indicated the world of lower-class people with boxing as a horizon to improve themselves and to build their own ways of life.

Like elsewhere in the world, Norbert Elias' theory has had a strong impact on French sociology of sport. Aspects of violence[3] are used to understand this macrohistorical and macrosociological evolution. The Eliasian approach to sport and physical activities has helped us understand the strict organization of rules against violence in the sport field. With it comes the progressive internalization of public control of violence by each person, and by each athlete. The public management of violence has increased and the sensitivity threshold to violence has been reduced. Recently, severe criticisms were pronounced against Elias's ethno- and sociocentric biases (Bodin & Robène, 2014).

With or without this theoretical approach, an interrogation about violence management has been developed in France with respect to risk in sport. Le Breton (1991) explained individual risky actions (such as climbing, competition sports, bodily self-injuries, speed, etc.) by examining aspects of social and collective support. Risky sports can become a space to prove oneself, as a rite of passage, or for other purposes in many different environments (Clavel, 2015; Collard, 1997; Laclémence, 1995; Routier & Soulé, 2012; Soulé, 2004). The question of what is an acceptable risk in sport today is a fascinating and common one in French research on sport.

NOTES

1. Which was his thesis title whose object was proposed in 1952 at Sorbonne University.
2. Vincent Nougier – Bilan CNU 2012–2015 – 19/02/2016. Accessed 03/26/2016.
3. Elias's book *The Quest for excitement* has been translated by "La civilisation des moeurs" *(civilization of manners)* in French.

FIVE KEY READINGS

1. **Duret, P., & Trabal, P. (2000).** *Le sport et ses affaires. Une sociologie de la justice de l'épreuve sportive.* **Paris: Métailié**.

Contemporary sports emphasize aspects of justice or injustice. Within institutions, sport actors tend to preserve their interest in behaviors like cheating and fraud. The logic of actions are negotiated and varied.

2. **Saouter, A. (2000).** *"Etre rugby". Jeux du masculin et du feminin.* **Paris: Payot**.

This study examines the gendered aspects of being a rugby player. The traditional Rugby (le monde de l'ovalie en Français) appears to be a initiatic ritual to become a man, with dominant relations but also ambivalent relations with females.

3. **Ferez, S., & Thomas, J. (Eds.) (2012).** *Sport et VIH. Un corps sous contrainte.* **Paris: Teraèdre**.

To live with a chronic disease can transform life and social relations. Living with AIDS and its strong collective representations are closely examined in this study.

4. **Routier, G., & Soulé, B. (2012). L'engagement corporel: une alternative au concept polythétique de sports à risque en sciences sociales,** *Movement & Sport Sciences*, **3(77), 61−71.**

Confronting danger and risk becomes a means of identity construction. Physicality and sport engagement seem to be at the same time a game and a stake (*jeu* and *enjeu* in the French language).

5. **Beauchez, J. (2014).** *L'empreinte du poing. La boxe, le gymnase et leurs hommes,* **Paris: Ed. EHESS.**

This ethnography examines the culture of boxing, with the boxing ring as a sharing scene, a true justice for people often in conflict with social institutions (family, school, work). Beauchez explains the mysteries of the physical and mental refinement required by the work of boxing. This is a study based on portraits, biographies, and extended observations.

REFERENCES

Adamkiewicz, E. (1988). *Des loisirs sportifs à La Part-Dieu, Implantation de micro sites de loisirs sportifs en milieu urbain. Projets d'équipements.* Lyon: Agence d'Urbanisme de Lyon/U.F.R.A.P.S.

Allain, B. (2010). *Des jeux de balle traditionnels au rugby professionnel: histoire d'une domination economique et politique des corps.* Saint-Quentin-en-Yvelines: thèse de l'université de Versailles.

Attali, M. (2015). Entre correspondant et sociologue: la fascination militante d'un écrivain. In T. Bauer (Ed.), *Georges Magnane: la plume et le sport* (pp. 80−97). Reims: EPURE.

Baillette, F. (1985). Révoltes sociales et orthopédie sportive (sport et normalisation de la déviance). *Quel Corps?*, 28−29 ("Sport et modernité"), n° 28/29, 83−95.

Baillette, F. (1987). Le sport de compétition devrait être banni des pays civilisés. In J.-P. De Modenard (Ed.), *Drogues et dopages* (pp. 277−312). Paris: Éditions Chiron.

Ballin, G. (1996). *Des jeux traditionnels au sport quilles et les mutations de la société aveyronnaise* (p. 2). Bordeaux: thèse STAPS de l'université de Bordeaux.

Baquet, M., Dumazedier, J., & Magnane, G. (1952). *Regards neufs sur les Jeux Olympiques.* Paris: Seuil.

Berthelot, J. M. (1982). Une sociologie du corps a-t-elle un sens? *Recherches sociologiques,* *13*(1−2), 59−65.

Berthelot, J. M. (1983). Corps et société. *Cahiers internationaux de sociologie*, *74*(2), 119−131.

Bodin, D., & Robène, L. (2014). Sport and civilisation: Violence mastered. From the lack of a definition for violence to the illusory pacifying role of modern sports. *International Journal of History of Sport*, *31*(16), 1939−1955.

Bodin, D., Robène, L., & Héas, S. (2004). *Sports et violences en Europe.* Strasbourg: Editions du Conseil de l'Europe, août.

Boltanski, L. (1971). Les usages sociaux du corps. *Annales. Économies, Sociétés, Civilisations,* *26*(1), 205–233.

Boltanski, L., & Thévenot, L. (1987). *De la justification. Les économies de la grandeur.* Paris: Gallimard.

Bouet, M. (1968). *Significations du sport.* Paris: Editions universitaires.

Bourdieu, P. (1979). *La distinction, critique sociale du jugement.* Paris: Editions de Minuit.

Brohm, J. M. (1976). *Sociologie politique du sport.* Paris: Ed. J.-P. Delarge.

Brohm, J. M. (1981). *Le mythe olympique.* Paris: Ed. Bourgois.

Brohm, J. M., & Caillat, M. (1984). *Les dessous de l'olympisme.* Paris: La Découverte, Collection Cahiers libres.

Bujon, T. (2002). *L'etoffe du champion: contribution a une sociologie de la grandeur* (p. 2). Lyon: thèse de sociologie et d'anthropologie de Lyon.

Caillois, R. (1958). *Les jeux et les hommes.* Paris: Gallimard.

Clavel, A. (2015). *Mega-évènements sportifs et gestion du risque: entre menace, sécurité et liberté. La Coupe du Monde 2006* (p. 11). Paris: thèse de l'université de Paris.

Clément, J. P. (1981). La force, la souplesse et l'harmonie. Etude comparée de trois sports de combat. In C. Pociello (Ed.), *Sports et société* (pp. 285–301). Paris: Vigot.

Clément, J. P. (1985). *Étude comparative de trois disciplines de combat (Lutte, Judo, Aikido) et de leurs usages sociaux* (p. 7). Paris: thèse de l'université de Paris.

Clouscard, M. (1963). Les fonctions sociales du sport. *Cahiers Internationaux de Sociologie,* *34,* 125–136.

Collard, L. (1997). *Risques sportifs, prises de risques et science de l'action motrice. Aspects sociologiques* (p. 5). Paris: thèse de l'université de Paris.

Corneloup, J. (Ed.). (2010). *Créativité et innovation dans les loisirs sportifs de nature. Un autre monde en émergence.* L'Argentière la Bessée: Edition du Fournel.

Corneloup, J., & Bourdeau, P. (2004). Les sports de nature Entre pratiques libres, territoires, marchés et logiques institutionnelles. *Cahier Espaces, 81,* 117–124.

Czornyj, A. (2012). *D'une pratique traditionnelle à un sport de combat: Ar Gouren ou la lutte bretonne.* Paris: L'Harmattan.

Davisse, A., & Louveau, C. (1991). *Sports, école, société: la part des femmes.* Joinville le pont: Actio.

Davisse, A., & Louveau, C. (1998). *Sports, école, société: la différence des sexes: féminin, masculin et activités sportives.* Paris: L'Harmattan.

Defrance, J. (1995). *Sociologie du sport.* Paris: La Découverte/Syros.

Defrance, J. (2011). Regards sur la sociologie du sport. *Savoir agir, 15,* 59–66.

Delalandre, M., & Collinet, C. (2013). Le Mixed martial arts et les ambiguïtés de sa sportification en France. *Loisir et Société, 35,* 293–316.

Dugas, E. (2002). Éducation physique et éducation informelle à l'école. *Éducation et Sociétés,* *2*(10), 21–34.

Dumazedier, J. (1959). Réalités du loisir et idéologies. *Esprit, 274*(6), 866–893.

Dumazedier, J. (1962). *Vers une civilisation du loisir.* Paris: Seuil.

Duret, P. (1993). *L'Héroïsme sportif.* Paris: Presses Universitaires de France.

Duret, P. (1999). *Les jeunes et l'identité masculine.* Paris: PUF.

Duret, P., & Roussel, P. (2003). *Le corps et ses sociologies* (p. 128). Paris: A. Colin, coll.

Duret, P., & Trabal, P. (2000). *Le sport et ses affaires. Une sociologie de la justice de l'épreuve sportive.* Paris: Métailié.

Epron, A. (2008). *Histoire du gouren (xixe-xxie siècles): l'invention de la lutte bretonne* (p. 2). Rennes: thèse STAPS de l'université Rennes.

Faure, J. M. (1987). *Sport, culture et classes sociales.* Nantes: thèse d'Etat de l'université de Nantes.

Feillet, R. (2000). *Pratiques sportives et résistance au vieillissement.* Paris: L'Harmattan.

Ferez, S., & Thomas, J. (Eds.). (2012). *Sport et VIH. Un corps sous contrainte.* Paris: Teraèdre.

Gasparini, W., & Talleu, C. (Eds.). (2010). *Sport et discriminations en Europe. Regards croisés de jeunes chercheurs et de journalistes européens.* Strasbourg: Editions du Conseil de l'Europe.

Gibout, C., & Lebreton, F. (2013). Cultures juvéniles et loisirs sportifs de rue: une approche par l'espace public. *Agora, 3*(68), 71–84.

Haridas, C. (2011). *Le developpement du potentiel humain par le sport: le cas de l'institut des sports guyanais.* Pointe-à-Pitre: thèse STAPS de l'université Antilles-Guyane.

Héas, S. (2010). *Les discriminations sportives dans les sports contemporains; entre inégalités, médisances et exclusions.* Nancy: PUN, collection Epistémologie du corps.

Heimbourger, Y. (2006). *Le BMX (Bicross) en France: organisation, culture, professionnalisation* (p. 1). Grenoble: thèse STAPS de l'université de Grenoble.

Henaff-Pineau, P.-C. (2008). *Pratiques physiques des seniors et vieillissement: entre raison et passion: analyse sociologique de la transformation des pratiques avec l'avancée en âge* (p. 11). Paris: thèse STAPS de l'Université de Paris.

Javerlhiac, S. (2010). *Pouvoir et vouloir se former. Les Sportifs de Haut Niveau face au processus de reconversion: entre strategies individuelles et contraintes institutionnelles, personnelles et systemiques* (p. 2). Rennes: thèse de l'université de Rennes.

Jelen, N. (2009). *La socialisation professionnelle en debut de carriere: le cas d'enseignants d'EPS.* Arras: thèse STAPS de l'université d'Artois.

Jeu, B. (1973). La contre-société sportive et ses contradictions. *Esprit, Nouvelle Série, 10*(428), 391–416.

Laclémence, P. (1995). *Le stade de football: espace d'ordre ou zone a risque pour les foules festives? Spectateurs, supporters, hooligans ou martyrs?* Reims: thèse Lettres et Sciences Humaines de l'université de Reims.

Le Breton, D. (1985). *Corps et sociétés: essai de sociologie et d'anthropologie du corps.* Paris: Méridiens-Klincksieck.

Le Breton, D. (1990). *Anthropologie du corps et modernité.* Paris: PUF.

Le Breton, D. (1991). *Passions du risque.* Paris: Métailié.

Lebreton, F. (2010). *Cultures urbaines et sportives "alternatives". Socio-anthropologie de l'urbanaité ludique.* Paris: L'Harmattan.

Lucq, J. (2007). *Sport, valeurs et régulations sociales.* Brest: thèse STAPS de l'université de Brest.

Magnane, G. (1959). Effets du sport sur le comportement social de l'adolescent. *International Review of Education, 5*(1), 98–104.

Magnane, G. (1964). *Sociologie du sport.* Paris: Gallimard.

Mennesson, C. (2005). *Être une femme dans le monde des hommes. Socialisation sportive et construction du genre.* Paris: L'Harmattan.

Michon, B. (1993). *L'espace des sciences et techniques des activites physiques et sportives: recours au corps et effets de corps.* Strasbourg: thèse d'Etat de l'université de Strasbourg.

Nache, C. (2004). *Activités physiques et sportives et consommation d'alcool chez les jeunes: approche sociologique des styles de vie.* Caen: thèse STAPS de l'université de Caen.

Negro, A.-L. (2008). *Sportifs de haut-niveau: reconversion* (p. 2). Lyon: thèse de sociologie de l'université de Lyon.

Nuytens, W. (2011). *L'épreuve du terrain. Violences des tribunes, violences des stades.* Rennes: PUR, coll. "Des Sociétés".

Parlebas, P. (1984). Le sport est-il un jeu naturel, universel et supérieur? *Ven, 387,* 4–15.

Parlebas, P. (1986). *Eléments de sociologie du sport.* Paris: PUF.

Parlebas, P. (1999). *Jeux, sports et sociétés. Lexique de praxéologie motrice.* Paris: INSEP Publications.

Pociello, C. (Ed.). (1981). *Sport et société.* Paris: Vigot.

Pociello, C. (1983). *Le rugby ou la guerre des styles.* Paris: Métailié.

Pociello, C. (1995). *Les cultures sportives.* Paris: PUF.

Quin, G., & Bohuon, A. (Eds.). (2015). *Les liaisons dangereuses de la médecine et du sport.* Paris: Glyphe.

Régnier, P. (2014). *Devenir cavalier: une expérience d'apprentissage par corps. Essai de socio-anthropozoologie des pratiques et techniques équestres.* Rennes: thèse de sociologie de l'université de Rennes.

Régnier, P. (2016). *Dans la peau d'un cavalier. Un acteur communicationnel par excellence?* Paris: L'Harmattan, coll. Des Haut&débat.

Routier, G., & Soulé, B. (2012). L'engagement corporel: une alternative au concept polythé-tique de sports à risque en sciences sociales. *Movement & Sport Sciences, 3*(77), 61–71. doi 10.3917/sm.077.0061

Saouter, A. (2000). *"Etre rugby". Jeux du masculin et du feminin.* Paris: Payot.

Sekulovic, A. (2013). *Profession: agent sportif: contribution à une théorie des modèles profes-sionnels* (p. 10). Paris: thèse STAPS de l'université de Paris.

Sempé, G. (2016). *Sports et prisons en Europe.* Strasbourg: Editions du Conseil de l'Europe.

Sirost, O., Evrard, B., & Fém1enias, D. (2011). *Rapport final. Les usages récréatifs de l'estuaire de la Seine* (Vol. 4, p. 101). Rouen: Projet SeineAval.

Soulé, B. (2004). *Sports d'hiver et sécurité. De l'analyse des risques aux enjeux de leur gestion.* Paris: L'Harmattan, Collection Sport en Société.

Tchirkov, V. (2012). *Déterminants du handicap moteur en République de Guinée: causes et consé-quences des déficiences des membres inférieurs chez les habitants de Conakry.* Strasbourg: thèse STAPS de l'université de Strasbourg.

Thomas, R. (1991). *Histoire du sport.* Paris: PUF, coll. que sais-je?

Thomas, R. (1993). *Sociologie du sport.* Paris: PUF, coll. que sais-je?

Thomas, R. (1998). *Psychologie du sport.* Paris: PUF, coll. que sais-je?

Verschave, G. (2012). *La socialisation par les sports collectifs: une approche conative auprès des enseignants d'éducation physique et sportive.* Dunkerque: thèse STAPS de l'université de Dunkerque.

Vial, J. (1952). Pour une Sociologie des Loisirs. *Cahiers Internationaux de Sociologie, 13,* 61–77.

Vigarello, G. (1978). *Le corps redressé.* Paris: J.P. Delarge.

Vigarello, G. (1988). *Une Histoire culturelle du sport. Techniques d'hier et … d'aujourd'hui.* Paris: R. Laffont/EPS.

Vigarello, G. (2002). *Du jeu ancien au show sportif. La naissance d'un mythe.* Paris: Seuil.

Wacquant, L. (2002). *Corps et âme: carnets ethnographiques d'un apprenti boxeur.* Paris: Agone.

CHAPTER 11

SOCIOLOGY OF SPORT: GERMANY AND SWITZERLAND

Markus Lamprecht, Siegfried Nagel and Hanspeter Stamm

ABSTRACT

This chapter examines the origins and institutionalization of sport sociology in Germany and Switzerland and provides an overview of the current state of research. It shows how academic chairs and research committees were established and how the first textbooks, anthologies, and journals appeared from the 1970s onwards. The institutionalization process of German-speaking sport sociology proceeded parallel to the establishment of sport science. With regard to its theoretical and empirical basis, German-speaking sport sociology is rooted in theories and concepts of general sociology. Studies using a system theory perspective, conceptualizing sport as a societal sub-system and examining its linkage with and dependence on economy, media, or politics are particularly common in the German-speaking region. In addition, actor theoretic perspectives are very popular, and French sociologists such as Bourdieu and Foucault have had a marked influence on German-speaking sport sociology. A large number of sport sociology studies are concerned with the changes in leisure and elite sports. In this context, the emergence of new trends in risk sports as well as the fitness boom and its implications on body

Sociology of Sport: A Global Subdiscipline in Review
Research in the Sociology of Sport, Volume 9, 187–206
Copyright © 2017 by Emerald Group Publishing Limited
All rights of reproduction in any form reserved
ISSN: 1476-2854/doi:10.1108/S1476-285420160000009015

perception are of special interest. Further areas of research refer to sport participation and the impact of social inequality, particularly with respect to gender differences and social integration. Finally, organization research focusing on change at the level of sport associations and clubs has a long tradition. Major challenges for the future of German-speaking sport sociology include its internationalization and an enhanced international linkage in order to improve the visibility of research results.

Keywords: Sport sociology in Germany and Switzerland; history; institutionalization; state of research; theories

INTRODUCTION: THE HISTORY OF THE SOCIOLOGY OF SPORT

Sociological research on sport has started comparatively late and somewhat hesitantly in the German-speaking countries. Even though some of the father figures of German sociology such as Georg Simmel, Max Weber, or Max Scheler mentioned sport in their respective works, their notes on the subject remained marginal. Yet, as early as 1921 a 100-page book entitled *Soziologie des Sports* (*Sociology of Sport*) was published. The book by Heinz Risse (1921) had originally been planned as a doctoral dissertation, but was rejected by its supervisor, Alfred Weber, on the ground that sport might not yet be a topic suitable for scientific study (Bette, 2011). As a result the book remained largely unnoticed and Risse himself withdrew the publication some years later because he no longer subscribed to his own sociological analysis of sport. As late as 1981 the book was reissued without the knowledge and consent of Heinz Risse and is now mainly remembered as the first German book on sport sociology, which included initial observations regarding sport's dependence upon industrial society.

The significance of sport in industrial society is also the core issue of an article by Helmuth Plessner from 1956, which initiated the first phase of German-speaking sport sociology. According to Plessner (1956) sport was a way to compensate for the demands of industrial society such as lack of physical activity, unilateral strains, and alienation. Plessner's hypothesis triggered a controversial discussion regarding the relationship of sport and society and, in the end, was empirically rejected by Linde and Heinemann (1968). Jürgen Habermas, for example, argued that sport does not compensate but rather extends the demands of work into the sphere of leisure (Habermas, 1967; Lamprecht & Stamm, 1994). For Habermas, sport was by no means an alternative realm but rather steeped in market mechanisms. As a result, the basic principles of industrial work such as differentiation, specialization, and the measurement of performance are reflected in sport (Rigauer, 1969).

In sum, the first phase of German-speaking sport sociology from the mid-1950s to the end of the 1960s was characterized by sociologists, (cultural) anthropologists, philosophers, historians, and economists who discovered sport as a testing ground for their theories (Bette, 2011).

The takeoff of German-speaking sport sociology occurred during the 1970s. Parallel to the growing societal importance of sport and as a side effect of the increasing scientification of sport, sport sociology as one of a number of specialized fields of sociological research emerged. At the beginning of the 1970s a phase of more intense public promotion of elite sports started that was further pushed ahead by the awarding of the Olympic Summer Games of 1972 to Munich. The Games in Germany were deemed to become a success in any respect, and funding as well as major public interest were available. To a large extent, Germany's huge interest in the Games was due to the fact that athletes from the German Democratic Republic (GDR) had won more medals than those from the Federal Republic of Germany (FRG) four years earlier in Mexico City. What was celebrated as a sign of superiority of socialism in the GDR, was a kind of "Sputnik shock" for sport in the FRG (Bette, 2011). To avoid repeating the "scandal of Mexico City," politics established and improved a number of sport science organizations. In 1970, the Bundesinstitut für Sportwissenschaft (BISp, Federal Institute for Sport Science) was established, which, little by little, started supporting research in sport sociology. The "sociology of sport" that up to that point saw itself as a critical and subversive discipline was converted into "sport sociology" as a part of sport science. Some of the new institutes for sport science established academic chairs for sport sociology. As a consequence, sport sociology became a mandatory part of sport science studies and various sport sociological research projects, mainly with a focus on elite sports, were carried out.

As a result, we can say that sport sociology in the German-speaking region has two main sciences of reference — namely, general sociology and sport science. During the establishment phase of sport sociology there was a shift from general sociology to sport science thus transforming sport sociology from a part of sociology into a part of sport science. The somewhat tense relationship between sociology and sport science was also evident during the institutionalization period of sport sociology, which started towards the end of the 1970s.

INSTITUTIONALIZATION OF SPORT SOCIOLOGY IN GERMANY

As a consequence of the development and differentiation of sport science and the establishment of "sport sociology" as a special discipline, the first introductory textbooks on sport sociology were published by Grieswelle (1978), Heinemann (1980/2007), Rigauer (1982) and, somewhat later, Cachay (1988) and Voigt (1992). At the same time the first anthologies illustrating the diversity of themes, theories, and methods of the still-young discipline appeared (see Hammerich & Heinemann, 1975; Kutsch & Wiswede, 1981; Lüschen & Weis, 1976; Winkler & Weis, 1995).

Sport sociology was established as a discipline within sport science and also became a part of the curriculum of physical education teachers. Within general sociology, however, sport sociology only played a marginal role. The new chairs were established in sport science rather than in sociological institutes. As a result, the scientific backgrounds of professors differ substantially. Some have studied general sociology and received their degrees for research on sport matters from a general sociological perspective. Others have developed sport sociology as their area of specialization within the interdisciplinary field of sport science. As mentioned above, new academic chairs were mainly established in sport science and, as a result, the number of persons that had been studying sport science with a special focus on sport sociology increased.

It is important to note, however, that only a small proportion of the about 60 German sport science institutes have in fact one or more chairs for sport sociology. Only in about one-quarter of the generally small institutes, with an average of three to four professorships, there are research units that explicitly examine the relationship of sport and society from a sport sociological point of view. Furthermore, as a rule there are no independent study courses focusing on sport sociology. Rather, sport sociology is a more or less important part of general sport science studies that are mainly aimed at teaching and management positions in sport. In these study courses, sport sociological issues offer important basic and reflective knowledge, however.

That sport sociology is better moored in sport science than in general sociology also becomes evident if one takes a look at journal publications.

The majority of all contributions by sport sociologists are published in sport science journals. Papers on sport sociology in general sociological journals are scarce and have often been written by sociologists whose main interest is not sport sociology (Hitzler, 1991; Honer, 1985).

A large number of sport sociological contributions are published in *Sportwissenschaft* (*The German Journal of Sports Science*). *Sportwissenschaft* was founded in 1971 by the sport scientist Ommo Grupe (who was also its managing editor for over three decades) and is the official journal of the BISp, the Deutscher Olympischer Sportbund (DOSB, German Olympic Sport Federation), and the Deutsche Vereinigung für Sportwissenschaft (dvs, German Association for Sport Science). The journal covers a broad range of topics such as sport sociology, physical education, sport psychology, sport history, sport economics, sport medicine, training and physical activity research, legislation, and technology.

In 2004 the journal *Sport und Gesellschaft* (*Sport and Society*) was established. It is the official journal of the section of sport sociology of the dvs and appears three times a year. Apart from contributions from sport sociology it also includes papers on sport philosophy, economics, and history. The first managing editor was Jürgen Baur, followed by Klaus Cachay, who was replaced by Thomas Alkemeyer in 2013.

Apart from this sport sociological journal, a number of book series publishing sport sociological dissertations and research reports were established. Particular mention needs to be made of the *Reihe Sportsoziologie* (*Sport Sociology Series*), which has been edited by Klaus Cachay and Helmut Digel since 2002 for Hofmann publishers. Other important series include the *Edition Global-lokale Sportkultur* (*Global and Local Sport Culture*, edited by Dieter Jütting) and *Sportentwicklung in Deutschland* (*Sport Development in Germany*, edited by Jürgen Baur and Wolf-Dietrich Brettschneider).

Due to the two points of reference of sport sociology in Germany (namely, general sociology and sport science), there are also two professional associations. Apart from the already mentioned sport sociology section of the dvs that publishes *Sport und Gesellschaft* (*Sport and Society*) there is also the Sociology of the Body and Sport section of the German Sociological Association (DGS) that is more closely associated with general sociology. The sport sociology section of the dvs was founded in the late 1970s shortly after the establishment of the dvs and has currently about 150 members that come from Germany, Switzerland, and Austria. The study group Sociology of Sport was initiated by Günter Lüschen and was recognized as a section of the DGS in 1984. In 2005 this section merged with the study group Sociology of the Body under the new label Sociology of the Body and Sport, which currently has about 100 members.

Both sport sociology groups organize sessions and conferences independently under the auspices of the dvs and the DGS. The conference themes range from social inequality in sport and organization research to issues of modern elite sport and thus illustrate the broad range of research interests. Apart from annual conferences with 80 to 100 participants there have also been workshops for young academics and postgraduates for about the past 10 years.

Up to this point, our remarks were concerned with the development of sport sociology in the Federal Republic of Germany (FRG). Even though the beginning of sport sociology in the German Democratic Republic (GDR) dates back to the early 1960s, it never managed to develop its own profile or to become an important part of academic studies. Sport sociology in the GDR was mainly confined to isolated contributions to management and coaching courses for foreigners at the Deutsche Hochschule für Körperkultur (DHfK) in Leipzig. In addition, general sociology in the GDR hardly took notice of sport sociology, and within sport science, sport sociology did not appear to contribute much to practical issues and was marginalized because of its close ties to the ideology of the SED (i.e., the ruling Socialist Unity Party of Germany). Against this background it is hardly surprising that sport sociology of the type developed in the FRG became dominant in the reunited Germany of the past few decades (Voigt, 1992).

INSTITUTIONALIZATION OF SPORT SOCIOLOGY IN SWITZERLAND

At the outset of this chapter we mentioned that sociological research on sport started relatively late and slowly in the German-speaking part of Europe. This observation is particularly true for Switzerland. With regard to the institutionalization of general sociology and the establishment of sport science and thus also regarding sport sociology Switzerland lagged behind other countries.

In Switzerland, the institutionalization of sport sociology started at the beginning of the 1990s. The research committee on sport sociology was founded in 1992 as an independent section of the Schweizerische Gesellschaft für Soziologie (SGS, Swiss Sociological Association). Markus

Lamprecht and Hanspeter Stamm have alternated in the management of the committee for the past 24 years. Christophe Jaccoud and Thomas Busset have been, and still are, the contact persons for French-speaking sociologists and sport scientists. From the beginning, the link-up of German- and French-speaking researchers was an important goal and feature of the committee. Still, French-speaking (sport) sociologists tend to be geared somewhat more towards France, whereas the German-speaking part of the committee developed links to Germany and the Anglo-Saxon region. However, the contact between the two language regions is being fostered in regular meetings that often take place in the context of the annual conferences of the SGS. The first such meeting took place in 1994 when the SGS conference theme was "sport" and well-known speakers from Germany, France, Belgium, and the United Kingdom were invited. Currently, the research committee has 30 members including sociologists, historians, economists, sport scientists, and planning experts.

In 1989 a sport sociology research unit was created at the Federal Institute of Technology (FIT) in Zurich. As there were no long-term perspectives at the FIT, Markus Lamprecht und Hanspeter Stamm, who manned the research unit together with Paul Ruschetti at that time, founded Lamprecht & Stamm Sozialforschung und Beratung AG, a private research firm that increasingly took over the tasks of the research unit, won public and private research contracts and founded the Swiss Observatory for Sport and Physical Activity in 2003. On behalf of the Federal Government and a number of further partner organizations the Observatory gathers and analyzes data on the development of sport in Switzerland and thus contributes to the continuous monitoring of sport and sport policy. Lamprecht and Stamm (2002) have also written the first introductory text on sport sociology in Switzerland.

In the French-speaking part of Switzerland, sport sociologists found their first institutional home at the International Center for Sports Studies (CIES), an independent study center located in Neuchâtel. The CIES was created in 1995 as a joint venture between the Fédération Internationale de Football Association (FIFA), the University of Neuchâtel, and the City and State of Neuchâtel.

Contrary to the situation in Germany, there was never a discussion as to whether sport sociology should be a part of general sociology or sport science in Switzerland. Here, sport sociology clearly emerged as a special discipline within general sociology whereas the Swiss Association for Sport Science was only founded in 2008. Until the early 2000s sport science had a very limited spot in the framework of study courses for physical education teachers. The first sport science institutes at the FIT and the Universities of Berne, Basel, and Lausanne were established only after the turn of the millennium. In the course of this process, two chairs for sport sociology were established. Since 2006 the French sport sociologist Fabien Ohl holds a chair at the University of Lausanne, and Siegfried Nagel has been a professor for sport science at the University of Berne since 2008. Both specialize in sport sociology in research and teaching, and their well-funded departments also render possible the promotion of young sport sociologists.

There is no special journal for sport sociology in Switzerland. Swiss sport sociologists publish in French, German, European, and international journals. In some instances, articles on sport sociology were published in the *Swiss Journal of Sociology* (Lamprecht & Zwicky, 1990).

In conclusion, mention must also be made of sport sociology in Austria. Here, the institutionalization started as early as 1968 when the Österreichischer Arbeitskreis für Soziologie des Sports und der Leibeserziehung (Austrian Work Group on the Sociology of Sport and Physical Education) that was later converted into the Österreichische Gesellschaft für Sportsoziologie (Austrian Society for Sport Sociology) was established. The Austrian group is moored in general sociology (as a section of the general association) as well as in sport science. As in Germany, there was a sharp increase in Austrian sport sociology publications during the 1980s. The first introductory book on sport sociology was written by Gilbert Norden and Wolfgang Schulz in 1988. In 1999, Otmar Weiss published *An Introduction to Sport Sociology*, which was revised and newly published in 2013 by Weiss and Norden.

MAIN APPROACHES TAKEN

From a theoretical and methodological point of view, sport sociology is mainly based on theories, notions, and methods of general sociology. Regarding theories and methods there is a great deal of pluralism. As a rule, general theories and approaches are used and adapted for questions referring to sport, but there is usually no in-depth discussion of theories (Rigauer, 2008). The theoretical concepts that are being used are usually taken from different sociological paradigms. Essentially, there are three approaches to the sociological study of sport-related phenomena in the German-speaking countries.

First, in German sport sociology there are a large number of studies that approach sport from a system theoretic perspective inspired by Niklas

Luhmann's seminal work. Special mention needs to be made of the studies and introductory texts by Cachay, Bette and Thiel (Bette, 1999, 2010; Cachay & Thiel, 2000). These authors view sport as a societal sub-system and as a special context of meaning based on performance-oriented communication for its own sake. A particular feature of this kind of analysis is sport's output on behalf of other sub-systems (e.g., education, health, economy). These Anschlussofferten (services rendered) have contributed to the emergence and differentiation of sport as a social system (Cachay, 1988). A great deal of system theory analyses refer to high-performance sports and its specific "win–lose" code under which doping, for example, poses a structural dilemma (Bette & Schimank, 2006).

Second, there are a number of actor-centered approaches that focus on the actions of individual actors within a social structure and suggest that social action and social structure are interrelated continuously over time (Giddens, 1984; Schimank, 2000). An important contributor to this discussion is Uwe Schimank, who bridges the gap between system and action theory. He is currently also the only well-known and respected German general sociologist who has taken an in-depth look at sport in several of his works (Bette & Schimank, 2006; Schimank, 1992). Schimank's ideas have been taken up by a number of sport sociologists. In an international comparative study, Hartmann-Tews (1996), for example, has examined the policy goal of sport-for-all in the context of actor interests and inclusion politics. Nagel (2006) has conceptualized sport clubs as interest organizations and proposes a multi-level model for the analysis of the development of clubs that is based on Esser's (1993) ideas regarding the logic of sociological explanations. Finally, the seminal contributions by Jürgen Baur and Ulrike Burmann, who suggested a heuristic frame of reference for socialization in sport that is based on an interactionist and socialization theoretic model (Hurrelmann, 2006), need to be mentioned (Baur, 1989; Baur & Burrmann, 2008).

Finally, the contributions of "critical" sport sociologists and notions regarding the body and praxeology (Alkemeyer, 2008; Gugutzer, 2004; Hortleder & Gebauer, 1986) have often been inspired by French sociologists such as Michel Foucault or Pierre Bourdieu. These studies look at the interrelation of social action and social structure by, for example, using Bourdieu's notion of habitus in which physicalness plays an important role for the understanding of social practices. Several studies on sport and social inequality also include multiple references to Bourdieu (Haut, 2011; Lamprecht & Stamm, 1994, 1995; Nagel, 2003). Conversely, the use of figurational concepts in the vein of Norbert Elias is comparatively rare in German-speaking sport sociology.

Empirical studies use a variety of different methods. On the one hand, there are a number of large, quantitative surveys examining the population's sport participation and the situation of sport organizations and their members. On the other hand, qualitative methods ranging from interviews and case studies of organizations to anthropological studies are important. In this connection it is worth mentioning that there is no German textbook on the methods of sport sociology. Rather, the general standards, methods, instruments, and analysis strategies of empirical social research constitute the fundamental framework for research.

MAIN AREAS OF RESEARCH

Our discussion of theoretical approaches, as well as the overview of important contributions at the end of this chapter, demonstrates that German-speaking sport sociology has examined a wide range of topics and issues. To simplify the following short overview of research areas we shall follow Thiel, Seiberth, and Mayer (2013) who have identified three broad perspectives of sport sociology research (see also Heinemann, 1980/2007):

1. At the macro-level we find studies looking at the differentiation, development, and change of modern sport.
2. At the meso-level there are studies examining social structures, in particular organizations and teams in sport.
3. Studies at the micro-level deal with social action and particularly with sport participation and its repercussions on individuals.

As social action and social structure in sport are dependent upon each other, it is at times difficult to assign studies clearly to one of the three perspectives mentioned above. In spite of this restriction, the model is a good frame of reference for a short recapitulation of important perspectives and broadly discussed issues in German-speaking sport sociology.

1. *Change in Modern Sport*
   At the macro-level, general developments in sport are being described and analyzed. This also includes the questions as to how society shapes sport and whether sport has an impact on societal developments. Fundamental studies examine the differentiation of sport into different fields or models of sport (Dietrich & Heinemann, 1989; Digel, 1986). Apart from traditional competitive sport in clubs and high-performance sport these contributions also mention instrumental health sport and

expressive leisure and trend sport. With regard to the differentiation of health sport, Cachay (1988) has published a seminal system theoretical study that looks at the increasing significance of sport in the context of the historical development of the health system.

While there are only few studies concerning health sport, the development of trend sport (Breuer & Michels, 2003; Jaccoud, 1998; Lamprecht & Stamm, 1998; Schwier, 2000; Wopp, 2006) as well as risk and adventure sport (Bette, 2004) have attracted considerable attention. Apart from describing and classifying trends (Schwier, 2000) and the analysis of development patterns (Lamprecht & Stamm, 1998) the causes of the differentiation of these new sports have been examined. In doing this, a number of general societal developments such as the shift in values (Digel, 1986) and individualization (Bette, 1999) are discussed, which are identified as prerequisites and as drivers of developments in sport. The sociology of the body perspective (Gugutzer, 2004) stresses the rediscovery of the body in modern society, which appears to have led to an increasing importance of fitness and a "body boom." In this context, sport and particularly trend sports can contribute to the development of one's identity in modern society.

Development processes and problems have been studied particularly well with regard to elite sports. An important contribution to this kind of research was Bette and Schimank's (2006) analysis of the doping problem as a dilemma that results from the system-specific win code and the interlacing of elite sport with the economy and the media. In their studies, Bette and Schimank also discuss possibilities to resolve the doping problem (regarding doping, see also the study by Ohl, Fincoeur, Lentillon-Kaestner, Defrance, and Brissonneau, 2015). The research group around Klaus Cachay has published several studies on the issue of the compatibility of top-level sport with school, academic studies, and profession (e.g., Borggrefe, Cachay, Riedl, 2009; Teubert, Borggrefe, Cachay, & Thiel, 2006; see also Nagel, 2002; Wippert, 2002). Digel (2013) has compared the organizational structure of top-level sport in eight countries (e.g., Australia, Germany, Russia, the United States) in a large international study, and a study by Thiel, Mayer, und Digel (2010) examined health in top-level sport. Other sociological studies have explored the relationship between (top-level) sport and the media (Schierl, 2007; Schwier & Schauerte, 2008), and in Switzerland, Raffaele Poli's Football Observatory (within the CIES) has published a number of studies on the development of professional soccer (particularly with respect to the demography within teams).

2. *Organizations and Groups in Sport*

At the meso-level studies on the organizational structure of sport, and particularly on sport clubs, are of great importance. Initiated and funded by the German Sport Association and the BISp, a first representative survey of the structural features of sport clubs in Germany was undertaken in the 1970s (Schlagenhauf, 1977; Timm, 1979). These so-called financial and structural analyses (FISAS) were continued in the 1990s (Emrich, Pitsch, & Papathanassiou, 2001; Heinemann & Schubert, 1994), and over the past 10 years a continuous monitoring of the situation of sport clubs at two-year intervals was established under the direction of Christoph Breuer and under the label "Sportentwicklungsbericht" ("sport development report") (Breuer, 2015; Wicker & Breuer, 2013). In Switzerland, Lamprecht and Stamm have been carrying out several national association and club studies in close co-operation with the German studies (Lamprecht & Stamm, 2012; Stamm & Lamprecht, 1998).

Contrasting with these representative studies, Nagel examines the interests and situation of club members and their linkage to structural data of clubs on the basis of case studies (Nagel, Conzelmann, & Gabler, 2004; Schlesinger, Klenk, & Nagel, 2014). The multi-level analyses of Schlesinger and Nagel (2013, 2015) take a particular interest in issues of members' commitment to the club and individual and structural factors influencing voluntary engagement in sport clubs. Emrich's working group, too, investigates the reasons for and against voluntary work (Flatau, 2009; Flatau, Emrich, & Pierdzioch, 2014).

Jütting and collaborators have submitted several studies on voluntary work in sport clubs that characterize sport clubs as organizations of the third sector and see voluntary engagement as an important societal commitment (Jütting, van Bentem, & Oshege, 2003; Schulze, 2004; Strob, 1999). In addition, Braun has published a number of studies looking at voluntary work in the context of citizen participation in civil society (Braun, 2013).

As opposed to sport clubs, there are only few studies on the development of sport associations, that is, umbrella organizations (Fahrner, 2008; Winkler & Karhausen, 1985) or regarding professionalization in clubs and associations (Horch, Niessen, & Schütte, 2003; Thiel, Meier, & Cachay, 2006).

Studies on teams and sport groups take a particular interest in social conflict. Thiel (2002) examines conflict in elite-level team sport (see also the studies by Cachay, 1980; Lenk, 1964, on the significance of conflict in sport teams), and Pilz (2008) has taken close looks at (spectator) violence in sport. Violence and extremism in sport was also the theme of Busset's Swiss studies (Busset, Besson & Jaccoud, 2014; Busset, Jaccoud, Dubey, & Malatesta, 2008).

Finally, mention must be made of the studies of Alkemeyer's work group, which see sport as social practice and look at action contexts and body practices in different settings such as training groups or scenes (Brümmer, 2015).

3. *Participation in Sport*

An important question that has been examined since the 1970s refers to the determinants of sport participation. An important frame of reference of these studies are conventional notions of social inequality and the investigation of the impact of structural variables such as age, gender, education, social background, and ethnicity on sport participation (for overviews, see Lamprecht & Stamm, 1994; Nagel, 2003). Klostermann and Nagel (2012) analyze the linkage of sport participation during one's youth with sport participation in the second half of life. In Switzerland, the Sport Switzerland surveys of 2000, 2008, and 2014 by the Swiss Observatory for Sport and Physical Activity are of particular importance for the analysis of sport participation and the interest the population takes in sport (Lamprecht, Fischer, & Stamm, 2014).

In Germany large-scale population surveys on sport participation are lacking. Apart from a number of recent Eurobarometer studies, data are only available at the communal level where they are used for sport development planning (for an overview, see Rütten, Nagel, & Kähler, 2014).

In numerous studies, gender researchers (e.g., Petra Giess-Stuber, Ilse Hartmann-Tews, Marie-Luise Klein, Bettina Rulofs) have examined social structural characteristics and constellations that are of importance for gender-specific participation in different sport contexts (for overviews, see Hartmann-Tews & Rulofs, 2006; Sobiech & Günter, 2016 and in Switzerland Aceti & Jaccoud, 2012).

Another interesting research question refers to whether participation in sport also entails a specific form of social integration. Baur and Braun (2003) look at the integrative performance of sport clubs from a member perspective. An important issue in this connection is how and by which integration processes migrants can be included in sport clubs (Burrmann, Mutz, & Zender, 2015; Kleindienst-Cachay, 2007; Mutz, 2012; Poli, Berthoud, Busset, & Kaya, 2012). The current discussion also takes an interest in the possibilities and limitations of the inclusion of handicapped persons into sport (Radtke, 2011; Tiemann, 2008).

CHALLENGES AND PERSPECTIVES

Mainly due to the increasing institutionalization of sport science, sport sociology in Germany and Switzerland, as well as in Austria, is currently well established and has produced a large number of relevant contributions in the area of sport and society. Yet, compared to other social and behavioral science disciplines (such as sport education or psychology) there are comparatively few academic chairs. In addition, in cases where new appointments become due, the positions are often no longer dedicated to sport sociology as such but are changed into general social science, economics, or sport management chairs. As a result, it is a challenge to preserve the actual number of sport sociology positions for the future.

To this end it is necessary to make clear that sociological perspectives are important for sport science curricula and to ensure the continuation of research of a high academic standard and of access to funding. With respect to the latter, researchers should not only rely on sport-specific funding available from, for example, the BISp (Germany) or the Federal Office for Sport (Switzerland), but should also seek funding from general public research organizations or from third parties (e.g., sport associations). To be able to tap into these sources, sport sociology has to demonstrate its relevance for society and its high scientific standards.

Another important challenge is the institutionalization and international recognition of German-speaking sport sociology. Even though some German sport sociologists have made important contributions to the development of the International Sociology of Sport Association (ISSA), German-language research and results are scarcely noticed internationally. To improve its international profile, German-speaking sport sociology needs more publications in English and a stronger involvement in the international sport sociology community. An important step in this process was the creation of the European Association for Sociology of Sport (EASS) in 2002 whose development was fostered by its founding president, Otmar Weiss, and other German-speaking sport sociologists (e.g., Georg Anders). It is also noteworthy that the EASS's official publication, the *European Journal for Sport and Society*, has been exclusively edited by German sport sociologists (Dieter Jütting, Bernd Schulze, Siegfried Nagel, Ansgar Thiel) since its establishment in 2004. This is an indication that German-speaking sport sociology might increase its output of English publications in the foreseeable future.

FIVE KEY READINGS

1. **Bette, K.-H. (2010).** *Sportsoziologie.* **Bielefeld: transcript.**

   The book is an introductory text and a research study at the same time. Bette examines the establishment and development of sport sociology, its causes and effects, sport in society, research approaches and theories, opportunities and limitations, as well as threats to modern sport on the basis of system theory.

2. **Heinemann, K. (2007).** *Einführung in die Soziologie des Sports.* **Schorndorf: Hofmann.**

   In 2007, Klaus Heinemann has published the fifth extended and revised edition of his introductory text from 1980. Heinemann was one of the first German sociologists to examine sport in a differentiated manner and has thus contributed greatly to the establishment of sport sociology in Germany. The book provides a systematic introduction to the subjects and problems of the sociology of sport. Particular emphasis is placed on sport as an action sphere with its own special features and sport's institutional arrangements, social processes, and representations.

3. **Lamprecht, M., & Stamm, H. (2002).** *Sport zwischen Kultur, Kult und Kommerz.* **Zürich: Seismo.**

   The textbook from Switzerland offers an entertaining and well-illustrated introduction to the issues and approaches of sport sociology. Highlights include discussions of the fitness boom and current "body cult," the development of trend sports, the history of (women's) sport, and the functioning of highly professional and perfectly staged, economically relevant media sport events.

4. **Thiel, A., Seiberth, K., & Mayer, J. (2013).** *Sportsoziologie: Ein Handbuch in 13 Lektionen.* **Aachen: Meyer & Meyer.**

   The book offers an introduction to the different perspectives and issues of sport sociology and is also suitable for self-study. The 13 lessons provide in-depth answers to fundamental questions of sport sociology concerning the development (e.g., elite sport, trends in sport) and organizational structure of sport (e.g., sport clubs), as well as sport participation (e.g., social inequality, integration in sport).

5. **Weis, K., & Gugutzer, R. (2008).** *Handbuch Sportsoziologie.* **Schorndorf: Hofmann.**

The first German-language compendium of sport sociology provides an encompassing and systematic overview of the current state of the art of sport sociology. The book includes 40 articles by renowned sport sociologists from Germany, Austria, and Switzerland, which cover the following general research areas: development and change of modern sport, social structure and sport, social action in sport, and special settings (e.g., youth sports).

REFERENCES

Aceti, M., & Jaccoud, C. (2012). *Sportives dans leur genre? Permanences et variations des constructions genrées dans les engagements corporels et sportifs.* Bern: Lang.

Alkemeyer, T. (2008). Sport als soziale Praxis. In K. Weis & R. Gugutzer (Eds.), *Handbuch der Sportsoziologie* (pp. 220–229). Schorndorf: Hofmann.

Baur, J. (1989). *Körper- und Bewegungskarrieren. Dialektische Analysen zur Entwicklung von Körper und Bewegung im Kindes- und Jugendalter.* Schorndorf: Hofmann.

Baur, J., & Braun, S. (2003). *Integrationsleistungen von Sportvereinen als Freiwilligenorganisationen.* Aachen: Meyer & Meyer.

Baur, J., & Burrmann, U. (2008). Sozialisation zum und durch Sport. In K. Weis & R. Gugutzer (Eds.), *Handbuch der Sportsoziologie* (pp. 230–238). Schorndorf: Hofmann.

Bette, K.-H. (1999). *Systemtheorie und Sport.* Frankfurt a. M.: Suhrkamp.

Bette, K.-H. (2004). *X-treme. Zur Soziologie des Abenteuer- und Risikosports.* Bielefeld: transcript.

Bette, K.-H. (2010). *Sportsoziologie.* Bielefeld: transcript.

Bette, K.-H. (2011). *Sportsoziologische Aufklärung. Studien zum Sport der modernen Gesellschaft.* Bielefeld: transcript.

Bette, K.-H., & Schimank, U. (2006). *Doping im Hochleistungssport.* Frankfurt a. M.: Suhrkamp.

Borggrefe, C., Cachay, K., & Riedl, L. (2009). *Spitzensport und Studium. Eine organisationssoziologische Studie zum Problem dualer Karrieren.* Schorndorf: Hofmann.

Braun, S. (2013). *Der Deutsche Olympische Sportbund in der Zivilgesellschaft. Eine sozialwissenschaftliche Analyse zur sportbezogenen Engagementpolitik.* Wiesbaden: Springer VS.

Breuer, C. (2015). *Sportentwicklungsbericht 2013/2014: Analyse zur Situation der Sportvereine in Deutschland.* Köln: Strauss.

Breuer, C., & Michels, H. (2003). *Trendsport. Modelle, Orientierungen und Konsequenzen.* Aachen: Meyer & Meyer.

Brümmer, K. (2015). *Mitspielfähigkeit. Sportliches Training als formative Praxis.* Bielefeld: transcript.

Burrmann, U., Mutz, M., & Zender, U. (2015). *Jugend, Migration und Sport. Kulturelle Unterschiede und die Sozialisation zum Vereinssport.* Wiesbaden: Springer VS.

Busset, T., Besson, R., & Jaccoud, C. (2014). *L'autre visage du supportérisme. Autorégulations, mobilisations collectives et mouvements sociaux.* Bern: Lang.

Busset, T., Jaccoud, C., Dubey, J.-P., & Malatesta, D. (2008). *Violence et extrémisme dans le football. Perspectives européennes.* Lausanne: Editions Antipodes.

Cachay, K. (1980). Gruppen und soziale Konflikte im Sport. In O. Grupe (Ed.), *Sport. Theorie in der gymnasialen Oberstufe. Arbeitsmaterialien für den Sportunterricht* (pp. 231–301). Schorndorf: Hofmann.

Cachay, K. (1988). *Sport und Gesellschaft: Zur Ausdifferenzierung einer Funktion und ihrer Folgen.* Schorndorf: Hofmann.

Cachay, K., & Thiel, A. (2000). *Soziologie des Sports: Zur Ausdifferenzierung und Entwicklungsdynamik des Sports der modernen Gesellschaft.* Weinheim: Juventa.

Dietrich, K., & Heinemann, K. (1989). *Der nichtsportliche Sport: Beiträge zum Wandel im Sport.* Schorndorf: Hofmann.

Digel, H. (1986). Über den Wandel der Werte in Gesellschaft, Freizeit und Sport. In K. Heinemann & H. Becker (Eds.), *Die Zukunft des Sports: Materialien zum Kongress Menschen im Sport 2000* (pp. 14–43). Schorndorf: Hofmann.

Digel, H. (2013). *Sociological aspects of modern sports.* Aachen: Meyer & Meyer.

Emrich, E., Pitsch, W., & Papathanassiou, V. (2001). Die Sportvereine. Ein Versuch auf empirischer Grundlage. Schorndorf: Hofmann.

Esser, H. (1993). *Soziologie. Allgemeine Grundlagen.* Frankfurt: Campus.

Fahrner, M. (2008). *Sportverbände und Veränderungsdruck.* Schorndorf: Hofmann.

Flatau, J. (2009). Zum Zusammenhang von Sozialisation und ehrenamtlicher Mitarbeit in Sportvereinen: Erste Überlegungen unter Anwendung der Rational-Choice-Theorie. *Sport und Gesellschaft, 6*(3), 259–282.

Flatau, J., Emrich, E., & Pierdzioch, C. (2014). Einfluss unterschiedlicher Motive auf den zeitlichen Umfang ehrenamtlichen Engagements in Sportvereinen. *Sportwissenschaft, 44*(1), 10–24.

Giddens, A. (1984). *The constitution of society: Outline of the theory of structuration.* Cambridge: Polity Press.

Grieswelle, D. (1978). *Sportsoziologie.* Stuttgart: Kohlhammer.

Gugutzer, R. (2004). *Soziologie des Körpers.* Bielefeld: transcript.

Habermas, J. (1967). Soziologische Notizen zum Verhältnis von Arbeit und Freizeit. In H. Plessner, H.-E. Bock, & O. Grupe (Eds.), *Sport und Leibeserziehung: Sozialwissenschaftliche, pädagogische und medizinische Beiträge* (pp. 28–46). München: Piper.

Hammerich, K., & Heinemann, K. (1975). *Texte zur Soziologie des Sports.* Schorndorf: Hofmann.

Hartmann-Tews, I. (1996). *Sport für alle!? Strukturwandel europäischer Sportsysteme im Vergleich: Bundesrepublik Deutschland, Frankreich, Grossbritannien.* Schorndorf: Hofmann.

Hartmann-Tews, I., & Rulofs, B. (2006). *Handbuch Sport und Geschlecht.* Schorndorf: Hofmann.

Haut, J. (2011). *Soziale Ungleichheiten in Sportverhalten und kulturellem Geschmack. Eine empirische Aktualisierung der Bourdieuschen Theorie symbolischer Differenzierung.* Münster: Waxmann.

Heinemann, K. (1980/2007). *Einführung in die Soziologie des Sports.* Schorndorf: Hofmann.

Heinemann, K., & Schubert, M. (1994). *Der Sportverein: Ergebnisse einer repräsentativen Untersuchung.* Schorndorf: Hofmann.
Hitzler, R. (1991). Ist Sport Kultur? *Zeitschrift für Soziologie, 20*(6), 479−487.
Honer, A. (1985). Beschreibung einer Lebens-Welt. Zur Empirie des Bodybuilding. *Zeitschrift für Soziologie, 14*(2), 131−139.
Horch, H.-D., Niessen, C., & Schütte, N. (2003). *Sportmanager in Vereinen und Verbänden.* Köln: Strauss.
Hortleder, G., & Gebauer, G. (1986). *Sport − Eros − Tod.* Frankfurt a. M.: Suhrkamp.
Hurrelmann, K. (2006). *Einführung in die Sozialisationstheorie.* Weinheim: Beltz.
Jaccoud, C. (1998). *Action publique et nouvelles pratiques sportives: Roller et skate dans deux villes suisses.* Neuchâtel: Editions CIES.
Jütting, D., van Bentem, N., & Oshege, V. (2003). *Vereine als sozialer Reichtum: Empirische Studien zu lokalen freiwilligen Vereinigungen.* Münster: Waxmann.
Kleindienst-Cachay, C. (2007). *Mädchen und Frauen mit Migrationshintergund im organisierten Sport.* Baltmannsweiler: Schneider.
Klostermann, C., & Nagel, S. (2012). Changes in German sport participation: Historical trends in individual sports. *International Review for the Sociology of Sport, 49*(5), 609−634.
Kutsch, T., & Wiswede, G. (1981). *Sport und Gesellschaft. Die Kehrseite der Medaille.* Königstein: Hain.
Lamprecht, M., Fischer, A., & Stamm, H. (2014). *Sport Schweiz 2014. Sportaktivität und Sportinteresse der Schweizer Bevölkerung.* Magglingen: Bundesamt für Sport BASPO.
Lamprecht, M., & Stamm, H. (1994). *Die soziale Ordnung der Freizeit: Soziale Unterschiede im Freizeitverhalten der Schweizer Wohnbevölkerung.* Zürich: Seismo.
Lamprecht, M., & Stamm, H. (1995). Soziale Differenzierung und soziale Ungleichheit im Breiten- und Freizeitsport. *Sportwissenschaft, 25*(3), 265−284.
Lamprecht, M., & Stamm, H. (1998). Vom avantgardistischen Lebensstil zur Massenfreizeit. Eine Analyse des Entwicklungsmusters von Trendsportarten. *Sportwissenschaft, 28*(3−4), 370−387.
Lamprecht, M., & Stamm, H. (2002). *Sport zwischen Kultur, Kult und Kommerz.* Zürich: Seismo.
Lamprecht, M., & Stamm, H. (2012). *Die Schweizer Sportvereine. Strukturen, Leistungen, Herausforderungen.* Zürich: Seismo.
Lamprecht, M., & Zwicky, H. (1990). Sportsoziologie in der Schweiz. Forschungsfragen und Entwicklungsperspektiven unter besonderer Berücksichtigung des Verhältnisses von Sport und sozialer Ungleichheit. *Schweizerische Zeitschrift für Soziologie, 16*(2), 195−222.
Lenk, H. (1964). Konflikt und Leistung in Spitzensportmannschaften. Soziometrische Strukturen von Wettkampfachtern im Rudern. *Soziale Welt, 15*(4), 307−343.
Linde, H., & Heinemann, K. (1968). *Leistungsengagement und Sportinteresse.* Schorndorf: Hofmann.
Lüschen, G., & Weis, K. (1976). *Die Soziologie des Sports.* Darmstadt: Luchterhand.
Mutz, M. (2012). *Sport als Sprungbrett in die Gesellschaft? Sportengagement von Jugendlichen mit Migrationshintergrund und ihre Wirkung.* Weinheim: Beltz/Juventa.
Nagel, M. (2003). *Soziale Ungleichheiten im Sport.* Aachen: Meyer & Meyer.
Nagel, S. (2002). *Medaillen im Sport − Erfolg im Beruf? Berufskarrieren von Hochleistungssportlerinnen und Hochleistungssportlern.* Schorndorf: Hofmann.

Nagel, S. (2006). *Sportvereine im Wandel: Akteurtheoretische Analysen zur Entwicklung von Sportvereinen*. Schorndorf: Hofmann.

Nagel, S., Conzelmann, A., & Gabler, H. (2004). Sportvereine – Auslaufmodell oder Hoffnungsträger? Tübingen: Attempto.

Norden, G., & Schulz, W. (1988). *Sport in der modernen Gesellschaft*. Linz: Trauner.

Ohl, F., Fincoeur, B., Lentillon-Kaestner, V., Defrance, J., & Brissonneau, C. (2015). The socialization of young cyclists and the culture of doping. *International Review for the Sociology of Sport, 50*(7), 865–882.

Pilz, G. (2008). Gewalt im Sport. In K. Weis & R. Gugutzer (Eds.), *Handbuch der Sportsoziologie* (pp. 287–297). Schorndorf: Hofmann.

Plessner, H. (1956). Die Funktion des Sports in der industriellen Gesellschaft. *Wissenschaft und Weltbild, 9,* 262–274.

Poli, R., Berthoud, J., Busset, T., & Kaya, B. (2012). *Football et intégration. Les clubs de migrants albanais et portugais en Suisse*. Bern: Lang.

Radtke, S. (2011). Inklusion von Menschen mit Behinderung im Sport. *Politik und Zeitgeschichte, 16*(19), 33–38.

Rigauer, B. (1969). *Sport und Arbeit. Soziologische Zusammenhänge und ideologische Implikationen*. Frankfurt a. M.: Suhrkamp.

Rigauer, B. (1982). *Sportsoziologie. Grundlagen, Methoden, Analysen*. Reinbek: Rowohlt.

Risse, H. (1921). *Soziologie des Sports*. Berlin: Reher.

Rütten, A., Nagel, S., & Kähler, R. (2014). *Handbuch Sportentwicklungsplanung*. Schorndorf: Hofmann.

Schierl, T. (2007). *Handbuch Medien, Kommunikation und Sport*. Schorndorf: Hofmann.

Schimank, U. (1992). Grössenwachstum oder soziale Schliessung? Das Inklusionsdilemma des Breitensports. *Sportwissenschaft, 22*(1), 32–45.

Schimank, U. (2000). *Handeln und Strukturen. Einführung in die akteurtheoretische Soziologie*. Weinheim: Juventa.

Schlagenhauf, K. (1977). *Sportvereine in der Bundesrepublik Deutschland. Teil I: Strukturelemente und Verhaltensdeterminanten im organisierten Freizeitbereich*. Schorndorf: Hofmann.

Schlesinger, T., Klenk, C., & Nagel, S. (2014). *Freiwillige Mitarbeit im Sportverein. Analyse individueller Faktoren und organisationaler Entscheidungen*. Zürich: Seismo.

Schlesinger, T., & Nagel, S. (2013). Who will volunteer? Analysing individual and structural factors of volunteering in Swiss sports clubs. *European Journal of Sport Science, 13,* 707–715.

Schlesinger, T., & Nagel, S. (2015). Does context matter? Analysing structural and individual factors of member commitment in sport clubs. *European Journal for Sport and Society, 12,* 53–77.

Schulze, B. (2004). *Ehrenamtlichkeit im Fussball*. Münster: Waxmann.

Schwier, J. (2000). *Sport als populäre Kultur*. Hamburg: Czwalina.

Schwier, J., & Schauerte, T. (2008). *Soziologie des Mediensports*. Köln: Strauss.

Sobiech, G., & Günter, S. (2016). *Sport & Gender – (Inter-)nationale sportsoziologische Geschlechterforschung. Theoretische Ansätze, Praktiken und Perspektiven*. Wiesbaden: Springer VS.

Stamm, H., & Lamprecht, M. (1998). *Sportvereine in der Schweiz: Probleme – Fakten – Perspektiven*. Chur: Rüegger.

Strob, B. (1999). *Der vereins- und verbandsorganisierte Sport: Ein Zusammenschluss von (Wahl-)Gemeinschaften?* Münster: Waxmann.

Teubert, H., Borggrefe, C., Cachay, K., & Thiel, A. (2006). *Spitzensport und Schule. Möglichkeiten und Grenzen einer strukturellen Kopplung in der Nachwuchsförderung.* Schorndorf: Hofmann.

Thiel, A. (2002). *Konflikte in Sportspielmannschaften des Spitzensports. Entstehung und Management.* Schorndorf: Hofmann.

Thiel, A., Mayer, J., & Digel, H. (2010). *Gesundheit im Spitzensport. Eine sozialwissenschaftliche Analyse.* Schorndorf: Hofmann.

Thiel, A., Meier, H., & Cachay, K. (2006). *Hauptberuflichkeit im Sportverein. Voraussetzungen und Hindernisse.* Schorndorf: Hofmann.

Thiel, A., Seiberth, K., & Mayer, J. (2013). *Sportsoziologie. Ein Lehrbuch in 13 Lektionen.* Aachen: Meyer & Meyer.

Tiemann, H. (2008). Soziologie des Behindertensports. In K. Weis & R. Gugutzer (Eds.), *Handbuch der Sportsoziologie* (pp. 379−388). Schorndorf: Hofmann.

Timm, W. (1979). *Sportvereine in der Bundesrepublik Deutschland. Teil II: Organisations-, Angebots- und Finanzstruktur.* Schorndorf: Hofmann.

Voigt, D. (1992). *Sportsoziologie, Soziologie des Sports.* Frankfurt a. M.: Diesterweg.

Weiss, O. (1999). *Einführung in die Sportsoziologie.* Wien: WUV-Universitätsverlag.

Weiss, O., & Norden, G. (2013). *Einführung in die Sportsoziologie.* Münster: Waxmann.

Wicker, P., & Breuer, C. (2013). Understanding the importance of organizational resources to explain organizational problems: Evidence from nonprofit sport clubs in Germany. *Voluntas, 24*(2), 461−484.

Winkler, J., & Karhausen, R.-R. (1985). *Verbände im Sport. Eine empirische Analyse des Deutschen Sportbundes und ausgewählter Mitgliedsorganisationen.* Schorndorf: Hofmann.

Winkler, J., & Weis, K. (1995). *Soziologie des Sports. Theorieansätze, Forschungsergebnisse und Forschungsperspektiven.* Opladen: Westdeutscher Verlag.

Wippert, P.-M. (2002). *Karriereverlust und Krise.* Schorndorf: Hofmann.

Wopp, C. (2006). *Handbuch zur Trendforschung im Sport.* Aachen: Meyer & Meyer.

CHAPTER 12

SOCIOLOGY OF SPORT: HUNGARY

Tamás Dóczi and Andrea Gál

ABSTRACT

The history of Hungarian sociology of sport can be divided to two periods, which are different in terms of conditions but show similarities in many other ways. In the period between the mid-1960s and 1989, the intensive development of the discipline was hindered by the repression of sociology and the lack of interest in sport on the part of social scientists. However, the unique social functions of (elite) sport still created a demand for scientific inquiry. In the second period, from 1989 to the present day, the conditions of research freedom were established; yet, sport as an area for research failed to attract the attention of social scientists. In this respect, today's scholars of sociology of sport face similar problems as the founders of the discipline, although the changing economic conditions in terms of research funding and institutionalization provide a more favorable environment for the scientific investigation of sport-related social issues. As a result, the number of sport sociological publications has steadily increased in the past decade and Hungarian scholars have the opportunity to participate in international conferences and

Sociology of Sport: A Global Subdiscipline in Review
Research in the Sociology of Sport, Volume 9, 207–225
ISSN: 1476-2854/doi:10.1108/S1476-285420160000009016

research projects. This chapter reviews sociology of sport in Hungary, with a focus on historical heritage, institutionalization, the current situation, and barriers to development.

Keywords: Sociology of sport; Hungary; 1989–1990 transition; interdisciplinary research; sport sciences

INTRODUCTION: HISTORY OF THE SOCIOLOGY OF SPORT IN HUNGARY

The status of sociology of sport in any country depends on what traditions sport is built on and what functions it has in that society, as well as how the political, economic, and cultural environments have determined the development of social sciences and sociology in particular and the degree of freedom related to practicing sociology. In Hungary, this development was mainly influenced by (1) the unique social functions of (elite) sport, (2) the repression of sociology during state socialism, (3) the lack of interest in sport on the part of social scientists, and (4) the changing context after the 1989–1990 political and economic transition, in terms of research funding and institutionalization.

In Hungary, sport, especially elite sport, has always had an important political function, as a means of gaining international prestige and domestic legitimacy, and the 168 Olympic gold medals won between 1896 and 2012 by Hungarian athletes contributed to the recognition of this small (93,000 km^2) Central-Eastern European country with a population of 10 million as a sports nation. At the same time, these successes have also served as one of the most important sources of national pride among the citizens (Dóczi, 2012).

After World War II, in Hungary, as a state socialist country, sport was assigned unique social functions: health education, defense, patriotism, productivity, modernization, social integration, and international recognition (Riordan, 1990). While in Western societies the development of civil society was not restricted by the state and the business sectors, in the east, civil society, similarly to other areas of social life, was governed by politics (Andorka, 1993). Even so, in the four decades of socialism, sport was one of the few areas of culture where fundamental values could not be influenced by state intervention.

As a source of political legitimacy, elite sport, in many ways, had a privileged status in the socialist system. This was reflected in substantial state support mainly through the ownership of clubs by large state-owned companies, and in athletes' opportunities to be quasi professional, enjoy a better-than-average standard of living, and travel more freely than the general public. After the 1989–1990 political and economic transition, the previously existing channels of state support ceased, and the ownership of clubs shifted from public to private, which posed a serious challenge to sport stakeholders, who considered sport to be a loser of the transition (Földesi, 1993).

Contrary to sport, the evolution and functioning of the social sciences (among them sociology) took a much different path in the four decades of state socialism, in terms of political intervention and social functions. After 1948, in the countries of the communist bloc, the political regimes used social sciences to serve the aims of politics and, with the exception of Poland, research and education in sociology was banned. Therefore, the contradictions and the social dynamics of the sport system could not be revealed until the ban was lifted in some states, when dictatorships began to crumble. Since this process started relatively early and was more effective in Hungary compared to other Eastern European states, sociology was reborn, and sport sociology could also gain ground from the 1960s onward, decades earlier than, for example, in East Germany, or Romania (Földesiné, Gál, & Dóczi, 2010).

The First 25 Years: A Tolerated Discipline in a Soft Dictatorship

Due to the political restrictions on social sciences, in spite of the rich sporting traditions of the country, at the time of the early evolution of sociology of sport worldwide, social scientific investigations were not carried out in Hungarian sport. This forced intermission had a negative effect on the establishment of the discipline, even if it was one of the first branches of sociology to evolve when sociological research was given permission, although to a limited extent, from the mid-1960s. The presence of the official Marxist-Leninist ideology at research and educational institutions meant an obstacle, as well as the lack of methodologically proficient sociologists, international literature, and research organizations with traditions.

Sport sociological issues were first dealt with by physical education teachers, coaches, and philosophers (Földesi, 2015), whose efforts deserve recognition because they laid the foundations of the discipline and started to explore social phenomena related to sport amid the aforementioned obstacles. The sport sociological approach as an imperative was not emphasized by institutions; research began on the basis of individual interest based on a kind of social demand. The first school of sport sociology was formed around János Schiller at the University of Physical Education; it is mainly thanks to Schiller that the university was among the first higher education institutions to include a compulsory course of general sociology in the curriculum. Furthermore, it introduced sociology of sport as a specialized subject for physical education teachers and coaches. In 1965, when the International Committee for the Sociology of Sport (ICSS, predecessor of ISSA) was founded, the Hungarian Ferenc Hepp was among the first members. The first Hungarian sport sociological committee was established in 1968, relatively early in international comparison, within the framework of the Physical Education Scientific Committee, and played an active role in the promotion and development of sport sociology in the country.

The transition of sociology of sport from the group of banned sciences to that of tolerated, or even supported, sciences was somewhat fostered by the fact that in socialist countries, in the hope of elite sport success, even stricter dictatorships made some concessions to scientific research. It was a turning point in the spread of the discipline when in 1974 a compilation of sport sociological papers could be published (Balyi & Takács, 1974), allowing interested scholars in the field to look into foreign literature and read about international trends in theory and practice. This was further boosted by the visit of Barry D. McPherson and Gerald Kenyon to Eastern Europe in the mid-1970s who, with the aim of disseminating the sub-discipline in the region, gifted sport sociology books to scholars in Budapest. In the years prior to the 1989–1990 transition, intellectuals working in the sport system did not initiate reforms or protest against existing conditions, because even if they were aware of the shortcomings, they knew that compared with other sectors, sport was in a much better position (Földesi & Egressy, 2005). Therefore, until the 1980s, there were only a few attempts to challenge the prevailing political and ideological dogmas. From the middle of the decade, with the erosion of state socialism, more critical writings on the condition and crisis of Hungarian sport were published (Frenkl, 1986), and some previously taboo topics, such as the issue of doping, or social inequalities existing in sport, could also be put on the agenda (Földesiné, 1984; Frenkl, 1982). This tendency certainly reflects an increasing level of professional freedom, even more so, if contrasted with general sociological publications of the time.

The Second 25 Years: Between Sociology and Sport Science — Progress to Institutionalization and Scientific Recognition

After the 1989—1990 political and economic transition, ideological restrictions broke down, which made it possible to conduct research in a much wider range of topics and publish results for a wider public than in the previous regime. In many areas of sociology, researchers see it as a positive consequence of the transition that international relations could be established with foreign researchers and institutions without political restrictions. Although Hungarian sport sociologists had relatively better opportunities for establishing international connections even in the 10—15 years before the political transition, their more frequent participation in conferences and exchange programs had mainly financial barriers. These issues can still be considered as a challenge, but Hungarian and EU grants have been useful incentives for sociologists dealing with sport to join large-scale international research projects.

After the political and economic transition, Hungarian sociology of sport managed to keep the reputation it gained in the 1970s and 1980s. The circle of partners extended, researchers were invited to participate in international projects and to serve international organizations in various positions. Its strong international position also contributed to the recognition of the discipline in Hungary. From the 1990s, sociology of sport was represented in various scientific organizations. As a section of the Hungarian Sociological Association, and from the mid-2000s, it is also present among the sociological sub-committees of the Hungarian Academy of Sciences.

Nevertheless, Hungarian sport sociology was not only present in sociological associations, but also, and maybe in a more articulate way, became a respected branch in sport sciences. The sport sociological sub-committee of the Hungarian Society of Sport Science was established in the early 1990s and has been active since that time. The first president of the sport sociological sub-committee was Gyöngyi Szabó Földesi, and the secretary was Gábor Gáldi, both with a background in sociology and physical education. The committee had approximately 10—12 members, and mainly dealt with issues such as the integration of sociology of sport in university curricula, potential areas of research, and creating the frameworks for future publications. However, the enthusiastic professional community could not become stronger with the progress of time, mainly because the funding opportunities for research remained limited, which proved to be an obstacle of further, organizational-level professionalization. From the beginning of the 2000s, the EU integration of Hungary, the transformation of higher education (Bologna process), and the opportunities for higher education institutions to participate in national and EU projects have resulted in sport sociologists being engaged in their research activities primarily in their workplace, isolated from one another.

Teamwork is mainly characteristic in large-scale EU-funded projects, where the workload requires such cooperation, but typically it is not only sociologists, but also experts in economy, management and pedagogy that are joined in a team. In recent years it has also become more frequent that sport sociologists are invited to contribute to the projects of national and international sport organizations, partly because of the theoretical knowledge they have, and partly because of the methods they can mobilize for data collection and analysis.

NUMBER OF SCHOLARS: A SMALL COMMUNITY IN A LOOSE NETWORK

In Hungary, sport sociologists have not established an independent professional organization, which can be explained by the low number of scholars with a degree in sociology (active in sport-related research), or a PhD in sport science (with a sociological focus); their numbers can be estimated as between 10 and 20 in the country. It has to be added that a much broader circle of social scientists dealing with sport (specialists of education, management, psychology, history, etc.) deal with sport sociological topics and use the methods of the discipline to investigate them.

The fact that very few mainstream sociologists deal with sport issues is also reflected in the fact that the topic of sport is scarcely included in general sociological training programs and curricula, and it is not characteristic of PhD programs in general sociology to include sport as a topic for scientific enquiry. Contrary to this, sport sociological training and research are much more embedded in higher education institutions specialized in sport, where it is included as a separate subject in the master's and bachelor's programs of physical education teachers, coaches, recreation specialists, and sport managers.

The number of sport sociological investigations significantly increased after the Hungarian Accreditation Committee accepted the PhD program of the Hungarian University of Physical Education in 1997. The program incorporates three sub-programs, one devoted to social sciences, and there have been a number of PhD dissertations (approximately 20) written in a sport sociological topic (not necessarily by qualified sociologists), and several others utilizing the methodological tools of sociology.

Owing to its traditions in sport-related research and the presence of emblematic figures in Hungarian sociology of sport, the University of Physical Education[1] in Budapest, the leading sport science higher education institution of the country, has been the center of the Hungarian sociology of sport movement, with the intellectual leadership of Gyöngyi Szabó Földesi. The university runs the only doctoral school where a PhD can be obtained in sport sciences and sociology of sport in particular, which has made it possible for researchers with various backgrounds to join the small community of sport sociologists. The majority of them now work at different regional sport science centers in the countryside (e.g., Debrecen, Szeged, Pécs) and earned their doctoral or PhD degrees at this university, under Földesi's supervision. On the other hand, there are only a few scholars working at non-sport faculties and institutions who still have a stronger connection with the discipline.

Although most of the people involved in sport sociological research know each other personally, there has been no interest in establishing a formalized nationwide professional network. Nevertheless, since the circle of the profession is very small, sport sociologists follow each other's work and engage in a scientific dialogue. In recent years, the conferences of the Hungarian Society of Sport Science have been the most important regular events for sport sociologists working in different institutions of the country to exchange ideas and research results. In addition to these conferences, occasional international conferences and the defenses of PhD dissertations in a sport sociological topic, or book launch events, have also provided a platform for professional encounters.

THE RESEARCH ENVIRONMENT IN HUNGARY: BARRIERS AND FACILITATORS

Since its infancy, sociology of sport in Hungary has had an ambivalent reception, which could simplistically be explained by the fact that although elite sport success has always been important for the public, the majority of social scientists have underestimated the social significance of sport and failed to consider it as a serious research area (Földesi, 2015). At the same time, people working in the field of sport do agree that political, economic, social, and cultural factors fundamentally define the functioning of sport.

However, the usefulness of sociology of sport is still often questioned, since the research results of sociology do not directly contribute to performance enhancement. As a consequence, sociology of sport can be considered as the stepchild of sociology and sport sciences, which of course, has also had an impact on its perspectives and prestige.

This marginalized situation is still more manifested in mainstream sociology, whereas in sport scientific research, due to the spread of interdisciplinary approach, sociology of sport has also gained ground. This is further boosted by the tendency that while in the period of state socialism, sport policy was almost exclusively focused on elite sport performance and the efficiency of the sport talent management system, since the 1989–1990 transition, other areas of sport have also been given more attention. Therefore, sociological investigations have been carried out in the field of school physical education and sport, university sport, sport for people with disabilities, and leisure sport, which were financially supported through various calls for proposals.

The latter area came into the focus of research because physical activity is increasingly seen as a crucial factor in the demographic situation and health status of the population. Yet, a contradiction can still be marked in the fact that although leisure sport development has become a more emphatic goal of sport policy (at least in rhetoric), the results of sport sociological research are not necessarily relied on during the implementation of related action plans. This contradiction could not be resolved, even when the emblematic figure of Hungarian sociology of sport, Gyöngyi Szabó Földesi, was the president of the National Leisure Sport Federation, and was a member of the National Sports Council, the advisory organization of the government.

Since the world of sport is more interested in research results that can be benefited from in the short term, these attitudes have limited the range of research topics and researchers' intellectual-theoretical activity as well. Notwithstanding this, there have been attempts to establish a theoretically and empirically based sport sociology that can challenge existing paradigms, but so far, these efforts have not managed to achieve this paradigm shift (Földesi, 2015).

Nevertheless, sociology of sport did make some progress toward academic recognition in Hungary. Shortly after the PhD program of the University of Physical Education was launched, the Sport Science Committee of the Hungarian Academy of Sciences was established within the Committee on Preventive Medicine in the Section of Medical Sciences. For years, the aforementioned Gyöngyi Szabó Földesi was a member of the committee, ensuring the representation of social sciences in general and sociology of sport in particular in the Academy. Her academic doctoral thesis, accepted in 2006, has so far been the single one in a sport sociological topic.

SOCIOLOGICAL INVESTIGATIONS OF SPORT: FROM LIMITED SCOPE SOCIOGRAPHY TO INTERDISCIPLINARY RESEARCH

In the 1960s and 1970s, the first generation of Hungarian sport sociologists, mainly coming from a physical education or sport background, conducted empirical research in all areas of sport that were considered as important (elite sport, leisure sport, school sport, and physical education), but with a limited scope (sport socialization, sporting habits, equal opportunities, social stratification and mobility in sport, motivations, values, lifestyle, and career of elite athletes). Investigations were mostly carried out on a micro level, and made it possible to form moderate conclusions and ad hoc theories (Földesi, 1989).

Owing to the accidental nature of topic selection for scientific enquiry, the significance of critical essays and columns, as well as sociographic writings, increased in the professional discourse on social issues in sport. Sociography at that time was generally used as a substitute for sociology, with writings in literary rather than scientific style. Between 1960 and 1989, Hungarian authors published 10 books and nearly 200 papers and book chapters, which reflects a fair level of productivity, even when comparing it to other areas of sociology or sport sciences. These contributions mostly relied on empirical research. However, the standard of papers highly varied and the majority of them could rather be labeled as popular science. Even so, between 1978 and 1989, 17 university doctoral dissertations were written in a sport sociological topic, indicating some improvement in quality, although the majority of candidates, after obtaining their degree, did not continue their scientific activity (Földesi, 1989; Földesiné et al., 2010).

After the 1989–1990 political and economic transition, sport sociologists in Hungary were facing the transformation of social conditions and the restructuring of the sport system at the same time. As the field of sport was by and large ignored by general sociology, sport sociologists had to undertake the task of analyzing what was happening in sport. As the political-ideological restrictions ceased, the range of research areas increased, and publications in international journals and books became more frequent, mostly in English.

Some sport sociologists were investigating the impact of the political transition on the sport system (Bakonyi, 2007; Földesi, 1993, 1996c; Földesi & Egressy, 2005; Laki & Nyerges, 2006), or the place of Hungarian sport in the context of the European Union and globalization (Dóczi, 2012; Földesi, 2003). Others turned to exploring general social issues in the field of sport, such as social inequalities and social mobility (Földesi, 2004a; Velenczei & Gál, 2011), the sport participation and the place of sport in lifestyle (Földesi, 1991; Földesiné, Gál, & Dóczi, 2008; Gáldi, 2004; Kozma, Bács, & Perényi, 2015; Piko & Keresztes, 2008), or the value orientation of sport participants (Perényi, 2010a, 2010b; Piko & Keresztes, 2006).

The gender aspects of sport were also given attention (Béki & Gál, 2013; Földesi, 1998; Gál, 2008; Gál, Velenczei, & Kovács, 2010), as well as the situation of university sport and students' participation (Baltatescu & Kovács, 2012, 2013; Földesi, 2005; Kovács, 2013, 2015). A number of sport sociologists dealt with the issue of fandom, social/national identity, and football hooliganism (Dóczi, 2012; Földesi, 1996a, 1996b, 2001; Hadas, 2000; Molnar, 2010), and research focusing on the unique situation of Hungarian football has also emerged (Molnar, 2011, 2014; Molnar, Doczi, & Gál, 2011; Szerovay, Itkonen, & Vehmas, 2015). Recently, some researchers have turned to specific types of "postmodern" sporting activities and phenomena (Dóczi, 2009; Földesi, 2004b; Perényi, 2015; Pólus-Thiry & Rédei, 2012), and the social consequences of the recently introduced measure of daily physical education in schools (Vámos & Dóczi, 2015).

Increasing specialization within the social sciences has brought about the emergence of new disciplines whose topics may overlap with sport sociological themes (Földesi, 2015). This tendency can mostly be observed in the case of public health, marketing, and management, which, although from a different angle, are all interested in topics of sport sociological relevance, such as sport participation and consumption, sport policy, intervention programs and evaluation, or mega sport events.

It is a general tendency that sport sociological research results are not very well known outside the small circle of experts, and are mostly published in sport science journals and books. However, in spite of the scientific-professional isolation of the discipline, some sport sociologists are invited by the media to discuss sport-related topics of public interest, which is much less characteristic of sociologists in general, who do not often appear in the media as "talking heads," lagging behind economists and political scientists when it comes to the discussion of broader social issues.

APPROACHES IN THEORY AND RESEARCH

As mentioned above, sociology of sport in Hungary did not have adequate human resources in terms of quality or quantity to develop theories that could contribute to the progress of the discipline on the international level. The imbalance between theory and evidence has been characteristic throughout the history of sociology of sport in Hungary, and it is a general tendency that sport sociologists, when looking for a theoretical basis for their research, draw on theories of general sociology.

Owing to the institutional embeddedness of sociology of sport (that is, its stronger affiliation with sport sciences), empirical studies are predominantly carried out using quantitative methods. The reason behind this is that sport sciences, despite their interdisciplinary nature, imply a natural scientific imperative, which is reflected in the requirements of PhD theses and the guidelines for scientific journals in terms of structure and content as well. Therefore, while in international sociology of sport, qualitative methods such as interviews, anthropological observations, and discourse analyses have been emerging in the past few decades, these research methods are not part of the mainstream research protocol in Hungarian sport sciences, which rather accept them as complementary methods to large-scale quantitative investigations. The outcome of this contradiction is that sport sociologists, when accommodating themselves to one context, may have difficulties in publishing their results in the other.

THE CONTRIBUTION OF VARIOUS GENERATIONS TO THE DEVELOPMENT OF SOCIOLOGY OF SPORT

The first significant publication that made a great contribution to the development of sociology of sport in Hungary was the collection of studies published in 1974 and edited by István Balyi and Ferenc Takács, who were working at the University of Physical Education. The volume included studies by internationally well-known sport sociologists. Four years later, Schiller (1978) published his book *Some Questions of Sport Sociology*, which was an effort to underline the importance of the sociological approach of sport as a complex social phenomenon. This idea was strengthened by Frenkl (an academic in sports medicine with a deep interest in the social aspects of sport) in his book on the sport of the next century (1979), in which he referred to the importance of interdisciplinary analysis and the role of sport sociology. In parallel with this, an increasing number of critical studies were published about social issues in sport (Földesiné, 1984; Frenkl, 1986).

From the 1980s, the physical education teacher and sociologist, Földesi became the leading figure on Hungarian sociology of sport. Throughout her career, she has published more than 80 studies (including 10 in the *International Review for the Sociology of Sport*) and 13 books between 1976 and 2016. In these, she dealt with elite sport and Olympic athletes (1984), university sport (2005), the situation of leisure sport and sport for all in different social groups (1998, 2009, 2010, 2011), and sport consumption (Földesi, 1996b; Földesiné et al., 2008). Her edited volume *The Intellectual Panorama of Hungarian Sport* (1996) is one of the most important books from the 1990s, compiling prominent sport scientists' analyses of the impact of the 1989—1990 transition on sport. In 2006, she was the first sport sociologist to receive an academic doctoral degree with her dissertation written on the same topic. She has received several awards for her career from national and international organizations, including an honorary membership to ISSA. In 2010, a volume containing her most important publications was published (Földesiné, 2010), and in the same year, she was the co-author of the first course book of sociology of sport in Hungarian (Földesiné et al., 2010).

As a professor at the University of Physical Education, she has had an important role in guiding and mentoring young researchers from Hungary and abroad alike, by fostering publication activity and PhD thesis supervision; her former mentees are active in higher education and research, as well as in sport organizations. Their scientific progress has resulted in valuable publications, which broadened the spectrum of research topics in Hungary.

Two of her former PhD students (the authors of this chapter) have become her colleagues, and this group has published a number of important books (Földesi & Dóczi, 2011; Földesi & Gál, 2005; Földesiné et al., 2008, 2010), including the previously mentioned first Hungarian course book. Andrea Gál conducted her PhD research in connection with the media representation of men's and women's sport, contributing to the international project entitled "A Global Content Analysis of Sport

Newspaper Coverage" (Gál et al., 2010). In addition to gender-related topics, her main research focus has been on leisure sport participation and policy implications (2010, 2014). In his PhD research, Tamás Dóczi explored the relationship between sport and national identity in the context of globalization and the 1989–1990 transition (2012), and since then, has been focusing on sport and social inclusion (2014). In 2015, to pay respect to their mentor, they edited a collection of studies from the former students, colleagues, and friends of Gyöngyi Szabó Földesi, including several sport sociological papers.

Another example coming from the same scientific school is Bakonyi, whose book *State, Civil Society, Sport* (2007) analyzed the characteristics and tendencies of sport policy before and after 1989. Perényi, also a former student, has been active in research on sport participation and value preferences (2010a, 2010b, 2014, 2015; Kozma et al., 2015), and is currently working at the University of Debrecen.

In recent years, undertaking research projects with neighboring countries has also become popular among Hungarian sport sociologists. A highlight of such cooperation was the 2011 conference entitled "Sport and Society in the V4 Countries,"[2] where social scientists exchanged ideas about the situation of sport in the region. Another successful project was the Romanian, Ukrainian, and Hungarian joint research investigating the sporting habits of university students living in the cross-border area, and the relationship between healthy and unhealthy behavior, subjective well-being, achievement, and sport as a protective factor, with the contribution of talented Hungarian sport sociologist, Kovács (Baltatescu & Kovács, 2012, 2013; Kovács, 2013, 2015).

THE FUTURE OF HUNGARIAN SOCIOLOGY OF SPORT

Contemporary sociologists of sport are in a unique situation in Eastern Europe as "participant observers" of the recent political changes and their effects on sport. It is a particular challenge for sport sociology in the region is to identify and critically analyze the intended and unintended consequences of the political and economic transition of sport (Földesi, 2015). Although the functions of sport changed, the evolution of sport as a social sub-system and sport policy can be characterized with continuity; the

success of elite sport remained a key objective in spite of the limited financial possibilities (Dóczi, 2012). Consequently, the Hungarian sport system
has remained Olympics-centered, which is also reflected in the fact that
while the Hungarian Olympic Committee is financially and strategically
responsible for all areas of sport, its activity, as well as managerial recruit-
ment, reflects a strong elite sport bias. The sport system in Hungary shows
the characteristics of a unique sub-culture with special mechanisms and
beliefs, in which leaders, having been socialized in the privileged elite sport
system of state socialism, continue to expect state support and maintain a
discourse of success in exchange. However, in this kind of discourse, critical, out-of-the-box thinking is not much encouraged by decision-makers,
which narrows the opportunities for funding sociologically relevant
research in sport.

It is a precondition of the scientific recognition of the discipline that its
relations with sociology be strengthened through the investigation of
sport as a social sub-system in a broader context. The other precondition
of development lies in decreasing the imbalance between empirical
research and general social theory by promoting a more intellectual
approach. It is likely that the spectrum of sport sociological research will
continue to broaden and previously less explored areas of sport, such as
university sport, or sport and disability, will also get more attention.
Complying with international trends it can also be expected that research
methodology will be more diversified, with more emphasis on qualitative techniques.

Today, Hungarian sociology of sport possesses the traditions and the
international embeddedness necessary for its future development, which is
well illustrated by the fact that the 2016 World Congress of Sociology of
Sport is to be held in Budapest. This event will hopefully contribute to the
recognition of the discipline in Hungary, foster exchange between
Hungarian and international scholars, and open a global perspective to the
young generation of researchers in the country.

NOTES

1. Between 2000 and 2014, the University was integrated into the Semmelweis
(Medical) University, as the Faculty of Physical Education and Sport Science; since
September 2014, it has been independent again.
2. V4 stands for the Visegrád 4 countries: Poland, Czech Republic, Slovakia,
and Hungary.

FIVE KEY READINGS

1. Földesi, G. S. (1989). **Past and present state of sport sociology in Hungary.** *International Review for the Sociology of Sport, 1,* 1–16.

Földesi's paper provides information on the development of sociology of sport in Hungary prior to the 1989–1990 political and economic transition, with regard to political-ideological restrictions, social and theoretical influences, and institutionalization.

2. Földesi, G. S. (2015). **Assessing the sociology of sport: On world inequalities and unequal development.** *International Review for the Sociology of Sport, 4–5,* 442–447.

Földesi's article reflects on the development of sociology of sport from an Eastern European perspective and on some special challenges of sociology of sport in the region.

3. Földesi, G. S., & Egressy, J. (2005). **Post-transformational trends in Hungarian sport (1995–2004).** *European Journal for Sport and Society, 2,* 85–96.

This paper provides a comprehensive analysis of the situation of sport in Hungary after the 1989–1990 political and economic transition from modernization perspectives, in the dimensions of over-politicization, re-centralization, and paternalism.

4. Gál, A. (2008). **Social status of Hungarian (sports)women before and after the 1989–1990 political system change.** *European Journal for Sport and Society, 2,* 195–210.

Gál's article focuses on the situation of Hungarian sportswomen, and how the politics of "state feminism" was manifested in reality. The dimensions of the analysis include the financial situation, studying opportunities, preparation for civil life, social capital, and the opportunities to translate social capital to economic capital.

5. Dóczi, T. (2012). **Gold fever(?) Sport and national identity – The Hungarian case.** *International Review for the Sociology of Sport, 47*(2), 163–180.

Dóczi's paper analyzes the relationship between sport and national identity in Hungary, in the context of globalization and the 1989–1990 political and economic transition. It offers an insight into the unique social functions of sport in Hungary and the discourses defining the way of thinking in sport policy.

REFERENCES

Andorka, R. (1993). The socialist system and its collapse in Hungary: An interpretation in terms of modernisation theory. *International Sociology, 3*, 317–337.

Bakonyi, T. (2007). *Állam, civil társadalom, sport [State, civil society, sport].* Budapest: Kossuth Kiadó Zrt.

Baltatescu, S., & Kovács, K. (2012). Sport participation and subjective well-being among University students in the Hungarian-Romanian-Ukrainian Cross-border area. In G. Pusztai, A. Hatos, & T. Ceglédi (Eds.), *Third mission of higher education in a cross-border region. Educational research in central and Eastern Europe I* (pp. 134–148). Debrecen: CHERD-H, University of Debrecen.

Baltatescu, S., & Kovács, K. (2013). Sport and subjective well-being among Romanian and Hungarian students. The mediation of resilience and perceived health. In E. Zamfir & F. Maggino (Eds.), *The European culture for human rights: The right to happiness* (pp. 174–191). Newcastle: Cambridge Scholars Publishing.

Balyi, I., & Takács, F. (1974). *Sportszociológia [Sociology of sport].* Budapest: Közgazdasági és Jogi Könyvkiadó.

Béki, P., & Gál, A. (2013). Rhythmic Gymnastics vs. Boxing: Gender stereotypes from the two poles of female sport. *Physical Culture and Sport. Studies and Research, 58*(1), 5–16.

Dóczi, T. (2009). Active sport tourism in the Hungarian population: Current trends and perspectives. *Physical Culture and Sport. Studies and Research, 46*(1), 261–267.

Dóczi, T. (2012). Gold fever(?) Sport and national identity – The Hungarian case. *International Review for the Sociology of Sport, 2*, 163–180.

Dóczi, T. (2014). *Sport és hátrányos helyzet [Sport and social disadvantage].* In J. Farkas (Ed.), *A fizikai aktivitás és a sport magyarországi dimenzióinak feltárása* (pp. 104–128). Budapest: Magyar Sporttudományi Társaság.

Frenkl, R. (1979). *A jövő század sportja [Sport of the next century].* Budapest: Sportpropaganda.

Frenkl, R. (1982). *Nem fog fájni [It will not hurt].* Budapest: Sport Kiadó.

Frenkl, R. (1986). A magyar sport eltékozolt évtizede [The wasted decade of Hungarian sport]. *Valóság, 10*, 24–34.

Földesi, G. S. (1989). Past and present state of sport sociology in Hungary. *International Review for the Sociology of Sport, 1*, 1–16.

Földesi, G. S. (1991). From mass sport to the "Sport for All" movement in the socialist countries in Eastern Europe. *International Review for the Sociology of Sport, 4*, 239–258.

Földesi, G. S. (1993). The transformation of sport in Eastern Europe: The Hungarian case. *Journal of Comparative Physical Education and Sport, 1*, 5–21.

Földesi, G. S. (1996a). Football, racism and xenophobia in Hungary: Racist and xenophobic behaviour of football spectators. In U. Merkel & W. Tokarski (Eds.), *Racism and xenophobia in European football* (pp. 169–186). Aachen: Meyer und Meyer Verlag.

Földesi, G. S. (1996b). Social and demographic characteristics of Hungarian football fans and their motivations for attending matches. *International Review for the Sociology of Sport*, 4, 395–412.

Földesi, G. S. (1996c). Sports policy in Hungary. In L. Chalip, A. Johnson, & L. Stachura (Eds.), *National sports policies. International handbook* (pp. 187–221). Westport, CT: Grenwood Press.

Földesi, G. S. (1998). Life style and aging: The Hungarian case. *Women Sport and Physical Education Journal*, 1, 171–190.

Földesi, G. S. (2001). Aggression and violence in sport from sociological perspective. In H. Ruskin & M. Lämmer (Eds.), *Fair play: Violence in sport and society* (pp. 13–29). Jerusalem: The Hebrew University of Jerusalem.

Földesi, G. S. (2003). Sport and European integration: The Hungarian case. In J. Kosiewicz & K. Obodynski (Eds.), *Sport in the mirror of the values* (pp. 50–58). Rzeszow: EASS.

Földesi, G. S. (2004a). Social status and mobility of Hungarian elite athletes. *International Journal of the History of Sport*, 5, 711–726.

Földesi, G. S. (2004b). Sport tourism: New circumstances-new strategies. In J. Kosiewicz & K. Obodynski (Eds.), *Sport in changing Europe* (pp. 197–215). Rzeszov: KORAW.

Földesi, G. S. (2005). University sport from a sociological perspective. In J. Kosiewicz (Ed.), *Sport, culture and society* (pp. 345–356). Warsawa: AWF.

Földesi, G. S. (2009). Class or mass: (Sport for all) policy at a crossroads. *Physical Culture and Sport. Studies and Research*, 1, 147–156.

Földesi, G. S. (2010). Social exclusion/inclusion in the context of Hungarian sport. *Physical Culture and Sport Studies and Research*, 1, 44–59.

Földesi, G. S. (2011). Hungary. In M. Nicholson, R. Hoye, & B. Houlihan (Eds.), *Participation in sport. International policy perspectives* (pp. 76–90). London: Routledge.

Földesi, G. S. (2015). Assessing the sociology of sport: On world inequalities and unequal development. *International Review for the Sociology of Sport*, 4–5, 442–447.

Földesi, G. S., & Dóczi, T. (Eds.). (2011). *The interaction of sport and society in the V4 Countries*. Budapest: MSTT.

Földesi, G. S., & Egressy, J. (2005). Post-transformational trends in Hungarian sport (1995–2004). *European Journal for Sport and Society*, 2, 85–96.

Földesi, G. S., & Gál, A. (Eds.). (2005). *New social conditions in sport 1990–2005*. Budapest: MSTT.

Földesiné, Sz. Gy. (1984). *Magyar olimpikonok önmagukról és a sportról [Hungarian Olympic athletes about themselves and sport]*. Budapest: Közgazdasági és Jogi Könyvkiadó.

Földesiné, Sz. Gy. (Ed.). (1996). *A magyar sport szellemi körképe [Intellectual Panorama of Hungarian Sport]*. Budapest: OTSH-MOB.

Földesiné, Sz. Gy. (2010). *Fejezetek a magyar sportszociológia múltjából és jelenéből [Chapters from the past and present of Hungarian sociology of sport]*. Budapest: Double Printing Kft.

Földesiné, Sz. Gy., Gál, A., & Dóczi, T. (Eds.). (2008). *Társadalmi riport a sportról 2008 [Social report on sport 2008]*. Budapest: ÖM-MSTT.

Földesiné, Sz. Gy., Gál, A., & Dóczi, T. (2010). *Sportszociológia [Sociology of sport]*. Budapest: SE-TSK.

Gál, A. (2008). Social status of Hungarian (sports) women before and after the 1989–1990 political system change. *European Journal for Sport and Society*, 2, 195–210.

Gál, A. (2010). Elite sport and leisure sport in Hungary: The double trouble. *Physical Culture and Sport. Studies and Research*, *1*, 72–77.

Gál, A. (2014). A nők sportjának jellegzetességei [Characteristics of women's sport]. In J. Farkas (Ed.), *A fizikai aktivitás és a sport magyarországi dimenzióinak feltárása* (pp. 84–103). Budapest: Magyar Sporttudományi Társaság.

Gál, A., Velenczei, A., & Kovács, Á. (2010). Hungary. An unchanged situation in a changing society: The Hungarian case. In T. Bruce, J. Hovden, & P. Markula (Eds.), *Sportswomen at the Olympics: A global content analysis of newspaper coverage* (pp. 141–152). Rotterdam: Sense Publishers.

Gáldi, G. (2004). *Szabadidő-struktúra és fizikai rekreáció Magyarországon 1963–2000 között, életmód-időmérleg vizsgálatok tükrében [Structure of leisure and physical recreation in Hungary between 1963 and 2000, in the mirror of time use studies]*. PhD-dissertation, Semmelweis Egyetem, Budapest.

Hadas, M. (2000). Football and social identity: The case of Hungary in the 20th century. *Sports Historian*, *2*, 43–66.

Kovács, K. (2013). Bourdieu, Hradil és Bandura elméleteinek vizsgálata a sportra vonatkozóan: A társadalmi, környezeti és egyéni tényezők hatása a partiumi régió hallgatóinak sportolására [Examining the theories of Bourdieu, Hradil and Bandura in relation to sport: Effect of social, environmental and individual factors on students' sporting habits in the Hungarian-Romanian cross border area]. *Társadalomkutatás*, *2*, 175–193.

Kovács, K. (2015). A sportolás mint támogató faktor a felsőoktatásban. *[Sport activity as a supportive factor in higher education]* Oktatáskutatók könyvtára (p. 2). Debrecen: CHERD.

Kozma, G., Bács, Z., & Perényi, Sz. (2015). Differences and similarities in sports participation: Analysis considering regions and settlements in case of Hungary and European Union. *Journal of Physical Education and Sport*, *3*, 551–560.

Laki, L., & Nyerges, M. (2006). Changing of political system and role of sport – Competitive sport – In Hungary. *Kalokagathia*, *1–2*, 13–27.

Molnar, G. (2010). Re-discovering Hungarianness: The case of elite Hungarian footballers. In P. Dine & S. Crosson (Eds.), *Sport, representation and evolving identities in Europe* (pp. 239–262). Witney: Peter Lang.

Molnar, G. (2011). From the Soviet Bloc to the European community: Migrating professional footballers in and out of Hungary. In J. Maguire & M. Falcous (Eds.), *Sport and migration* (pp. 56–70). London: Routledge.

Molnar, G. (2014). The league of retirees: Foreigners' perception of Hungarian pro football. In R. Elliott & J. Harris (Eds.), *Football and Migration: Perspectives, places, players* (pp. 106–124). Oxon: Routledge.

Molnar, G., Doczi, T., & Gál, A. (2011). Socio-cultural organisation of Hungarian football. In H. Gammelsæter & B. Senaux (Eds.), *The organisation and governance of top football across Europe* (pp. 253–267). London: Routledge.

Perényi, Sz. (2010a). On the fields, in the stands, in front of TV – Value orientation of youth based on participation in, and consumption of, sports. *European Journal for Sport and Society*, *1*, 41–52.

Perényi, Sz. (2010b). The relation between sport participation and the value preferences of Hungarian youth. *Sport in Society: Cultures Commerce Media Politics*, *6*, 984–1000.

Perényi, Sz. (2014). *A mozgás szabadsága: A szabadidősport társadalmi, gazdasági és egészségü- gyi megközelítései. [Freedom of movement: social, economic and health care approaches to sport].* Debrecen: Debreceni Egyetem Gazdaságtudományi Kar.

Perényi, Sz. (2015). Hungary: The popularisation and expansion of amateur running culture. In J. Scheerder, K. Breedveld, & J. Borgers (Eds.), *Running across Europe: The rise and size of one of the largest sport markets* (pp. 63–86). Basingstoke: Palgrave Macmillan.

Piko, B. F., & Keresztes, N. (2006). Physical activity, psychosocial health and life goals among youth. *Journal of Community Health, 2,* 136–145.

Piko, B. F., & Keresztes, N. (2008). Sociodemographic and socioeconomic variations in leisure time physical activity in a sample of Hungarian youth. *International Journal of Public Health, 6,* 306–310.

Pólus-Thiry, É., & Rédei, Cs. (2012). Value orientation of people involved in action or extreme sports in Hungary. *European Journal for Sport and Society, 1–2,* 105–117.

Riordan, J. (1990). Commentary: A bright future shrouded in Mist. Sport in Eastern Europe. *Journal of Sport History, 1,* 69–74.

Schiller, J. (1978). *A sportszociológia néhány kérdése [Some questions of sport sociology].* Budapest: Sport Kiadó.

Szerovay, M., Itkonen, H., & Vehmas, H. (2015). 'Glocal' processes in peripheral football countries: A figurational sociological comparison of Finland and Hungary. *Soccer & Society,* doi:10.1080/14660970.2015.1067785

Vámos, Á., & Dóczi, T. (2015). Everyday physical education: Functional and dysfunctional consequences in Hungarian public education. *Physical Culture and Sport. Studies and Research, 1,* 20–30.

Velenczei, A., & Gál, A. (2011). New challenges, old answers in Hungarian sport: The case of talent management. *European Journal for Sport and Society, 4,* 281–297.

CHAPTER 13

SOCIOLOGY OF SPORT: ITALY

Caterina Satta

ABSTRACT

This chapter offers insight into Italian sociology of sport. It first describes the fragmented history from the 1990s to the present of a discipline that has never developed as a truly mature field in the academic environment, and then outlines some main areas of research strengths and outcomes. Four strands can be highlighted: fandom and organized soccer supporters (Ultras); changes in sport through the forces of television, new media, sponsorship, and globalization; hybridization of sport, mass media, and politics with Berlusconi's entrance into the Italian political scene and the advent of the era of "football politics"; and lastly, the body, bodywork, formal/informal sport activities, and gym culture with a microsociological perspective. However, despite their sociological relevance, these topics have had no regular, substantial development. They constitute separate fields of knowledge appearing in the sociological landscape in conjunction with social alarms, mainly related to soccer violence, or the emergence of new mass sport events or trends. It is difficult to predict what the future will hold. There is currently emerging attention to new urban sports and some sporadic in-depth ethnographic investigations of sport in micro arenas, such as soccer pitches, fitness gyms, and dance schools. Otherwise, Italian sociology of sport is folded into

Sociology of Sport: A Global Subdiscipline in Review
Research in the Sociology of Sport, Volume 9, 227–243
Copyright © 2017 by Emerald Group Publishing Limited
All rights of reproduction in any form reserved
ISSN: 1476-2854/doi:10.1108/S1476-285420160000009017

physical education science and is only considered as a field of inquiry for
physical health and wellbeing.

Keywords: Sociology of sport; Italy; sport; fandom; media; body

NOT PROPERLY GROWN UP YET: THE MISSING
HISTORY OF THE SOCIOLOGY OF SPORT IN ITALY

Sport has always received such scant, intermittent attention in sociological research in Italy that we could say that it is not young enough to be "a new field" and not developed enough to be considered a mature field. We could describe the history of the discipline as a missed opportunity for scientific reasons that I will seek to outline in this chapter.

In 2000, in *Rassegna Italiana di Sociologia*, Pippo Russo highlighted the problems in defining sociological studies on sport and their place within sociology and, as further evidence of this difficulty in Italy, wrote only a half page in the section called "The Sociology of Sport in Italy and New Strands of Research" (p. 311). One year later, in the same journal, Laura Balbo, a prominent Italian sociologist, called on the scientific community to reflect on the sociological relevance of sport, inexplicably left on the sidelines of the sociological debate. But these appeals have been largely ignored, considering the limited number of works published as a result.

With the exception, in the 1990s, of the works of Dal Lago (1990) and Roversi (1992) on soccer stadiums and fandom as ritual expression of social conflict (see also De Biasi, 1998; Roversi & Triani, 1995), and later, Porro's political analysis of social sport cultures (2001, 2013), and Lo Verde's work on leisure studies (2014), sport, seen within a Marxist division between work and free time, is commonly considered a minor activity, at best a "safety valve" for a society increasingly pressurized by a hyper-productive view of life.

The fact that sport, and Italian soccer in particular, is a popular cultural phenomenon, in the common sense of the term "popular" and not in a cultural studies perspective, may start to explain this "oversight." This fact has likely fostered an elitist attitude among social sciences concerned with everyday life, which have neglected sport. Whether this happens for extra-scientific reasons or due to "academic mechanisms that organize subject areas and knowledge, with their more or less implicit hierarchy of relevance and scientific respectability" (Balbo, 2001, p. 485), the exclusion of sport is a point of fact.

However, it would be unfair to the Italian scientific community to disregard the vast proliferation of studies on sport, especially in the field of education sciences (Farnè, 2008, and for sport in the urban environment, Zoletto & Wildemeersch, 2012) or in the academically younger area called *scienze motorie* ("physical education and sport science," dominated by psychology and physiology), but these disciplines keep a particular attitude toward sport. Education regards it as instrumental to the achievement of educational goals, while physical education and sport science is struggling to carve out an autonomous space, "caught in the difficult balance between anatomy and physiology and psychosocial and psychocultural analysis" (Simonicca, 2008, p. 10). We still have the challenge of saying something sociological about sport, not in order to multiply disciplinary boundaries, but because sport is already a social fact in itself, rich in implications that can be read within a sociological frame (Dunning & Elias, 1986).

Among the various fields of specialization and sociological analytical perspectives and interpretations in which sport can be framed (cultural studies, gender studies, studies on deviance, media and communication of sports events), the one that has grown most intensely is related to the mediatization and spectacularization of sport, mainly of soccer. Due to the "hybridization of sport, mass media and politics" (Porro & Russo, 2000, p. 348) in Italy starting in the 1990s, we could argue that Italian sociology of sport has clearly shifted toward sociology of communications and media research.

In contrast to the attention focused on mediated sport, sport grounded and practiced in place by diverse social actors and its relationship with urban studies has been the subject of little scholarly inquiry.

The connections between urban space and sport have been addressed in the international area of studies on youth subcultures, ethicized to varying degrees, referring to all those bodily practices that are conducted in an urban setting and are termed urban sports (Borden, 2001). Skateboarding, inline skating, or the newer discipline of parkour constitute new forms of sportsmanship (Ferrero Camoletto, 2008) in which, unlike in traditional sports, learning is not controlled and imparted by an expert, but is transmitted by improvisation and an autonomous exploration of space through the body and of the body through space. These experiences have usually been read through the lens of lifestyle (and the Italian debate is no exception), or the contrast between a dominant urban culture and a subordinate one (often young, male, and of foreign origin) trying to be included in the

public space through its specific codes and to give new meanings to space
(Queirolo Palmas, 2009). Among the (still) few Italian scholars who took
on this "new" topic of urban sports, we could mention the work of
Sebastiano Benasso conducted in Genoa (2015), the work by De Martini
Ugolotti (2015) in Turin, and, with a gender perspective on body construction, the work by Stagi (2015). They all sought to investigate the role of
sport/leisure practices and urban spaces in the processes of citizenship
construction amongst groups of young people (both native and of migrant
origins) in Italian cities and give us a picture not only of mainstream and
underground body practices but also of the city's dominant urban
dynamics and politics.

Alongside these new sport trends, traditional forms of sport are still
practiced regularly on a small scale, to the almost total indifference of the
social sciences. The only exception, which we will discuss later, is the work
based on Roberta Sassatelli's research on fitness gyms (2000, 2010).

With these few exceptions, most of the attention has been focused on
soccer, "both because it is the country's most popular sport and because it
has led trends affecting other major sports including cycling and motor
racing" (Lewis, 2009, p. 96).

An Archipelago in the Italian Peninsula: The Place of Sport Scholars in Academia

The dispersion of sociology of sport scholars in the Italian university landscape is evidence of the field's difficulty in emerging and the discipline's
resistance to accepting it. Rather than a condensed (even if minority) presence in one or more academic institutions, there are a few, isolated scholars. The few sociologists of sport, or more accurately, sociologists who
teach sociology of sport (as there is no official discipline group for sociology of sport, but it is included in three macrosectors of disciplines in political and social sciences, specifically general sociology and sociology of
cultural and communicative processes) work in different universities and
are primarily centered within physical education and sport science. This is
perhaps the main reason that sociology of sport has never developed as an
autonomous field of inquiry within Italian sociology. Sport has been
squeezed into a view of the body that is merely physical, kinetic, and medical, or in a psychosocial−psychocultural perspective. With few exceptions
Italian academia has yet to take on sport's cultural challenge.

These sociologists cannot be said to constitute a critical mass in academia. Unlike other subdisciplines, such as the history of sport and the psychology of sport, which have their own specialized associations (the SISS, Italian Society of Sport History, and SIPsiS, the Italian Society of Sport Psychology, respectively), there is no professional association in the field of Italian sociology of sport, and within the Italian Sociological Association (AIS), there are no research committees for the sociology of sport, or examples of intersections of working-thematic groups that have studied the subject of sport. Confirming the paucity of sport studies, we see that publications (such as the aforementioned work by Dal Lago) are from sociologists who do not include sport among their primary research interests. This is proof of how much sport has been predominantly perceived as a phenomenon unto itself, one to be considered mainly in conjunction with a rise in widespread public opinion, or more often, by full-fledged moral panics such as that caused by stadium violence by soccer fans. Many Italian-published works have predominantly focused on Italian soccer fans, doing so in a historical period starting in the early 1990s, the era of a mainly media-driven emergence of stadium violence (Dal Lago, 1990; Dal Lago & De Biasi, 1994; Dal Lago & Moscati, 1992; De Biasi, 1998; Roversi, 1990, 1992), to the 2000s. As De Biasi has noted, "We can see how [...] the sociology of the soccer fan, with few exceptions, stops at trying to respond to social alarm" (1998, p. 433).

The Academic Environment and Barriers to Research

We can say that sport is taken seriously in Italy and is widespread, again especially soccer, not only in terms of active sport participants, but also in terms of sports media consumption, as we see by the great popularity of sport newspapers and broadcasts, especially pay TV. However, the same cannot be said for sport in the academic environment. This could be an interesting aspect of Italian sociology of sport because the passion for soccer that crosses class and cultural background lines has nonetheless not succeeded in passing an "unconsciously aristocratic view that prevents researchers from using sport – a much more diverse phenomenon and richer in sociological implications than it appears to academic observation – as an extraordinary change sensor" (Porro, 2001, p. 9).

Though sport is one of the most popular topics of discussion for laymen, when we try to shift it to the academic environment, it has a greater stigma than other sociological topics for being a point of everyday conversation.

To quote Bourdieu, the sociology of sport "scorned by sociologists ... is despised by sportspersons" (1988, p. 153).

We see a gap between society and the academic sociological discipline that may be difficult to explain if not perhaps by considering the conditioning effect of the Marxist orientation that dominated the humanities and social sciences around the 1970s and ignored any object of study related to the sphere of leisure rather than work. Cultural studies was late to take root in Italy, as seen in the fact that the *Studi Culturali* (*Cultural Studies*) journal was established only in 2004 by a major Italian publisher (Il Mulino), which could have opened the way to such research. But in its 12 years, there have actually been very few articles on sport, even though in the editorial of its first issue, sport was among the topics of cultural analysis on which the journal intended to work. This lack is not the fault of the journal, other than for not promoting knowledge on the topic by translating essays and disseminating the debate happening outside of Italy. The fault lies in an actual scarcity of studies and research on sport from a cultural perspective. Moreover, the last and only work showing both an interest and an investment in this subsection of social sciences was a voluminous 1995 anthology edited by Roversi and Triani that collected a wide selection of foreign essays translated into Italian. The book provided an updated look at the significant understandings of different sports (not only soccer) and the different directions of research developed by the classics of sociology of sport, aiming to "convey the idea that sport and sports, far from banal activities whose sociological significance is infinitely less than 'serious' aspects of economic and political life, are indeed an area of considerable social meaning" (Roversi & Triani, 1995, p. 6). Both the authors' introduction and the work of translation itself (never repeated again) gave cause to think that the discipline would develop more productively. Now 20 years later, we can say that this did not happen and, most significantly, it never again gained the amount of attention within sociology as a whole that it had then.

The same cannot be said for disciplines such as pedagogy and psychology, which took up the topic much more seriously and focused study and specific teaching on it (such as game and sport pedagogy). These disciplines worked in support of national sports organizations to promote sport, the right to sport and a sport culture "for all." Pedagogy and psychology have a clear stance on sport; that is, they take a "positive" perspective on sport as a source of psychological and physical wellbeing, a tool of social inclusion, and an antidote to unhealthy eating habits. Though they have often identified enemies within sport, such as doping and extreme competitiveness, they always do so in the name of sport's intrinsic positive essence. Even sociology, with its qualitative research methods, such as participatory observation and in-depth interviews, teaches us to have a "certain viewpoint" on social phenomena (i.e., observing and experiencing the world as a participant, while retaining an observer's eye for analysis) and understand the facets and dimensions of individual or collective action that are more complex than "it's good for you" or "it's bad for you." Nonetheless, with the exception of a few areas that we will discuss in the next section, sociology has often suffered from a kind of cultural subalternity, merely copying a pedagogical approach and giving up on the challenge of building its own discourse on sport to be integrated with other disciplines.

Outside of academia, we find studies and statistical reports such as those by the Italian National Statistical Institute (ISTAT) in the findings of periodic surveys like "Multipurpose Study of Families" and "Aspects of Everyday Life," the Italian National Olympic Committee (CONI), and organizations like Italian Union of Sport for All (UISP), which examine Italians' sport practices and consumption. They work mainly through publications that statistically investigate trends in inclination to sport, actual sports practiced, preferences between athletic disciplines, the existence of sporting associations and facilities, and the economic value of sport in terms of employment and businesses directly tied to sport.

MAIN AREAS OF RESEARCH

Whereas, for the reasons given, we cannot consider sociology of sport in Italy as a *structured* research field, with established approaches and methods that are continuous over time, we can try to describe through areas of research the contribution that sociology has given over the last 25 years to building a field of research that we could say is "about" sport, even if only indirectly.

The main areas we can identify include those regarding fandom and Ultras groups, the relationship between sport and media (and recently between sport, media, and market), the political, organizational, and local and international governance of sport and, lastly, considerations of Foucauldian production of the body through new sport practices in fitness gyms. All of these sociological examples should be set in a historical context because they emerged from certain social phenomena, including (1) the rise of stadium violence with a scope (or, perhaps more precisely, with a scope of media coverage) not fitting the dominant cheerful image in Italy of Sundays at the stadium; (2) the increasingly central role played by media, especially starting in the 1990s, particularly television, both in representing sport, with complete matches broadcast on the small screen and new recording methods, and even the very production of sport, which started to change its internal organization to meet the growing desires of media consumers of sport (e.g., the number of matches played, match schedules, and even the recent introduction of channels dedicated to certain Series A teams, television filming of "behind the scenes" of the match and players; (3) the specific features that mediated sport took on with the appearance of Silvio Berlusconi on the public scene as a means through which to do politics, building a successful social—political—sport communication system that would deeply change Italian politics itself; and, lastly, (4) the mass fitness boom around the 1980s (or the 1990s in Italy) which, with the advent of complete commercial centers for physical exercise, promoted new moral ideas of health and beauty of the body through new techniques controlling people's bodies and leisure time.

Alessandro Dal Lago stands out among the authors who first developed the first of these topics through social ethnography on soccer, focusing on soccer support in the stadium, as a collective ritual that "condenses and transfigures deep social meanings [...] evoking the staging of a battle" (Dal Lago, 2001, p. 8) and celebrating warlike conflict. The author sought to look at this sport phenomenon from within to analyze and deconstruct the dominant viewpoint that considered fandom a mere expression of a violent youth subculture. Dal Lago adopted Geertz's interpretive theory of culture (1973), Goffman's phenomenological approach of ritual and frame analysis (1974), and an ethnographic method with participant observation, in-depth interviews, and document analysis, creating research unique in Italy on fan behavior. The focus was on "what fans do" rather than on their sociological profile or their organization. This study is still a reference point, though dated, considering the major changes to the soccer phenomenon over the last 20 years. For example, 20 years afterwards, Scalia's article (2009) sets Ultras groups (organized soccer supporters) in a more complex system relationships in which the Ultras "are not an isolated phenomenon that threatens Italian football from outside" (Scalia, 2009, p. 41), but garner legitimacy and support both from their clubs as well as from politicians. And there is the recent book by Testa and Armstrong (2010), which through an in-depth ethnographic investigation into the social movement of Ultras, and specifically of the groups in support of the Rome's two soccer clubs (AS Roma and SS Lazio), showed the connection between soccer fandom and the language and values of neo-fascism.

In contrast, Roversi studied the phenomenon with a more traditional approach that labels Ultras as a violent marginal mob (1988; 1992), where the interest is not in soccer, but in deviant behavior. Furthermore, as Bromberger (1999) pointed out, the focus of studies about fans is almost exclusively on those who adopt violent behavior.

Subsequently, even after major changes in soccer with the huge entrance of media in constructing the events, research focused primarily on the communication of sport, mainly regarded as a cultural/media phenomenon (Porro, 1997; Russo, 2004). Many sociology of communication scholars focus on sport communications, social cultural aspects of "mediated" sport, or on the public of large sport events (Olympics, World Cup) (Martelli, 2010). Just to give an idea of how much sport has become part of the Italian debate as a social media phenomenon more than as a sporting practice, we could mention one of the recent issues of the journal from Il Mulino, *Problemi dell'informazione*. The journal, which is concerned with topics related to information and media systems, recently dedicated a special issue to the topic of *Il Calcio e i Campionati Mondiali tra Informazione. Comunicazione e Spettacolo* (Soccer and the World Cup: Information, Communication, and Spectacle; 2015/1). As mentioned, we cannot find such interest in other sociology journals, which have only sporadically published articles related to sport.

A gender perspective has also come into sport, but primarily in studies of communication, which have investigated the construction of Italian masculinity by studying media images of men in sport, mainly in soccer (Boni, 2007). It takes sport as the aesthetic performance of a virile body; the athlete as a new model of masculinity in which the spectacularization of the athletic body has created, both in everyday life and in sociological studies, greater attention to the mediatized body (to the processes of body construction) rather than to the sport experience. In other words, when gender studies encounter sport, with a few exceptions that we will discuss later, they do so through the medium of communication studies and sport becomes a means for investigating other issues.

But the true particularity of Italian sociology of sport was created by the phenomenon of Berlusconism (the past tense is now obligatory), as he made the intersection between media, politics, and sport key ingredients of his success and durability. The expression "football politics" (Porro & Russo, 2000, p. 348) perfectly sums up one of the configurations that soccer took in Italy, while expressing an interpretive lens through which soccer was considered a cultural and political expression. Sport in Italy, as noted by McCarthy (2000), a British Professor of European Studies whose interests and expertise focused mainly on contemporary Italy's social and political transformations, including sport and the sociology of sport, is (or perhaps was) an important factor of analysis of the political scene. This is true not only for metaphorical reasons but because, since Berlusconi, the political discourse has been full of "symbols, metaphors and signifiers that deliberately echoed the world of sport" (Porro & Russo, 2000, p. 349).

Only in 2000, with the publication of Roberta Sassatelli's *Anatomia della Palestra*, was sport studied in its phenomenological dimension through an ethnomethodological and interactional approach. After Dal Lago's ethnography of fandom in the stadium, here we have an ethnography of fitness culture deployed inside gyms. This approach and research method have the advantage of studying organizations from the inside, observing the practices of actors within their specific space and time context. In this study, the macrocategories of the individualization and commodification, the sportification of society or the "reflexive turn" on the body, are discussed not in an ontological or almost essentialist way, but as socially rooted phenomena locally organized by specific institutions that guide the body processes and with which individuals come into relationship. We can say that with Roberta Sassatelli's study — a revised, updated version was translated in English in 2010 and republished in a paperback version in 2014, also by Palgrave — the foundations were laid in Italy for a cultural and interpretative shift about sport, away from a functionalist approach. However, we should say that, aside from other studies also published by Sassatelli (2002, 2015), also from a gender perspective (2003, 2012), this research did not give rise to a school of qualitative empirical studies on sport. Among the few exceptions, in addition to the mentioned studies on parkour, there is the ethnomethodological and phenomenological approach of Bassetti's work (2014) on theatrical dance, the body and the processes of embodiment, and the processes of constructing masculinity in ballrooms in Italy (2013). The originality of her work lies in the study of the body in action, analyzing the practice involved in the process of learning to dance and the role of embodied knowledge in those practices, starting from dance, a discipline even more neglected than sport in sociology.

Also following Sassatelli's research, Satta's work takes the perspective of the new sociology of childhood (Corsaro, 2005), using a phenomenological and interactional approach, to investigate children's participation in soccer and the importance of the body in defining their social and spatial position in society (Satta, 2015a, 2015b). The relationship between sport and childhood has also been completely neglected by Italian sociology of sport (unlike in the international realm; see Messner (2009) and, with an approach of social anthropology, Dyck, 2012) and delegated to pedagogy, which certainly investigates it with different aims if not with different research tools. Organized or informal sport activities are actually practiced most by children and young people, according to recent statistics about Italians' everyday life (ISTAT, 2014). As such, the lack of a generational perspective in the study of sport is an omission that pertains both to the sociology of childhood and the sociology of sport.

WHAT NEXT FOR THE SOCIOLOGY OF SPORT IN ITALY?

After the hard-won, vacillating progress of recent years, it is difficult to predict how the sociology of sport in Italy could develop. All the research we described here ultimately gave sociological attention to sport mainly when it took on mass proportions, or when the attention of media and public opinion is aroused and it becomes a cultural phenomenon or cause of social alarm, as in the case of violent fandom.

Apart from the ongoing work by Porro, who promotes sociological attention to sport through his studies and several handbooks written for students, there seems to be nothing that could be defined as a well-established sociology of sport. There are authors who have taken up and studied sport, but mostly in other frames, such as deviance, youth subcultures, or as a political, mass media or (recently) urban phenomenon, or within studies on the body and gender. Perhaps now is the time to ask ourselves what sport is? We could ask if sport is ultimately all of this: a mediatic, political, economic, cultural, urban, educational (local and global) phenomenon, and a matter of body and gender concern. Or perhaps, in saying that, we run the risk of continuing to make sport parenthetical, forever relegating it to medicine and education science, as we see happening in Italy. Comparison with international literature confirms sport's minority status (not just in Italy), as seen in the pages of the *Sociology of Sport Journal*, where Alan Bairner wrote: "It is vital that the sociology of sport be defended against the tyranny of the natural sciences. This project, however, must not be disaggregated from the requirements to fight for greater acceptance from mainstream sociology and to address our own shortcomings by extending the sociology of sport in potentially exciting ways" (2012, p. 102). Nascent studies on urban sports (lifestyle sports), especially on parkour, would suggest that body practice in urban space could be a path for studying sport in Italy, though the focus is more on the dynamics of inclusion or exclusion from the public sphere of its practitioners (mostly young and very young, some of foreign origin).

In summary, the sociology of sport seems to have become well established within physical education and sport science as an area of analysis of health, or rather wellbeing, through body practices. The passing of the Berlusconi era, which was tied to a growth in the literature of studies on communication and politics seen through sport, has partly marked a drop of interest in political sociology and in sociology of communications for sport as a lens for understanding Italian society; though the dominance of sport language in the political discourse seems to have outlived the decline of Berlusconi. However, there is still attention to communication in sport, which has shifted toward large-scale events, such as the Olympics and world championships, including studies of new channels of communication through the Internet. Given sport's increasingly marked professionalization and its economic importance, it has also become an area of study for legal scholars and sociologists of organization. Sport is now investigated in the realm of organization studies regarding the growing sector of sport management especially in soccer clubs — increasingly complex and global — the international and internal sport governance and laws, and the relationship between sport, media, and the market (Lo Verde, 2015).

What seems to be missing, particularly in the Italian context, is ethnographic attention to sport activities and places dedicated to physical activity, which constitute areas of learning, production, and reproduction of new knowledge about the body and through which the body can become the means of belonging to a community (Satta & Scandurra, 2015b). Not enough attention has been given to how the "inhabitants" of these urban gyms (differentiated by sex, age, national origin, social class, biographical paths, etc.) give meaning to a sport that cannot be reduced to a "simple" physical activity.

Although internationally there appears to be a repositioning of "sports studies," which is leading to the emergence of the field of physical cultural studies (Silk & Andrews, 2011), I believe that in Italy a reflection anchored to ethnography on the intersections between the body, sports, and urban areas would be of great benefit: not only for purely academic purposes, but to enrich a reflection on public space that arises from those places (gyms, sports fields, as well as city squares and parks) where canons of corporeality/subjectivity are built and rebuilt, defining which bodies may legitimately occupy public space and which are to be excluded or marginalized. The special issue of the journal *Modern Italy* recently edited by Satta and Scandurra (2015a) with the aim of investigating the role of sports practices and urban spaces in processes of citizenship construction in Italian cities, explores exactly these processes in the framework of Italy's complex urban network, made up mainly of small and medium-sized cities and to which the social sciences have rarely paid attention. Identifying and linking the intersections between the body, sports/leisure, space, and citizenship could also be a way to innovate studies on sport, starting from what has been left on the margins. This could be a way of closely connecting substantial, strong concepts and minor practices, in keeping with a phenomenological perspective on everyday life.

We cannot know whether this special issue will spawn new studies, but for now we can recognize that it has brought together scholars who have studied sport in an interdisciplinary perspective. And perhaps there is good reason for this. If a perspective on sport, as an independent social field and cultural fact, has had trouble taking off, perhaps the only way to escape the confines of a discipline that has not yet flourished is to dialogue with other disciplines and build a new field of inquiry.

FIVE KEY READINGS

1. **Sassatelli, R. (2010).** *Fitness culture: Gyms and the commercialisation of discipline and fun.* **Basingstoke, UK: Palgrave.**

   Sassatelli's book on fitness culture offers insight into the broad fitness phenomenon, tackling its global expansion and institutional consolidation within fitness gyms. Based on a solid multisite ethnography spanning 15 years in several commercial gyms in two European countries (Italy and Britain), it explores the specificity of fitness as instrumental leisure and looks at gyms as places of consumption, where producers and users contribute to the fitness culture development as an ongoing "local/global dialectic."

2. **Porro, N., & Russo, P. (2000). Berlusconi and other matters: The era of 'football-politics'.** *Journal of Modern Italian Studies*, **5(3), 348–371.**

   Porro and Russo's article describes the specific features that mediated sport took on with the appearance of Silvio Berlusconi on the public scene as a means through which to do politics, building a successful social–political–sport communication system that would deeply change Italian politics itself. Their expression "football politics" perfectly sums up one of the main configurations that soccer took in Italy as a cultural and political phenomenon.

3. **Testa, A., & Armstrong, G. (2010).** *Football, fascism and fandom. The ultras of Italian football.* **London: Bloomsbury Publishing.**

Testa and Armstrong's book presents a rich account of the Italian hard-core fan culture. Through in-depth ethnographic research into the social movement of Ultras, and specifically of two of the keenest groups in support of the Rome's soccer clubs (AS Roma and SS Lazio), it shows the connection between soccer fandom and the language and values of neo-fascism.

4. **Lo Verde, F.M. (2014).** *Sociologia dello sport e del tempo libero.* **Bologna: il Mulino.**

Lo Verde's book offers an updated overview of his attempts to fill the gap between sociological thinking about sport and leisure and promote sociological understanding of sport through the lens of leisure studies. The book gives an insight into the practice of sport in Europe and Italy, drawing attention to the case of extreme sport as a new trend in sport/leisure consumption, as well as into mediated sport with its increased professionalization and the rise of sporting celebrities.

5. **Satta, C., & Scandurra, G. (2015). Introduction: Sport and public space in contemporary Italian cities. Processes of citizenship construction through body-related practices.** *Modern Italy, 20*(3), 229–236.

Satta and Scandurra's edited special issue on sport and public space in contemporary Italian cities, investigating the role of sports practices and urban spaces in processes of citizenship construction, develops a discourse on sport at the intersections between the body, sports/leisure, space, and citizenship. It offers an overview of the latest research, deployed in Italy with an ethnographic approach, on sport and its practitioners.

REFERENCES

Bairner, A. (2012). For a sociology of sport. *Sociology of Sport Journal, 29*(1), 102−117.

Balbo, L. (2001). Parlare della sociologia (scelte, gerarchie, esclusioni) partendo dal mondo dello sport. *Rassegna italiana di Sociologia, 42*(3), 485−492. doi:10.1423/2579

Bassetti, C. (2013). Male dancing body, stigma and Normalising processes. Playing with (bodily) signifieds/ers of masculinity. *Recherches Sociologiques et Anthropologiques, 44*(2), 69−92. Retrieved from http://rsa.revues.org/1048

Bassetti, C. (2014). The knowing body-in-action in performing arts. Embodiment, experiential transformation and intersubjectivity. In T. Zembylas (Ed.), *Artistic practices. Social interactions and cultural dynamics* (pp. 91−111). London: Routledge.

Benasso, S. (2015). Giardini Govi is our spot! When parkour meets Genoa. *Modern Italy, 20*(3), 285−294. doi:10.1080/13532944.2015.1065238

Boni, F. (2007). Sport, mascolinità e media. In E. Dell'Agnese & E. Ruspini (Eds.), *Mascolinità all'italiana. Costruzioni, narrazioni, mutamenti* (pp. 79−102). Torino: Utet.

Borden, I. (2001). *Skateboarding, space and the city: Architecture of the body.* London: Berg.

Bourdieu, P. (1988). Program for a sociology of sport. *Sociology of Sport Journal, 5*(2), 153−161.

Bromberger, C. (1999). *La partita di calcio. Etnologia di una passione.* Roma: Editori riuniti (Original work published 1996).

Corsaro, W. A. (2005). *The sociology of childhood.* Thousand Oaks, CA: Pine Forge Press.

Dal Lago, A. (1990). *Descrizione di una battaglia. I rituali del calcio.* Bologna: il Mulino.

Dal Lago, A. (2001). Preface to. In A. Dal Lago (Ed.), *Descrizione di una battaglia. I rituali del calcio* (2nd ed.). Bologna: il Mulino.

Dal Lago, A., & De Biasi, R. (1994). Italian football fans: Culture and organization. In R. Giulianotti, N. Bonney, & M. Hepworth (Eds.), *Football, violence and social identity* (pp. 71−86). London: Routledge.

Dal Lago, A., & Moscati, R. (1992). *Regalateci un sogno: miti e realtà del tifo calcistico in Italia.* Milano: Bompiani.

De Biasi, R. (1998). Sociologie del tifo estremo. *Rassegna Italiana di Sociologia, 39*(3), 427−434. doi:10.1423/2497

De Martini Ugolotti, N. (2015). Climbing walls, making bridges: Children of immigrants' identity negotiations through capoeira and parkour in Turin. *Leisure Studies, 34*(1), 19−33. doi:10.1080/02614367.2014.966746

Dunning, E., & Elias, N. (1986). *The quest for excitement. Sport and leisure in the civilizing process.* London: Basil Blackwell.

Dyck, N. (2012). *Fields of play: An ethnography of children's sports.* Guelph, Ontario: University of Toronto Press.

Farné, R. (Ed.) (2008). *Sport e formazione.* Milano: Guerini.

Ferrero Camoletto, R. (2008). Giocare col limite. La costruzione del corpo nelle nuove forme di sportività. *Equilibri, 12*(1), 37−46. doi:10.1406/26845

Geertz, C. (1973). *The interpretation of cultures: Selected essays.* New York, NY: Basic Books.

Goffman, E. (1974). *Frame analysis. An essay on the organization of experience.* Cambridge, MA: Harvard University Press.

ISTAT (2014). *Annuario statistico italiano 2014*. Rome: Istat. Retrieved from http://www.istat.
    it/it/archivio/134686

Lewis, A. (2009). From alpine clubs to Baggio and Berlusconi: Italy reflected through sport.
    Journal of Modern Italian Studies, 14(1), 96–103. doi:10.1080/13545710802647890

Lo Verde, F. M. (2014). *Sociologia dello sport e del tempo libero*. Bologna: il Mulino.

Lo Verde, F. M. (2015). Sport, media e mercato. L'intreccio indissolubile. *Problemi dell'infor-
    mazione, 40*(1), 167–193. doi:10.1445/79612

Martelli, S. (2010). *Lo sport "mediato". Le audience di Olimpiadi, paralimpiadi e Campionati
    europei di calcio (2000–2008)*. Milano: Franco Angeli.

McCarthy, P. (2000). Sport and society in Italy today. *Journal of Modern Italian Studies, 5*(3),
    322–326. doi:10.1080/1354571X.2000.9728257

Messner, M. A. (2009). *It's all for the kids: Gender, families and youth sports*. Berkeley, CA:
    University of California Press.

Porro, N. (Ed.) (1997). *L'Italia in Tv agli Europei '96. Il calcio come identità e rappresentazione*.
    Roma: Rai-ERI, Vqpt.

Porro, N. (2001). *Lineamenti di sociologia dello sport*. Roma: Carocci.

Porro, N. (2013). *Movimenti collettivi e culture sociali dello sport europeo. Le stagioni della
    sportivizzazione*. Acireale-Roma: Bonanno.

Porro, N., & Russo, P. (2000). Berlusconi and other matters: The era of 'Football-politics'.
    Journal of Modern Italian Studies, 5(3), 348–371. doi:10.1080/1354571X.2000.9728259

Queirolo Palmas, L. (2009). *Dentro le Gang. Giovani, Migranti e Nuovi Spazi Pubblici*. Verona:
    Ombre corte.

Roversi, A. (1988). Calcio e violenza in Italia. *Il Mulino, 4*, 676–700. doi:10.1402/13749

Roversi, A. (1992). *Calcio, tifo e violenza. Il teppismo calcistico in Italia*. Bologna: Il Mulino.

Roversi, A., & Triani, G. (Eds.) (1995). *Sociologia dello sport*. Napoli: Edizioni
    Scientifiche Italiane.

Russo, P. (2000). L'analisi sociologica dello sport. *Rassegna italiana di sociologia, 41*(2),
    303–314. doi:10.1423/2542

Russo, P. (2004). *Sport e società*. Roma: Carocci.

Sassatelli, R. (2000). *Anatomia della palestra. Cultura commerciale e disciplina del corpo*.
    Bologna: il Mulino.

Sassatelli, R. (2002). Corpi in pratica: "habitus", interazione e disciplina. *Rassegna Italiana di
    Sociologia, 43*(3), 429–458. doi:10.1423/4582

Sassatelli, R. (2003). *Lo sport al femminile nella società moderna*. Roma: Enciclopedia dello
    Sport Treccani. Retrieved from http://www.treccani.it/enciclopedia/lo-sport-al-femminile-
    nella-societa-moderna_(Enciclopedia-dello-Sport)/

Sassatelli, R. (2010) (2014 with new preface). *Fitness culture. gyms and the commercialisation of
    discipline and fun*. Basingstoke: Palgrave.

Sassatelli, R. (2012). Body politics. In K. Nash & A. Scott (Eds.), *Blackwell companion to poli-
    tical sociology* (pp. 347–358). Oxford: Blackwell.

Sassatelli, R. (2015). Healthy cities and instrumental leisure: The paradox of fitness gyms as
    urban phenomena. *Modern Italy, 20*(3), 237–249. doi:10.1080/13532944.2015.1065239

Satta, C. (2015a). Embodying citizenship. Children's spatial and bodily experience in a football
    club academy. *Modern Italy, 20*(3), 273–284. doi:10.1080/13532944.2015.1061487

Satta, C. (2015b). La città e il calcio dei bambini. Diventare calciatori in una scuola calcio di
    serie A. *La Ricerca Folklorica, 70*, 65–76.

Satta, C., & Scandurra, G. (2015a). Introduction: Sport and public space in contemporary Italian cities. Processes of citizenship construction through body-related practices. *Modern Italy*, *20*(3), 229–236. doi:10.1080/13532944.2015.1072966

Satta, C., & Scandurra, G. (2015b). Introduzione. Comunità di pratica, sport e spazi urbani. *La Ricerca Folklorica*, *70*, 3–11.

Scalia, V. (2009). Just a few rogues?: Football ultras, clubs and politics in contemporary Italy. *International Review for the Sociology of Sport*, *44*(1), 41–53. doi:10.1177/1012690208101682

Silk, M. L., & Andrews, D. L. (2011). Toward a physical cultural studies. *Sociology of Sport Journal*, *28*(1), 4–35.

Simonicca, A. (2008). Introduzione. In H. Bausinger (Ed.), *La cultura dello sport* (pp. 9–34). Roma: Armando.

Stagi, L. (2015). Crossing the symbolic boundaries: Parkour, gender and urban spaces in Genoa. *Modern Italy*, *20*(3), 295–305. doi:10.1080/13532944.2015.1061486

Testa, A., & Armstrong, G. (2010). *Football, fascism and fandom. The ultras of Italian football.* London: Bloomsbury Publishing.

Zoletto, D., & Wildemeersch, D. (2012). Public playgrounds as environments for learning citizenship. *Pedagogia oggi*, *1*, 78–86.

CHAPTER 14

SOCIOLOGY OF SPORT: THE NETHERLANDS

Annelies Knoppers

ABSTRACT

Sociology of sport does not exist as a (sub)discipline or course of study in the Netherlands. Scholars who call themselves sport sociologists engage in a variety of research and related publication activities. Many of these might not strictly fit under some understandings of the title "sociology" since they focus on sport management, policy implementation, and change. In this chapter, I describe how sociology of sport research tends to be defined and how that research is used to defend government spending on sport participation. This instrumental approach means the results of Dutch research using critical perspectives are often heard only internationally. I explain how the structure of Dutch academia, which limits the number of associate professors and professors, relies primarily on external funding for research and makes such funding difficult to obtain if it does not fit within a specified perspective, and limits who is able to engage in research and the type of research that is produced. I show how this structure in combination with the emphasis on an instrumental function of sport has largely shaped much of the research and has limited the use of a variety of theoretical frameworks and the

Sociology of Sport: A Global Subdiscipline in Review
Research in the Sociology of Sport, Volume 9, 245–263
ISSN: 1476-2854/doi:10.1108/S1476-285420160000009018

development of a robust and coherent body of knowledge about the sociology of sport in the Netherlands.

Keywords: Instrumental; fragmentation; participation; funding

INTRODUCTION

Since the term "sociology of sport" is loosely used in the Netherlands and no program of study, journal, or organization has this as its focus, in the following I often use it synonymously with the expression "the social aspects of sport" since that is the heading or theme with which sociology of sport is often associated in Dutch academia. Dutch or national/local literature in this area is very difficult to find since there are few outlets for accessible or peer-reviewed publication. Most studies are commissioned by a specific group/organization. The resulting data, discussion, and implications/recommendations tend to pertain primarily to the group that commissioned the study. The resulting reports tend to be descriptive and end with policy recommendations aimed at the specific group.

This situation is further complicated because scholars who call themselves "sport sociologists" engage in a variety of research publication activities, many of which might not strictly fit under some understandings of the title "sociology" since they focus on sport management, policy implementation, and change and are published or produced primarily for a specific organization instead of for national or international scholarly public consumption. I therefore base the following analysis primarily on the available literature published by Dutch scholars, especially the international literature. I do not pretend that this version is complete and do not intend to provide an exhaustive list of all that has been written in this area but rather to cite examples of literature (that I usually limit to two per topic). I describe more of this context in which the study of sociology of sport takes place in the Netherlands in the following sections. This chapter reflects my perspective as an insider/outsider. I have worked in Dutch academia for about 20 years, was not educated in the Netherlands, and have a North American habitus with respect to the sub-discipline. My description and analysis may therefore be quite different from an account that might be written by someone who has a Dutch academic and sport habitus.

HISTORY OF SOCIOLOGY OF SPORT IN THE NETHERLANDS

Although its performance in elite sport has given the Netherlands visibility in the global arena, the Netherlands has a very uneven and fragmented history concerning the study of the sociology of sport. As I show throughout this chapter, this history is in part determined by meanings and functions ascribed to sport participation, by the ways in which research on sport has been funded and by the structure of academia.

In 1928, the Netherlands hosted the Olympic Games. An international conference on research on sport was held at the same time but this concerned primarily dimensions of physical performance (De Heer, 2000). The funds for these games and conference came from private sources and not the government. There is no record of scholarly attention being paid to social dimensions of sport at this conference. This systematic neglect of the study of sport characterized the next 50 years (see also Stokvis, 2004).

The first recorded scholarly attention given to social aspects of sport in the Netherlands came 10 years later. Johan Huizinga published *Homo Ludens* in 1938, a book in which he wrote about the social significance of play. According to him, the content of play reflected a culture. In the following 50 years little attention was paid by the Dutch government or scholars to social aspects of sport, which may reflect Huizinga's thesis and perhaps says something about Dutch culture at that time. Sport was considered to be play and not an object of scholarly study or government funding (Stokvis, 2004, 2010). If sport was not play, then it was far removed from this ideal and not worth studying.

When sport became a social object to be studied, the focus initially tended to be on socio-historical development in which scholars used Eliasian perspectives. Miermans (1955) was one of the first to do so in his dissertation about the societal and sporting aspects of soccer. He emphasized the role of class and religious differences in this development. About 20 years later, Stokvis (1979) also wrote a socio-historically focused dissertation on the history of sport development in the Netherlands with special attention to struggles about the desirability of maintaining amateurism as opposed to increasing professionalism and about the need to focus on recreational sport for all as opposed to the necessity to provide a necessary basis for elite sport. However, these studies were rarities. Attention began to be paid to sport but not to a social scholarly study of it. Despite the struggles as described by Stokvis, however, participation in recreational sport increased steadily over the years as individuals began to have more leisure time (Breedveld, 2014).

Sport clubs played a major role in this growth. These tended to be locally based and were organized and managed by volunteers. These clubs played a major role in this development of and continue to be a major venue for amateur sport for people/youth of all ages today. Anyone could and can start a club in any sport, think of a name, recruit members, find a place to play, and incorporate (see Verweel & Knoppers, 2006 for a further explanation of this manner of organizing sport). Each club created age and gender categorizations for its teams. Currently, licenses to play have to be obtained from the relevant national sport association if teams want to engage in competition with other clubs. All these clubs were and continue to be led and managed by volunteers.[1] Teams were, however, primarily created for boys and men (see also Derks, 1999). Sport participation for women became a significant factor beginning in the 1970s so that now the number of women and men participating in recreational sport clubs/teams is about equal (www.sportdeelname.nl). This increase in participation did not go unnoticed by scholars and the government and was conflated with other societal developments and governmental emphases on encouraging integration/cohesion and healthy lifestyles.

One of the first available government-sponsored research projects that focused on sport participation was conducted by Manders and Kropman (1974) who examined where/how people participated in sport. They found that much sport participation took place outside of sport clubs. Since the government saw sport clubs as places where individuals, and especially youth, could be socialized into Dutch values and norms, this was cause for concern. This conclusion required more research, however. Such research on sport needed to focus on large groups so that its findings could contribute to the wellbeing of its citizens (Jacobs & Kamphorst, 1976). Jacobs and Kamphorst also argued that this research needed to be scholarly and empirical in nature and that its results should be applicable to practice. Subsequently, Manders and Kropman (1982) reported on obstacles and facilitators of sport participation, especially with respect to sport clubs. Buisman (1987) introduced youth sport as a topic for discussion with his book about fair play. This emphasis on sport as a site for teaching societal norms and values led to other projects also funded by the government. Similarly, Crum (1991) wrote a report about the ways in which society was becoming what he called "sporticized."

This scholarly attention to sport by way of these reports resulted in increased government interest in sport and the study of it. In addition to funding such scholarly projects, the government continued to be interested in harnessing what were seen as the positive values that could come about through sport participation. For example, in 1991 Hedy d'Acona, the Minister of Welfare, Health and Culture, requested a public discussion about the quality and changing nature of sport practices. This request led to the publication of several other studies. The social importance of sport as a possible source of inspiration was addressed and confirmed by the Kearney (1992) report for which 80 scholars, government officials, and those working in sport, especially at the highest levels, were interviewed. Notably athletes were not interviewed. This report and similar studies such as that by Van Bottenburg and Schuyt (1996) convinced the government that it needed to pay attention to social aspects of sport and the study of it.

The government visibly showed its interest in sport by changing the name of the Ministry of Health, Welfare and Culture to the Ministry of Health, Welfare and Sport in 1994. The combination of the three names in the title also shows the assumed connection between them. Sport was assumed to contribute to both the welfare of citizens and the nation and to the health of individuals, and was possibly seen as more important than a focus on "culture" (see also VWS, 1996a, 1996b).

During the 1990s this scholarly interest in sport was a bi-national endeavor involving academics from both Belgium and the Netherlands. In 2001 Belgian and Dutch colleagues spearheaded a scholarly project (Steenbergen, de Knop, & Elling, 2001) on the values of and norms in youth sport. This resulted in one of the first Belgian–Dutch collaborative scholarly books on the topic and indicated the interests of scholars in the study of sport.[2] Although individual scholars in both Belgium and the Netherlands still occasionally engage in a joint project, this collaboration became less important over time as both Belgium and the Netherlands set different priorities in their focus and emphases.

The 1990s, therefore, represented an increase in attention by the government and scholars to social aspects of sport. This shift in attention by the government and scholars has not diminished over time but instead has steadily increased. An independent institute, Mulier Institute, was established in 2002 as a center for research in the social science of sport. It has monitored sport participation including that of marginalized groups, has organized debates on social issues in sport, and has served as an archive for the many social science projects in the area of sport. Since the funding of the Mulier Institute is based on grants from the government and sport organizations, most of the topics of research tend to be determined by demand from the field. Many of its scholars have, however, used such data to also publish articles about social aspects of sport in international peer-reviewed journals (e.g., Hoekman, Breedveld, & Kraaykamp, 2016; Peeters & Elling, 2015). An annual day for the presentation of sport research, where scholars in this area could present their findings, was begun in 2010.

The greatest focus of Dutch sport policy and research in the last 20 years on social aspects of sport has consistently been on the importance or function of sport, and especially on sport participation, to society. Henry (2009) studied the various ways in which sport was configured in European countries and concluded that the Dutch sport system had a unique focus on effectiveness and capacity building. This emphasis on effectiveness and capacity building is reflected in much of the research on the social aspects of Dutch sport. Every five years a knowledge plan or agenda is produced by a hybrid group of scholars, policy makers, and government and sport officials (see Breedveld, Molleman, Smits, & Reijgersberg, 2010). This plan includes the areas designated as requiring "social" research, specifically, participation, vitality (lifelong healthy living), and achievement/winning.[3] The focus of much of the needed research described in this knowledge acquisition plan pertaining to the social aspects of sport is therefore on monitoring participation; on ascertaining the motivation to participate in sport; on identifying best practices that can be used to encourage participation by various social groups; and, the value of sport in its contribution of sport to social cohesion, to integration, and to the disciplining of youth and people of all ages into healthy lifestyles. As I shall detail further on, most research projects therefore aim to show how effective sport can be in reinforcing these dimensions and how sport can be strengthened as an institution (capacity building).

Although there is a great deal of emphasis on sport as a necessary and valued social institution, sociology of sport does not formally exist as a recognized field or (sub)discipline, there are people who call themselves sport sociologists such as Koen Breedveld, Maarten van Bottenburg, Agnes Elling, Ramón Spaaij, Ruud Stokvis, and Annelies Knoppers. Those who research this area tend to come from diverse backgrounds. Two scholars have a background in movement sciences/kinesiology. Other scholars who identify as sport sociologists or as social sport scholars have backgrounds in cultural anthropology, sociology, philosophy, and pedagogy, and have rarely followed courses in sociology of sport. Few such courses exist.[4] Sport may, however, be a topic addressed in courses in media or communication studies courses.

There is also no national association with a focus on sociology of sport. An informal network called INSPIRE is used to notify members of upcoming events and calls for papers via email. Those especially interested in sport sociology tend to be members of the International Sociology of Sport Association (ISSA) and/or the European Association for Sport Sociology (EASS).

APPROXIMATE NUMBER OF SCHOLARS AND WHERE LOCATED

Scholars are scattered across six universities, often working in a department that does not have sport in its title such as in the Departments/Faculties of Governance and Organization Studies (Utrecht), Humanities (Groningen), Human Movement (Free University), Communication Studies (Erasmus University), Sociology and Policy (University of Nijmegen), and Sociology (University of Amsterdam). The largest concentration of scholars in the social aspects of sport works at the Utrecht University School of Governance (USG). At USG Maarten van Bottenburg occupies the chair in sport development,[5] Paul Verweel has held a chair in sport sponsored by the Krajicek Foundation, and Annelies Knoppers has held the chair for pedagogy of/in sport and physical education. Various scholars at USG work in the area of the social aspects of sport including sport management, sport policy development, and sociology of sport. The unique emphasis on sport scholarship at USG is on looking critically at social issues in sport including the ways sport clubs function, the trend towards consumerism in sport clubs, gender/diversity in sport governance and organizations, and the role of bodies/embodiment in organizational research and practices and how this may inform other societal dynamics and issues. This critical approach is also evident in the work of Ramón Spaaij and Ruud Stokvis at the University of Amsterdam, Agnes Elling at Mulier Institute, and Jacco van Sterkenburg at Erasmus University.

ACADEMIC ENVIRONMENT AND BARRIERS TO RESEARCH

The Dutch structure of higher education determines to a large extent which bodies of knowledge receive scholarly attention and are taught. Since the country is small and students can easily commute to other universities,

universities must have areas of interest that are unique to the Netherlands. They cannot duplicate each other's programs/majors. Only one university therefore has a program of study in movement science (Free University). Although its focus is primarily on performance/skill development and draws on bodies of knowledge from natural sciences and psychology, it also offers courses in philosophy of sport.

Most positions at Dutch universities are teaching positions. Each university/department has a set number of associate professors; this number is even smaller for professors who occupy a chair and therefore become professor (usually one per university in sport, if at all). This means that some academics will remain assistant professors during their entire academic career. Since assistant professors usually have a 100% teaching assignment, their opportunities for conducting research and publishing in international refereed journals is limited.

Another factor that determines the direction of research and at the same time inhibits the development of a significant and robust body of research around a topic is the program for doctoral students. There are two ways to be a doctoral student – by being a graduate assistant or by being a part-time student while working full time elsewhere such as at a university of applied sciences. The number of graduate assistantships for doctoral students in the area of sociology of sport is very small. Most doctoral students are, therefore, part time. The primary requirement that needs to be met to attain a doctoral degree is to write an acceptable dissertation, that is, students do not follow any course work or specific training in the subdiscipline of sociology of sport and rarely, if at all, systematically attend scholarly international conferences. A dissertation can be written as a book or consist of a compilation of articles that have been published in international peer-reviewed journals. Those that choose the book option usually write it in Dutch and rarely publish internationally nor do they conduct research on a specific theme after their graduation. Those who have been graduate assistants tend to be better versed in theoretical frameworks since they are required to follow course work. That course work is, however, based on the parent discipline of their department. This means doctoral students at USG, for example, have to take several courses in governance and public administration in which the word "sport" rarely is taken as an object of study. Thus their knowledge and understanding of sociology of sport is also limited.

Another factor that limits the growth of the field of sociology of sport is that only those holding a chair (i.e., are professors) are allowed to supervise doctoral students. This means that the interests and preferred theoretical framework of the person holding the chair guide the direction of research. In addition, with one exception, the five to six chairs in sport are temporary; that is, they are held for 5–10 years, after which someone else will take over (if there is sufficient funding) with his or her own interests. Consequently there is relatively little continuity in topic or theoretical development in the type of research that is conducted.

Research time must literally be earned, primarily through obtaining funds. A great deal of the scholarship in social aspects of sport in the Netherlands is dependent on funding since much of the research time at universities and universities of applied sciences tends to be given on the basis of funded projects. Questions for research usually come from sport organizations or the government.[6] These questions usually pertain to increasing sport participation and using sport to address (and solve!) social problems. In other words, the field tends to determine the research agenda and ensures the dominant theoretical perspective used is instrumental (see further on as well).[7] The primary national source for academic grants in the Netherlands is the Netherlands Organization for Scientific Research (NWO). The competition for scholarly grants from NWO is fierce since all researchers from all universities write these (time-consuming) applications of which only a few (1–15%) get funded (see also Van Calmthout, 2015). Other sources of grants are the Ministry of Health, Welfare and Sport (VWS) or national or local sport organizations.[8] These grants usually require applied work in which time is only allotted for collecting data and writing a report or for recommending policy. Consequently, such grants leave little time for scholars to write a scholarly article.

Ironically, doctoral students who elect to write articles instead of a book tend to be quite productive since in order to graduate they publish four to five such articles based on a specific theme.[9] After their graduation, however, they often disappear from the national/international scholarship and publishing scene as they then tend to engage in primarily locally applied research as I described earlier due to lack of funding/time. Unless a person has a chair/becomes a professor (or sometimes associate professor), the opportunities for continuing to develop a specific area or oneself as an international scholar are small. This means that much of Dutch scholarly research in sociology of sport is not only marked by its instrumental focus but also by its lack of continuity. As a result, the body of knowledge about and in sociology of sport is quite fragmented.

MAIN AREAS OF RESEARCH STRENGTH

As I indicated above, most of the funding for research comes from the government directly (including national, provincial, and local governments) or via the Dutch National Olympic Committee (NOC*NSF) and only a very small number via the less instrumentally and more theoretically focused NWO. In this section I describe the themes that have emerged in Dutch research in sociology of sport in the last 15 years. Funding has come for research that shows how sport is or can become a practice that can be used to address societal problems and research that tries to find/locate obstacles to sport participation. Some of these take a critical debunking approach to governmentally defined social issues such as obesity (e.g., Van Amsterdam, Knoppers, Claringbould, & Jongmans, 2012a, 2012b) and delinquency among youth (e.g., Spaaij, 2009a) while others look for ways to enable sport to address the integration of immigrants (e.g., Krouwel, Boonstra, Duyvendak, & Veldboer, 2006; Verhagen & Boonstra, 2014).

This emphasis on sport as a positive force does not mean that the negative or shadow side of sport is ignored. Attention is paid to the dark or shadow side of sport, especially violence in and around soccer matches (e.g., Schaap, Postma, Jansen, & Tolsma, 2015; Spaaij, 2007, 2008), doping (Van Hilvoorde, Vos, & de Wert, 2007), and abuse of athletes by coaches (Smits Jacobs & Knoppers, 2016; Vertommen et al., 2016). The findings of such research, however, tend to be used to create regulatory policies that seem to address symptoms rather than exploring possible causes. For example, after a report about the emotionally abusive behavior of coaches was given to the national association governing the sport (Knoppers, Smits, & Jacobs, 2015), those coaches were taught positive coaching methods (personal communication, Vander Weg, December 1, 2014). Little attention was paid to the reasons for this behavior, namely the emphasis on winning, competition among coaches and club directors for the few outstanding athletes, the age and gender of the athletes, etc. The assumption seemed to be that the problems described in the report could be solved if coaches learned to frame their instructions in a different way. Funds for research that might give insights into underlying processes or use other than functional theoretical frameworks, therefore, tend to be rare unless given by NWO.

MAIN APPROACHES TAKEN

The most frequently used theoretical approach (often unnamed) is structural functionalism. Much research focuses on why people participate in sport, who is excluded, and how to increase participation and the barriers to participation (see Breedveld, 2014 for a summary). There has also been some use of figuration theories by professors such as Stokvis and Van Bottenburg, who have situated current developments within a historical framework.

Those who have looked at the social capital that accumulates through club membership have situated this primarily in the work of Goffman and Putnam and often take a symbolic interactionist perspective. For example, research was used to explore the social capital accumulated through bonding and bridging by those belonging to an immigrant sport club (as opposed to a nonimmigrant club) and the ways in which local neighborhood sport projects contributed to neighborhood cohesion and integration of immigrants (e.g., Boessenkool, Leisink, & Verweel, 2003; Janssens & Verweel, 2014; Slobbe, Vermeulen & Koster, 2013; Spaaij, 2009a, 2009b; Vermeulen, 2011; Vermeulen & Verweel, 2009).

A third focus of research in Dutch universities with respect to social aspects of sport is on the development of sport at elite and recreational levels and how local sport clubs (can) facilitate this (e.g., Scheerder et al., 2011). This focus on development includes an emphasis on how sport involvement, and sport as an institution, have become essential contributors to Dutch civil society, how this is reflected in sport policies and adds to or strengthens what are known as common or public values (see, e.g., Leisink, Boselie, Hosking, & Van Bottenburg, 2013; Van der Roest, Vermeulen, & Van Bottenburg, 2015). Another strand in this research is a focus on elite top sport and the identification of national factors (Sports Policy Factors Leading to International Sporting Success, or SPLISS) that can lead to improved performance (i.e., more medals) (e.g., De Bosscher, De Knop, Van Bottenburg & Shibil, 2006; De Bosscher, Shibil, Westerbeek, & Van Bottenburg, 2015). This international focus using SPLISS is a joint Belgian–Dutch project.

A fourth and generally more (nationally) marginalized perspective than those described above is that which uses a critical theoretical/poststructural/postmodern approach. It has been used to tease out the assumptions made about sport and to make visible underlying processes that lead to exclusion and/or enable white heterosexual men to shape dominant discourses about sport/physical education and knowledge production in the Netherlands. This perspective is dominant in Dutch research that aims to add to understandings on how discourses about gender, ethnicity, and sexuality shape sport participation and governance. Examples of this are found in the area of sexuality and gender (e.g., Elling & Janssens, 2009; Elling-Machartzki, 2015), on the topic of sport leadership (e.g., Claringbould & Knoppers, 2013;

Dortants & Knoppers, 2016; Elling & Claringbould, 2005; Knoppers, 2011), ethnicity and media (e.g., Van Sterkenburg, 2013; Van Sterkenburg, Knoppers, & De Leeuw, 2010, 2012), and the body (e.g., Van Amsterdam et al., 2012a, 2012b). This body of research points out how sport practices may be oppressive and sustain societal discourses that construct what women and minorities do and think as being less important or of less value as compared to white heterosexual abled men. Since Dutch policy makers assume that sport participation has a positive effect on youth, a strand of scholarly research grounded within a poststructural approach has also looked at coaches and their work (e.g., Claringbould, Knoppers, & Jacobs, 2015; Jacobs, Smits, & Knoppers, 2016; Smits et al., 2016). Overall, however, the use of such a critical perspective on sport and the results of such research often are not incorporated or integrated into accepted ways of thinking and sustainable practices and policy making.

KEY CONTRIBUTORS AND KEY PUBLICATIONS

What can be defined as the best-known or the most influential work and as being main exemplars of the field is dependent on the eye of the beholder. Many of the key research endeavors have been cited above. It is my impression that research situated in poststructural perspectives (see above) tends to receive more attention in international circles than in the Netherlands itself. In part, this lack of interest in findings from these studies is evident in ways in which grants are (not) awarded and where work is cited. Possibly this critical approach does not fit into the dominant discourse that sees sport primarily in a functional/instrumental manner. In addition, since the Netherlands does not have many venues for publication, much of the critical work is published in international peer-reviewed journals. Although many universities emphasize open access of publications, those who do not work at a university or similar institution may not always have access to such research.

THE FUTURE

As increasingly more individuals who are working in higher education are encouraged to work on their doctoral degree, and since more tend to do this by publishing papers instead of writing a book, the Netherlands should continue to have an international presence in the sociology of sport. At the same time, the absence of a definable body that marks sociology of sport as a subdiscipline in the Netherlands and as a legitimate and scholarly subject of study means that the future of much research and knowledge production in this area will depend on funding and the scholarly interests of those holding one of the six chairs that have a focus on the social aspects of sport. The recent (2014) creation of an interdisciplinary university-wide focus area called Sport & Society at the University of Utrecht in partnership with the Utrecht University of Applied Sciences and the Technical University of Eindhoven also holds promise.[10] This focus area seeks to promote interdisciplinary research that looks critically at the relationship/interaction between society and sport in order to create a body of knowledge about ways public values are created in and through sport. Specifically, the objective for the creation of Sport & Society is to focus more on the complexity of sport than on ways of increasing sport participation. The recent selection of Ramon Spaaij to a special chair in sociology of sport at the University of Amsterdam will hopefully strengthen this body of research since his work could best be described as hybrid in both subject matter and theoretical perspectives. Overall, however, due to issues of funding and the structure of academia, sport sociology research in the Netherlands will continue to be dominated by an instrumental or functionalist approach with a primary focus on improving sport practice in terms of participation and policy development and strengthening sport governance. Sport sociology will continue to be a body of knowledge that is fragmented and lacks continuity.

NOTES

1. Although many Dutch adults are involved in volunteer work, the most volunteers are found in sport (Schmeets & te Riele, 2014).
2. This collaboration was later extended to a jointly published book on sport sociology (De Knop, Scheerder, & Van Reusel, 2006).
3. The other areas that are seen as separate from the "social research" designation are achievement/elite sport and vitality (health/lifelong participation).
4. Current exceptions are an undergraduate course at the University of Utrecht and a graduate course at the Free University of Amsterdam.
5. This is the only permanent university chair or professor position in the Netherlands that has sport in its title. All the other sport-related chairs or professor positions are "special" chairs and therefore temporary.
6. The NOC*NSF is not only the Olympic committee but is also the umbrella organization for all national sport associations. It often partners with the

government in suggesting research themes. Consequently it has a strong voice in determining what does and does not receive attention in the social area of sport and will be funded.

7. See, for example, projects that were funded from 2013 to 2016 by the Netherlands Organization for Scientific Research (NWO): Onderzoeksprojecten binnen het Programma Sport – Pijler Meedoen (Research Projects in Sport Participation; www.nwo.nl).

8. The European Research Council (ERC) is another source of research grants but here the competition is even greater than at the national level.

9. Those who are not graduate assistants but who work at universities of applied sciences usually receive 1–2 days per week to do their research and to work on publishing their results. After they graduate, however, they often lose this research time and/or need to use it to engage in applied research that does not allow time for publication as described earlier.

10. See http://www.uu.nl/en/research/sport-and-society

FIVE KEY READINGS

1. **Claringbould, I., & Knoppers, A. (2013). Understanding the lack of gender equity in leadership positions in (sport) organizations. In Leisink, P., Boselie, P., Hosking, D. M., & Van Bottenburg, M. (Eds.)** *Managing social issues: A public values perspective* **(pp. 162–182). Abingdon Oxon: Edward Elgar Publishing**.

Claringbould and Knoppers draw on both the extant and sport management/organization literature and Acker's theory of gender in organizations to explore why little has changed in gender diversity in sport organizations over the last 20 years. They show how various processes work together to maintain the status quo of male dominance. They also suggest that several other concepts such as liminality and privilege may play a role in these processes and need scholarly attention.

2. **Elling, A., & Janssens, J. (2009). Sexuality as a structural principle in sport participation negotiating sports spaces.** *International Review for the Sociology of Sport,* ***44***(1), 71–86.

In this article Elling and Janssens present the results of a Dutch study that compares sport participation among self-identified gay/bisexual men and women and a matched group of heterosexual men and women. In contrast to much of the literature in this area, Elling and Janssens used quantitative data. The results show how the type of sport and physical site shaped the sport history of both heterosexual and nonheterosexual women and men. Nonheterosexual men and women tended to participate in mainstream sport and to avoid LGBT sport clubs and in this way engaged in heteronormative compliance.

3. **Spaaij, R. (2009). Sport as a vehicle for social mobility and regulation of disadvantaged urban youth lessons from Rotterdam.** *International Review for the Sociology of Sport*, *44*(2–3), 247–264.

Spaaij addresses the assumption that sport for development programs contributes to the social mobility of sport participants, especially those from disadvantaged backgrounds. He analyzes a sport intervention program specifically designed to enhance the development of capital for disadvantaged youth in Rotterdam, the Netherlands, and that subsequently purports to improve their social position. Although a few participants experienced social mobility, others experience relatively modest changes in their social, economic, and/or cultural capital. Spaaij concluded that such programs not only led to expanded opportunities, they also became part of an effort to create social order in these inner city neighborhoods. These programs therefore also served as a source of social regulation and control.

4. **Van Bottenburg, M. (1994).** *Verborgen competitie: Over de uiteenlopende populariteit van sporten. [Hidden competition: Differences in sport popularity.]* **Amsterdam: Bert Bakker.**

Van Bottenburg uses figuration theory to explore differences in the worldwide spread and growth in popularity of about 30 sports during the last hundred years. He first assesses and tries to explain the popularity of these sports. Subsequently he examines differences in the popularity of these sports across the five continents. He attributes these differences to social and international relations rather than to the nature of the sport itself. An English version of his findings (*Global Games*) was published by University of Illinois Press in 2001.

5. **Verweel, P. (2006) Sensemaking in sport organizations. In A. Knoppers & A. Anthonissen (Eds)** *Making sense of diversity in organising sport* **(pp. 18–28). Maastricht: Shaker.**

This chapter sketches an interpretive approach called sensemaking and shows how it can be used to study cultural dynamics of sport organizations. Verweel explores seven dimensions of sensemaking and demonstrates how they are dependent on frames and cues. This chapter illustrates how a theoretical framework from outside of the sport literature can be applied to an analysis of the culture of sport organizations. The results can provide insights into an organizational culture and into ways its members explain or justify their actions and those of others.

REFERENCES

Boessenkool, J., Leisink, P., & Verweel, P. (2003). Commitment and community in organizations. In W. Koot, P. Leisink, & P. Verweel (Eds.), *Organizational relationships in a networking age: The dynamics of identity formation and bonding* (pp. 21–44). Cheltenham: Edward Elgar.

Breedveld, K. (2014). *Sportparticipatie: uitdagingen voor wetenschap en beleid. [Sport participation: Challenge for research and policy.]* Nijmegen: Inaugural address.

Breedveld, K., Molleman, G., Smits, F., & Reijgersberg, N. (2010). *Kennisagenda sport 2011–2016.* Den Haag: ZonMW & Mulier Instituut.

Buisman, A. (1987). *Jeugdsport en fair play. [Youth sport and fair play.]* Haarlem: De Vriesborch.

Claringbould, I., & Knoppers, A. (2013). Understanding the lack of gender equity in leadership positions in (sport) organization. In P. Leisink, P. Boselie, D. M. Hosking, & M. van Bottenburg (Eds.), *Managing social issues: A public values perspective* (pp. 162–182). Abingdon Oxon: Edward Elgar Publishing.

Claringbould, I., Knoppers, A., & Jacobs, F. (2015). Young athletes and their coaches: Disciplinary processes and habitus development. *Leisure Studies, 34*(3), 319–334.

Crum, B. (1991). *Over versporting van de samenleving. [Sporticization of society.]* Rijswijk, NL: WVC.

De Bosscher, V., De Knop, P., Van Bottenburg, M., & Shibil, S. (2006). A conceptual framework for analysing sports policy factors leading to international sporting success. *European Sport Management Quarterly, 6*(2), 185–215.

De Bosscher, V., Shibil, S., Westerbeek, H., & Van Bottenburg, M. (2015). *Successful elite sport policies: An international comparison of the Sportspolicy Factors Leading to International Sporting Success (SPLISS 2.0) in 15 nations.* Aachen: Meyer & Meyer Verlag.

De Heer, W. (2000). *Sportbeleidsontwikkeling: 1945–2000. [The development of sport policies: 1945–2000.]* Haarlem: De Vrieseborch.

De Knop, P., Scheerder, J., & Van Reusel, B. (2006). *Sportsociologie: Het spel en de spelers. [Sociology of sport: The game and the players.]* (2nd ed.). Maarsden: Elsevier Publishing.

Derks, M. (1999). Hard gras. Sekse, identiteit en voetbalgeschiedenis. [Hard grass: Gender, identity and history of soccer.] *Tijdschrift voor Genderstudies, 2*(4), 5–15.

Dortants, M., & Knoppers, A. (2016). The organization of diversity in a boxing club: Governmentality and entangled rationalities. *Culture and Organization, 22*, 245–260.

Elling, A., & Claringbould, I. (2005). Mechanisms of inclusion and exclusion in the Dutch sports landscape: Who can and wants to belong? *Sociology of Sport Journal, 22*(4), 498.

Elling, A., & Janssens, J. (2009). Sexuality as a structural principle in sport participation negotiating sports spaces. *International Review for the Sociology of Sport, 44*(1), 71–86.

Elling-Machartzki, A. (2015). Extraordinary body-self narratives: Sport and physical activity in the lives of transgender people. *Leisure Studies.* Early print. doi: 10.1080/02614367.2015.1128474

Henry, I. (2009). European models of sport. Governance, organisational change and sport policy in the EU. *Hitotsubashi Journal of Arts and Sciences, 50*, 41–52.

Hoekman, R., Breedveld, K., & Kraaykamp, G. (2016). A landscape of sport facilities in the Netherlands. *International Journal of Sport Policy and Politics, 8*, 305–320.

Huizinga, J. (1938). *Homo ludens.* Abingdon Oxon: Routledge. trans 1994.

Jacobs, F., Smits, F., & Knoppers, A. (2016). 'You don't realize what you see!': The institutional context of emotional abuse in elite youth sport. *Sport in Society*, 1–18. Early print. doi: 10.1080/17430437.2015.1124567

Jacobs, H., & Kamphorst, T. (1976). *Onderzoekwensen op sportgebied. [Preferences for research in sport.]* Utrecht.

Janssens, J., & Verweel, P. (2014). The significance of sports clubs within multicultural society. On the accumulation of social capital by migrants in culturally "mixed" and "separate" sports clubs. *European Journal for Sport and Society, 11*(1), 35.

Kearney, A. T. (1992). *Sport als bron van inspiratie voor onze samenleving. [Sport as a source of inspiration for society.]* Amsterdam: A.T. Kearney/ NOC*NSF.

Knoppers, A. (2011). Giving meaning to sport involvement in managerial work. *Gender, Work & Organization, 18*(s1), e1–e22.

Knoppers, A., Smits, F., & Jacobs, G. F. (2015). *Turnonkruid: Gemaaid maar niet gewied: Onderzoek naar het dames (sub)turntopsportklimaat. [Weeds in gymnastics: Mown but not extinguished. The culture in elite women's gymnastics.]* Rapport geschreven in opdracht van de Koninklijke Nederlandse Gymnastiek Unie (KNGU) en het Veilig sportklimaat (VSK). Utrecht School of Governance, Utrecht University.

Krouwel, A., Boonstra, N., Duyvendak, J. W., & Veldboer, L. (2006). A good sport? Research into the capacity of recreational sport to integrate Dutch minorities. *International Review for the Sociology of Sport, 41*(2), 165–180.

Leisink, P., Boselie, P., Hosking, D. M., & Van Bottenburg, M. (Eds.) (2013). *Managing social issues: A public values perspective* (pp. 162–182). Abingdon Oxon: Edward Elgar Publishing.

Manders, T., & Kropman, J. (1974). *Sportbeoefening en zijn organisatiegraad. [The organization of sport practices.]* Nijmegen: Instituut voor Toegepaste Sociologie.

Manders, T., & Kropman, J. (1982). *Sportbeoefening : drempels en stimulansen. [Sport practices: Obstacles and facilitators.]* Nijmegen: Instituut voor Toegepaste Sociologie.

Miermans, C. (1955). *Voetbal in Nederland: Een onderzoek naar de maatschappelijke en sportieve aspecten. [Soccer in the Netherlands: Research on the societal and sporting aspects.]* Assen: Van Gorcum.

Peeters, R., & Elling, A. (2015). The coming of age of women's football in the Dutch sports media, 1995–2013. *Soccer & Society, 16*(5–6), 620–638.

Schaap, D., Postma, M., Jansen, L., & Tolsma, J. (2015). Combating hooliganism in the Netherlands: An evaluation of measures to combat hooliganism with longitudinal registration data. *European Journal on Criminal Policy and Research, 2 1*(1), 83–97.

Scheerder, J., Vandermeerschen, H., Van Tuyckom, C., Hoekman, R., Breedveld, K., & Vos, S. (2011). *Understanding the game: Sport participation in Europe: Facts, reflections and recommendations.* Research Unit of Social Kinesiology & Sport Management of the K.U. Leuven, Faculty of Kinesiology and Rehabilitation Sciences, Belgium: K.U.Leuven.

Schmeets, H., & te Riele, S. (2014). Declining social cohesion in the Netherlands? *Social Indicators Research, 115*(2), 791–812.

Slobbe, M. V., Vermeulen, J., & Koster, M. (2013). The making of an ethnically diverse management: Contested cultural meanings in a Dutch amateur football club. *Sport in Society, 16*(10), 1360–1374.

Smits, F., Jacobs, F., & Knoppers, A. (2016). 'Everything revolves around gymnastics': Athletes and parents make sense of elite youth sport. *Sport in Society*, 1–18. Ahead of print. doi: 10.1080/17430437.2015.1124564

Spaaij, R. (2007). Football hooliganism in the Netherlands: Patterns of continuity and change. *Soccer & Society, 8*(2–3), 316–334.

Spaaij, R. (2008). Men like us, boys like them: Violence, masculinity, and collective identity in football hooliganism. *Journal of Sport & Social Issues, 32*(4), 369–392.

Spaaij, R. (2009a). Sport as a vehicle for social mobility and regulation of disadvantaged urban youth lessons from Rotterdam. *International Review for the Sociology of Sport, 44*(2–3), 247–264.

Spaaij, R. (2009b). The social impact of sport: Diversities, complexities and contexts. *Sport in Society, 12*(9), 1109–1117.

Steenbergen, J., de Knop, P., & Elling, A. (Eds.) (2001). *Values and norms in sport: Critical reflections on the meaning and position of sport in society.* Oxford: Meyer & Meyer Sport.

Stokvis (1979). *Strijd over sport: Ideologische en maatschappelijke ontwikkelingen. [Struggles in sport: Ideological and organizational developments.]* Deventer: Van Loghum.

Stokvis, R. (2004). Sport en sportsociologie. [Sport and sportsociology.] *Amsterdams Sociologisch Tijdschrift, 31*(4), 542–558.

Stokvis, R. (2010). The genesis of sport history in the Low countries. In S. Pope & J. Nauright (Eds.), *The Routledge companion to sports history* (pp. 350–359). New York, NY: Routledge.

Van Amsterdam, N., Knoppers, A., Claringbould, I., & Jongmans, M. (2012a). A picture is worth a thousand words: Constructing (non-)athletic bodies. *Journal of Youth Studies, 15*(3), 293–309.

Van Amsterdam, N., Knoppers, A., Claringbould, I., & Jongmans, M. (2012b). 'It's just the way it is ...' or not? How physical education teachers categorise and normalise differences. *Gender and Education, 24*(7), 783–798.

Van Bottenburg, M., & Schuyt, K. (1996). *De maatschappelijke betekenis van sport. [The social significance of sport.]* Arnhem: NOC*NSF.

Van Calmthout, M. (2015). Wetenschappers zijn tot een derde van hun tijd kwijt aan geld zoeken. [Scholars spend about a third of their time looking for grants.] *De Volkskrant.* Retrieved from http://www.volkskrant.nl/wetenschap/wetenschappers-zijn-tot-een-derde-van-hun-tijd-kwijt-aan-geld-zoeken~a3869400/. Accessed on February 20.

Van der Roest, J. W., Vermeulen, J., & Van Bottenburg, M. (2015). Creating sport consumers in Dutch sport policy. *International Journal of Sport Policy and Politics, 7*(1), 105–121.

Van Hilvoorde, I., Vos, R., & de Wert, G. (2007). Flopping, klapping and gene doping: Dichotomies between 'natural' and 'artificial' in elite sport. *Social Studies of Science*, *37*(2), 173−200.

Van Sterkenburg, J. (2013). National bonding and meanings given to race and ethnicity: Watching the football World Cup on Dutch TV. *Soccer & Society*, *14*(3), 386−403.

Van Sterkenburg, J., Knoppers, A., & De Leeuw, S. (2010). Race, ethnicity, and content analysis of the sports media: A critical reflection. *Media, Culture and Society*, *32*(5), 819−839.

Van Sterkenburg, J., Knoppers, A., & De Leeuw, S. (2012). Constructing racial/ethnic difference in and through Dutch televised soccer commentary. *Journal of Sport & Social Issues*, *36*(4), 422−442.

Verhagen, S., & Boonstra, N. (2014). Bridging social capital through sports: An explorative study on (improving) inter-ethnic contact at two soccer clubs in the Netherlands. *Journal of Social Intervention: Theory and Practice*, *23*(4), 23−38.

Vermeulen, J. (2011). The bridge as playground: Organizing sport in public space. *Culture and Organization*, *17*(3), 231−251.

Vermeulen, J., & Verweel, P. (2009). Participation in sport: Bonding and bridging as identity work. *Sport in Society*, *12*(9), 1206−1219.

Vertommen, T., Schipper-van Veldhoven, N., Wouters, K., Kampen, J., Brackenridge, C., Rhind, D., … Van Den Eede, F. (2016). Interpersonal violence against children in sport in the Netherlands and Belgium. *Child Abuse & Neglect*, *51*, 223−236.

Verweel, P., & Knoppers, A. (2006). What is going on? In A. Knoppers & A. Anthonissen (Eds.), *Making sense of diversity in organizing sport* (pp. 9−17). Oxford: Meyer & Meyer Sport.

VWS. (1996a). *Sport en allochtonen 1986−1995*. [Sport and immigrants, 1986−1995.] Rijswijk, NL: VWS, Directie sport.

VWS. (1996b). *Wat sport beweegt. [What moves sport?]* Den Haag: Sdu.

CHAPTER 15

SOCIOLOGY OF SPORT: NORWAY, SWEDEN AND DENMARK

Jorid Hovden and Kolbjørn Rafoss

ABSTRACT

This chapter reviews the sociology of sport as a subdiscipline in the Scandinavian countries of Norway, Sweden, and Denmark. The review is based on analyses of central documents, scholarly contributions, as well as interviews with some key scholars in the field. The review describes both similarities and differences across the three countries. The sociology of sport as a subdiscipline and research field is a relatively new area. Among the decisive factors that prompted the field to grow were the expansion of higher education and the institutionalization of sport studies as an academic field during the 1970s. Each country today has approximately 15—20 scholars who identify themselves as sport sociologists. None of the Scandinavian countries have special research programs for research funding in the social sciences of sport, and the main funding derives mostly from the research resources linked to the scholars' professorships/scholarships and external funding. The research trajectories of the field are mostly concentrated around areas like youth sport, participation studies, sport politics, and team sports. Besides scholars involved in gender studies and body culture, most of the key contributors also belong to these areas. Scholars make use of multifaceted theoretical

Sociology of Sport: A Global Subdiscipline in Review
Research in the Sociology of Sport, Volume 9, 265—283
ISSN: 1476-2854/doi:10.1108/S1476-285420160000009019

and methodological approaches. One of the main future challenges of the research field is to maintain and strengthen its critical traditions against the strong influence from neoliberal sport management discourses.

Keywords: Scandinavia; affiliation; theoretical perspectives; key areas; key contributions

INTRODUCTION

In the Scandinavian countries of Norway, Sweden, and Denmark, sociology of sport has, as an academic discipline, been highly influenced by international trends and shows parallels to many other Western countries (Åkesson, 2014; Fasting & Sisjord, 2001). As in several other countries, critical perspectives and issues of social stratification have been at the center from the very beginning. Nevertheless, and in contrast to other countries, Scandinavian studies of social stratification have mostly been concerned with disparities of gender (Hovden, 2007; Messner & Sabo, 1990). Similar to the general trend in the field, studies of sport organizations, governance, and sport politics were scarce until the end of the 1980s, but since then this research has flourished and today represents several trajectories rooted in different approaches and paradigms (Slack, 1997).

In this chapter we will review the main features of sociology of sport in the Scandinavian countries by describing key components such as historical characteristics, number of scholars, main areas of research, key contributions, institutionalization processes as well as future visions and challenges. The review is mainly based on analyses of central documents and scholarly contributions, as well as interviews with some key scholars in the field today.[1] Our descriptions will highlight both similarities and differences across the Scandinavian countries. These countries are often seen as a unit/region, because of many significant societal and cultural similarities, which we address below.

The Scandinavian countries have languages with similar (Germanic) roots, which means that they are understandable to most people across the region. The countries are well known as democratic welfare states and have among the lowest social inequalities in the world. Sweden has the biggest population with about 9 million, followed by Denmark with about 5.7 million, and Norway with about 5.2 million. In all three countries, voluntary organizations as part of the civil society play a significant role as social glue (Selle, 1993). The biggest voluntary organizations of the region are sport organizations, and we find sport clubs widespread in all local communities (Ibsen & Seippel, 2010). The sport organizations are nonprofit, democratic, and voluntary organizations. Norway and Sweden have umbrella organizations (the Norwegian Confederation of Sport and the Swedish Confederation of Sport), which have a monopoly in organizing sport, while Denmark has three main organizations – the Danish Sport Confederation, the Danish Association for Gymnastics and Sports, and the Association for Company Sports. Despite various other differences, the organizational structures, level of participation, types of activities, financial structures, and relation to the public sector are quite similar (Seippel, 2010).

HISTORICAL LANDMARKS

In Scandinavia the sociology of sport as a research field was established at the beginning of the 1970s. Relative to many other academic subfields, it can be seen as a new discipline. The research body had from the very beginning different points of departure due to contextual preconditions. In Denmark, research was rooted in German and French traditions, while Anglo-American traditions were dominant in Norway and Sweden (Fasting & Sisjord, 2001). There were several reasons why research in the sociology of sport appeared in this period and continues to grow.

Among the main factors that prompted the field to grow was the expansion in higher education in Scandinavia at the end of the 1960s and the beginning of the 1970s. This expansion led, among other things, to the institutionalization of sport studies as an academic field where social sciences became integrated. In addition, an explosive increase in participation of organized sport occurred. This increase was mainly caused by the inclusion of new population groups such as women and children. This situation created needs and possibilities to develop new and extended knowledge on sociological issues of sports. In all Scandinavian countries the sociology of sport was as an academic subdiscipline founded by scholars affiliated with departments of universities and teacher training colleges, running studies in sport sciences and/or physical education. However, the institutionalization processes developed somewhat differently across the three countries.

In Norway, the first studies seen as sociological sport studies were conducted by Svein Stensaasen (Stensaasen, 1976) and Kari Fasting (Fasting, 1975), both affiliated with the recently established Norwegian School for Sport Sciences (1968) in Oslo. Initial studies highlighted issues on participation and socialization in sport and physical activity as well as feminist issues. Fasting was one of the first scholars globally to publish academic articles on social stratification on gender.

In Sweden the institutionalization of the discipline seems, among other factors, to stem from the foundation of the Research Council for Studies of Sport in 1970 (Åkesson, 2014). This research council was initiated by the state and the Swedish Confederation of Sports with the objective to initiate, support, and coordinate academic scholarship, including research on social studies of sport. Research on the sociology of sport was, however, very limited in Sweden in the 1970s and 1980s. Most of the social research was conducted in the fields of sport pedagogy and sport psychology (Åkesson, 2014). Even though sociological studies of sport have increased significantly in Sweden since 2000, the trend is still that other social science disciplines are more dominant. In 1988 the Research Council for Studies of Sport was replaced by the Center for Sport Research, which, in most respects, was given similar mandates.

In 1975 the Center for Sport Research established at the Gerlev College of Sports Studies in Denmark. The Center was mainly funded by the Ministry of Culture. The main aim of this research center was to conduct research on the economic, political, and social role of sport in the Danish society and, in particular, sports at the local level (Kokkonen, 2000). From the beginning, mostly researchers from other disciplines than sociology were recruited − from psychology, history, and political science, for instance. Despite this, these scholars were among the first to apply sociological theories to the analysis of sport in Denmark (Eichberg, 1988; Jespersen & Riiskjær, 1980; Kempf, Møller, & Riiskjær, 1983; Korsgaard, 1997). In 2004, the Center for Sport Research was replaced by the Danish Institute for Sport Studies. This Institute was located in Copenhagen and funded by the Ministry of Culture. Its mandate was to conduct and disseminate research on the social sciences in sport.

None of the Scandinavian countries currently have organizations/associations within the field of the sociology of sport. However, the countries have had or have different interdisciplinary associations in the social sciences of sport: in Norway, the Norwegian Association for Sport Research (1983−2005); in Sweden, the Swedish Association for Behavioral and Social Research on Sport (from 1975); and in Denmark, the Forum of Sport, History and Society (1985−2007). The latter changed its name in 2008 to the Society for Sport History, Body and Culture. Despite the fact that Scandinavia has no associations within the sociology of sport, during recent years there have been several initiatives to establish a Nordic network for sport sociologists. However, none of these initiatives has succeeded in maintaining a sustainable network over time.

SCHOLARS AND INSTITUTIONAL AFFILIATION

In Scandinavia, sociology of sport scholars are both scattered across institutions and grouped into "critical masses" (Nordforsk/Academy of Finland, 2012). Norway has about 20 scholars who identify themselves as sport sociologists scattered across different universities and university colleges. Norway has three universities and two university colleges, offering master's degree programs where sociological approaches are central. The Norwegian School of Sport Sciences ran a program in the sociology of sport from 1998 to 2010. Thereafter, the profile was changed to sport management. The most sociological master's degree program today is affiliated with the Sociology Department at the Norwegian University of Science and Technology. This is the only program in Scandinavia belonging to a sociology department. The Norwegian School of Sport Sciences has offered a PhD program in social sport sciences since 1991. The first sociological doctoral thesis arrived in 1993 (Sisjord, 1993), and the first professorship in 1997.

Approximately 18 scholars can be categorized as sport sociologists in Sweden. Besides the group of scholars affiliated to Malmö University, the others are scattered across different Swedish universities (Åkesson, 2014). The first doctoral thesis in sociology in Sweden was written by Schelin (1985). Since then, only five scholars have graduated in sociology, four of them affiliated to sociology of sport department. Malmö University established the first doctoral program in the social sciences of sport in 2010.

In Denmark, like Norway, scholars engaging in the sociology of sport are scattered across the four Danish universities, teaching in bachelor's and master's programs where again sociological issues are central. The first PhD program in sport sciences was established at the University of Copenhagen in 1995. This program also included sociological trajectories, and is still the most sociologically profiled program at the PhD level in Denmark.

During recent years the first textbooks in Scandinavian languages (in Danish and Norwegian) have been published (Lesjø, 2008; Thing & Wagner, 2011). This may signal a strengthening of the sociology of sport as an academic discipline in Scandinavia.

THE ACADEMIC ENVIRONMENT AND BARRIERS
TO RESEARCH

In Scandinavia, the research funding from the national research councils for a subdiscipline like the sociology of sport tends to be very limited. Thus, seen from this point of view the research field is not taken very seriously. The main funding base for most sport sociologists derives from the research resources linked to their own academic positions. A university professorship has normally about 50% of their working time dedicated to research, but nowadays this type of position is rare.

Between 1997 and 2007, Norway had a research program for research in the social sciences of sport funded by the Norwegian Research Council. Even though the program had a low financial status compared to most other research programs, it enabled the financing of several scholarships and many national research projects. The evaluation of the program was on the whole positive, but the program was not maintained.

In Sweden the situation has been and still is somewhat different. The state annually supports the Center for Sport Research with over 2 million euros, of which 37% supports the social sciences (Åkesson, 2014). This funding finances PhD scholarships and postdoctoral positions, as well as research projects. The Swedish Confederation of Sports still plays a central role in the distribution of this annual money by deciding for which activities and projects half the grant should be used. In Sweden, the Center for Sport Research and the Swedish Confederation of Sports both contribute toward sport research and sport literature.

Denmark has no central program for sport research in the social sciences of sport. On the other hand, Denmark receives significant funding both from the Ministry of Culture and from other public and private sources. For example, Denmark has recently established a Center for Ball Games Research, where several scholars are engaged in sociological studies, partly financed by a private sponsor (Skagen Fondene). The Danish situation features an infrastructure with a close relationship among sport organizations, ministries, municipalities, and the private sector. This results in an emphasis on applied research that, in some respects, seems to represent a barrier to the use of critical sociological perspectives and the production of international publications.

Despite the fact that Scandinavia lacks specific sociological research programs, we can nevertheless trace an increasing numbers of scholars within the sociology of sport across the various countries. Among other factors, we consider this increase as a result of well-established PhD programs in all three countries.

MAIN AREAS OF RESEARCH STRENGTH

The sociology of sport in Scandinavia has mostly been concentrated around areas like youth sport, participation studies, sport politics, and ball games. However, these topics demonstrate both similarities and differences across the three countries. The research on the youth segment can be seen as a special research interest in Scandinavia, since the sport organizations mainly justify their societal role and mission around the high involvement of children and youth in organized sport. The main research trajectories in the field of youth sport seem to be surveys of participation and drop-out patterns in organized sport as well various types of studies on social stratification, socialization, and sporting identities (e.g., Engström, 2010; Fundberg, 2003; Peterson, 2011; Sisjord, 2009; Skille, 2005; Thing, Nielsen, & Ottesen, 2015; Walseth & Strandbu, 2014).

Recently, the Scandinavian countries have developed different types of national surveys mapping national participation patterns and changes in physical activity and sports in the population (e.g., Breivik, 2013; Breivik & Rafoss, 2012; Engström, 1999; Larsen, 2003; Pilgaard, 2012). These surveys have made it possible to make comparisons and examine developmental trends over time. All countries have cohort studies showing a substantial increase in physical activity in the populations since the 1980s. Engström's surveys (1999) in Sweden also contain longitudinal data, indicating how socialization from childhood to adulthood influences lifelong participation. National authorities and sport organizations frequently apply this research body as a knowledge base for policy-making.

The Scandinavian countries are also characterized by an extensive research body on sport politics. One of the central aspects comprises governance analyses and particularly studies that in various ways examine the adequacy of the Scandinavian sport model (e.g., Bergsgard, 2005; Bergsgard & Norberg, 2010; Ibsen & Eichberg, 2012; Tangen, 2015). Another popular policy concern is research on sport facilities (e.g., Bundgaard Iversen, 2015; Høyer-Kruse, 2013; Rafoss, 2015; Rafoss & Tangen, 2009; Sjöblom, 2006). These studies revolve mostly around the use and distribution of facilities and whether political priorities mirror the needs of the population and thus contribute to supporting sport for all. Another policy field given much scholarly attention is gender policy. This research field has an emphasis on aspects like gender equity issues, the gendering of sport leadership, and strategies of inclusion and exclusion of women in sports (e.g., Apelmo, 2012; Fasting, 1987; Hovden, 2010, 2012; Lippe, 2010; Olofsson, 1989; Pfister, 2006; Wickman, 2008).

Another popular research trajectory in Scandinavia is sociological studies of ball games (e.g., Ronglan, 2000; Thing, 1999), and particularly studies of football (soccer) and football cultures (e.g., Billing, Franzén, & Peterson, 2004; Hjelseth, 2006; Hognestad & Hjelseth, 2012; Ottesen, Jeppesen, & Krustrup, 2010; Radmann, 2015; Rasmussen, Joern, & Havelund, 2010; Skogvang, 2009). Swedish contributions, mostly about men's football seem, however, to represent the bulk of research in this field, covering a wide range of topics like talent selection processes, processes of professionalization and commercialization, as well as studies on masculinities and hooliganism (e.g., Andersson, 2014; Billing et al., 2004; Carlsson, 2009; Fundberg, 2003; Peterson, 2014; Radmann, 2015). Several scholars have also offered significant studies on women's football, comprising, for example, various aspects of female top players' conditions and possibilities (e.g., Agergaard, Andersson, Carlsson, & Skogvang, 2013; Pfister, 2015).

This profiled research may also indicate, compared to the global research profile, that several areas are weakly represented or mostly left out in Scandinavia. Among the weakly represented areas are critical studies on globalization and commercialization of sport, multifaceted media studies, studies on sport and development, and studies of social inequalities from an intersectional perspective.

MAIN THEORETICAL AND
METHODOLOGICAL APPROACHES

Theoretical approaches applied in Scandinavian sociology of sport represent a multifaceted landscape. Despite this, we trace dominance around sociologists like Bourdieu, Luhmann, and Putnam. Feminist scholarship tends to draw, however, on more diverse perspectives. Regarding methodological approaches, we note an emphasis on both quantitative and qualitative methods. Nevertheless, looking at the recent production of doctoral theses, we tend to see a turn toward more context-based sociological studies.

Probably the most dominant sociologist applied in analyses of sport in Scandinavia is Pierre Bourdieu. His theoretical framework is used in both quantitative and qualitative studies – in studies by people such as Christensen (2009), Engström (2010), Skille (2005), and Langseth (2012). For example, Engström (2008) demonstrates how Bourdieu's theory of practice explains patterns of social stratification in studies of sport participation in the Swedish population. Another sociologist with significant theoretical influence, especially in Norway, is Nicolas Luhmann (e.g., Ronglan, 2000; Storm, Hoberman, & Wagner, 2010; Tangen, 1997, 2004). For example, Tangen's doctoral thesis (1997) illustrates how Luhmann's system theoretical approach allows us to understand the historical processes that influence sport as an independent societal subsystem. Several sociological studies on sport in Denmark and Norway are influenced by Putnam's theoretical framework, and in particular his conceptualization of "social capital" (e.g., Ibsen, 1996; Seippel, 2008b). Such studies discuss the role of social capital in sport as part of a civil society activity and show how the importance of social ties and networks influence social integration in and through sport (e.g., Ibsen, 1996; Ibsen & Seippel, 2010; Seippel, 2008a; Strandbu, 2006).

Scandinavian feminist studies in the sociology of sport are underpinned by various theories. Initial studies (e.g., Fasting, 1979; Lippe, 1982) were theoretically inspired by radical gender role discourses developed by the Norwegian sociologist Harriet Holter (Hovden, 2007). However, from the end of the 1980s we trace an epistemological shift toward more relation-oriented and social constructivist feminist perspectives deriving from theorists such as Beauvoir, Butler, Connell, Haavind, and Lorber. These perspectives gave rise to various contextual studies on how gender is produced and reproduced in sporting contexts and organizations (e.g., Hovden, 2010; Ottesen, Skirstad, Pfister, & Habermann, 2010; Pfister, 2006) as well as several phenomenological and poststructural gender studies on embodiment, emotions, and identity (e.g., Apelmo, 2012; Eng, 2003; Fundberg, 2003; Thing, 1999; Wickman, 2008).

Methodological approaches applied are shaped by a diversity of quantitative and qualitative designs. Within quantitative methodologies we observe a development from descriptive statistical analyses toward multivariate analyses or regression analyses, a development often demonstrated in studies of sport participation (Breivik, 2013; Pilgaard, 2012; Seippel, 2016). Qualitative methodologies are also applied. The most dominant approach used is undoubtedly interviewing, but also several ethnographic studies are conducted (Fundberg, 2003; Hovden, 2000; Ronglan, 2000). Recently, we also see an increase in the use of different types of discourse analyses. One of the

most comprehensive and classical studies, using a Foucauldian approach, is
conducted by the Norwegian sociologist Augestad (2003), who analyzes how
the mutual relationship between knowledge and power influences the historical development of physical education in Norway.

KEY CONTRIBUTORS AND PUBLICATIONS

In Scandinavia most of the key contributors in the sociology of sport are
best known domestically within their national contexts or Scandinavia per
se. This is, among other factors, caused by the fact that many significant
publications are written in Scandinavian languages. Several key contributors and key publications are worthy of note.

Gender and Sport

It seems likely that the best-known sociology of sport contributions from
Scandinavia focus on gender and sport. Besides the two most leading
figures (Kari Fasting and Gertrud Pfister), there are at least 18 other scholars with PhDs and/or international publications, most of them from
Norway. The most well known globally is Kari Fasting – a foundational
scholar on gender and sport. For example, Fasting has been president of
the International Association for the Sociology of Sport and a founding
member of Women's Sports International. Recently, Fasting's research
efforts have mostly been concentrated on sexual harassment and abuse in
sports. In this field she has worked as an expert consultant for several organizations, including the International Olympic Committee. This indicates
how, during her career, Fasting has emphasized a close link between
research, politics, and practice. Among her key publications in the field of
sexual harassment are empirical articles, often coauthored with Cecilia
Brackenridge and others (e.g., Fasting, Brackenridge, & Knorre, 2010;
Fasting, Brackenridge, & Sundgot-Borgen, 2004).

In Norway we also find several other influential contributors. Among
the most internationally well known are Jorid Hovden, Gerd von der
Lippe, and Mari Kristin Sisjord. Hovden has mostly contributed to the
field via her studies on the gendering of sport organizations and sport leadership (Hovden, 2006, 2010). Lippe's most profiled sociological works
comprise gender relations in the sports media (Lippe, 2001, 2010).
Recently, Sisjord's work highlights lifestyle sport and gender and focuses
mostly on the gendering of snowboarding (e.g., Sisjord, 2009, 2013, 2015).

The most international profiled scholar in gender studies of sport in Denmark is Gertrud Pfister. In recent years Pfister is probably the most productive scholar in Danish sociology of sport. Her scholarly work embraces books and articles of various topics. For example, she has published key contributions about women in sport leadership, female coaches, women's football, female fans, and Muslim women's barriers and opportunities in sport (e.g., Pfister, 2006, 2010; Pfister, Lenneis, & Mintert, 2013).

Sweden has also some key contributors in the field of sport and gender. Olofsson (1989) wrote the first doctoral thesis on women and sport in Scandinavia. The thesis was a historical sociological analysis of the development of women's sport in Sweden. Among other studies, there are two recently published doctoral theses (Apelmo, 2012; Wickman, 2008) worth mentioning. Both studies offer intersectional analyses of how meanings of gender and disability are interwoven into disabled athletes' sporting experiences.

Sport and Body Cultures

Most Scandinavian sociological work is empirically oriented. Theoretically oriented contributions are scarce. Nevertheless, the Danish scholar with possibly the most well-known publications globally, Henning Eichberg, has, in his four-decade career, worked with many core theoretical issues in the sociology of sport. He has continually questioned positivistic approaches and raised new theoretical and critical issues. His most influential contributions are concentrated around topics like body and movement cultures, play and games, democracy, and identities in sport. Among other things, Eichberg has paved the way for radical conceptualizations of sport practices based on comparative studies of body cultures. His most recognized books include *Die Veränderung des Sports ist Gesellschaftlich: Die Historische Veraltensforschung in der Diskussion* (1986); *Body Cultures: Essays on Sport, Space and Identity* (1998); and *Bodily Democracy: Towards a Philosophy of Sport for All* (2010).

Football Studies

Another research field with several key contributors is sociological football (soccer) studies. Most of the key contributions on male football are located at Malmö University; Tomas Peterson is one of the key figures. Many of the core publications are, however, in Swedish and thus not internationally well known. The contributions mirror a variety of studies on modern football such as historical sociological analyses (Andersson, 2014), analyses of juridification processes (Carlsson, 2009), analyses of identities and masculinities (Fundberg, 2003), professionalization processes (Billing et al., 2004), talent selection systems in youth football (Peterson, 2014), and studies of hooliganism (Radmann, 2015). A few of these scholars have also contributed to sociological studies on women's football (Agergaard et al., 2013; Kjær & Agergaard, 2013). The latter area has, however, mostly key publications by Danish and Norwegian scholars such as Agergaard (2013) and Skogvang (2006, 2009).

Governance and Sport Politics

The Scandinavian sport model is built on a close relationship between voluntary sport organizations and the State. This relationship has spawned an extensive research body on sport governance and sport politics, especially in Denmark and Norway. In Denmark, the key contributor to this field has been, and remains, Bjarne Ibsen. His most influential works (Ibsen, 1996; Ibsen & Eichberg, 2012) comprise analyses on how changes and political reforms in the Danish voluntary sector have shaped local sport policies as well as overall political strategies in the Danish sport system. In Norway the main contributor is, among others, Nils Asle Bergsgard. Besides his doctoral thesis (Bergsgard, 2005), his best-known works are probably his cross-national comparative analyses of different sport systems (Bergsgard, Houlihan, Mangset, Nødland, & Rommetvedt, 2007; Bergsgard & Norberg, 2010).

FUTURE VISIONS

It is never easy to predict future developments, particularly within a complex and multifaceted field like the sociology of sport. However, as concluding remarks, we will put forward some suggestions based on a few trends and future visions.

Our review mirrors a field where many scholars identify themselves more as social science researchers of sports rather than "pure" sociologists of sport per se. Nevertheless, almost all of the scholars mentioned in this chapter can be considered "critical" scholars. The scholars are rooted in different critical paradigms and examine sociological issues where power structures, democracy, and social inclusion and exclusion in sports are central points of entry.

We hope that this trend will shape future research, even though the future research body will certainly embrace new empirical fields as well as more diverse and complex theoretical and methodological approaches. In Scandinavian research today, as is the case globally, we can trace a trend toward more studies providing intersectional analyses of social inequalities, aiming to grasp, for example, how meanings of race and social class are intertwined (Andersson, 2008; Massao & Fasting, 2010, 2014).

In Scandinavia as in many other countries today, we note how sociological research agendas are challenged by an increasing dominance of (neo-liberal) management discourses. This challenge creates ideological tensions and hegemonic struggles regarding priorities of study programs as well as requiring greater scrutiny regarding which approaches and perspectives belong to the field of sociology versus the field of sport management. This situation may in the future hold potential to revitalize and strengthen critical sociological perspectives, but will most probably contribute to a weakening of sociological concerns. The latter will influence future research agendas and make them to a greater extent infected by theoretical frameworks underpinned by positivistic logics and models of new managerialism. Thus studies holding critical sociological paradigms will need to fight harder for their survival. Nevertheless, the vision we have for the future is that critical sociological paradigms will maintain their current positions in Scandinavia, and continue to represent a counterbalance to mainstream sport management discourses by demystifying neoliberal ideologies.

NOTE

1. We are deeply grateful to Professor Bjarne Ibsen, University of Southern Denmark; Professor Mari Kristin Sisjord, Norwegian School of Sport Science; Professor Ørnulf Seippel, Norwegian School of Sport Science; Professor Eivind Skille, Hedmark University College, Norway; and Professor Tomas Peterson, Malmö University, Sweden for their valuable contributions to this chapter.

FIVE KEY READINGS

1. **Eichberg, H. (2010).** *Bodily democracy: Towards a philosophy of sport for all.* **London: Routledge.**

This book includes a discussion on how the study of "sport for all" may open up new ways of phenomenological knowledge, moving bottom-up from sport to the philosophy of "the individual," of event, of nature, and of human energy. Based on Scandinavian experiences, the book presents studies about festivities of sport, outdoor activities, song and movement, and play and games.

2. **Engström, L. M. (2008). Who is physically active? Cultural capital and sports participation from adolescence to middle age—A 38-year follow-up study.** *Physical Education and Sport Pedagogy, 13*(4), 319–343.

This article is based on a very unique longitudinal study of participation in physical activity and sport. The study demonstrates how differences in sports experiences during childhood and adolescence and differences in cultural capital are reflected in exercise habits in middle age. It illustrates how a middle-aged individual's level of exercise in Sweden is closely linked to that person's social position and, accordingly, to his or her educational capital.

3. **Fasting, K., Brackenridge, C., & Sundgot-Borgen, J. (2004). Prevalence of sexual harassment among Norwegian female elite athletes in relation to sport type.** *International Review for the Sociology of Sport, 4*, 373–386.

This empirical study is one of the most extensive in this research area and tests the widespread assumption that the prevalence of sexual harassment varies by sport. The study includes female elite athletes participating in 56 different sports. The conclusion is that sexual harassment occurs in every sport group and when it comes to female athletes' experiences of sexual harassment, sport type matters far less than sport participation per se.

4. **Ottesen, L., Skirstad, B., Pfister, G., & Habermann, U. (2010). Gender relations in Scandinavian sport organizations – A comparison of the situation and the policies in Denmark, Norway and Sweden.** *Sport in Society, 13*(4), 657–675.

This study represents the first comparative research in Scandinavia on this subject. It examines the underrepresentation of females on executive boards in sport in the Scandinavian countries. The similarities and differences in Denmark, Norway, and Sweden are explained in the light of gender policy in society at large and within the respective sports organizations and gives plausible explanations for why female Danish sports leaders are less concerned with equality questions than their colleagues in Sweden and Norway.

5. **Ibsen, B., & Seippel, Ø. (2010). Voluntary organized sport in Denmark and Norway.** *Sport in Society, 13*(4), 593–608.

Sport organized through voluntary organizations is widespread in the Scandinavian countries. Few studies have, however, explored similarities and differences among various countries. This essay attempts to understand and discuss similarities, differences, and future challenges for voluntary organized sport in Denmark and Norway. The two cases are compared along a set of dimensions including organizational structures, level of participation, type of activity and ideology, resources, and relations to the public sector.

REFERENCES

Agergaard, S., Andersson, T., Carlsson, B., & Skogvang, B. O. (2013). Scandinavian women's football in a global world: Migration, management and mixed identity. *Soccer & Society, 14*(6), 769–780.

Åkesson, J. (2014). Idrottens akademisering. Idrottsvetenskapleg kunnskap inom forskning, utbildning och på arbetsmarknaden. PhD, Malmö Högskola, Malmø.

Andersson, M. (2008). *Flerfarget idrett: Nasjonalitet, migrasjon og minoritet.* Bergen: Fagbokforlaget.

Andersson, T. (2014). The 1958 world cup in Sweden: Between modernity and idyll. In S. Rinke & K. Schiller (Eds.), *The FIFA world cup 1930–2010: Politics, commerce, spectacle and identities.* Göttingen: Wallstein.

Apelmo, E. (2012). Som vem som helst. Kön, funktionalitet och idrottande kroppar. PhD, Lund University.

Augestad, P. (2003). *Skolering av kroppen: om kunnskap og makt i kroppsøvingsfaget.* Institutt for idretts- og friluftslivsfag. Bø:Høgskolen i Telemark.

Bergsgard, N. A. (2005). *Idrettspolitikkens maktspill: Endring og stabilitet i den idrettspolitiske styringsmodellen.* Oslo: Universitetet i Oslo.

Bergsgard, N. A., Houlihan, B., Mangset, P., Nødland, S., & Rommetvedt, H. (2007). *Sport policy.* Hoboken: Taylor and Francis.

Bergsgard, N. A., & Norberg, J. R. (2010). Sports policy and politics – The Scandinavian way. *Sport in Society, 13*(4), 567–582.

Billing, P., Franzén, M., & Peterson, T. (2004). Paradoxes of football professionalization in Sweden: A club approach. *Soccer & Society, 5*(1), 82–99.

Breivik, G. (2013). *Jakten på et bedre liv. Fysisk aktivitet i den norske befolkningen 1985–2011.* Oslo: Universitetsforlaget.

Breivik, G., & Rafoss, K. (2012). *Fysisk aktivitet; omfang, tilrettelegging og sosial ulikhet – En oppdatering og revisjon.* Oslo: Helsedirektoratet.

Bundgaard Iversen, E. (2015). Bedre kommunal styring af idrætsfaciliteter – Hvordan kan ønskede målsætninger nås via anvendelse af forskellige styringsmodeller. PhD, Syddansk Universitet, Odense.

Carlsson, B. (2009). Insolvency and the domestic juridification of football in Sweden. *Soccer & Society, 10*(3–4), 477–494.

Christensen, M. K. (2009). "An eye for talent": Talent identification and the "practical sense" of top-level soccer coaches. *Sociology of Sport Journal, 26*(3), 365–382.

Eichberg, H. (1988). *Det løbende samfund: Idrætssociologi ud fra kroppen.* Slagelse: Bavnebanke.

Eichberg, H. (2010). *Bodily democracy: Towards a philosophy of sport for all.* London: Routledge.

Eichberg, H., Bale, J., Philo, C., & Brownell, S. (1998). *Body cultures: Essays on sport, space and identity.* London: Routledge.

Eichberg, H., & Hopf, W. (1986). *Die veränderung des sports ist gesellschaftlich: Die historische veraltensforschung in der diskussion.* Münster: Lit.

Eng, H. (2003). *Sporting sex/uality: Doing sex and sexuality in a Norwegian sports context.* Oslo: Norwegian University of Sport and Physical Education.

Engström, L. M. (1999). *Idrott som social markör.* Stockholm: HLS Förlag.

Engström, L. M. (2008). Who is physically active? Cultural capital and sports participation from adolescence to middle age—A 38-year follow-up study. *Physical Education and Sport Pedagogy, 13*(4), 319–343.

Engström, L. M. (2010). *Smak for mosjon − Fysisk aktivitet som livsstil och social markör.* Stockholm: Stockholms universitetsforlag.

Fasting, K. (1975). *Fysisk aktivitet og idrettsinteresse i den norske befolkning* (Vol. 32). Oslo: Norges idrettshøgskole.

Fasting, K. (1979). *Kvinners og menns idrettsengasjement sett i forhold til det tradisjonelle kjønnsrollemønsteret* (Vol. 58). Oslo: Norges idrettshøgskole.

Fasting, K. (1987). Sports and women's culture. *Women's Studies International Forum, 10*(4), 361–368.

Fasting, K., Brackenridge, C., & Knorre, N. (2010). Performance level and sexual harassment prevalence among female athletes in the Czech Republic. *Women in Sport & Physical Activity Journal, 19*(1), 26.

Fasting, K., Brackenridge, C., & Sundgot-Borgen, J. (2004). Prevalence of sexual harassment among Norwegian female elite athletes in relation to sport type. *International Review for the Sociology of Sport, 4*, 373–386.

Fasting, K., & Sisjord, M. K. (2001). Fremveksten av idrettssosiologi som eget fagfelt. *Sosiologi Idag, 31*(1), 88–94.

Fundberg, J. (2003). *Kom igen, gubbar!: Om pojkfotboll och maskuliniteter.* Stockholm: Stockholm universitet.

Hjelseth, A. (2006). Mellom børs, katedral og karneval: Norske supporteres forhandlinger om kommersialisering av fotball. PhD, Universitetet i Bergen, Bergen.

Hognestad, H., & Hjelseth, A. (2012). *Kampen om tribunen: Fotball, identitet & makt.* Trondheim: Akademika.

Hovden, J. (2000). *Makt, motstand og ambivalens: Betydningar av kjønn i idretten.* Tromsø: Universitetet i Tromsø.

Hovden, J. (2006). The gender order as a policy issue in sport: A study of the Norwegian sport organizations. *Nordic Journal of Women's Studies, 14*(1), 41–52.

Hovden, J. (2007). *Feminist sociology of sport in Norway: With a side look to other nordic countries* (pp. 46–55). Jyväskylä: University of Jyväskylä.

Hovden, J. (2010). Female top leaders − Prisoners of gender? The gendering of leadership discourses in Norwegian sports organizations. *International Journal of Sport Policy*, *2*(2), 189−205.

Hovden, J. (2012). Discourses and strategies for the inclusion of women in sport − In case of Norway. *Sport in Society*, *15*(3), 283−286.

Høyer-Kruse, J. (2013). Kommunal planlægning af idrætsfaciliteter. PhD, Syddansk Universitet, Odense.

Ibsen, B. (1996). Changes in local voluntary associations in Denmark. *Official Journal of the International Society for Third-Sector Research*, *7*(2), 160−176.

Ibsen, B., & Eichberg, H. (2012). Dansk idrætspolitik − Mellem frivillighed og statslig styring. In H. Eichberg (Ed.), *Idrætspolitik i komparativ belysning − National og international* (pp. 147−210). Odense: Syddansk Universitetsforlag.

Ibsen, B., & Seippel, Ø. (2010). Voluntary organized sport in Denmark and Norway. *Sport in Society*, *13*(4), 593−608.

Jespersen, E., & Riiskjær, S. (1980). *Idrætsfaciliteter i ringsted kommune* (Vol. 1). Slagelse: Bavlebanke.

Kempf, J., Møller, J., & Riiskjær, S. (1983). *Idræt og holdning: 15−19 årige og 40−49 årige i tal og tale* (Vol. 3). Slagelse: Bavnebanke.

Kjær, J. B., & Agergaard, S. (2013). Understanding women's professional soccer: The case of Denmark and Sweden. *Soccer & Society*, *14*(6), 816−833.

Kokkonen, J. (2000). *Research in sport and physical education in the nordic countries*. Helsinki: The Finnish Society for Research in Sport and Physical Education.

Korsgaard, O. (1997). *Kampen om kroppen: Dansk idræts historie gennem 200 år.* København: Gyldendal.

Langseth, T. G. (2012). *Spenningssøkingens sosialitet: En sosiologisk undersøkelse av verdisystem i risikosport.* PhD, Norges idrettshøgskole, Oslo.

Larsen, K. (2003). *Idrætsdeltagelse og idrætsforbrud i Danmark.* Aarhus: Klim.

Lesjø, J. H. (2008). *Idrettssosiologi. Sportens ekspansjon i det moderne samfunn.* oslo: Abstrakt forlag.

Lippe, G. v. d. (1982). *Kvinner og idrett: Fra myte til realitet.* Oslo: Gyldendal.

Lippe, G. v. d. (2001). *Idrett som kulturelle drama: Møteplasser i idrettssosiologi og idrettshistorie.* Oslo: Cappelen.

Lippe, G. v. d. (2010). *Et kritisk blikk på sportsjournalistikk: Medier og idrett i en globalisert verden.* Kristiansand: Universitetsforlaget.

Massao, P. B., & Fasting, K. (2010). Race and racism: Experiences of black Norwegian athletes. *International Review for the Sociology of Sport*, *45*(2), 147−162.

Massao, P. B., & Fasting, K. (2014). Mapping race, class and gender: Experiences from black Norwegian athletes. *European Journal for Sport and Society*, *11*(4), 331−352.

Messner, M. A., & Sabo, D. F. (1990). *Sport, men, and the gender order: Critical feminist perspectives.* Champaign, IL: Human Kinetics Books.

Nordforsk/Academy of Finland. (2012). *Sport sciences in Nordic countries* (Vol. 1/12). Helsinki: Nordforsk and Academy of Finland.

Olofsson, E. (1989). *Har kvinnorna en sportslig chans?: Den svenska idrottsrörelsen och kvinnorna under 1900-talet.* Umeå: Pedagogiska institutionen, Umeå universitet.

Ottesen, L., Jeppesen, R. S., & Krustrup, B. R. (2010). The development of social capital through football and running: Studying an intervention program for inactive women. *Scandinavian Journal of Medicine and Science in Sports*, *20*, 118.

Ottesen, L., Skirstad, B., Pfister, G., & Habermann, U. (2010). Gender relations in Scandinavian sport organizations – A comparison of the situation and the policies in Denmark, Norway and Sweden. *Sport in Society*, *13*(4), 657–675.

Peterson, T. (2011). *Talangutveckling eller talangavveckling?* Stockholm: SISU.

Peterson, T. (2014). *The double articulation of relative age effect on Swedish football.* Idrottsforum.org

Pfister, G. (2006). Gender issues in Danish sports organizations – Experiences, attitudes and evaluations. *NORA – Nordic Journal of Feminist and Gender Research*, *14*(1), 27–40.

Pfister, G. (2010). Outsiders: Muslim women and Olympic games – Barriers and opportunities. *The International Journal of the History of Sport*, *27*(16–18), 2925–2957.

Pfister, G. (2015). On women and football. *International Review for the Sociology of Sport*, *50*(4–5), 563–569.

Pfister, G., Lenneis, V., & Mintert, S. (2013). Female fans of men's football – A case study in Denmark. *Soccer & Society*, *14*(6), 850–871.

Pilgaard, M. (2012). *Flexible sports participation in late-modern everyday life.* PhD, University of Southern Denmark, Odense.

Radmann, A. (2015). Hit and tell – Swedish hooligan narratives. *Sport in Society*, *18*(2), 202–218.

Rafoss, K. (2015). *Hall i nord: En studie av beslutningsprosesser, anleggsbruk og idrettsdeltakelse knyttet til bygging av store innendørshaller i lokalsamfunn i Nord-Norge.* PhD, Norges teknisk-naturvitenskapelige universitet, Trondheim.

Rafoss, K., & Tangen, J. O. (Eds.). (2009). *Kampen om idrettsanleggene: Planlegging, politikk og bruk.* Bergen: Fagbokforl.

Rasmussen, K., Joern, L., & Havelund, J. (2010). *Fotboll och huliganism i skandinavien* (Vol. 8). Malmö. Idrottsforum.org

Ronglan, L. T. (2000). *Gjennom sesongen: En sosiologisk studie av det norske kvinnelandslaget på og utenfor banen.* PhD, Norges idrettshøgskole, Oslo.

Schelin, B. (1985). *Den ojämlika idrotten: Om idrottsstratifiering, idrottspreferens och val av idrott (67).* Lund: Lunds universitet, Sociologiska institutionen.

Seippel, Ø. (2008a). Public policies, social capital and voluntary sport. In M. Nicholson & R. Hoye (Eds.), *Sport and social capital.* Oxford: Butterworth-Heimenann.

Seippel, Ø. (2008b). Sports in civil society: Networks, social capital and influence. *European Sociological Review*, *24*(1), 69–80.

Seippel, Ø. (2010). Professionals and volunteers: On the future of a Scandinavian sport model. *Cultures, Commerce, Media, Politics*, *13*(2), 199–211.

Seippel, Ø. (2016). Sprek, vakker og kjedelig? Trening og mening blant ungdom: 1985–2013? In Ø. Seippel, M. K. Sisjord, & Å. Strandbu (Eds.), *Ungdom og idrett* (pp. 93–112). Oslo: Cappelen.

Selle, P. (1993). Voluntary organisations and the welfare state: The case of Norway. *Official Journal of the International Society for Third-Sector Research*, *4*(1), 1–15.

Sisjord, M. K. (1993). *Idrett og ungdomskultur: Bø-ungdom i tall og tale.* PhD, Norges idrettshøgskole, Oslo.

Sisjord, M. K. (2009). Fast-girls, babes and the invisible girls. Gender relations in snowboarding. *Cultures, Commerce, Media, Politics*, *12*(10), 1299–1316.

Sisjord, M. K. (2013). Women's snowboarding – Some experiences and perceptions of competition. *Leisure Studies*, *32*(5), 507–523.

Sisjord, M. K. (2015). On lifestyle sport and gender. *International Journal for the Sociology of Sport*, *50*(4−5), 596−600.

Sjöblom, P. (2006). *Den institutionaliserade tävlingsidrotten: Kommuner, idrott och politik i Sverige under 1900-talet*. Stockholm: Almqvist & Wiksell.

Skille, E. Å. (2005). *Sport policy and adolescent sport: The Sports City Program*. PhD, Norwegian School of Sport Sciences, Oslo.

Skogvang, B. O. (2006). *Toppfotball: Et felt i forandring*. PhD, Norges idrettshøgskole, Oslo.

Skogvang, B. O. (2009). The sport/media complex in Norwegian football. *Soccer & Society*, *10*(3−4), 438−458.

Slack, T. (1997). *The changing nature of voluntary organizations: Opportunities and constraints*. Paper presented at ISSA Symposium, Oslo, June 26−30.

Stensaasen, S. (1976). *Leisure and sport among youngsters: Glimpses from a current, Nordic project* (Vol. 39). Oslo: Norges idrettshøgskole.

Storm, R. K., Hoberman, J. M., & Wagner, U. (2010). *Observing sport: Modern system theoretical approaches* (Vol. 19). Schorndorf: Hofmann.

Strandbu, Å. (2006). *Idrett, kjønn, kropp og kultur: Minoritetsjenters møte med norsk idrett*. PhD, Universitetet i Oslo, Oslo.

Tangen, J. O. (1997). *Samfunnets idrett: En sosiologisk analyse av idrett som sosialt system, dets evolusjon og funksjon fra arkaisk til moderne tid*. Universitetet i Oslo.

Tangen, J. O. (2004). *Hvordan er idrett mulig?: Skisse til en idrettssosiologi*. Kristiansand: Høyskoleforlaget.

Tangen, J. O. (2015). «Nasjonale strateger», «familiemedlemmer», «spillets spillere» eller «systemets lakeier»? Norsk idrettspolitikk i lys av Slagstad, Selle, Bourdieu og Luhmann. *Sosiologisk Tidsskrift*, (4), 215−237.

Thing, L. F. (1999). *Sport: En emotionel affære: Kvinder, holdsport og aggression*. PhD, Københavns Universitet København.

Thing, L. F., Nielsen, S. F., & Ottesen, L. (2015). Are young people caught in the time bind? A sociological analysis of how young people in an upper secondary school view the issue of finding time to do sports or exercise in their spare time. *Annals of Leisure Research*, *18*(1), 9−24.

Thing, L. F., & Wagner, U. (2011). *Grundbog i idrætssociologi*. København: Munksgaard.

Walseth, K., & Strandbu, Å. (2014). Young Norwegian-Pakistani women and sport. *European Physical Education Review*, *20*(4), 489−507.

Wickman, K. (2008). *Bending mainstream definitions of sport, gender and ability: Representations of wheelchair racers*. PhD, Umeå universitet, Umeå.

CHAPTER 16

SOCIOLOGY OF SPORT: SPAIN

Núria Puig and Anna Vilanova

ABSTRACT

The chapter begins by examining the origins of sociology of sport in Spain, which dates back to the transition to democracy, during which period sport became transformed progressively from an object of social concern into an object of sociological study. It then goes on to analyse the main factors of activation in particular processes of university teaching staff accreditation which acted as catalysts for the set of processes that fostered the emergence of sociology of sport in Spain. Lastly, the principal study fields are analysed by grouping them into three areas: sport and society, social attitudes to sport and sport facilities and organisations. In the conclusion, an assessment is made of contributions made to the speciality as well as of sociology of sport's progressive internationalisation, a rare phenomenon prior to 2005 which is now regarded as a major indicator of the maturity of the discipline.

Keywords: Origins; factors of activation; sociological and methodological pluralism; internationalisation

Sociology of Sport: A Global Subdiscipline in Review
Research in the Sociology of Sport, Volume 9, 285–301
ISSN: 1476-2854/doi:10.1108/S1476-285420160000009020

INTRODUCTION: THE ORIGINS OF SOCIOLOGY OF SPORT IN SPAIN

Sociology of sport in Spain has been the object of analysis on a number of occasions (Moscoso, 2006; Mosquera & Puig, 2003; Puig, 1995, 2005). Given the limited space available to us, we shall cite only the most recent studies on each theme, since these contain earlier bibliographical information.

The first step towards constituting a field of sociology of sport within sport sciences as a whole was the transformation of sport from an object of social concern into an object of scientific study, placed in a removed way from everyday events and pressures. Sport ceased to be regarded as a 'social issue' and started to be seen as a 'sociological issue'. This process took place during the last years of the Franco regime and the period of political transition (1975–1983), a historical moment which greatly conditioned people involved in sport and gave rise to a set of issues posed in accordance with a strong spirit of revindication. The dividing lines between sociology of sport and desires to improve the prevailing situation were far from clearly defined, a characteristic typical of periods of political uncertainty, of change and of transition, as Lefebvre wrote in 1958.

Early in the 1980s a slight change took place in this context. Published works began to be more theoretical in tone or at least denoted greater technical rigour. In 1980 the first survey was conducted on the sporting habits of the Spanish population. Several censuses were published on sport facilities in the country and the first 'Sport in Contemporary Society' symposium was held in Madrid in 1983. Some authors at that time were attracted to the school of thought which emerged in France around 1968 with the Partisans group. What mattered was not so much a concrete theoretical perspective as the examination of a hitherto practically unquestioned reality.

In our view, the first sociology of sport studies to appear at this time were those by Cagigal (1975, 1981) and Manuel García Ferrando. During the transition years, the latter was already producing texts on sociological problems. In 1982, he saw the publication of his *Deporte y Sociedad* (Sport and Society), the first empirical study in a series on the sporting habits and attitudes of the Spanish people. Previously he had published *Los Problemas Sociales del Trabajo Deportivo* (*The Social Problems of Sport Work*) and *Feminidad, Deporte y Conflicto de Roles* (*Femininity, Sport and Role Conflict*). García Ferrando was the first to establish a link between Spanish academic sociology and the then emerging sociology of sport.

From the mid-1980s, sociology of sport began to acquire its own identity in sport sciences as a whole. Themes became progressively diversified and methodological rigour and theoretical reflection increased. It is now worth examining the factors which made the activation of this field possible.

FACTORS OF ACTIVATION

Several factors have influenced the evolution described above: growing awareness of the importance of sport as part of people's everyday habits; the role of the 1992 Barcelona Olympics, which contributed to applying measures to foster the development of sport; the increase in international exchanges (the fruit of European integration); and the creation of an institutional framework which has acted as support to the whole process. This last aspect is fundamental in that it has acted ultimately as a catalyst to all the other factors.

An essential issue in the development of a scientific discipline as such is the existence of an institutional framework of reference which acts as a meeting point for all initiatives. A space is needed to endow the whole with coherence and foster the emergence of a 'critical mass'; that is, the set of human, economic, administrative and other factors necessary for the development of scientific work.

Sociology of sport has managed to develop in Spain thanks to the sport sciences faculties. At the time of writing, 43 faculties exist where sport science courses are offered. Sociology of sport is a compulsory subject in the curriculum and, consequently, a body of teachers specialises in the subject. Furthermore, in a number of cases this subject is taught in master's degree programmes, none of which, however, focus exclusively on this discipline. Moreover, from the information available to us at present, approximately 20 research teams are associated principally with these faculties in which research is conducted into sociology of sport and we estimate that approximately 100 people are linked to them. Nonetheless, what has undoubtedly contributed most to raising the standard of Spanish sociology of sport and to its internationalisation are the accreditation processes which since 2002 are periodically compulsory for university teaching staff.

The publication by Spain's best academic publishing house of the *Sociología del Deporte* handbook, edited by García Ferrando, Puig and Lagardera in 1998, to which contributions were made by many of the people who teach sociology of sport at universities, was a great opportunity to share knowledge. Now in 2016 the fourth edition is currently in preparation (García Ferrando, Puig, Lagardera, Llopis, & Vilanova).

Scientific associations have strengthened the critical mass by fostering exchange between scholars. Several of these focus on this discipline, and we list them below in order of seniority.

The AEISAD (Asociación Española de Investigación Social Aplicada al Deporte, or Spanish Association of Social Research Applied to Sport; http://www.aeisad.org) was founded in 1991. Rather than focusing exclusively on sociology of sport, the association extends its research to other disciplines including anthropology, history, education and management. From the outset, it has organised a twice-yearly public congress and published a newsletter and the congress proceedings.

The Asociación Española de Ciencias del Deporte (Spanish Sport Sciences Association; http://www.cienciadeporte.com/) was created in 1998. Prominent among its activities are the organisation of a two-yearly international congress, publication of the journal *Motricidad, European Journal of Human Movement* and convening a national award for young researchers. Sociology of sport constitutes one of its main fields.

The Federación Española de Sociología (FES; Spanish Sociology Federation) has had a sociology of sport committee since 2007 (http://www.fes-sociologia.com/sociologia-del-deporte/comites/29/). The committee has been assigned a section in the congresses organised by the FES and carries out tasks of dissemination in the field of sociology of sport.

Sociology of sport in Spain has attained a respectable degree of maturity thanks in particular to its full acceptance as a university discipline. The main barrier we have faced hitherto is discrimination against sociology of sport and other social sciences in favour of the experimental sciences in terms of academic evaluation and financial support in the research field. Those of us who work in this sphere are forced to legitimise our work and defend the territory we have managed to conquer, because the hegemonic thinking characteristic of the sport sciences tends not to acknowledge our achievements. This attitude is clearly not exclusive to Spain, however.

We shall now examine the main areas of research and the main approaches adopted.

MAIN AREAS OF RESEARCH AND APPROACHES ADOPTED

It is difficult to offer an exhaustive overview here given the great number of people who work in sociology of sport in Spain. We therefore apologise in advance if we have overlooked any contributions that should have been included in this chapter.

We have organised the information in to three categories: *sport in society*, *social attitudes to sport* and *sport facilities and organisations.*

Sport in Society

Lagardera (1992), further to the proposals put forward by Elias and Dunning, Parlebas and Luhmann, examines the meaning of the sport phenomenon from an historical perspective in order to reach an understanding of its present and of its future trends. His aim was to generate a model to reveal the processes by which different sport practices are incorporated into the sport system. Although he acknowledges diversity, he states that all kinds of sport practice tend to enter into processes of institutionalisation and homogenisation.

By contrast, the heterogeneous nature of the sport system and its transformation from a closed system into an open system lie at the basis of reflections on the part of Puig and Heinemann (1991), Durán (1995) and Martos and Salguero (2009) enriched empirically thanks to the results of successive surveys on sporting habits (García Ferrando & Llopis, 2011).

Given this evolution of sport towards an increasingly heterogeneous system, traditional sport structures now co-exist with others. García Ferrando and Llopis (2011) speak of a post-modern twist in the sport system that reveals the transformation of values traditionally associated with sport, such as discipline and the pursuit of performance, which co-exist with others like hedonism, adventure and emotion. Other studies corroborate these findings. Urteaga and Aldaz (2013) analyse the meaning of sport practices in the light of the liquid modernity that has arisen as the outcome of three significant interrelated historical processes: that of technification, that of acculturation and that of reconstruction and reinstitutionalisation.

This evolution is also reflected in football, a sport that mobilises a great number of players and spectators in Spain. In *Spanish Football and Social Change*, Llopis (2016) regards this sport as enjoying a supremacy which 'converts it into a paradigm of the contradictions and ambivalences that characterise sport in a globalised world' (García Ferrando & Llopis, 2011, p. 22). A great many studies also associate football with the construction of the different national identities currently existing in Spain (Quiroga, 2013; Rodríguez, 2016; Rojo-Labaien, 2014), while a number of others address the theme of racism in this sport (Durán & Jiménez, 2006; Llopis, 2013).

This post-modern twist must not mask continuing inequality in access to sport (García Ferrando & Puig, 2002; Rodríguez, 2008). As in other areas of society, in the first quarter of the twenty-first century, inequality also persists in the sport system, an issue that several authors have examined. Besides the work coordinated by Barbero (1993), we should mention the ones coordinated by Devís (2001), Sicilia and Fernández-Balboa (2004) and Monteagudo and Puig (2004) and the study by Rodríguez (2008). According to Rodríguez, sport is not divorced from relationships of power; it is a social construct in which the conflicts and forms of co-existence between the social agents of sport put their aspirations and negotiating abilities to the test.

From the perspective of sport as a leisure experience, Olivera and Olivera (2016) propose a conceptual classification of activities in the natural environment. Latiesa, Martos, and Paniza (2001) present the major connections that exist between sport and tourism, as well as tourist policies, planning and sustainable tourism.

The media and sport is a further theme that has attracted the attention of many authors. One of the first studies in this field is the one by Moragas, Rivenburgh, and Larson (1995) on the opening ceremony of the 1992 Barcelona Olympics, in which they highlight television's ability to create new realities. For his part, González-Ramallal (2004) focused on the spectacular dimension of modern sport in the media.

More recent are the studies on how the media treat women's sport (Crolley & Teso, 2007; López-Díaz, 2011; Martín, 2009, 2010; Sainz de Baranda Andújar, 2013). In this context, Martín proposes that the issue be analysed using the post-structuralist sexual difference approach based on French philosopher Luce Irigaray's theory of sexual difference.

The sport job market has attracted a great deal of attention, above all in the light of the difficult recession we are currently experiencing. Martínez del Castillo, Puig, Fraile, and Boixeda (1991) and Martínez del Castillo et al. (1992) addressed the theme of the sport job market and its prospects up until the year 2000. More recent studies include Campos-Izquierdo, González-Rivera, and Taks (2016), Observatori Català de l'Esport, Viñas, and Pérez (2014) and Paramio and Zofío (2008). Labour situations are very heterogeneous and are reproduced in and adapted to the open sport system.

All of these processes take place in a globalised society. In 2005 García Ferrando and Moscoso and Alonso published their respective texts on the subject. In 2010 Puig and Gomes edited a special issue of the *European Journal for Sport and Society* on the global/local dialectic. In 2016, Llopis and García Ferrando published an article on the Olympic movement understood as a new social world-object based on the theory of Serres (2006). According to these authors, the Olympic Games represent a paradigmatic example of the globalisation of sport that has been taking place since the end of the last century.

Social Attitudes to Sport

Between 1980 and 2010, every five years García Ferrando directed a survey on sport participation, which marked the evolution of attitudes to the practice of sport (García Ferrando & Llopis, 2011).

Understanding gender differences in access to sport was undoubtedly the issue to which he devoted most of his efforts. A great many of the studies are based on feminist theories of difference, further developed by Martín (2012) and Soler (2009). There are also studies, however, that approach women's sport practice from the perspective of theories of inequality and oppression. Time after time, cases are reported of the unequal treatment women receive in sport (Pujadas et al., 2016). Furthermore, a high degree of sensitivity exists regarding sexual harassment in sport (Chroni et al., 2012; Martín & Juncà, 2014).

More recently, studies have appeared on masculinity in sport (Llopis, 2008; Moscoso, 2008) and initial debates are taking place on the study of non-binary terms of gender relationships (Martín, 2015; Pérez, Fuentes, Pereira, & Devís, 2016).

A tradition exists of studies on the different stages in the human life cycle. Regarding young people, prominent analyses are those by Fraile and De Diego (2006) and Moscoso, Sánchez, Martín, and Pedrajas (2015), and with respect to the elderly, by Aldaz, Arribas, Gil, Montes, and de Cos (2010), Martínez del Castillo, Jiménez-Beatty, Graupera, and Rodríguez (2006) and Serrano, Biedma, Moscoso, and Martín (2013).

Concern with the dual career of top-level sportspersons has generated many studies. Vilanova and Puig (2014) analyse the *strategies* developed by sportspersons in order to undertake a dual career. Efforts have been made to understand the circumstances in which this group lives and to ease the transition to a second career (Álvarez-Pérez, Pérez, González-Ramallal, & López-Aguilar, 2014; López de Subijana, Barriopedro, & Conde, 2015).

Sensitivity towards people who risk social exclusion is high and has increased since 2009. The structures of what has become a weak welfare state are tottering, leaving many people in a state of poverty and threatened by social exclusion. An example of such concern is the monographic issue of the journal *Anduli* on Sport, Inclusion and Social Diversity, which features articles that relate sport with, among others, the elderly, immigrants, the disabled and the homeless (Moscoso & Muñoz, 2012). To these we might add studies that propose measures as well as others that address the theme of sport initiatives set in motion in a spirit of solidarity. Recent publications include the guidebook on *Deporte, Actividad Física e Inclusión Social* (*Sport, Physical Activity and Social Inclusion*), coordinated in 2011 by Gaspar Maza, and the work coordinated by Abadía in 2014.

Though they are less numerous, we should also mention studies on violence in sport (Durán, 1996; Mosquera, 2004), emotions in sport (Lavega, Alonso, Etxebeste, Lagardera, & March, 2014; Puig & Vilanova, 2011) and specific profiles of sportspersons such as runners (Llopis & Vilanova, 2015a), skateboarders (Camino, 2013) and rollerbladers (Capell, 2016).

Sport Facilities and Organisations

Regarding this subject we should highlight the three National Sport Facilities Censuses, published in 1986, 1996 and 2005. A comparison between these periods has made it possible to ascertain the scope of investments made and rationalise construction policies in terms of new facilities (Gallardo, Burillo, García-Tascón, & Salinero, 2009; Martínez del Castillo, 1998).

Sport facilities, however, have been the object of other approaches. Martínez del Castillo and Puig (2005) provide an overview that encompasses their history, social uses and impact on the territory. In 2009 Paramio studied the construction of football stadiums and, in 2013, the processes of urban regeneration through sport. The fact that 45% of the population does not use the corresponding facilities to engage in sport has led to reflections on the use of such facilities, its importance in the realm of social relations (Puig & Maza, 2008) and analyses of the impact of sport practice on the natural environment (Funollet, 2004; Inglés & Puig, 2015).

Heinemann (1999, 2002) has made major theoretical contributions to the study of sport organisations.

Municipal councils have been the object of much attention because they constitute the entities most responsible for promoting sport. Studies have been published on their characteristics and specific aspects (Arboledas & Puig, 2012; Gallardo, 2002; Martínez & Camps, 2008).

Regarding voluntary organisations, attention has focused on describing the characteristics of clubs and their relations with the public sector (Esteve, Di Lorenzo, Inglés, & Puig, 2011; Llopis & Vilanova, 2015b). There is no tradition of the study of commercial organisations.

Tapiador (2008) proposes a model by which to analyse sport policies since the Transition period. Studies have focused on research into the development of the welfare state and into interactions between the agents involved in such development. As the democratising process has advanced, the central role of the public sector has decreased, while its interactions with other stakeholders, voluntary organisations in particular, have increased (Burriel & Puig, 1999; Puig, Sarasa, Junyent, & Oro, 2003). Dissent exists as regards the interpretation of this process, as reflected in the current debate between Moscoso, Rodríguez, and Fernández (2015) and Puig (under review).

CONCLUSION

In this chapter we began by tracing the origins of sociology of sport in Spain which emerged during the transition to democracy. We then went on to analyse the main factors of activation, highlighting the accreditation processes of university teaching staff. The main study areas have been grouped together under the headings of sport and society, social attitudes to sport and facilities and organisations.

The study areas are related to social matters. Most probably for this reason, the sphere in which we have encountered most literature is that of social attitudes to sport: women (less represented than men in sport), the elderly (increasingly numerous and with low purchasing power), immigrants or people threatened by social exclusion and so on. There are practically no studies on doping and violence in sport, despite the fact that they are very much in the news.

There are no clear theoretical or methodological trends. In general, Spanish sociology of sport is characterised by theoretical and methodological pluralism. Theories and methods are chosen on the basis of the initial questions posed by researchers. Nonetheless, we would highlight Martín's contributions to the feminist theories of difference and those of García Ferrando and Llopis when it comes to providing a theoretical framework with which to analyse the sporting habits of the population.

A major problem has arisen, however, related to the sporting habits surveys and the facilities censuses. Every five years since 1980, the surveys had been directed by García Ferrando. Inexplicably, however, the 2015 survey was conducted by other researchers using a different questionnaire. Consequently, the resulting data could not be compared with that of the previous surveys, which created a void as regards the evolution of sporting habits since 2010. Something similar has occurred with the Sport Facilities Census. The Consejo Superior de Deportes modified its criteria, as a result of which each autonomous community has conducted its own census using different parameters. Sociology of sport has therefore lost two invaluable databases. We can only hope that these decisions are temporary ones.

All in all, there can be no doubt that we have now entered fully into the theoretical debate, into a process of fine-tuning methodologies and into optimising the methods by which we may obtain greater empirical knowledge of the sociological aspects of Spanish sport.

In earlier assessments (Puig, 1995, 2005) we expressed concern with the low degree of internationalisation of the discipline. The situation has changed for the better, however. People working in the sociology of sport field publish in international journals, attend congresses organised by European or world associations and participate in projects involving several countries. The discipline has therefore become fully consolidated, enjoying a fine state of health with prospects of ongoing development in view.

ACKNOWLEDGEMENT

The translation into English of this chapter was supported by the Institut Nacional d'Educació Física de Catalunya (INEFC).

FIVE KEY READINGS

1. **García Ferrando, M., Puig, N., Lagardera, F., Llopis, R., & Vilanova, A. (Eds.). (in preparation).** *Sociología del deporte* [*Sociology of Sport*] **(4th ed.). Madrid: Alianza Editorial.**

   This is the fourth edition of the handbook used in faculties that offer the subject of sociology of sport, with contributions from people who work in this field. The main themes are addressed from a pedagogical viewpoint to introduce students to the subject.

2. **García Ferrando, M., & Llopis, R. (2011).** *Ideal democrático y bienestar personal. Encuesta sobre los hábitos deportivos en España 2010 [Democratic Ideal and Personal Wellness: A Survey on Sporting Habits in Spain, 2010].* **Madrid: Consejo Superior de Deportes & Centro de Investigaciones Sociológicas.**

The culmination of successive analyses of the sporting habits surveys. The authors speak of a twist in the sport system that reveals the transformation of values associated with sport, in the sense that traditional and post-modern values now co-exist. They argue that sport is an area in which citizens may exercise their sovereignty in the first person, though in a limited way, in the context of a democratic society (hence the title of the book).

3. **Moscoso, D., & Puig, N. (2006). Sociología del Deporte. [Special issue].** *Revista Internacional de Sociología, XIV(44).*

This special issue features the main current research areas, namely sporting habits, gender, the elderly, top-level sportspersons, tourism and so on, which bring to light the plurality of theoretical and methodological approaches.

4. **Moscoso, D., & Muñoz, V. (2012). Deporte, inclusión y diversidad social. [Special issue].** *Anduli, 11.*

This is a special issue that focuses on those sectors of society threatened by exclusion. Experts in the field successively address the issues of the elderly, immigrants, convicts, the disabled, post-conflict social contexts, Romani women and the homeless.

5. **Puig, N., & Maza, G. (2008). El deporte en los espacios públicos urbanos. [Special issue].** *Apunts Educació Física i Esports, 91.*

The result of research conducted in Barcelona on the use of urban public spaces for sport. Seen from a variety of perspectives, the core idea considers public space as an environment in which to learn to become a citizen, that is, where people may discover how to acquire commitment in the face of conflicts.

REFERENCES

Abadía, S., Medina, F. X., Sánchez, R., Bantulà, J., Fornons, D., Bastida, N., & Pujadas, X. (2014). Entre el boom atlético y la cooperación social. Las carreras solidarias y el ejemplo de la Trailwalker España 2013. *Península, 9*(1), 105–123. doi:10.1016/s1870-5766 (14)70122-9

Aldaz, J., Arribas, S., Gil, L., Montes, D., & de Cos, I. L. (2010). Transformación de los hábitos de práctica de actividad física y deporte de la población mayor de 65 años en Gipuzkoa. *Retos. Nuevas tendencias en Educación Física, Deporte y Recreación, 17*, 122–125.

Álvarez-Pérez, P. R., Pérez, D., González-Ramallal, M. E., & López-Aguilar, D. (2014). La formación universitaria de deportistas de alto nivel: análisis de una compleja relación entre estudios y deporte. *Retos: nuevas tendencias en educación física, deporte y recreación, 26*, 94–100.

Arboledas, D., & Puig, N. (2012). Análisis comparativo de los servicios deportivos municipales de Andalucía y Cataluña. *Revista Internacional de Ciencias del Deporte, 29*(8), 223–244. doi:10.5232/ricyde2012.02903

Barbero, J. I. (1993). *Materiales de sociología del deporte.* Madrid: La Piqueta.

Burriel, J. C., & Puig, N. (1999). Responsabilidades y relaciones entre el sector público y el privado en el sistema deportivo. In J. Subirats (Ed.), *¿Existe sociedad civil en España?. Responsabilidades colectivas y valores públicos.* Madrid: Fundación Encuentro.

Cagigal, J. M. (1975). *El deporte en la sociedad actual.* Madrid: Editora Nacional.

Cagigal, J. M. (1981). *¡Oh deporte! Anatomía de un gigante.* Valladolid: Miñón.

Camino, X. (2013). La irrupción de la cultura skater en el espacio público de Barcelona. *Arxiu d'Etnografia de Catalunya, 13*, 11–38.

Campos-Izquierdo, A., González-Rivera, M. D., & Taks, M. (2016). Multi-functionality and occupations of sport and physical activity professionals in Spain. *European Sport Management Quarterly, 16*(1), 106–126. doi:10.1080/16184742.2015.1108990

Capell, M. (2016). *Qui són els patinadors urbans? Esport, identitat i passió a la Barcelona Contemporània.* Barcelona: Blanquerna. Retrieved from http://www.tdx.cat/handle/10803/360331

Chroni, S., Fasting, K., Hartill, M., Knorre, N., Martín, M., Papaefstathiou, M., & Zurc, J. (2012). *Prevention of sexual and gender harassment and abuse in sports: Initiatives in Europe and beyond.* Germany: Deutsche Sportjugend.

Crolley, L., & Teso, E. (2007). Gendered narratives in Spain: The representation of female athletes in Marca and El País. *International Review for the Sociology of Sport, 42*(2), 149–166. doi:10.1177/1012690207084749

Devís, J. (Ed.). (2001). *La Educación Física, el Deporte y la Salud en el siglo XXI.* Alcoy: Editorial Marfil.

Durán, J. (1995). Análisis evolutivo del deporte en la sociedad española (1975–1990): Hacia una creciente complejidad y heterogeneidad deportiva. *Revista Española de Educación Física y Deportes, 1*, 15–24.

Durán, J. (1996). *El vandalismo en el fútbol. Una reflexión sobre la violencia en la sociedad moderna.* Madrid: Gymnos.

Durán, J., & Jiménez, P. J. (2006). Fútbol y Racismo: un problema científico y social. *Revista Internacional de Ciencias del Deporte, 2*(3), 68–94.

Sociology of Sport: Spain   297

Esteve, M., Di Lorenzo, F., Inglés, E., & Puig, N. (2011). Empirical evidence of stakeholder management in sports clubs: The impact of the board of directors. *European Sport Management Quarterly, 11*(4), 423–440. doi:10.1080/16184742.2011.599210

Fraile, A., & De Diego, R. (2006). Motivaciones de los escolares europeos para la práctica del deporte escolar: Un estudio realizado en España, Italia, Francia y Portugal. *Revista Internacional de Sociología, 64*(44), 85–109.

Funollet, F. (2004). La necesidad de las actividades deportivas en el medio natural. *Tándem, 16*, 7–19.

Gallardo, L. (2002). Características generales de los servicios deportivos municipales en Castilla-La Mancha. *Revista Motricidad, 9*, 165–191.

Gallardo, L., Burillo, P., García-Tascón, M., & Salinero, J. J. (2009). The ranking of the regions with regard to their sports facilities to improve its planning in sport: The case of Spain. *Social Indicators Research, 94*(2), 297–317.

García Ferrando, M. (2005). Globalización y deporte: paradojas de la globalización. In A. Ariño (Ed.), *Las encrucijadas de la diversidad cultural* (pp. 453–468). Madrid: Centro de Investigaciones Sociológicas.

García Ferrando, M., & Llopis, R. (2011). *Ideal democrático y bienestar personal. Encuesta sobre los hábitos deportivos en España 2010*. Madrid: Consejo Superior de Deportes & Centro de Investigaciones Sociológicas.

García Ferrando, M., & Puig, N. (2002). Postmodernity and inequality in the sporting habits of the Spanish population. In M. Friederici, H. D. Horch, & M. Schubert (Eds.), *Sport, Wirtschaft und Gesellschaft* (pp. 53–66). Schorndorf: Hofmann.

García Ferrando, M., Puig, N., & Lagardera, F. (Eds.). (1998). *Sociología del deporte*. Madrid: Alianza Editorial.

García Ferrando, M., Puig, N., Lagardera, F., Llopis, R., & Vilanova, A. (Eds.). (in preparation). *Sociología del deporte* (4th ed.). Madrid: Alianza Editorial.

González-Ramallal, M. E. (2004). El reflejo del deporte en los medios de comunicación en España. *Revista Española de Sociología, 4*, 271–280.

Heinemann, K. (1999). *Sociología de las Organizaciones Voluntarias. El ejemplo del club deportivo*. Valencia: Tirant lo Blanch, Asociación Española de Investigación Social Aplicada al Deporte.

Heinemann, K. (2002). *Las organizaciones deportivas: Un reto para la gestión*. Barcelona: UB Virtual – Universitat de Barcelona.

Inglés, E., & Puig, N. (2015). Sports management in coastal protected areas. A case study on collaborative network governance towards sustainable development. *Ocean & Coastal Management, 118*(B), 178–188. doi:10.1016/j.ocecoaman.2015.07.018

Lagardera, F. (1992). De la aristocracia gimnástica al deporte de masas. *Sistema: Revista de ciencias sociales, 110–111*, 9–36.

Latiesa, M., Martos, P., & Paniza, J. L. (Eds.). (2001). *Deporte y cambio social en el umbral del Siglo XXI*. Madrid: Librerías Deportivas Esteban Sanz-AEISAD.

Lavega, P., Alonso, J. I., Etxebeste, J., Lagardera, F., & March, J. (2014). Relationship between traditional games and the intensity of emotions experiences by participants. *Research Quarterly for Exercise and Sport, 84*, 457–467.

Lefebvre, H. (1958). *Critique de la vie quotidienne*. Paris: L'Arche editeur.

Llopis, R. (2008). Learning and representation: The construction of masculinity in football. An analysis of the situation in Spain. *Sport in Society: Cultures, Commerce, Media, Politics, 11*(6), 685–695. doi:10.1080/17430430802283948

Llopis, R. (2013). Racism, xenophobia and intolerance in Spanish football: Evolution and responses from the government and the civil society. *Soccer & Society*, *14*(2), 262−276. doi:10.1080/14660970.2013.776461

Llopis, R. (2016). *Spanish football and social change. Sociological investigations.* London: Palgrave Macmillan.

Llopis, R., & García Ferrando, M. (2016). Los Juegos Olímpicos como NOMS. El olimpismo en la sociedad deportivizada global. *Revista Española de Sociología*, *25*(1), 109−131.

Llopis, R., & Vilanova, A. (2015a). Spain: A sociological analysis of the evolution and characteristics of running. In K. Breedveld & J. Borgers (Eds.), *Running across Europe. The rise and size of one of the largest sport markets.* London: Palgrave Macmillan.

Llopis, R., & Vilanova, A. (2015b). Sports clubs in Spain − A sociological analysis. In C. Breuer, R. Hoekman, S. Nagel, & H. van der Werff (Eds.), *Sport clubs in Europe. A cross-national comparative perspective* (pp. 381−400). London: Springer.

López de Subijana, C., Barriopedro, M., & Conde, E. (2015). Supporting dual career in Spain: Elite athletes' barriers to study. *Psychology of Sport and Exercise*, *21*, 57−64. doi:10.1016/j.psychsport.2015.04.012

López-Díaz, P. (2011). *Deporte y mujeres en los medios de comunicación. Sugerencias y recomendaciones.* Madrid: Consejo Superior de Deportes.

Martín, M. (2009). An analysis of Amaya Valdemoro's portrayal in a Spanish newspaper during Athens 2004. In P. Markula (Ed.), *Olympic women and the media* (pp. 185−213). London: Palgrave Macmillan.

Martín, M. (2010). Spain. In T. Bruce, J. Hovden, & P. Markula (Eds.), *Media coverage of women at the 2004 Olympic games. Missing in action* (pp. 127−140). Rotterdam: Sense Publishers.

Martín, M. (2012). The (im)possible sexual difference: Representations from a rugby union setting. *International Review for the Sociology of Sport*, *47*(2), 183−199.

Martín, M. (2015). Assessing the sociology of sport: On gender identities in motion and how to de-essentialize difference(s). *International Review for the Sociology of Sport*, *50*(4−5), 542−546.

Martín, M., & Juncà, A. (2014). El acoso sexual en el deporte: el caso de las estudiantes-deportistas del grado de Ciencias de la Actividad Física y el Deporte de Cataluña. *Apunts. Educación Física y Deportes*, *115*(1), 72−81. doi:10.5672/apunts.2014-0983.es. (2014/1).115.07

Martínez, I., & Camps, A. (2008). La externalización de los servicios deportivos municipales. Estudio de caso en Bizkaia. *Apunts. Educación Física y Deportes*, *92*(2), 74−80.

Martínez del Castillo, J. (1998). *Las Instalaciones Deportivas en España. II Censo Nacional de Instalaciones Deportivas de 1997.* Madrid: Consejo Superior de Deportes.

Martínez del Castillo, J., Jiménez-Beatty, J. E., Graupera, J. L., & Rodríguez, M. L. (2006). Condiciones de vida, socialización y actividad física en la vejez. *Revista Internacional de Sociología*, *64*(44), 39−62. doi:10.3989/ris.2006.i44.27

Martínez del Castillo, J., & Puig, N. (2005). Espacio y tiempo en el deporte. In M. García Ferrando, N. Puig, & F. Lagardera (Eds.), *Sociología del deporte* (pp. 159−186). Madrid: Alianza editorial.

Martínez del Castillo, J., Puig, N., Fraile, A., & Boixeda, A. (1991). *La estructura ocupacional del deporte en España. Encuesta realizada sobre los sectores de Entrenamiento, Docencia, Animación y Dirección.* Madrid: Consejo Superior de Deportes.

Martínez del Castillo, J., Puig, N., Fraile, A., Navarro, C., Jiménez, J., Martínez, J., & De Miguel, C. (1992). *Deporte, sociedad y empleo. Proyección del mercado deportivo laboral en la España de los noventa. En los sectores de entrenamiento, docencia, animación y dirección.* Madrid: Ministerio de Educación y Ciencia, Consejo Superior de Deportes.

Martos, P., & Salguero, A. (2009). Análisis de los modelos deportivos en la sociedad actual. In A. Vilanova, J. Castillo, A. Fraile, M. González, J. Martínez del Castillo, N. Puig, … S. Soler (Eds.), *Deporte, Salud y medio ambiente* (pp. 131−141). Madrid: Librerías Deportivas Esteban Sanz.

Maza, G. (Ed.). (2011). *Deporte, actividad física e inclusión social. Una guía para la intervención social a través de las actividades deportivas.* Madrid: Consejo Superior de Deportes.

Monteagudo, M. J., & Puig, N. (2004). *Ocio y deporte. Un análisis multidisciplinar.* Bilbao: Universidad de Deusto.

Moragas, M., Rivenburgh, N. K., & Larson, J. F. (1995). *Television in the Olympics.* London: John Libbey.

Moscoso, D. J. (2006). La sociología del deporte en España. Estado de la cuestión. *Revista Internacional de Sociología, 64*(44), 177−204.

Moscoso, D. J. (2008). The social construction of gender identity amongst mountaineers. *European Journal for Sport and Society, 5*(2), 187−194.

Moscoso, D. J., & Alonso, V. (2005). Globalización y deporte. Una propuesta de investigación a través del fútbol en Canarias. *Cultura, ciencia y deporte: revista de ciencias de la actividad física y del deporte de la Universidad Católica de San Antonio, 1*(3), 125−130.

Moscoso, D. J., & Muñoz, V. (2012). Deporte, inclusión y diversidad social, antecedentes. *Revista Andaluza de Ciencias Sociales, 11*, 13−19.

Moscoso, D. J., Rodríguez, Á., & Fernández, J. (2015). Elitist rhetoric and the sports gap. Examining the discourse and reality of sport in Spain. *European Journal for Sport and Society, 12*(1), 33−53.

Moscoso, D. J., Sánchez, R., Martín, M., & Pedrajas, N. (2015). ¿Qué significa ser activo en una sociedad sedentaria? Paradojas de los estilos de vida y el ocio en la juventud española. *EMPIRIA. Revista de Metodología de Ciencias Sociales, 30*(1), 77−108. doi: empiria.30.2015.13886

Mosquera, M. J. (2004). *No violencia en el deporte y en la vida. Guía para docentes y personas interesadas.* A Coruña: Xunta de Galicia.

Mosquera, M. J., & Puig, N. (2003). Sociología de la actividad física y el deporte en España. In J. Dosil (Ed.), *Ciencias de la Actividad Física y el Deporte* (pp. 91−126). Madrid: Síntesis.

Observatori Català de l'Esport, Viñas, J., & Pérez, D. (2014). *El mercat de treball de l'esport a Catalunya. Especial incidència a la província de Barcelona.* Barcelona: INDE.

Olivera, J., & Olivera, A. (2016). Adventure Physical Activities in Nature (APAN): Review of the Taxonomy (1995−2015) and Tables for Classification and Identification of Practices. *Apunts. Educación Física y Deportes, 124*, 53–70.

Paramio, J. L. (2009). ¡Ha llegado el football¡ Campos y estadios de fútbol en Madrid (1885−1966). *Ilustración de Madrid, 13*, 11−18.

Paramio, J. L. (2013). Sport and urban regeneration. In I. Henry & L.-M. Ko (Eds.), *Routledge handbook of sport policy* (pp. 275−288). Abingdon: Routledge.

Paramio, J. L., & Zofío, J. L. (2008). Labor market duality and leisure industries in Spain quality of life versus standard of living. *American Journal of Economics and Sociology, 67*(4), 683−717.

Pérez, V., Fuentes, J., Pereira, S., & Devís, J. (2016). Abjection and alterity in the imagining of transgender in PE and sport: A pedagogical approach in higher education. *Sport, Education and Society*, *21*(7), 985–1002. doi:10.1080/13573322.2014.981253

Puig, N. (1995). The sociology of sport in Spain. *International Review for the Sociology of Sport*, *30*(2), 123–139. doi:10.1177/101269029503000201

Puig, N. (2005). La Sociología del Deporte en España. In Á. M. González (Ed.), *Avances en las Ciencias del Deporte* (pp. 153–174). Bizkaia: Universidad del País Vasco. Servicio Editorial.

Puig, N. (under review). Sport for all and elitist sports in Spain. Reply to David Moscoso-Sánchez, Álvaro Rodríguez-Díaz and Jesús Fernández-Gavira. *European Journal for Sport and Society*.

Puig, N., & Gomes, R. (2010). Sport, between local and global. *Special Issue of European Journal for Sport and Society*, *7*, 177–302.

Puig, N., & Heinemann, K. (1991). El deporte en la perspectiva del año 2000. *Papers. Revista de Sociología*, *38*, 123–141. doi:10.5565/rev/papers/v38n0.1613

Puig, N., & Maza, G. (2008). El deporte en los espacios públicos urbanos. Reflexiones introductorias. *Apunts. Educación Física y Deportes*, *91*(1), 3–8.

Puig, N., Sarasa, S., Junyent, R., & Oro, C. (2003). Sport and the welfare state in the democratisation process in Spain. In K. Heinemann (Ed.), *Sport and welfare policies*. Schorndorf: Hofmann, The Club of Cologne.

Puig, N., & Vilanova, A. (2011). Positive functions of emotions in achievement sports. *Research Quarterly for Exercise and Sport*, *82*(2), 334–344. doi:10.1080/02701367.2011.10599761

Pujadas, X., Garai, B., Gimeno, F., Llopis, R., Ramírez, G., & Parrilla, J. M. (2016). Sports, morality and body: The voices of sportswomen under Franco's dictatorship. *International Review for the Sociology of Sport*, *51*(6), 679–698. doi:10.1177/1012690214551182

Quiroga, A. (2013). *Football and national identities in Spain. The strange death of Don Quixote*. London: Palgrave Macmillan.

Rodríguez, Á. (2008). *El deporte en la construcción del espacio social*. Madrid: Centro de Investigaciones Sociológicas.

Rodríguez, V. (2016). Soccer, nationalism and the media in contemporary Spanish society: La Roja, Real Madrid & FC Barcelona. *Soccer & Society*, *17*, 628–643. doi:10.1080/14660970.2015.1067793

Rojo-Labaien, E. (2014). Football and the representation of Basque identity in the contemporary age. *Soccer & Society*. [Published online]. doi:10.1080/14660970.2014.980741

Sainz de Baranda Andújar, C. (2013). *Mujeres y deporte en los medios de comunicación. Estudio de la prensa deportiva española (1979–2010)*.

Serrano, R., Biedma, L., Moscoso, D. J., & Martín, M. (2013). Perceived health, physical activity and sport among the elderly of Spain. *Advances in Applied Sociology*, *3*(2), 151–156. doi:10.4236/aasoci.2013.32020

Serres, M. (2006). *Récits d'humanisme*. Paris: Le Pommier.

Sicilia, A., & Fernández-Balboa, J. M. (2004). *La otra cara de la investigación: reflexiones desde la educación física*. Sevilla: Wanceulen Editorial Deportiva.

Soler, S. (2009). Los procesos de reproducción, resistencia y cambio de las relaciones tradicionales de género en la educación física: el caso del fútbol. *Cultura y Educación*, *21*, 23–42.

Tapiador, M. (2008). Evolución de los sistemas deportivos locales en España desde la transición hasta la actualidad. Un modelo de análisis. *Cultura Ciencia y Deporte*, *3*(9), 155–160.

Urteaga, E., & Aldaz, J. (2013). Practiques sportives et usages liquides. *Sociétés*, *120*(2), 147–157. doi:10.3917/soc.120.0147

Vilanova, A., & Puig, N. (2014). Personal strategies for managing a second career: The experiences of Spanish Olympians. *International Review for the Sociology of Sport*. doi:10.1177/1012690214536168

CHAPTER 17

SOCIOLOGY OF SPORT: UNITED KINGDOM

John Horne and Dominic Malcolm

ABSTRACT

Sociology of sport in the United Kingdom is as old as the subdiscipline itself but was uniquely shaped by the prominence of football hooliganism as a major social issue in the 1970s and 1980s. While it remains a somewhat niche activity, the field has been stimulated by the growing cultural centrality of sport in UK society. This quantitative and qualitative development has been recognized in recent governmental evaluations of research expertise. Current research reflects this expanded range of social stratification and social issues in sport both domestically and on a global level, while the legacy of hooligan research is evident in the continuing concentration on studies of association football. Historically, this empirical research has largely been underpinned by figurational, Marxist/neo-Marxist, or feminist sociological theories, but there is now a greater emphasis on theoretical synthesis and exploration. As a consequence of the expansion of the field, allied to its empirical and theoretical diversity, there is a burgeoning literature produced by UK sociologists of sport that spans entry-level textbooks, research monographs, and the editorship of a significant number of specialist journals. The chapter concludes by noting the future prospects of the sociology of sport in the

Sociology of Sport: A Global Subdiscipline in Review
Research in the Sociology of Sport, Volume 9, 303–319
Copyright © 2017 by Emerald Group Publishing Limited
All rights of reproduction in any form reserved
ISSN: 1476-2854/doi:10.1108/S1476-285420160000009021

United Kingdom in relation to teaching, research, and relations with other sport-related subdisciplines and the sociological mainstream.

Keywords: Figurational sociology; neo-Marxist theory; football hooliganism; Leicester School; Chelsea School

INTRODUCTION: A HISTORY OF SOCIOLOGY OF SPORT IN THE UNITED KINGDOM

As Malcolm argues (2012, 2014), identifying the emergence of a new field is an imprecise and contested process. Normally, however, emergence is evaluated relative to a field's literary and/or organizational manifestations. According to either criterion, the sociology of sport in the United Kingdom emerged as early as it did anywhere else. The first publications by UK-based sociologists of sport were Peter McIntosh's *Sport in Society* (1960), Dunning's (1963) history of association football and Elias and Dunning's (1966) analysis of the interdependence of agency and structure through an exploration of the dynamics of team sports. In 1969 Elias and Dunning first published their thesis on the *Quest for Excitement in Leisure*, which sought to explain why sport had such social significance in contemporary society (Elias & Dunning, 1986). However, the first English language text to bear the title, *The Sociology of Sport*, was Dunning's (1971) edited collection. Organizationally, McIntosh, Elias, and Dunning attended the initial meetings of the International Committee for the Sociology of Sport (ICSS), and an ICSS symposium was held in Leicester in 1968.

The underlying tension between physical educationalists and sociologists in the wider development of the subdiscipline (Sage, 1997) was relatively quickly resolved in the United Kingdom. McIntosh soon withdrew from organizational affairs and Dunning's alliance with Elias (who would subsequently become recognized as a major figure in sociological theory per se) cemented the sociological credentials of the subdiscipline. However, uniquely perhaps to the United Kingdom, football hooliganism played a key role in stimulating the field's growth. Social and political concern over the frequency and scale of spectator disorder broadened academic interest in sport and resonated particularly with the emerging British cultural studies scholars interested in working-class leisure cultures more broadly. In addition to Ian Taylor, who wrote a preliminary, Marxist, analysis of football hooliganism for Dunning's anthology, John Clarke, Chas Critcher, and even Stuart Hall from the Birmingham Center for Contemporary Cultural Studies contributed to the debate. Dunning, Murphy, and Williams (1988) attracted significant research funding, exhibited a considerable media presence, and produced publications that came (as close as anything) to establishing a hegemonic perspective on the sociology of football crowd disorder (see below).

Despite the acceptance and defense of some disciplinary distinctions, the development of the sociology of sport in the United Kingdom was aided by scholars in adjacent academic fields who shared a focus on sport. With no critical mass of sociologists of sport, there was a degree of interchange with historians (notably Tony Mangan, Tony Mason, and Dick Holt), geographers (John Bale), political scientists (Lincoln Allison), and media analysts (Garry Whannel). In addition there was recognition of some synergies and also distinct differences with scholars whose focus was more broadly leisure (Stan Parker, Ken Roberts). Concomitantly the empirical focus of the field expanded, examining aspects of race (Cashmore, 1982), gender politics (Hargreaves, 1994), and the commercial interests and implications of sport (Tomlinson & Whannel, 1984, 1986). The first sociology of sport research monograph was *Barbarians, Gentlemen and Players* (Dunning & Sheard, 1979), the first text to outline competing sociological theories of sport/leisure was Rojek's *Capitalism and Leisure Theory* (1985), and the first student textbook was Cashmore's *Making Sense of Sport* (1990).

Despite these indications of growth the UK field remained organizationally underdeveloped. This may have been due to theoretical differences (see below), or because the field of leisure and recreation provided an alternative forum for research dissemination. The British Sociological Association (BSA) established a Leisure and Recreation Group and the Leisure Studies Association (LSA) was formed in 1975. Scholars at the University of Brighton Chelsea School (see below) helped organize its first major international conference (1984). UK sociologists have also been outward facing: in addition to having had a continued presence in the ICSS/ISSA executive, a number of UK-born sociologists have been influential in developing the subject in North America, such as Alan Ingham, Peter Donnelly, Kevin Young, and most recently David Andrews. It was not until 1995 that a specific and explicit association for the sociology of sport was founded in the United Kingdom. The BSA Sport Study Group (BSA SSG) continues to have a presence at the annual BSA conference, has periodically held its own regional seminars and has maintained an annual postgraduate forum since 2003.

APPROXIMATE NUMBER OF SCHOLARS AND WHERE LOCATED

As sport has developed into a multibillion-dollar, mass mediated, global industry, the attention paid to it by sociologists and other social scientists has grown. Of course, practicing sociologists of sport have remained a small minority of BSA members — the BSA SSG list contained 180 members out of a total BSA membership of nearly 2,500 in March 2016, and approximately half of the list membership was not BSA members. But the academic study of sport has flourished in British universities.

As Horne, Tomlinson, Whannel, and Woodward (2013, p. xiii) noted: "In the late 1970s only a very few colleges or universities offered degree programs in sport-related subjects. Over the following three decades, more than a hundred institutions moved into this field." The importance of the field was also recognized in its research profile. In 1996 the higher education funding bodies of Britain (in their Research Assessment Exercise, or RAE) recognized sport-related subjects as a discrete and distinct area of research activity; in 2011, these bodies confirmed "sport and exercise sciences, leisure and tourism" as a specialist subpanel, or unit of assessment (UoA) 26, within the renamed research assessment process, the 2014 Research Excellence Framework (REF). According to the overview report published after the assessment had taken place, the scope of the subpanel, "stretched from sociology through biomechanics and medicine" (HEFCE, 2015, p. 2).

The growth in the academic study of sport, and the volume of research into specialist aspects of sport, culture and society, has "produced a burgeoning literature, in books and specialist journals" (Horne et al., 2013, p. xiii). Most UoAs submitted to the 2014 REF saw either a reduced number of staff submitted, or a modest increase. The exception was UoA 26, which the Higher Education Funding Council for England (HEFCE) overview report noted was "clearly a growing discipline" (HEFCE, 2015, p. 3). Since the 2008 RAE the number of academics submitting to the sport panel grew by 58% and the number of universities grew from 39 to 51 (HEFCE, 2015, p. 4). More particularly, the report noted that "[t]he social science of sport was dominated by sociological research … it is clear that the UK is the world leader in the sociology of sport" (HEFCE, 2015, pp. 116–117).

While critical of the predominance of football-related research, the panel further noted that "… social science research in sport and leisure was reaching wider academic audiences through its publication in single disciplinary journals in geography and sociology" (HEFCE, 2015, p. 117). Moreover, "other social science disciplines had not developed at the rate seen in sociology and there were few outputs submitted from the social science disciplines of anthropology, economics and geography" (HEFCE, 2015, p. 117).

The sociological study of sport can be found in all kinds of universities in the United Kingdom: research-intensive universities, those that aspire to develop their research profile, and predominantly teaching-oriented institutions. Notable clusters of academics doing sociological research can be found in Loughborough, Brighton, and Leeds Beckett, but other institutions also have excellent sociological research. While the distance learning postgraduate program in sociology of sport run by the University of Leicester no longer operates, there are several opportunities to study sociology of sport at the master's and postgraduate research levels at several universities in the United Kingdom.

ACADEMIC ENVIRONMENT AND BARRIERS TO RESEARCH

Sport and fitness loom large in the British media. Sport programs, dedicated sport channels, sports pages and sport supplements in newspapers, specialist sport magazines, and sport-related websites have become increasingly prominent. Although only a small minority of the population are active participants, a great many more have some degree of interest in following sport. The images derived from sport play a significant role in constituting our notions of the body and how it should, ideally, look. In both representational forms and lived practices, sport is one of the cultural spheres that most distinctively mark gender identities and differences. The activities of top sport stars are highly publicized, and debate rages about the extent to which they are role models with a wider social responsibility.

At the end of the 20th century there were several good books on sport in the United States and in other societies and countries, and on sport in cross-cultural and political contexts; research monographs, including detailed and illuminating social historical studies, also enhanced our understanding of sport in modern society. But there was a surprising lack of books attempting to produce an integrated sociocultural analysis of sport in modern Britain. The textbooks by Cashmore (1990) and Horne, Tomlinson,

and Whannel (1999) were the first to offer such an analysis from the
United Kingdom.

MAIN AREAS OF RESEARCH STRENGTH

British-based sociology of sport research provides a relatively accurate
reflection of the broader field. Generally speaking, areas of substantive
research can be divided into two key subsections: social stratification and
social issues in sport. Research has sought to capture the increasingly international manifestation of sport; however, a particularly notable feature of
UK sociology of sport research has been a continuation of the trend
initiated by the study of hooliganism, the aforementioned prevalence of
"football studies."

Traditionally there has been good coverage of the impact on sports
engagement/participation of all of the major axes of social stratification.
Social class, particularly as it related to issues of amateurism and professionalism, was well served in earlier sociological work. This focus was in
part fueled by the work of social historians concerned to chart the role of
sport in working-class cultures. Attention to gender and race issues has perhaps been more enduring. The former was pioneered in the United
Kingdom by Hargreaves (1994) and displayed important synergies with the
physical education community, in particular scholars such as Sheila
Scraton and Margaret Talbot. It has since developed to encompass the con-
tiguous field of athlete abuse/human rights and exhibit theoretical innovation, particularly in regard to poststructural feminism. UK studies of men
and masculinities in sport remain relatively underdeveloped compared to
North America in particular. Race and ethnicity has similarly been a constant feature of UK sociology of sport, perhaps a consequence of Britain's
imperial past. From Cashmore's early study of *Black Sportsmen* (1982)
analyses have ranged from sport in apartheid South Africa to a more recent
focus on the sporting experience and impact of male and female British-
Asians (including British-Muslims). There is also a critical mass of scholars
of disability and parasport in the United Kingdom, displaying synergies
with the politics and management of sport, as well as the embodied experience of disability.

The various "social issues" explored by UK sociologists of sport are
oriented around economic dimensions (commercialization, mediatization,
consumer culture) political dimensions (nationalism), and subcultural

dimensions (drug use, deviance, violence, pain and injury, and, latterly, the development of lifestyle sports). A significant number of research projects have sought to span these three dimensions. Initially these were underpinned by a focus on the impact of the globalization of sport but subsequently, and with London's staging of the 2012 Olympics acting as a catalyst, a focus on the multidimensional social impact of staging mega-events.

As noted above, perhaps the most notable feature of empirical research in UK sociology of sport has been the propensity to subject a broad spectrum of football-related issues to detailed scrutiny. Starting with football hooliganism, research developed to embrace supporter cultures more generally (King, 1998), the politics of the international game (Sugden & Tomlinson, 1998), the manifestation of race (Burdsey, 2007) and gender (Dunn, 2014), football as an occupational subculture, football and national identity, the commercialization and mediatization of football, as well as the impact of processes of European integration and globalization (Giulianotti, 1999; Millward, 2011). A primary reason for the strength of this strand of research is that football might reasonably be considered the "national sport" in two of the four constituent nations of the United Kingdom (England and Scotland). However, it is probably also true that this bias stemmed from the expansion of university education in the United Kingdom in the 1970s, the demographic backgrounds of the personnel this brought in to the discipline, and the broader emphasis in sociology/cultural studies on the importance of understanding working-class subcultures. While to some extent the focus on elite male football mirrors broader societal interest in sport (as portrayed by the media), it also undoubtedly reflects the gender dynamics of the field. UK sociology of sport has historically been male dominated and to some extent remains so.

MAIN APPROACHES TAKEN

Sociology of sport in the United Kingdom has traditionally been relatively strong in terms of theoretical application and development. As Malcolm (2012) points out, UK scholars have produced a significant number of textbooks devoted to social theory, especially relative to the size of the UK community in relation to the field at large (and North America in particular). This is probably a consequence of the relative independence of the field from the traditionally more atheoretical physical education community but, it should be noted, there has been a cost associated with this.

Giulianotti (2004, p. 1), for instance, has described the "rancorous exchanges" that have characterized the field and the sometimes highly personal nature of these conflicts have been a source of bemusement to an "outsider" to these conflicts.

Within the United Kingdom the subdiscipline has traditionally been dominated by scholars with a commitment either to Eliasian figurational sociology or Marxist/neo-Marxist variants of cultural studies (Horne, 1992, p. 147). The former featured in some of the first "British" sociology of sport literature to emerge, and figurational sociology (of sport) became closely associated with Leicester, the city in which Elias acquired his first professorial post. This connection strengthened with the christening of the "Leicester School" of football hooliganism during the 1980s. While at the beginning of the millennium Dunning (2002) identified "five generations" of figurational sociologists of sport, this now seems both an outdated simplification and descriptively insufficient to capture the role and dispersion of scholars within UK sociology of sport who broadly advocate this perspective.

A UK Marxist sociology of sport began with Ian Taylor's preliminary analysis of football hooliganism. Subsequently a significant number of sociologists of sport saw the British cultural studies development as a spiritual home and important source of academic legitimacy. With Alan Tomlinson and John Sugden as prime movers, a number of scholars working in this tradition gravitated toward the University of Brighton. *Power Games*, edited by Sugden and Tomlinson (2002) and incorporating colleagues at Brighton and from the broader field, attempted to delineate the core principles of the "Chelsea School." A somewhat tangential but logically correlative development of this tradition has been the recent advocacy of a physical cultural studies paradigm by British-born sociologists of sport on both sides of the Atlantic (Silk & Andrews, 2011). Notably though, to date, there has not been an especially strong uptake for this perspective in the United Kingdom itself.

The paradigmatic polarization of the field has to some extent weakened in recent times. Most publications seek to demonstrate the applicability of theory to particular empirical subjects, and exhibit little by way of theoretical innovation through sport-applied research (Carrington, 2010). Figurational sociologists are increasingly open to other perspectives and theoretical synthesis, while explicitly Marxist work has become less prominent. There has been a manifest engagement with a broader range of theories including Bourdieu, Foucault, Giddens, Butler and poststructural feminism more broadly, Bauman and critical race theory; although a call for scholars to get "back to [Marxist] basics" has been issued (Bairner, 2007). British sociologists of sport have become more "ends driven" (perhaps as a consequence of increasing state regulation of academic research), avoiding controversies that might reduce the likelihood of publication. They largely exist in a state of harmonious theoretical difference. There are relatively few open debates about the relative merits of theories and little explicit critique of comparative approaches.

KEY CONTRIBUTORS AND KEY PUBLICATIONS

The growth in the sociological study of sport, and the volume of research into specialist aspects of sport and society, has produced a burgeoning literature, of books, edited collections, and specialist journals. UK-based academics have produced some of the most significant publications in the sociology of sport, ranging from general overviews, textbooks, handbooks, and dictionaries. Some of the most widely cited journals, while not restricted to UK authors, are also published in the United Kingdom (Horne, 2015). The rest of this section outlines the contribution of UK scholars to theories of sport in society, research on social divisions and identities, football (soccer), politics and social control, globalization, mass media and consumption, and sports mega-events.

Textbooks that have emerged since Horne et al. (1999) include Coakley and Pike (2014), Giulianotti (2015a, first edition 2005), and Jarvie and Thornton (2012, first edition 2006). Horne et al. (2013) updates the previous textbook and has a focus on the sociocultural and historical development of sport in the United Kingdom. Two readers – Tomlinson (2007) and Scraton and Flintoff (2002) – and the collection by Giulianotti (2015b) also contain valuable work. Malcolm's (2008) dictionary contains fairly detailed entries on all key topics and issues in the study of sport in social context, while Tomlinson's (2010) version contains a mixture of short and long entries covering a much broader range of topics.

The following journals are published in the United Kingdom and often publish sociology of sport articles: *Sport in Society*, *Sport, Education and Society*, *Leisure Studies*, and *Soccer & Society*. Two other journals occasionally publish articles relevant to the sociology of sport (*International Journal of the History of Sport* and *Sport in History*).

The classic works of the sociology of sport, especially from the United Kingdom, exemplify the importance of history to sociology in understanding the development of the relationships between sport, culture, and society. A seminal work on the origins of British sport is Dunning and Sheard (1979), a study of the development of rugby football, in which they develop a typology of "the structural properties of folk-games and modern sports." This classification focuses upon the general characteristics of sports in the transformative period of industrialization. Many of the core characteristics of modern sports were shaped in the British public schools of the 19th century. This is widely acknowledged and useful accounts and discussions abound including Holt (1989) and Hargreaves (1986). Hargreaves' social and historical analysis of popular sports in Britain stresses that the story of the formation of modern sport in the 19th century is primarily one of bourgeois suppression. The definitive source for an understanding of the nature and impact of the public schools' approach to games, sport, and physical activity remains the work of Mangan (1981). Hargreaves' (1994) classic work on women's involvement in sport is a valuable corrective to the male focus of much sport history and sociology.

Many books that attempt to discuss theories of sport and leisure (e.g., Giulianotti, 2004; Giulianotti, 2015a; Jarvie & Maguire, 1994) were written with senior-level sociology students in mind. Textbooks pitched at year one and two undergraduates that include useful introductory discussions about theories are Molnar and Kelly (2013), and Coakley and Pike (2014). Most of the textbooks deal with the leading theoretical approaches in studying sport in society – functionalism, Marxism, interpretive sociology, figurational sociology, feminism, and postmodernism. Elias and Dunning (1986) brings together in one volume several articles that the two had written separately or together in previous decades. Each chapter provides an insight into the distinctive approach to sport (and leisure) that the figurational sociological perspective offers.

Historians and sociologists have investigated the way that social class has played a major role influencing participation in, and the construction, organization, consumption of, modern sport. Class was central to the formation of modern sports culture and sport is a powerful symbol of mobility and change in social status. Research by sociologist Tony Bennett and colleagues (Bennett et al., 2009) offers insight into the role that social class plays in influencing participation and interest in sport and other forms of physical cultural leisure activity in contemporary Britain. Other British sociologists (Carrington, 2010) consider the social construction of "racial" and ethnic difference that leads to the "naturalization" of genetic and even cultural differences. They ask whether sports reproduce or challenge the stereotypes that reproduce racism. Although not all research on gender divisions is conducted with self-declared feminist researchers, the questions raised by feminist and nonfeminist approaches to sport alike include: Why do fewer women take part in sport than men? Why are there so few women in senior sports leadership positions? The aforementioned Jennifer Hargreaves has investigated the history and sociology of women's involvement in sport. In later work she also examines the importance of patriarchal discourses and gender performances (Hargreaves, 2001). Sport offers both a place for the reproduction of patriarchal values and a means of resisting them. A similar dialectic can be found at work in the position of disabled people and sport (see, e.g., Thomas & Smith, 2009).

Further contributions explore the ways in which sport is necessarily political. Sugden and Bairner (1993) suggest that the state seeks to exert a degree of influence over sport because sport has come to play an influential part in an individual's socialization and the construction of notions of community in modern life. The authors showed how in Northern Ireland every significant aspect of life was bound up with the politics of division, and sport was no exception.

How is sport being transformed by globalization? How is sport contributing to globalization? How does the globalization of sport affect sport at the national and local levels? These are three key questions that British sociologists of sport have examined (Bairner, 2001; Giulianotti & Robertson, 2009). In addition, they ask to what extent globalization is a useful term with which to try to understand the development of modern sport. Other researchers have drawn attention to the existence of "global commodity chains" in much sports-goods manufacturing (Maguire, 1999). In addition to the movement of goods, globalization has been researched in terms of the flows of sports people, including migrant sports labor from the Global South to the Global North (Darby, 2001).

Sport is both modern, as practice, and postmodern, as part of media culture. The development of professional spectator sports predates 20th century advances in radio and television broadcasting, but the relationship between the mass media and sport has always been vital (Whannel, 1992). In the United Kingdom, as elsewhere in advanced capitalist economies, an enormous increase in the media coverage of sport has been evident. The media help to construct what is meant by sport. Sport may be both a commercial spectacle and used as a means of resisting commercial values. Professional sport has become increasingly allied to the consumption of goods and services. Hargreaves (1986, p. 134) argued that "What links up consumer culture with sports culture so economically is their common concern with, and capacity to accommodate, the body as a means of expression." These issues are taken up in works on the nature of contemporary sporting celebrity. Sports stars' relationships with the media and with the sporting establishment is taken up by Whannel (2002) in a series of case studies of British and American sportsmen. In his earlier book *Fields in Vision* Whannel (1992) considers the historical development of sport on television, the growth of sponsorship and the way that television and sponsorship have reshaped sport in the context of the enterprise culture. Boyle and Haynes (2004) examine the battle for control of football in the United Kingdom as media, business, and fans all seek to redefine the sport. Horne (2006) provides a distinctive way of understanding the position of sport in consumer society.

New mass communication technologies, especially the development of satellite television, have created the basis for global audiences for sports mega-events. The expansion of mega-events has seen the formation of a sport—media—business alliance that transformed professional sport generally in the late 20th century. Interest in hosting sports mega-events proliferated because they have become seen as valuable promotional opportunities for nations, cities, and regions. Yet there has also been ongoing controversy about the value, impact, and legacy of global mega-events, with critics questioning their effectiveness as avenues for economic development and the gap between the rhetoric and reality of the mega-event "effect." Sugden and Tomlinson (1998) provided the first full-length study of the Fédération Internationale de Football Association (FIFA) and its role in framing and controlling world football. Horne and Whannel (2016) apply a critical sociological and cultural studies lens to a wide range of issues and controversies that have surrounded the Olympic movement. These topics will continue to be central to the sociology of sport in the future.

THE FUTURE OF SOCIOLOGY OF SPORT IN THE UNITED KINGDOM

The landscape of UK higher education is dominated by a neoliberal governmental agenda that has seen a general shift from state- to self-funded provision and from professionally proscribed curricula to consumerism. This process has been softened by a residual desire to intervene in the market for STEM (science, technology, engineering, and mathematics) subjects based on perceptions about their relative value to the broader economy. This creates a challenging environment for all social science. Conversely, however, the continuing/increasing social significance of sport in the United Kingdom presents opportunities for growth. Claims about the broader potential of sport as a social engineering tool (ironically critiqued by many UK sociologists of sport) remain politically influential and the legacy of hosting the 2012 London Olympics is still being felt. Within this broader context the future of the subdiscipline in the United Kingdom can be assessed relative to its prospects in the following three areas.

Teaching: Sport-related subjects remain popular among the new consumer-students and generally recruit good numbers. Social science subjects also have the benefit of being relatively cheap to teach, posing few infrastructural resource demands, and are relatively amenable to the newer learning technologies. The central challenge is in terms of explicitly articulating the relationship between the sociology of sport and an employability agenda that has grown as part of the increasing consumerism of UK higher education. What this does mean, however, is that UK sociology of sport continues to attract significant numbers of very talented and highly motivated young scholars.

Research: The post-financial crisis emphasis on austerity has seen already limited research income become increasingly scarce. Because there are few "natural" commercial funders of sociology, and because the diminished government funding for research is increasingly likely to be distributed to STEM subjects, social science will have to fight to retain a share of the distributed funds. Conversely however, government funding now prioritizes research that can demonstrate impact (as assessed by the commercial and public sectors), thereby requiring the development of more extensive collaborations, which, in turn, creates new opportunities for sociologists. Impact necessarily requires a social application, and multidisciplinarity continues to be flagged as the future of research, even if it remains a somewhat elusive goal. This may ultimately see the demise of a more autonomous, theoretical, and critical sociology (of sport). However, the convergence of funding priorities, broader social change, and the demonstrable value of social science means that there are future growth areas, for instance in physical activity related health research or the sport for development and peace sector.

Relations with other disciplines and mainstream sociology: One notable trend over the 50 years that the UK sociology of sport has existed is the "retreat" of sport researchers from mainstream sociology to sports science and physical education departments. This development is, however, symptomatic of broader challenges for the subdiscipline, manifest in the relocation of many sociologists into schools of education, management, and health and life sciences. A comparable challenge comes from the sport-related social sciences that are more amenable to neoliberalism, namely psychology and management. The former appeals to the propensity to desocialize individuals' behavior, the latter to the desire for more direct forms of social engineering promised by economic evaluation and social policy.

FIVE KEY READINGS

1. **Carrington, B. (2010).** *Race, sport and politics: The sporting Black diaspora.* **London: Sage.**

   This book addresses sport's role in "the making of race," its place within black diasporic struggles for freedom and equality, and its contested location in relation to the politics of recognition within contemporary multicultural societies. Carrington shows how the idea of "the natural black athlete" was invented in order to make sense of and curtail their political impact and cultural achievements but recently, "the black athlete" as sign has become a highly commodified object within contemporary sports-media culture.

2. **Elias, N., & Dunning, E. (1986).** *Quest for excitement—Sport and leisure in the civilizing process.* **Oxford: Basil Blackwell.**

   This book reviews aspects of sport in society through the ages, and develops a theory of leisure that encompasses sociological, psychological, and biological perspectives. The book asks: why do people choose to spend their leisure time in sports that verge on violence? What impulses are involved? Does the violence in and around sport, and the group behavior sport gives rise to, reflect social and psychological trends? What role does sport play in the creation of masculine identities?

3. **Hargreaves, J. A. (1994).** *Sporting females—Critical issues in the history and sociology of women's sports.* **New York, NY: Routledge.**

   Sporting Females won the North American Society for the Sociology of Sport (NASSS) book award in 1994. Uses both a historical and sociological perspective in analyzing women's sport. The book puts women and their sporting experiences at the forefront of importance. This remains the most comprehensive book on women and sport.

4. **Hargreaves, J. (1986).** *Sport, power and culture—A social and historical analysis of popular sports in Britain.* **Cambridge: Polity Press.**

Hargreaves traces the changing relations between sport and social power. He pays particular attention to the ways in which sporting activities of different kinds relate to divisions of class, sex, and race. He analyzes the significance of sport as a means of exercising power on the body, situating this analysis in the context of a general discussion of the role of sport in education and consumer culture.

5. **Whannel, G. (1992).** *Fields in vision: Television sport and cultural transformation.* **London: Routledge.**

Fields in Vision is a classic analytical study of the international phenomenon of television sports coverage. *Fields in Vision* explains the development of television sport by linking its economic transformation with the cultural forms through which it is represented, offering a study encompassing not simply the sports world, but our relationship with television and the media industries as a whole.

REFERENCES

Bairner, A. (2001). *Sport, nationalism and globalization. European and North American perspectives.* Albany, NY: State University of New York Press.

Bairner, A. (2007). Back to basics: Class, social theory, and sport. *Sociology of Sport Journal*, *24*, 20–36.

Bennett, T., Savage, M., Silva, E., Warde, A., Gayo-Cal, M., & Wright, D. (2009). *Culture, class, distinction.* London: Routledge.

Boyle, R., & Haynes, R. (2004). *Football in the new media age.* London: Routledge.

Burdsey, D. (2007). *British Asians and football: Culture, identity, exclusion.* London: Routledge.

Carrington, B. (2010). *Race, sport and politics: The sporting black diaspora.* London: Sage.

Cashmore, E. (1982). *Black sportsmen.* London: Routledge & Kegan Paul.

Cashmore, E. (1990). *Making sense of sport.* London: Routledge & Kegan Paul.

Coakley, J., & Pike, E. (2014). *Sports in society* (2nd ed.). Boston, MA: McGraw-Hill.

Darby, P. (2001). *Africa, football and FIFA: Politics, colonialism and resistance.* London: Frank Cass.

Dunn, C. (2014). *Female football fans: Community, identity and sexism.* London: Palgrave Pivot.

Dunning, E. (1963). Football in its early stages. *History Today*, December.

Dunning, E. (Ed.). (1971). *The sociology of sport.* London: Frank Cass.

Dunning, E. (2002). Figurational contributions to the sociological study of sport. In J. Maguire & K. Young (Eds.), *Theory, sport and society* (pp. 211–238). Oxford: Elsevier Science.

Dunning, E., Murphy, P., & Williams, J. (1988). *The roots of football hooliganism. An historical and sociological study.* London: Routledge and Kegan Paul.

Dunning, E., & Sheard, K. (1979). *Barbarians, gentlemen and players: A sociological study of the development of Rugby football*. London: Routledge.

Elias, N., & Dunning, E. (1966). Dynamics of sports groups with special reference to football. *British Journal of Sociology, 17*(4), 388–402.

Elias, N., & Dunning, E. (1986). *Quest for excitement—Sport and leisure in the civilizing process*. Oxford: Basil Blackwell.

Giulianotti, R. (1999). *Football: A sociology of the global game*. Cambridge: Polity Press.

Giulianotti, R. (Ed.). (2004). *Sport and modern social theorists*. London: Palgrave Macmillan.

Giulianotti, R. (2015a). *Sport: A critical sociology* (2nd ed.). Cambridge: Polity.

Giulianotti, R. (Ed.). (2015b). *Routledge handbook of the sociology of sport*. London: Routledge.

Giulianotti, R., & Robertson, R. (2009). *Globalization and football*. London: Sage.

Hargreaves, J. (1986). *Sport, power and culture—A social and historical analysis of popular sports in Britain*. Cambridge: Polity Press.

Hargreaves, J. A. (1994). *Sporting females—Critical issues in the history and sociology of women's sports*. New York, NY: Routledge.

Hargreaves, J. A. (2001). *Heroines of sport: The politics of difference and identity*. London: Routledge.

HEFCE. (2015). *REF 2014 overview report by main panel c and sub-panels 16 to 26*. Bristol: Higher Education Funding Council for England.

Holt, R. (1989). *Sport and the British. A modern history*. Oxford: Oxford University Press.

Horne, J. (1992). Sociology of sport. In M. Shoebridge (Ed.), *Information sources in sport & leisure* (pp. 147–160). London: Bowker-Saur.

Horne, J. (2006). *Sport in consumer culture*. Basingstoke: Palgrave.

Horne, J. (2015). *Sports*. Oxford Bibliographies. Retrieved from http://www.oxfordbibliographies.com/view/document/obo-9780199756384/obo-9780199756384-0130.xml?rskey=AvJoXZ&result=121

Horne, J., Tomlinson, A., & Whannel, G. (1999). *Understanding sport: An introduction to the sociological and cultural analysis of sport*. London: Spon.

Horne, J., Tomlinson, A., Whannel, G., & Woodward, K. (2013). *Understanding sport: A socio-cultural analysis* (2nd ed.). London: Routledge.

Horne, J., & Whannel, G. (2016). *Understanding the Olympics* (2nd ed.). London: Routledge.

Jarvie, G., & Maguire, J. (1994). *Sport and leisure in social thought*. London: Routledge.

Jarvie, G., & Thornton, J. (2012). *Sport, culture and society* (2nd ed.). London: Routledge.

King, A. (1998). *The end of the terraces: The transformation of English football in the 1990s*. London: Leicester University Press.

Maguire, J. (1999). *Global sport. Identities, societies, civilizations*. Cambridge: Polity Press.

Malcolm, D. (Ed.). (2008). *The Sage dictionary of sports studies*. London: Sage.

Malcolm, D. (2012). *Sport and sociology*. London: Routledge.

Malcolm, D. (2014). The social construction of the sociology of sport: A professional project. *International Review for the Sociology of Sport, 49*(1), 3–21.

Mangan, J. A. (1981). *Athleticism in the Victorian and Edwardian public school—The emergence and consolidation of an educational ideology*. Cambridge: Cambridge University Press.

McIntosh, P. (1960). *Sport in society*. London: C.A. Watt.

Millward, P. (2011). *The global football league: Transnational networks, social movements and sport in the new media age*. Basingstoke: Palgrave Macmillan.

Molnar, G., & Kelly, J. (2013). *Sport, exercise and social theory*. London: Routledge.

Rojek, C. (1985). *Capitalism and leisure theory*. London: Tavistock Publications.

Sage, G. (1997). Physical education, sociology and sociology of sport: Points of intersection. *Sociology of Sport Journal, 14*(4), 317–339.

Scraton, S., & Flintoff, A., (Eds.). (2002). *Gender and sport: A reader*. London: Routledge.

Silk, M., & Andrews, D. (2011). Toward a physical cultural studies. *Sociology of Sport Journal, 28*(1), 4–35.

Sugden, J., & Bairner, A. (1993). *Sport, sectarianism and society in a divided Ireland*. Leicester: Leicester University Press.

Sugden, J., & Tomlinson, A. (1998). *FIFA and the contest for world football: Who rules the people's game?* Cambridge: Polity.

Sugden, J., & Tomlinson, A. (Eds.). (2002). *Power games: A critical sociology of sport*. London: Routledge.

Thomas, N., & Smith, A. (2009). *Disability, sport and society: An introduction*. London: Routledge.

Tomlinson, A. (Ed.). (2007). *The sport studies reader*. London: Routledge.

Tomlinson, A. (Ed.). (2010). *Oxford dictionary of sports studies*. Oxford: Oxford University Press.

Tomlinson, A., & Whannel, G. (1984). *Five ring circus: Money, power and politics at the Olympic games*. London: Pluto Press.

Tomlinson, A., & Whannel, G. (1986). *Off the ball: The football world cup*. London: Pluto Press.

Whannel, G. (1992). *Fields in vision: Television sport and cultural transformation*. London: Routledge.

Whannel, G. (2002). *Media sport stars: Masculinities and moralities*. London: Routledge.

NORTH AMERICA

CHAPTER 18

SOCIOLOGY OF SPORT: CANADA

Parissa Safai

ABSTRACT

This chapter explores the emergence, growth, and current status of the sociology of sport in Canada. Such an endeavour includes acknowledging the work and efforts of Canadian scholars — whether Canadian by birth or naturalization or just as a result of their geographic location — who have contributed to the vibrant and robust academic discipline that is the sociology of sport in Canadian institutions coast-to-coast, and who have advanced the socio-cultural study of sport globally in substantial ways. This chapter does not provide an exhaustive description and analysis of the past and present states of the sociology of sport in Canada; in fact, it is important to note that an in-depth, critical and comprehensive analysis of our field in Canada is sorely lacking. Rather, this chapter aims to highlight the major historical drivers (both in terms of people and trends) of the field in Canada; provide a snapshot of the sociology of sport in Canada currently; and put forth some ideas as to future opportunities and challenges for the field in Canada.

Keywords: Canada; critical intellectual tradition; politics of language; legacy; public intellectuals

Sociology of Sport: A Global Subdiscipline in Review
Research in the Sociology of Sport, Volume 9, 323–342
Copyright © 2017 by Emerald Group Publishing Limited
All rights of reproduction in any form reserved
ISSN: 1476-2854/doi:10.1108/S1476-285420160000009023

INTRODUCTION

In 2015, Paris, France was the backdrop to the World Congress of Sociology of Sport, aptly titled 'The Sociological Lens and the Well-being of Sport', during which time the 50th anniversary of the International Sociology of Sport Association (ISSA) and *International Review for the Sociology of Sport* (IRSS) was heartily celebrated. As is customary, time had been carved out of the scientific programme to honour the accomplishments of emerging and established members of the sociology of sport community. On this particular occasion, because of the significant anniversary of the association and journal, a special tribute for ISSA Honorary Members from 1965 to 2015 was organized and capped by a group photograph of the hundreds of attendees indicating a 'five' and a 'zero' with their hands in the air. On stage, Gyongyi Szabo Foldesi (Hungary), Kari Fasting (Norway) and John W. Loy (Canada) joined the most recent recipients of the Honorary Member award, Jay Coakley (United States), as then ISSA-President Elizabeth Pike (United Kingdom) spoke about their individual contributions to the sociology of sport as a body of knowledge as well as to the birth and growth of the association itself. As a member of the audience, the significance of the event in and of itself was most certainly not lost on me, nor did it escape my attention that I was enjoying the celebration alongside my own supervisor, Peter Donnelly (Canada) who, in turn, was enjoying the recognition of his supervisor, John W. Loy.

I appreciate that a close reading of the above paragraph may give some readers pause as I have identified both Loy and Donnelly as Canadians. For some readers, this may be understood as inaccurate as Loy was born in the United States, worked in the United States and in Canada, and then spent his last working years in New Zealand. Donnelly was born and initially worked in physical education in England, then studied in the United States, and has been working and living in Canada ever since. And yet, my decision to identify these two scholars in the introduction in this fashion is quite deliberate.

This chapter explores the emergence, growth, and current status of the sociology of sport in Canada and such an endeavour inevitably includes acknowledging the work and efforts of Canadian scholars – whether Canadian by birth, naturalization or just as a result of their geographic location – who have contributed to the vibrant academic discipline that is the sociology of sport in Canadian institutions coast-to-coast, and who have advanced the socio-cultural study of sport globally in substantial ways. Before delving into the task at hand, it is important to acknowledge that this chapter does not provide an exhaustive description and analysis of the past and present states of the sociology of sport in Canada; in fact, it is important to note that an in-depth, critical, and comprehensive analysis of our field in Canada is sorely lacking. Rather, this chapter aims to highlight the major historical drivers (both in terms of people and trends) of the field in Canada, provide a snapshot of the sociology of sport in Canada currently and put forth some ideas as to future opportunities and challenges for the field in Canada. Although I draw from numerous sources in mapping out the historical and contemporary dimensions of our field in Canada, I take full responsibility for any errors, misinterpretations, and missed recognition of individuals and/or groups. Further, I acknowledge that any historical or contemporary accounting of the field is informed and framed by my own social location and, drawing on the famous Frederick Jackson Turner quote, 'with reference to the conditions uppermost in [my] own time'.

HISTORY OF SOCIOLOGY OF SPORT IN CANADA

The historical development of the sociology of sport in Canada has, in many ways, been documented as part of the emergence and growth of the sociology of sport in North America and worldwide. Most historical accounts of the sociology of sport (as we know of it today) suggest that the process of its institutionalization began in the mid-1960s as informed by a series of major, interconnected trends. Coakley and Dunning (2000), Ingham and Donnelly (1997), Macintosh and Whitson (1990) and Malcolm (2012), to name but a few who have written of the history of the field nationally and internationally, suggest that a few key developments sparked and spurred on the development of the sociology of sport including: the growing recognition of sport and physical education as social practices by university teachers of physical education; an appreciation among some notable scholars and university teachers of sociology of the importance of understanding sport as a phenomenon worthy of sociological study; the general expansion of universities and the intensification of academic work (i.e. the 'publish or perish' imperative) including the momentum within physical education departments to build on Henry's (1964) call for 'disciplinized' physical education; the various counter-cultural rights and protest movements of the 1960s and early 1970s, which were informed by and supported left-of-centre or 'radical' ways of thinking about and studying social life (including sport); and the tensions associated with major geo-political events of the 1960s, 1970s and 1980s (e.g. the Vietnam War, the Cold War), which motivated a perceived need to better understand how sport contributed to the relations of power within and across nations.

It was out of this mélange of trends and events that the International Committee for Sport Sociology (ICSS, renamed ISSA in the late 1990s) and its house journal, the *IRSS*, were born. Canadian-based/Canadian scholars such as John W. Loy and Gerald Kenyon participated in these pivotal early meetings and their respective works over the next two decades, often done collaboratively together and with other founding members of the field including, most notably, Canadian Barry McPherson, helped to solidify and legitimize the sociology of sport nationally and internationally (Kenyon & Loy, 1965; Loy, McPherson, & Kenyon, 1978, 1979; McPherson, 1975, 1978). In fact, Coakley and Dunning (2000) note that Loy and Kenyon's *Sport, Culture and Society* (1969) was the first major English-language edited collection or reader — a critical developmental milestone in the institutionalization of any scholarly field. From the mid-1960s/early 1970s onwards, other notable Canadian and Canadian-based scholars emerged onto the nascent sociology of sport scene with contributions that: firmed up the contours of the subdiscipline (i.e. establishing sport as a legitimate category of inquiry) in North America; cleaved it away from its entanglements with social psychology or applied sociology; and, perhaps most significantly, began to shift and advance the theoretical paradigms in which early sociology of sport was oriented. Key Canadian/Canadian-based scholars of the 'network' (1965–1972) and 'cluster' (1973–1978) stages of the field (cf. Loy et al., 1979) include, but are not limited to (in alphabetical order): Rob Beamish, Hart Cantelon, Jim Curtis, Peter Donnelly, Rick Gruneau, M. Ann Hall, Jean Harvey, Bruce Kidd, Helen Lenskyj, Donald Macintosh, Robert Sparkes, Nancy Theberge and Dave Whitson. Depending on which system of periodization one chooses to use, these members of the early and late second generation or third generation of sociology of sport — some of whom were the students of first- or second-generation sport sociologists at Wisconsin or Massachusetts — ultimately returned or migrated to Canada, eventually becoming the supervisors and/or mentors of subsequent generations of scholars trained in Canadian universities.

Many note in their historical accounts of the development of the field that Canadian scholars were pivotal in advancing more critical analyses of sport and society in the nascent field. As Coakley and Dunning (2000,

p. xxx) note: '... Canadian scholars and others who had not been born in the United States were centrally involved in the left-radicalization of the sociology of sport which took place during the 1970s and 1980s' and Ingham and Donnelly pinpoint a 1979 symposium at Queen's University as 'the hallmark event for the counterhegemonic turn to political economy' in the sociology of sport (1997, p. 376). Canadian and Canadian-based scholars steered away from the more functionalist, applied and (ahistorical) positivist readings of the nature of sport in social life that figured heavily in mainstream American sociology of sport and embraced Marx, Weber, Mills, the Frankfurt School, Gramsci, Williams, interpretive sociology, British cultural studies, Foucault and Bourdieu (Cantelon & Gruneau, 1982; Ingham & Donnelly, 1990). Such a shift should not be surprising given that Canadian and Canadian-based scholars reside outside the 'imperial power' of the United States (Coakley & Dunning, 2000, p. xxx) and that many elements of Canadian social, cultural, political and economic life are influenced not just by its neighbours to the south but also by its long-standing (colonial) ties to Britain, France and other European nation-states (cf. Crossman & Scherer, 2015; see also Rowe, McKay, & Lawrence, 1997). When asked to comment on if Canadian scholarship in the sociology of sport has a particular reputation in the international sociology of sport community, one could easily argue that Canadian sociology of sport scholarship emerged and continues to operate from a critical intellectual tradition that 'consists of a complex and contradictory configuration of political economy, feminism, postmodernism/poststructuralism, neo-Marxism, British cultural studies, and critical media studies' (Rowe et al., 1997, p. 346); there has been and still is a decisively progressive and theoretically rich feel to the sociology of sport in Canada.

During the late 1970s and into the 1980s, Canadian and Canadian-based scholars such as Theberge, Lenskyj, Vertinsky (whose work as a social and cultural historian have had tremendous impact on the sociological study of sport), and Hall were also advancing critical feminist scholarship in the sociology of sport and actively grappling alongside and in conversation with other feminist scholars in the United States and in the United Kingdom through sites of tension and connection with historical materialist/political economic perspectives in the sociology of sport (Ingham & Donnelly, 1997; Theberge & Donnelly, 1984). By the late 1980s and into the 1990s, more points of synergy could be found between feminist and materialist explorations of sport as relational (as opposed to more categoric or distributive) analyses of gender proliferated (Hall, 1996; Lenskyj, 1986; MacNeill, 1988; Theberge, 1985,

1987) and as culture, the body, difference and identity politics – informed in some measure by the more active uptake of sub/cultural, feminist, Foucauldian, postmodernist/poststructuralist, postcolonial and queer theories (to name but a few) in the scholarship of some Canadian and Canadian-based scholars – became more central sites of academic investigation (cf. Donnelly & Young, 1988; Harvey, 1988, 1990; Harvey & Rail, 1995a; Harvey & Sparks, 1991; Pronger, 1992; Rail, 1998; Sparks, 1990). In addition to the continuing scholarship of Theberge, Vertinsky, Lenskyj, MacNeill and Rail, other notable (established and emerging) Canadian and Canadian-based scholars who continue to advance groundbreaking and innovative feminist and gender-based scholarship across a wide range of topics include, but are not limited to (in alphabetical order) Mary Louise Adams, Natalie Beausoleil, Christine Dallaire, Alex Dumas, Wendy Frisby, Caroline Fusco, Audrey Giles, Lyndsay Hayhurst, Michelle Helstein, Marg Holman, Cathy van Ingen, Shannon Jette, Samantha King, Pirkko Markula, Moss Norman, Brian Pronger, Heather Sykes, Ann Travers, Philip White and Kevin Young (again, but to name a few; see Young & White, 1999 for one of the first critical edited collections on sport and gender in Canada).

By the late 1990s and into the 2000s, Canadian and Canadian-based sociologists of sport had and were contributing to research in a wide variety of areas and vis-à-vis a broad range of theoretical and methodological perspectives, a trend that continues favourably unabated to this day. Throughout this period of time, more critical scholarship was starting to emerge on racialized peoples including, of particular note here, Aboriginal/Indigenous/First Nations sport in Canada and the experiences of Aboriginal/Indigenous Canadians in and through sport (see Forsyth & Giles, 2013 for a comprehensive review of the scholarship in this area). Victoria Paraschak's work on in this area has been seminal and other notable established and emerging Canadian and Canadian-based scholars exploring the intersections of race, ethnicity, identity and/or indigeneity include, but are not limited to (in alphabetical order): Sean Brayton, Janice Forsyth, Simon Darnell, Audrey Giles, Joanie Halas, Lyndsay Hayhurst, Michael Heine, Janelle Joseph, Courtney Mason, Yuka Nakamura and Michael Robidoux.

Canadian and Canadian-based scholars have also positively influenced the global sociology of sport landscape in other substantive areas as well, including (names of established and emerging scholars are offered in parentheses): analysis of sport subcultures (Michael Atkinson, Peter Donnelly, James Gillett, Jason Laurendeau, Brian Wilson, Kevin Young;

Atkinson's and Young's (2008) edited volume *Tribal Play* is a substantial collection of writing in this area); deviance, violence and risk (the late Michael Smith and Kevin Young (see Young, 2012) are two seminal writers in this area; Jason Laurendeau's research is also noteworthy); risk, injury and pain in sport (gender-based analyses of pain and injury tolerance published in the early 1990s by Kevin Young, Philip While and William McTeer remain, to this day, some of the most cited research in this area; see Young, White, & McTeer (1994) and Young & White (1995); other notable contributors include Michael Atkinson, P. David Howe, Parissa Safai and Nancy Theberge; see Young, 2004); the political economy of sport, including globalization and sport media (Rob Beamish, Hart Cantelon, Peter Donnelly, Richard Gruneau, Steve Jackson, Donald Macintosh, Margaret MacNeill, Brad Millington, Robert Pitter, Geneviève Rail, Michael Sam, Jay Scherer, Brian Wilson, David Whitson); sport and social movements, including sport for development and peace (Simon Darnell, Lyndsay Hayhurst, Bruce Kidd, Rob Millington, Brian Wilson); health, healthcare and physical activity/sport (Alex Dumas, Caroline Fusco, James Gillett, Jean Harvey, Shannon Jette, Samantha King, Suzanne Laberge, Margaret MacNeill, Lisa McDermott, Moss Norman, Geneviève Rail, Robert Sparkes, Nancy Theberge, Patricia Vertinsky); sport policy (Peter Donnelly; Jean Harvey; Bruce Kidd; Michael Sam); and disciplinary, theoretical, and/or methodological innovations in the sociology of sport (e.g. Michael Atkinson's writings have informed both the global debate around physical cultural studies as well as around methodological practice in the socio-cultural study of sport (see Atkinson & Young, 2012) and Wendy Frisby's commitment to participatory action research with vulnerable migrant and/or impoverished individuals and groups has been lauded nationally and internationally). This type of stocktaking is fraught with problems as: (1) there are many other names that can be added to the themes noted above; and (2) all the individuals that have been identified above have advanced the socio-cultural study of sport around numerous other substantive themes (both individually and in collaboration with one another). May it be enough to note, in gathering together the threads of this section, that Canadian and Canadian-based researchers have long been on the cutting edge of scholarship in the sociology of sport and continue to push the discipline's theoretical, methodological and substantive frontiers.

A SNAPSHOT OF THE CONTEMPORARY
SOCIOLOGY OF SPORT IN CANADA

Contemporary sociology of sport in Canada is alive and well, and sociologists of sport can be found in Canadian universities from coast-to-coast.[1] That said, Coakley and Dunning's (2000, p. xxv) comments still ring true in the Canadian context: 'The number of scholars doing research and teaching in the sociology of sport in [different] countries has increased. However, they do not constitute a critical mass large enough to present themselves as formal subsections in the major professional sociology associations in their countries'. Currently there is no distinct Canadian professional society or association in the sociology of sport, no distinct Canadian journal in the field, no annual national sociology of sport conference (although many individual institutions host relatively regular sociology of sport colloquia, workshops or lectures; e.g. the annual Donald Macintosh Memorial Lecture at Queen's University), and the sociology of sport is not an identified, singular research cluster in the Canadian Sociological Association (CSA). Most Canadian and Canadian-based sociologists of sport are members of ISSA and/or NASSS (the North American Society for the Sociology of Sport) – the latter of which mandates the inclusion of at least one Canadian member-at-large in its executive committee. Canadian and Canadian-based scholars routinely attend the annual conferences for both ISSA and NASSS, a number of which have been held in Canada over the years – for example, Canadian cities played host to NASSS in 1982 (Toronto, Ontario); 1987 (Edmonton, Alberta); 1993 (Ottawa, Ontario); 1997 (Toronto, Ontario); 2003 (Montréal, Québec); 2006 (Vancouver, British Columbia); 2009 (Ottawa, Ontario); and, most recently, 2013 (Québec City, Québec). Further, many Canadian and Canadian-based scholars have served on the governing boards of ISSA, NASSS, *IRSS* and *Sociology of Sport Journal* (*SSJ*) either as members of the editorial or editorial advisory boards, or even as editors-in-chief of the journals themselves; for example, Peter Donnelly (1990–1994), Chris Stevenson (1999–2001), Nancy Theberge (2002–2004), Pirkko Markula (2009–2011) and Michael Atkinson (2012–2014) have all served as editors of the *SSJ*.

Beyond the information that can be gleaned from memberships in professional societies or attendance at scholarly conferences, it is challenging to offer definitive data on the number of sociologists of sport and/or their location across the country. It may be safe to suggest that there are 50–75

Canadian and Canadian-based scholars (a figure that is exclusive of graduate students training in the field) who contribute to the sociological study of sport from coast-to-coast, but I offer this number very tentatively for two interconnected reasons. First, while physical education/kinesiology departments are the places where sociology of sport thrives (as will be discussed below), not all Canadian and Canadian-based sociologists of sport are located in these units and this makes it exceedingly difficult to determine the number of scholars in the field accurately. There is no one comprehensive national database that documents fields of study among all Canadian university researchers and teachers and, in the case of sociology of sport, many scholars in the area work out such diverse disciplinary departments as, to name a few, sociology, history, anthropology, child and youth studies, communication studies, education, international development studies, women's studies, or political science; this becomes additionally complicated when one attempts to take into account those sociologists of sport who hold cross-appointments in multiple units (e.g. kinesiology and sociology). Second, there are many Canadian or Canadian-based scholars who contribute to research and teaching in the critical sociological study of sport in Canada but who either do not identify themselves as sociologists or who straddle multiple disciplinary identities/approaches to the study of sport in social life. Patricia Vertinsky's work has already been noted as one such example, Russell Field is another colleague who bestrides sport history and sociology of sport, P. David Howe's (Loughborough) or Michael Robidoux's (Ottawa) work as social and cultural anthropologists are other examples, and there are some colleagues in the field of sport management (e.g. Lucie Thibault at Brock University) who actively participate in and contribute to research in the sociology of sport (Harvey, Thibault, & Rail, 1995).

As noted just above, the sociology of sport in Canada flourishes outside of sociology departments. This is not to suggest that there are no sociologists of sport in sociology departments but that

> ... even in countries where scholars have been using sociology to research sports, mainstream sociology has been slow at the institutional level to acknowledge the growing social and cultural significance of sports and sports participation. The tendency of sociologists to give priority to studies of work and other 'serious' subjects (politics, for example) over studies of play, sports, or leisure has accounted for much of the inertia in the parent discipline. (Coakley & Dunning, 2000, p. xxiv)

Out of the 17 Canadian universities that offer PhDs in sociology, none of them identify the study of sport as one of their central thematic areas and only one of them (University of Calgary, the home institution of Kevin Young, the editor of this book series) noted that their faculty did research in the area of the sociology of sport. What this means is that there are very few Canadian and Canadian-based scholars (Jason Laurendeau, Nancy Theberge and Kevin Young) who carry the proverbial flag for the subfield within the parent discipline.

Outside of mainstream sociology, the field is a far more established dimension of physical education/kinesiology units – or whatever mutation or combination of like words that have come to characterize these departments on Canadian campuses such as, to name but a few, Human Kinetics (Ottawa), Kinesiology and Health Sciences (York), Kinesiology and Health Studies (Queen's), Physical Education and Recreation (Alberta), Kinesiology and Physical Education (Lethbridge and Toronto), and Kinesiology and Recreation Management (Manitoba). In some of these departments, there may only be one sociologist of sport but there are some departments across the country (e.g. at the time of writing, British Columbia, Lethbridge, Alberta, Manitoba, York, Ottawa, Western and Toronto) where there is a 'critical mass' (which I define as three or more) of scholars all engaged in the socio-cultural study of sport and/or physical cultural studies (PCS). Some of these 'critical mass' hubs have been and/or continue to be particularly influential in the Canadian and international sociology of sport/PCS landscape including, from west to east, the University of British Columbia, University of Lethbridge, University of Calgary, University of Alberta, McMaster University, the University of Toronto, Queen's University and the University of Ottawa. The individual and collaborative work of scholars within and across these intellectual 'hubs' is significant and, in fact, one could dedicate a great deal of valuable time and energy mapping the flow(s) and influence of scholars across Canadian institutions.

Why though has the sociology of sport flourished outside of sociology departments? One factor for this trend has to do with the political machinations of the early generations of Canadian and Canadian-based scholars in the field who established themselves in their respective physical education departments as sociologists of sport, who established the importance of the discipline to the broad study of human movement (cf. Henry, 1964), and who were supported in doing so by high-ranked allies in their respective universities (i.e. department chairs, directors or even deans) – folks like Patrick Galasso or Earle Ziegler – who understood that well-rounded graduates of their programmes needed to have some sociological understanding of sport and physical education (Macintosh & Whitson, 1990).

Another factor contributing to the embeddedness of sociology of sport in physical education/kinesiology departments is the accreditation system developed by the Canadian Council of University Physical Education and Kinesiology Administrators (CCUPEKA). CCUPEKA serves as an accrediting body for physical education and kinesiology programmes in Canadian universities (see http://www.ccupeka.org/), and has actively protected the study of sport from the 'social sciences and humanities' perspective (i.e. psychology, history, philosophy, management and socio-cultural). This is particularly important for departments looking to prepare students for teaching. As teaching remains an extremely popular career destination for undergraduate students in Canada, CCUPEKA's accreditation system sets the standards for pre-teaching preparation such that departments who want CCUPEKA certification must meet particular targets around the number and variety of undergraduate course offerings in the socio-cultural area.

Although the focus of this chapter is on the emergence and state of sociology of sport in Canada as a field of research, it is important to add one additional and troubling comment on the state of teaching in the area in the country. As noted just above, not all Canadian and Canadian-based sociology of sport scholars enjoy a critical mass of colleagues in their units but rather are singular representatives of the field in their home departments. Notable scholars who have impacted the socio-cultural study of sport nationally and internationally while being, for all intents and purposes 'empires of one' (Theberge, personal communication, June 2009) in their home units, include Chris Stevenson, Robert Pitter, Nancy Theberge and Kevin Young. For some of these most isolated scholars, it is not uncommon for them to have to take on undergraduate teaching responsibilities not just in the area of the sociology of sport but also in such areas as history, philosophy or ethics. For some of these colleagues, these tangential topics may fit with their areas of expertise; for others, the need to teach in these areas, even occasionally, represents additional and substantial work and time away from teaching and research in the sociology of sport.

ACADEMIC ENVIRONMENT AND BARRIERS TO RESEARCH

Sport is taken seriously in Canada – sport headlines routinely make the front pages of the national and local newspapers; dedicated sport channels thrive on Canadian television and radio; and sport has been taken up by Canadian politicians as well as local grassroots or community-based individuals/organizations in the name of boosterism and civic life (see, e.g. Scherer & Davidson, 2011; Scherer & Sam, 2008; Wilson & White, 2002).[2] That said, this does not always mean that the sociological study of sport is always taken seriously in Canada. Compared to the earliest generations of sport sociologists, contemporary scholars in the field in Canada have certainly benefitted from an increased awareness of the social significance of sport amongst lay Canadians, government officials (including policy-makers and programme developers), as well as journalists (sport journalists or otherwise) and others (e.g. bloggers) in popular media. It is not uncommon to see sociologists of sport called upon as public intellectuals and subject matter experts in the media although this tends to happen at relatively predictable times; for example, in the lead-up to or during high-profile sporting events (e.g. Olympics or Paralympics) or when there is some scandal or controversy in the sporting world (Brown, 2014; Jenkins, 2014). Yet much of Canadian mainstream sport coverage on television and radio focuses on the plays of the game and the statistics of the sport, not necessarily or consistently the social and cultural dimensions of sport; although the regular inclusion of a sports culture panel on the Canadian Broadcasting Corporation's (CBC) very popular national radio broadcast 'q', as but one example, is evidence that social and cultural conversations about sport in the media are not completely absent.

Within political circles, it is not uncommon for federal, provincial/territorial and/or municipal government officials to call upon sociologists of sport to contribute to environmental scans of particular topics or to aid in the development of sport policies and guidelines (e.g. language). For example, as part of the renewal of the Canadian Sport Policy (CSP) in 2012 (colloquially referred to as CSP 2.0), Sport Canada (the federal branch responsible for sport in concert with the provincial/territorial sport ministries) engaged in a series of consultative meetings with a wide range of representatives from the Canadian government and sport communities, including policy-makers, community officials, regional sport leaders, coaches and sport science scholars. Five specific round tables were held across the country in efforts to gain insight and direction on enhancing sport participation for marginalized individuals and communities (official language minority communities; Aboriginal peoples; Canadians with a disability; ethno-cultural populations; and women) in Canada and, at each of these round table sessions, scholars from the socio-cultural study of sport community (e.g. Janice

Forsyth, Lynn Lavallee, Yuka Nakamura, Parissa Safai) were invited to participate and help inform CSP 2.0.

In addition to these opportunities for consultation, the federal government recognizes the value of social scientific study, including the sociology of sport, through various funding agencies. Arguably, the most relevant of these is the Social Sciences and Humanities Research Council of Canada (SSHRC), through which grants are awarded to promote and support research and research training in the humanities and social sciences in Canadian postsecondary educational institutions. In 2005, as part of a dedicated push for more comprehensive policy- and programme-relevant research, Sport Canada partnered with SSHRC to launch a joint initiative known as the Sport Participation Research Initiative (SPRI) (see http://www.sshrc-crsh.gc.ca/funding-financement/programs-programmes/sport_can-eng.aspx): 'Sport Canada is funding the SPRI to better evidence the benefits of, and barriers to, quality sport participation with the aim of improving Canadian sport policy outcomes' (retrieved from http://sirc.ca/resources/sport-science-sport-medicine-sport-research/scri-research).

Even with government funding and support for research in the sociocultural study of sport, there is a need for caution and vigilance among Canadian and Canadian-based scholars in the field to ensure its current and future health. Some of the concern arises from mounting pressures on academia broadly, including the corporatization of Canadian universities, the commercialization of research/knowledge and market-driven pressures on Canadian postsecondary institutions to focus more so on workforce preparation than on academic freedom or the stimulation of critical thinking and communication among students (see Brownlee, 2015; Westheimer, 2010). Additionally, variable (and oftentimes diminishing) financial support from federal and provincial/territorial governments to postsecondary education (including for research and research training) in Canada, in combination with the elimination of mandatory retirement in 2007−2008, has made for a sparse job market for new PhDs in the sociology of sport and extremely competitive research funding/grant application (including postdoctoral fellowship) cycles (see https://www.caut.ca/docs/default-source/education-review/educationreview13-1-en.pdf?sfvrsn = 2).

Some of the concern for sociology of sport in Canada also arises from the technocratic reconstruction of university physical education departments into kinesiology, as well as the alignment with and ascendance of health and health-related studies. With regard to the former, many have written about the specialization of academic disciplines within kinesiology, and the transformation of physical education departments into management-centric, performance-oriented or applied sport science units that de-emphasize the philosophical, ethical, social and cultural study of sport (see, e.g. Elliott, 2007; McKay, Gore, & Kirk, 1990; Pronger, 1995, 1996). Given the limited space and scope of this chapter, I urge readers to re/turn to Macintosh and Whitson's (1990) in-depth exploration of the transformation of physical education in universities in Canada − a phenomenon stimulated, in part, by government intervention into the high-performance sport system. Nearly 30 years later, their comprehensive analysis of the serious and troubling negative implications of the 'technicist tendency' (Aronowitz & Giroux, 1985, p. 197, as cited in Macintosh & Whitson, 1990, p. 134) in kinesiology departments for the critical academic study of sport still rings true. Adding to the precariousness of this situation is the primacy and alignment of many physical education and kinesiology departments with health and health pro-motion. While many sociologists of sport have contributed richly to the cri-tical study of health in and through sport in many ways, including the critical socio-cultural study of kinesiology as a regulated health profession and tool for individualistic health promotion strategies (cf. Harvey, 1983), not all Canadian and Canadian-based scholars do health-related sociology of sport research and yet often feel pressure to do more than study sport for the sake of sport.

FUTURE TRAJECTORIES: INFLUENTIAL FACTORS AND POSSIBILITIES

As I draw this chapter to a close, I reflect once again on the 50th anniver-sary celebrations of ISSA and *IRSS* in Paris in the summer of 2015. This chapter aimed to explore the development, growth and current status of the sociology of sport in Canada, as influenced by the work of specific indi-viduals as well as by broad social, cultural and political trends both within and outside of the academy. One chapter does not do justice to the breadth and depth of the field's history in Canada or to important contributions made by Canadian and Canadian-based scholars in the sociology of sport; I repeat myself in noting that an in-depth, comprehensive study of the his-torical and social development of the discipline in Canada is long overdue. Canadian and Canadian-based scholars have been active participants in the creation of our field and the celebrations in Paris paid tribute to that. Furthermore, Canadian and Canadian-based scholars continue to shape the sociology of sport as an area of research and scholarship as well as a community of professional members. As noted earlier, numerous Canadian and Canadian-based scholars have held key leadership positions in *IRSS* and *SSJ* as well as in ISSA and NASSS. Kevin Young, the editor of this volume and the series editor for *Research in the Sociology of Sport* served two different four-year terms as vice president of ISSA and occupied numerous roles within the NASSS Board and, as of 1 January 2016, Christine Dallaire assumed the presidency of ISSA until 2020.

When musing about the future possibilities for sociology of sport in Canada, three important current factors still need to be addressed. The first is the ongoing political struggle around language in research and scholarship, a particularly pressing issue for Francophone sociologists of sport in Canada (cf. Harvey & Rail, 1995b). The consequences of the hegemony of English in research and scholarship identified by Donnelly (2004) — including the 'politics of translation', 'the loss of meaning through translation', 'the ethnic cost for non-Anglophones', and 'the loss of/limitation on scientific/interpretive discourse' (pp. 5—6) — remain limiting factors on the publication and presentation records of many Franco-Canadian scholars in the field. A second influential current factor is the ongoing conversation (or clash, depending on one's perspective) between sociology of sport and physical cultural studies (PCS). For some Canadian and Canadian-based scholars, PCS complements the sociology of sport whereas others suggest the 'impending demise of the sociology of sport' with PCS as its 'successor' or 'potential rival' (Atkinson, 2011, pp. 136—138; see also Adams et al., 2016). While I do not want to suggest that sociologists of sport in Canada have never been witness to tensions between theoretical or paradigmatic camps among scholars, there is something about the contemporary debate elicited by opponents and proponents of PCS that gives one pause. The third influential current factor relates to methodological trends in the sociology in sport in Canada, specifically around the diminishing presence of quantitative research among Canadian and Canadian-based scholars. One need only scan the table of contents of sociology of sport journals to see what types of methods predominate (and, in fact, one could be forgiven for suggesting that statistical analysis is a dying breed) among current Canadian and Canadian-based scholars as compared to earlier generations (e.g. Jim Curtis, William McTeer, Philip White).

Where then does the future of sociology of sport in Canada lie? The short answer is that its future trajectories are limitless, defined only by the measure of inquisitiveness of Canadian and Canadian-based scholars to continue exploring sport and physical culture as social phenomena. My personal answer is that the sociologists of sport in Canada embrace their roles as public intellectuals and as advocates for research, scholarship and teaching that is grounded in people's lived realities and that helps advance social justice. The future trajectory for our discipline in Canada lies in how we champion, both personally and professionally, humane sport for all and how we craft our work in the community, whether locally or internationally, into extensions of our beliefs that sport and physical culture are vital parts of humanity, that must be considered rights worthy of protection, and that must be made accessible to all.

NOTES

1. This chapter focuses exclusively on sociology of sport in Canadian universities to the neglect of Canadian colleges. Faculty members at Canadian colleges tend not to engage in research and are more teaching-oriented in their focus. Additionally, college curricula in Canada tend to focus more so on applied or job-skills training, of which sociology of sport does not always apply.

2. Yes, while some may argue otherwise, hockey still reigns supreme in the social fabric of Canadian life and a number of scholars have produced remarkable analyses of Canada's national sport including, but not limited to Gruneau and Whitson (1993), MacNeill (1996), Robidoux (2001), Robidoux (2012), and Whitson and Gruneau (2006).

FIVE KEY READINGS

1. **Field, R. (Ed.). (2015).** *Playing for change: The continuing struggle for sport and recreation.* **Toronto: University of Toronto Press.**

   Conceived of as a festschrift in honour of Bruce Kidd, this collection of essays from scholars of the history and sociology of sport is notable both for its important examinations of a variety of substantive issues in the field of sport studies, and for its commentary on the significance and legacy of Bruce's scholarship, advocacy and activism within and beyond the critical academic study of sport nationally and internationally. Of particular note is Peter Donnelly and Michael Atkinson's chapter on the need for public sociology of sport (pp. 363–388).

2. **Gruneau, R. (1999).** *Class, sports and social development* **(2nd ed.). Champaign, IL: Human Kinetics.**

   Gruneau's seminal text is a book-length treatise locating sport in critical sociological theory. His argument that play and sport were 'social practices existing in, and constitutive of, historically shifting limits and possibilities that specify the range of powers available to human agents at different historical moments' (p. 102) was particularly provocative and ground-clearing in the field when first published (1983).

3. **Harvey, J., & Cantelon, H. (Eds.). (1988).** *Not just a game: Essays in Canadian sport sociology/sport et pouvoir: les enjeux sociaux au Canada.* **Ottawa: University of Ottawa Press.**

Written exclusively by Canadian scholars and published in both official languages, this collection of essays remains remarkably noteworthy in its breadth and depth of analysis of sport in Canada. With contributions that were theoretically rich and historically contextualized, this volume helped to put not just Canadian scholarship on the sociology of sport map but Canadian sport on the sociological map.

4. **Rail, G. (Ed.). (1998).** *Sport and postmodern times.* **Albany, NY: State University of New York Press.**

Rail's edited volume is but one example of her prodigious contribution to the socio-cultural study of sport and physical cultural studies globally. This particular book has been recognized as an invaluable collection of essays focused on postmodernist perspectives on sport, power and social inequality.

5. **Theberge, N. (2000).** *Higher goals: Women's ice hockey and the politics of gender.* **Albany, NY: SUNY Press.**

Winner of the 2001 NASSS Book Award, Theberge's *Higher Goals* offered the most extensive examination of women's experiences in sport of the times. Through its in-depth two-year ethnographic study of elite female hockey players in Canada, Theberge advanced critical feminist research in the sociology of sport in ways that highlighted and intertwined the social, political and cultural dimensions of women's hockey as well as the personal stories of her participants.

REFERENCES

Adams, M. L., Davids, J., Helstein, M. T., Jamieson, K. M., Kim, K. Y., King, S., ... Rail, G. (2016). Feminist cultural studies: Uncertainties and possibilities. *Sociology of Sport Journal, 33*(1), 75–91.
Aronowitz, S., & Giroux, H. (1985). *Education under Siege: The conservative, liberal and radical debate over schooling.* South Hadley, MA: Bergin and Harvey.

Atkinson, M. (2011). Physical cultural studies [redux]. *Sociology of Sport Journal, 28*(1), 135–144.

Atkinson, M., & Young, K. (2008). *Tribal play: Subcultural journeys through sport.* Bingley, UK: Emerald Group Publishing Limited.

Atkinson, M., & Young, K. (Eds.). (2012). *Qualitative research on sport and physical culture.* Bingley, UK: Emerald Group Publishing Limited.

Brown, I. (2014, February 14). Faster, stronger – Deadlier: Why do elite athletes sneer at risk and tempt the gods, and why do we encourage them? *The Globe and Mail.* Retrieved from http://www.theglobeandmail.com/sports/olympics/faster-stronger-deadlier-why-do-elite-athletes-sneer-at-risk-and-tempt-the-gods-and-why-do-we-encourage-them/article16903881/?page = all. Accessed on March 26, 2016.

Brownlee, J. (2015). *Academia, Inc: How corporatization is transforming Canadian universities.* Black Point, NS: Fernwood Publishing.

Cantelon, H., & Gruneau, R. (1982). *Sport, culture and the modern state.* Toronto: University of Toronto Press.

Coakley, J., & Dunning, E. (Eds.). (2000). *Handbook of sport studies.* London: Sage.

Crossman, J., & Scherer, J. (2015). Social dimen*sions of Canadian sport and physical activity.* Toronto: Pearson.

Donnelly, P. (2004). Editorial. *International review for the sociology of sport, 39*(1), 5–6.

Donnelly, P., & Young, K. (1988). The construction and confirmation of identity in sport subcultures. *Sociology of Sport Journal, 5*(3), 223–240.

Elliott, D. (2007). Forty years of Kinesiology: A Canadian perspective. *Quest, 59*(2), 154–162.

Forsyth, J., & Giles, A. R. (Eds.). (2013). *Aboriginal peoples and sport in Canada: Historical foundations and contemporary issues.* Vancouver: University of British Columbia Press.

Gruneau, R. S. (1983). *Class, sport and social development.* Amherst, MA: University of Massachusetts Press.

Gruneau, R., & Whitson, D. (1993). *Hockey night in Canada: Sport, identities and cultural politics.* Toronto: Garamond Press.

Hall, M. A. (1996). *Feminism and sporting bodies: Essays on theory and practice.* Champaign, IL: Human Kinetics.

Harvey, J. (1983). *Le corps programmé or la rhétorique de Kino-Québec.* Montreal: Éditions coopératives Albert Saint-Martin.

Harvey, J. (1990). De l'ordre au conflit: L'élargissement des perspectives théoriques en sociologie du sport. *Loisir et Société/Society and Leisure, 13*(1), 129–143.

Harvey, J., & Rail, G. (1995a). Body at work: Michel Foucault and the sociology of sport. *Sociology of Sport Journal, 12*(2), 164–179.

Harvey, J., & Rail, G. (1995b). Special issue: Sociology of sport in 'la Francophonie'. *Sociology of Sport Journal, 12*(2), 119–232.

Harvey, J., & Sparks, R. (1991). The politics of the body in the context of modernity. *Quest, 43*(2), 164–189.

Harvey, J., Thibault, L., & Rail, G. (1995). Neo-corporatism: The political management system in Canadian amateur sport and fitness. *Journal of Sport & Social Issues, 19*(3), 249–265.

Henry, F. (1964). Physical education: An academic discipline. *Journal of Health, Physical Education, and Recreation, 35*(7), 32–69.

time (see Fig. 1) but remain few and far between in spite of the increasing trend shown for the period 2010–2016. Furthermore, if we take the entire 63-year period spanning 1953–2016, the total number of sociological writings on sport in the Caribbean amount to 31, of which only 4 have been books (*Beyond a Boundary, Grass Roots Commitment, Caribbean Hoops, Social Roles of Sport in Caribbean Society*), 20 journal articles, 6 chapters in books, and 1 unpublished paper. In his examination of the number of academic studies on sport in the Caribbean, American sociologist Malec stated in 1995:

> A detailed review of computerized data bases in sociology, psychology, and education revealed surprisingly few studies of sports in the Caribbean. Apart from CLR James's (1983) classic, *Beyond a Boundary*, Manley's (1988) major work on cricket, and a handful of others there are few books on the topic. (1995b, p. 11)

Indeed, while the total number of publications in sport sociology has increased marginally from 11 to 15 since Malec made this observation in 1995, the situation has not changed significantly in the new millennium notwithstanding the increasing trend. This applies particularly to books, for none has been published since 1995.

However, the limited number of sociological writings on Caribbean sport is merely a reflection of the limited number of researchers in the field. In this regard, if we exclude the three early Caribbean authors (Brathwaite, James, and Matthews), who have since passed on, the number of scholars who have written on the sociology of Caribbean sport from the 1980s to the present amounts to just 11. These researchers can be further distinguished in terms of their geographical location, country of origin (re: birth), and sex. In terms of location, the majority are based in the United States (eight), one in the United Kingdom, one in Canada, and two in the Caribbean, of whom only three are women (one American, one Jamaican, and one of Antiguan-Barbudan parentage). However, only four were born in the Caribbean or are of Caribbean parentage, two of whom are from Trinidad and Tobago, one from Jamaica, and one from Antigua-Barbuda. In addition, for the most part, these scholars have worked independently of each other and while not all may still be active in doing sociological research on Caribbean sport, they have made an invaluable contribution to the creation of a body of knowledge on the sociology of sport in the region. Unfortunately, as a result of the very limited numbers, this has prevented the creation of a critical mass of sociological researchers or scholars on Caribbean sport sociology who can provide intellectual leadership in the development of this subspecialization.

MAIN CHARACTERISTICS OF RESEARCH IN THE ENGLISH-SPEAKING CARIBBEAN

The sociological study of Caribbean sport is not only very limited in terms of the number of publications, but also the range of sports and to a lesser extent, the various issues examined. For instance, the sports examined amount to just six: athletics, basketball, boxing, cricket, horseracing, and soccer. The major issues examined have related to race/ethnicity (Mandle & Mandle, 1988); class (Mandle, 1994; Mandle & Mandle, 1988, 1994); gender (Anderson, 1990; McCree, 2010a, 2011, 2014, 2015, 2016b); clientelism (Mandle & Mandle, 1988); democratization, ludic diffusion/athletic migration, cultural imperialism, and Caribbean integration (Mandle, 1994; Mandle & Mandle, 1988, 1990b, 1990c, 1990d, 1994; McCree, 2008a, 2014); globalization (McCree, 2008a); nationalism (McCree, 2010b, 2011, 2016a); "invented traditions" (McCree, 2016a); sport media (McCree, 2011, 2016a); governance (Tomlinson, 2007); community sport (Austin, 1990; Mandle & Mandle, 1988; McCree, 1990; Mitrano & Smith, 1990); spectatorship (Rampersad, 2011); professional, commercial sport (Mandle, 1994; Mandle & Mandle, 1988; McCree, 2000); amateurism/voluntarism (Mandle, 1994; Mandle & Mandle, 1988, 1990a, 1994; McCree, 2008a); Caribbean diasporic identity (Joseph, 2012); and parenting (McCree, 2016b). Given the diversity of topics, it is very challenging to indicate those that have been more popular or that have received more scholarly attention. This notwithstanding, the available evidence would suggest that issues of race/ethnicity, class, gender, community sport, amateurism, and commercialization have been some of the more salient topics examined in the extant literature on sport sociology in the ESC. Some of the issues or topics less focused on include sexuality, the environment, new media, educational performance, aging, disability, obesity, crowd disorder, and doping.

Notwithstanding its sparse nature, the literature has several methodological and theoretical characteristics. In terms of methodology, the research has been dominated by qualitative approaches, including ethnography, observation, documents, inclusive of newspaper reports, interviews, and life histories. While there has been some survey-type quantitative work, this has been rather minimal and limited to frequencies or simple bivariate analyses (Anderson, 1990; McCree, 1990). In this context, there is a lot of room for doing quantitative research on sport in the Caribbean in order to generate some degree of methodological pluralism in the local study of this social institution. However, in relation to theory, the small body of work offers a more eclectic mix of competing theoretical approaches but no particular framework stands out above the rest. These approaches include the use of "opportunity theory" (Austin, 1990); traditional functionalism (Mitrano & Smith, 1990); Gramscian hegemony (McCree, 2008a); Eliasian figurational sociology (McCree, 2008a, 2008b, 2010b); networks (McCree, 2014); exclusionary power (McCree, 2015); the expectancy value model of sport participation (McCree, 2016b); Raymond Williams' notions of "open cultural space" (Mandle, 1994; Mandle & Mandle, 1990c) as well as his notions of "residual," "pre-emergent," and "emergent" cultural forms (McCree, 2000); Gruneau's neo-Marxian, materialist, dialectical, and phenomenological framework derived from the study of Canadian sport (McCree, 2000); and Bourdieu's notions of "habitus, capital and field" (Rampersad, 2011). While it might be problematic or difficult to find some commonality amidst this theoretical diversity, the studies are connected by one major thread or undercurrent: they show how the process of identity formation and human agency in the development of sport in the ESC have been shaped by various factors of a political, economic, social, cultural, and organizational nature at a local, regional, and global level.

THE ACADEMIC ENVIRONMENT AND BARRIERS TO RESEARCH

Universities, private institutions, and the State (UPS) play a critical role in providing the appropriate support and creating an enabling environment for the development of teaching and research in any discipline. However, if we are to go by the previous indicators (e.g., number of publications and scholars), one can easily assert that the sociology of sport and the study of sport in general were never taken seriously by the high UPS in the ESC. Admittedly, while there has been some research on cricket, this has been driven largely by scholars in the discipline of history and, even there, the available literature is very limited in relation to themes and other academic disciplines. For instance, in relation to themes, the major focus has been the issue of identity formation in relation to nationalism, regionalism, race, and class (Beckles, 1998a, 1998b, 1998c; Beckles & Stoddart, 1995; James, 1963; Manley, 1988; Sandiford, 1998; Stoddart, 2004). As a result, the study of cricket and sport in general has suffered from a disciplinary and thematic lacuna due to the absence or lack of research across a broader range of disciplines.

However, this failure to take the study and research of sport seriously is not unique to the ESC, for it stemmed from a British-derived mindset that had constructed sport primarily as a physical activity associated with play, extracurricular activity, and the subject of physical education, which was accorded very low academic or intellectual value within the education system (Hargreaves, 1982a, 1982b; Horne, Jary, & Tomlinson, 1987). Sport therefore was something that you either played or watched in order to have a good time and generate feelings of pride, prestige, pleasure, passion, power, and patriotism by beating other nations, teams, or individuals in competition (McCree, 2008b). So conceived or constructed, sport was not something you studied either to test or generate theories and hypotheses in order to help understand and develop society or sport itself. As a result of this mindset, in Britain, the sociology of sport was described as a "ghetto subject" in the 1970s and 1980s (Horne et al., 1987). Where sport was taken seriously within either the education system or the society at large, this derived mainly from its supposed functionalist or normative value "… as a source of (i) moralism or character formation; (ii) recreation; (iii) health; (iv) unity, harmony, integration and (v) nationalism/nation building" (McCree, 2008b, p. 165).

Given the prominence of this received British narrative or paradigm concerning sport, since the University of the West Indies was first established by the British in 1948 as an extension of the University of London,[7] the study of sport in general and the sociology of sport in particular, never formed part of its traditional teaching, research, and development agenda. As a result of this, the University, across all of its three campuses in Trinidad and Tobago, Barbados, and Jamaica, for most of its history, has been a veritable bastion for the exclusion of sport as an area of study and research (McCree, 2008b). Moreover, even in the parent discipline of sociology itself, sport has been largely excluded as an area of study unlike education, religion, family, and crime. Such an environment was not conducive to the development of sport sociology or sport studies as a whole.

From the late 1990s, however, a confluence of factors led to the gradual emergence of academic sport programs at various higher educational institutions in the Caribbean (namely the University Technology of Jamaica, the University of the West Indies, the University of Trinidad and Tobago) at both the undergraduate and graduate levels.[8] These factors included the accelerated commercialization of sport globally, the decline of the once formidable West Indies cricket team, which had dominated world cricket for 15 years, and concerns over the governance of Caribbean sport in which soccer figured prominently (Beckles, 1998a, 1998b, 1998c; Patterson, McIntyre, & McDonald, 2007; Tomlinson, 2007).

The educational programs that were introduced, however, focused on three major disciplinary areas: sport management, sport sciences, and sport medicine. One of these programs included a FIFA diploma in sport management offered at the St. Augustine Campus of the University of the West Indies in collaboration with the International Center for Sport Studies (CIES) based in Neuchâtel, Sweden.[9] The introduction of these programs and, moreso, those relating to sport management, have benefited the sociology of sport as a discipline for it has been offered as a course in the undergraduate programs dealing with sport management as well as sport science. The deeper impact of these programs therefore is that they are helping to institutionalize the sociological study of sport in the region. For instance, this author has taught the sociology of sport as part of the BSc in Sport Management at the University of the West Indies, St. Augustine since 2001. However, while these teaching programs have helped to create an environment that is a little more conducive to the study of sport, research and publications in the sociology of sport and sport studies have lagged significantly behind (see Table 1). This lag can be attributed to both economic (e.g., absence of funding specifically for sport research) as well as noneconomic factors (e.g., lack of sport sociologists, persistence of traditional ideas concerning the study of sport, as well as a general failure to see the link between such research and sport development or sport for development).

In this context, therefore, the sociology of sport can hardly be considered as mature a field of study in the Caribbean as say the sociology of education, family, or religion. As a subdiscipline of sociology, the status and development of the sociology of sport in the ESC seem to have mirrored the historical experience of the sociology of sport around the world (Coakley, 1987; Dunning, 1999; Hargreaves, 1982a, 1982b; Horne et al., 1987; Ingham & Donelly, 1997; Malcolm, 2012).

THE FUTURE OUTLOOK

The future outlook for the sociology of sport in the ESC is rather mixed. On the one hand, there have been three positive developments. These include the introduction of undergraduate and graduate sport degree programs at universities across the region, the introduction of national sport policies in several countries of the ESC, and the emergence of a concern with sport for development.[10] These developments can help to institutionalize the academic study of sport sociology as a discipline in this region and also serve as an important catalyst to carry out research given the current importance attached to evidence-based public policy making. On the other hand, the future remains bleak as long as funding opportunities remain nonexistent and old-fashioned ideas toward the study and research of sport persist, as well as the failure to see its relevance to the development of sport or sport for development. The available evidence clearly suggests that while the English-speaking Caribbean was among the early pioneers of the intellectual and sociological study of sport, it now remains one of the regions where it is least developed. This will persist if a more enabling environment is not created for its development.

NOTES

1. This general English label is misleading since in some countries like St. Lucia and Dominica, while English is the official language of business and formal education, there exists the language of patois or French creole, which is a national language since it forms an integral part of everyday life.

2. These countries include Antigua-Barbuda, Bahamas, Barbados, Belize, Bermuda, Cayman Islands, Dominica, Grenada, Guyana, Jamaica, Montserrat, St. Kitts and Nevis, St. Lucia, St. Vincent and the Grenadines, St. Croix, St. Thomas, Turks and Caicos.

3. The 1953 article was part of a larger unpublished study entitled, *Trinidad in Transition: The Sociological Analysis of a Colonial Society*, fieldwork for which was carried out in 1951–1952 (Brathwaite, 1953/1975, p. 1).

4. The publication first appeared as an article in 1953 in the Caribbean-based journal of *Social and Economic Studies* (*SES*) and republished 22 years later in 1975, as a book. The original article amounted to 176 pages and was the sole article in that issue of the journal. While working as a research assistant to Professor Brathwaite in the late 1990s, he related to me that it was not published as a book because of a directive from the then British Colonial Office that he focus on articles instead of books.

5. http://sportsillustrated.cnn.com/si_online/features/2002/top_sports_books/2/

6. The first Caribbean countries to become politically independent of Britain were Jamaica and Trinidad and Tobago, which happened in 1962.

7. https://www.uwi.edu/history.asp

8. UWI, Cave Hill, https://www.cavehill.uwi.edu/sport/academics/degree-programmes.aspx, https://www.cavehill.uwi.edu/gradstudies/resources/brochures/sport-sciences-msc.aspx; UWI, Mona School of Business, http://www.mona.uwi.edu/msbm/diploma-sports-management; UWI, Mona, http://www.mona.uwi.edu/sports/teaching-programmes-sports

9. https://sta.uwi.edu/fss/dms/M.ScPGDip.inSportsManagement.asp
10. Caricom Secretariat, http://www.caricom.org/jsp/community_organs/human_social_sport.jsp?menu = cob; Government of Trinidad and Tobago, https://static.sport.gov.tt/images/pdf/programmes/national_sport_policy.pdf

FIVE KEY READINGS

1. **James, C. L. R. (1963).** *Beyond a boundary.* **London: Hutchinson.**

First published in 1963, this book is one of the early pioneering studies of the socio-political significance of sport in the Caribbean and has received international acclaim. Although it is based on the English sport of cricket, it is very useful for showing how sport was an active agent in not only facilitating various modes of domination (be it class, race, ethnic, British colonialism/imperialism) but also in challenging or resisting them through decolonization, independence, and regionalism. The author takes issue with the dismissive universal attitude to the intellectual study of sport which still haunts the field of sport studies.

2. **Mandle, J., & Mandle, J. (1988).** *Grass roots commitment: Basketball and society in Trinidad and Tobago.* **Parkersburg: Caribbean Books.**

This book is an ethnographic study of basketball in Trinidad and Tobago, which was the first of its kind in the English-speaking Caribbean. In it, the Mandles examined several issues relating to participation in the sport, its popularity, ethnic and class-based character, organization, and some of the constraints related thereto. To explain the popularity of the sport, the authors take issue with the notion of American cultural imperialism, seeing it instead as an expression of cultural diffusion since the game was voluntarily adopted by its grassroots participants due to its "inexpensive character" and the opportunity it afforded them to feel a sense of self-worth, control, and power, which they are denied in the wider society.

3. **Dunning, E. (1999).** *Sport matters: Sociological studies of sport, violence and civilization.* **London: Routledge.**

This book is centered on showing the relevance of one of the lesser-known sociological theories, figurational theory, to understanding a host of sporting phenomena that include notably, crowd violence, racism, sexism, and globalization. In addition, the book takes issue with the historical trivialization and "downgrading" of the study of sport in the sociological and intellectual mainstream by showing the prominent role of sport in shaping human identities, and relations between individuals, groups, and nations.

4. **Malcolm, D. (2012).** *Sport and sociology.* **London: Routledge**.

This recent book is ideal for students as well as faculty for it traces the history, growth, and development of the sociology of sport in both Europe and North America from the 1960s onward. In this regard, it examines how the discipline has become more organized, institutionalized, and legitimized although the longstanding issue of marginalization from the sociological and academic mainstream has not disappeared. However, while showing the discipline's theoretical, methodological, and thematic growth, differences remain over the definition of sport, the sub-field itself, as well as its intellectual and developmental purpose.

5. **Coakley, J. 2014.** *Sport in society: Issues and controversies.* **Columbus, OH: McGraw-Hill**.

This is one of the major international introductory texts for the sociology of sport that should be reader-friendly for both beginners and the converted alike. It covers a very wide range of issues that include the definition(s) of sport, the history of sport from indigenous to modern times, theories of sport, race, class, gender, the media, and commercialization, as well as deviant behavior like violence and doping in sport. Although it is American centered, it draws on relevant empirical data to examine these issues and provides very useful illustrations.

REFERENCES

Anderson, B. (1990). Sport, play and gender based success in Jamaica. *Arena Review*, *14*(1), 59−67.

Arbena, J. (1999). *Latin American sport: An annotated bibliography, 1988−1998.* Westport, CT: Greenwood.

Austin, R. (1990). A parkboy remembers colts, products of a subculture of sport. *Arena Review*, *14*(1), 75−85.

Bateman, A. (2009). "From far it looks like politics": C.L.R. James and the canon of English cricket literature. *Sport and Society, 12*(4–5), 496–508.

Beckles, H. (Ed.) (1998a). *A spirit of dominance: Cricket and nationalism in the West Indies.* University of the West Indies, Kingston: Canoe Press.

Beckles, H. (1998b). *The development of West Indies cricket: The age of nationalism* (Vol. 1). London: The University of the West Indies and Pluto Press.

Beckles, H. (1998c). *The development of West Indies cricket: The age of globalization* (Vol. 2). London: The University of the West Indies and Pluto Press.

Beckles, H., & Stoddart, B. (Eds.). (1995). *Liberation cricket: West Indies cricket culture.* Manchester: Manchester University Press.

Brathwaite, L. (1953/1975). *Social stratification in Trinidad and Tobago.* University of the West Indies, Kingston: ISER.

Caribbean Quarterly. Retrieved from http://www.uwi.edu/cq/subjectindex.aspx

Caricom Secretariat. Retrieved from http://www.caricom.org/jsp/community_organs/human_social_sport.jsp?menu=cob

Carrington, B. (2010). *Race, sport and politics: The sporting black diaspora.* London: Sage.

Carrington, B. (2013). The critical sociology of race and sport: The first fifty years. *Annual Review of Sociology, 39*, 379–398.

Coakley, J. (1987). Sociology of sport in the United States. *International Review for Sociology of Sport, 22*(1), 63–77.

Cudjoe, R. S., & Cain, W. E. (Eds.). (1995). *CLR James: His intellectual legacies.* Amherst, MA: University of Massachusetts Press.

Dunning, E. (1999). *Sport matters: Sociological studies of sport, violence and civilization.* London: Routledge.

Farred, G. (1996). *Rethinking C.L.R. James.* Oxford: Blackwell Publishers.

Government of Trinidad and Tobago. *National sport policy.* Retrieved from https://static.sport.gov.tt/images/pdf/programmes/national_sport_policy.pdf

Hargreaves, J. (1982a). Sport, culture and ideology. In J. Hargreaves (Eds.), *Sport, culture and ideology* (pp. 30–61). London: Routledge.

Hargreaves, J. (1982b). Theorising sport: An introduction. In J. Hargreaves (Ed.), *Sport, culture and ideology* (pp. 1–30). London: Routledge.

Hargreaves, J., & McDonald, I. (2000). Cultural studies and the sociology of sport. In J. Coakley & E. Dunning (Eds.), *Handbook of sport studies* (pp. 48–60). London: Sage.

Horne, J., Jary, D., & Tomlinson, A. (Eds.). (1987). *Sport, leisure and social relations.* London: Routledge and Kegan Paul.

Ian Randle Publishers. Retrieved from https://www.ianrandlepublishers.com

Ingham, A., & Donnelly, P. (1997). A sociology of North American sociology of sport: Disunity in unity, 1965 to 1996. *Sociology of Sport Journal, 14*, 362–418.

James, C. L. R. (1963). *Beyond a boundary.* London: Hutchinson.

James, C. L. R. (1983). *Beyond a Boundary.* New York, NY: Pantheon.

Joseph, J. (2012). Culture, community, consciousness: The Caribbean sporting diaspora. *International Review for the Sociology of Sport, 49*(6), 669–687.

Journal of Eastern Caribbean Studies. Retrieved from http://www.cavehill.uwi.edu/salises/publications/jecs.aspx

Malcolm, D. (2012). *Sport and sociology.* London: Routledge.

Malec, M. (Ed.). (1995a). *The social roles of sport in the Caribbean.* Amsterdam: Gordon and Breach Publishers.

Malec, M. (1995b). Neglected fields: Sports in the Caribbean. In M. Malec (Eds.), *The social roles of sport in the Caribbean* (pp. 1–13). Amsterdam: Gordon and Breach Publishers.

Mandle, J. (1994). *Caribbean hoops: The development of West Indian basketball.* Amsterdam: Gordon and Breach Publishers.

Mandle, J., & Mandle, J. (1988). *Grass roots commitment: Basketball and society in Trinidad and Tobago.* Parkersburg, WV: Caribbean Books.

Mandle, J., & Mandle, J. (1990a). Amateur basketball in Trinidad and Tobago. *Sociology and Social Research, 74*(2), 95−102.

Mandle, J., & Mandle, J. (1990b). Basketball, civil society, and the post colonial state in the commonwealth Caribbean. *Journal of Sport and Social Issues, 14*(2), 59−75.

Mandle, J., & Mandle, J. (1990c). Open cultural space: Grassroots basketball in the English-speaking Caribbean. *Arena Review, 14*(1), 68−74.

Mandle, J., & Mandle, J. (1990d). Grassroots basketball in Trinidad and Tobago: Foreign domination or local creativity? In J. A. Lent (Eds.), *Caribbean popular culture* (pp. 133–144). Bowling Green, OH: Bowling Green State University Popular Press.

Mandle, J., & Mandle, J. (1994). The failure of Caribbean integration: Lessons from grass roots basketball. *Studies in Latin American Popular Culture, 13*, 153−164.

Manley, M. (1988). *A history of West Indies cricket.* London: Deutsch.

Matthews, B. D. (1965). The evolution of football in Trinidad and Tobago, 1908−1962. Presidential Address delivered at the Hotel Normandie, Port of Spain, Trinidad, December 12.

McCree, R. (1990). Whither jets, hawks and civic? The organisation of sport in a community in Trinidad: The case of point Fortin, 1970−1986. *Arena Review, 14*(1), 86−100.

McCree, R. (1995). *Professionalism and the development of club football in Trinidad.* MSc Diss., The University of the West Indies, St. Augustine.

McCree, R. (2000). Professional soccer in the Caribbean: The case of Trinidad and Tobago, 1969−1983. *International Review for the Sociology of Sport, 35*(2), 199−218.

McCree, R. (2008a). Modern sport, middle classes and globalization in the post-war Caribbean 1945−1952: Variations on a theme. *International Journal of the History of Sport, 25*(4), 472−492.

McCree, R. (2008b). The social bases for exclusion of sport from Caribbean economic development: Identity formation vs capital accumulation. *Nordic Journal of Latin American and Caribbean Studies, 38*(1−2), 154−176.

McCree, R. (2010a). Female boxing and violence in Trinidad. *Journal for the Study of Sports and Athletes in Education, 4*(2), 43−58.

McCree, R. (2010b). Sport and multiple identities in post-war Trinidad: The case of McDonald Bailey. In E. Smith (Ed.), *The sociology of sport and social theory* (pp. 201−214). Champaign, IL: Human Kinetics.

McCree, R. (2011). The death of a female boxer: Media, sport, nationalism, and gender. *Journal of Sport and Social Issues, 35*(4), 327−349.

McCree, R. (2014). Student athletic migration from Trinidad and Tobago: The case of women's soccer. In S. Agergaard & N. C. Tiesler (Eds.), *Women, soccer and transnational migration* (pp. 73−85). London: Routledge.

McCree, R. (2015). The fight outside the ring: Female boxing officials in Trinidad and Tobago. In A. Channon & C. Matthews (Eds.), *Global perspectives on women in combat sports* (pp. 104−118). London: Palgrave Macmillan.

McCree, R. (2016a). In the crucible of change: Bailey, Britain and the post-war Olympic games. *Sport in Society*, 1−17. Retrieved from http://www.tandfonline.com/doi/full/10.1080/17430437.2015.1133594. Accessed on January 22, 2016.

McCree, R. (2016b). Female sport and parenting in the Caribbean. *Women, Gender and Families of Color, 4*(1), 36−56.

Mitrano, J. R., & Smith, R. E. (1990). And they're off: Sport and the maintenance of community in St Croix. *Arena Review, 14*(1), 45−78.

Patterson, P. J., McIntyre, A., & McDonald, I. (2007). *Committee on governance of West Indies cricket: Final report*. Kingston. Retrieved from http://www.windiescricket.com/sites/default/files/documents/Committee-on-Governance-of-West-Indies-Cricket-Final-Report.pdf

Rampersad, A. (2011). The social and cultural consequences of cricket world cup 2007: Poor spectatorship in Trinidad and Tobago. In L.-A. Jordan, B. Tyson, C. Hayle, & D. Truly (Eds.), *Sports event management: The Caribbean experience* (pp. 171−182). London: Ashgate.

Sandiford, K. (1998). *Cricket nurseries of colonial Barbados: The elite schools, 1865−1966*. Kingston: The Press University of the West Indies.

Small Axe. Retrieved from http://smallaxe.dukejournals.org

Smith, A. (2012). *CLR James and the study of culture*. London: Palgrave Macmillan.

Sports Illustrated. *Sports illustrated's the top 100 sports books of all time*. Retrieved from http://sportsillustrated.cnn.com/si_online/features/2002/top_sports_books/1/

Stoddart, B. (1990). CLR James: A remembrance. *Sociology of Sport Journal, 7*, 103−106.

Stoddart, B. (2004). Sport, colonialism and struggle: C.L.R. James and cricket. In R. Giulianotti (Eds.), *Sport and modern social theorists* (pp. 111−128). London: Palgrave Macmillan.

The Bulletin of Eastern Caribbean Affairs. Retrieved from http://www.cavehill.uwi.edu/salises/publications/ecbulletin/publications—bulletin-index.aspx

The University of the West Indies. *Cave Hill*. Retrieved from https://www.cavehill.uwi.edu/gradstudies/resources/brochures/sport-sciences-msc.aspx; https://www.cavehill.uwi.edu/sport/academics/degree-programmes.aspx

The UWI. *About the UWI: An institution rich with history*. Retrieved from https://www.uwi.edu/history.asp

The UWI, Mona. Retrieved from http://www.mona.uwi.edu/sports/teaching-programmes-sports

The UWI. Mona School of Business. Retrieved from http://www.mona.uwi.edu/msbm/diploma-sports-management

The UWI Press. Retrieved from http://www.uwipress.com/about_uwipress

The UWI, St. Augustine. *Department of management studies*. Retrieved from https://sta.uwi.edu/fss/dms/M.ScPGDip.inSportsManagement.asp

Tomlinson, A. (2007). Lord. Don't stop the carnival: Trinidad and Tobago at the 2006 FIFA world cup. *Journal of Sport and Social Issues, 31*(3), 259−282.

CHAPTER 20

SOCIOLOGY OF SPORT: UNITED STATES OF AMERICA

Jeffrey Montez de Oca

ABSTRACT

This chapter provides readers with a summary of sport sociology in the United States. It begins with a brief overview of sport in the United States before describing the development of the sociology of sport in the United States and some of the major contemporary patterns in sport research. They key movement in US sport sociology was the critical-cultural turn that took place during the 1980s and 1990s when critical theory and feminism became dominant approaches to research. Scholarship in the 21st century has largely developed upon that turn and is generally qualitative and cultural. Contemporary US sport sociology is a critical endeavor heavily influenced by cultural studies, post-structuralism, feminism, queer theory, critical race theory, post-colonial theory, and theories of globalization. Despite a fairly consistent approach to sport research in the United States, sport sociology remains contentious and in disunity. This chapter argues that the contention and disunity results from broader structural patterns that guide sport sociologists' social actions.

Keywords: United States; sport sociology; sport research; critical theory; North American Society for the Sociology of Sport

Sociology of Sport: A Global Subdiscipline in Review
Research in the Sociology of Sport, Volume 9, 361–375
Copyright © 2017 by Emerald Group Publishing Limited
All rights of reproduction in any form reserved
ISSN: 1476-2854/doi:10.1108/S1476-285420160000009025

INTRODUCTION

Although the sociological study of sport has roots in the 19th and early 20th centuries (Sage, 1997; Yiannakis, Melnick, & Morgan, 2015), the sociology of sport has only been a vibrant sub-discipline in the United States since the 1970s, when the North American Society for the Sociology of Sport (NASSS) was established. US sport sociology initially emerged in the 1960s as a quantitative and positivistic endeavor influenced by Parsonian functionalism (Montez de Oca, 2013; Nixon, 2010; Sage, 1997). While we should always be cautious of "origins" (Foucault, 1984), the formal start of US sport sociology is often dated from Gerald Kenyon and John Loy's "Toward a Sociology of Sport" (1965). The 1970s and 1980s saw the emergence of a group of critical scholars steeped in political economy and feminist approaches. These "younger" scholars were qualitatively inclined and made power relations, especially class and gender, central to their analyses (Nixon, 2010; Yiannakis et al., 2015). By the 1990s, the critical scholars had become the leading figures in the field, which shifted US sport sociology toward qualitative research concerned with identities and power (Ingham & Donnelly, 1997). Although the areas of focus have become more diverse in the 21st century, sport sociology remains largely cultural, qualitative, and concerned with identity relations and power. It also remains contentious and in a state of disunity.

This chapter provides readers with a summary of sport sociology in the United States. It begins with a brief overview of sport in the United States before moving into a discussion of the sociology of sport. They key movement in US sport sociology was the critical-cultural turn that took place during the 1980s and 1990s. Scholarship in the 21st century has largely developed upon that turn and maintained the tradition of disunity. It should be noted that while the subject of this chapter is the United States of America, sport sociology in the United States is intricately linked to scholarly developments outside of the country (Ingham & Donnelly, 1997; Yiannakis et al., 2015). As Coakley states: "The sociology of sport was born in an international context. And an important group of the early sport sociologists in the United States were formally and informally involved in Canadian and European developments" (1987, p. 63). To this day, US-based scholars tend to have extensive professional and personal relations with scholars in Canada as well as the United Kingdom, Australia, New Zealand, Japan, and South Korea. Therefore, this chapter discusses US sport sociology with regular reference to scholars who are either located outside of the United States or are not US nationals.

SPORT IN THE UNITED STATES OF AMERICA

The sport system in the United States includes not only high-profile professional and amateur leagues in a variety of different sports (e.g., US football, basketball, baseball, hockey, soccer, motor sports, golf, cycling, aquatics, alternative sports, adventure sports, tennis, etc.) but also a diverse array of organized and informal sports for both adults and youth in the public and nonprofit sector (e.g., schools, municipal parks, YMCAs, etc.) as well as the private sector (e.g., private parks, resorts, gyms, and leagues). Despite large investments in sport, the United States, unlike many other nations, lacks a sport ministry that sets national policies or regulates sport assets. Not only does the US sport system lack the rationality that many other national sport systems possess, it also means that many sport resources are market-based rather than in the public. It is not unusual for people in the United States to pay for a private gym membership, sign their children up for a soccer league run as a corporate franchise, take their family on vacation to a private ski resort, and pay special taxes for the stadium of a local professional sport franchise. In short, sport in the United States tends to be more consumer- than citizen-oriented.

The liberal sport model in the United States produces a wide array of options for both sport participants and spectators alike. Given its commercial nature, the market model is highly technological and results-oriented, which means that the United States produces some of the best, the most celebrated, and the most highly compensated athletes in the world. In many respects, the liberal model produces the same results as more state-centered models, such as high-level performance, scientific training, and negative physical and mental health outcomes of elite sport participation. But it also fosters the inter-penetration of sport and corporations, and pushes many of the system's costs onto citizens as the literature on stadium construction demonstrates (Baade & Dye, 1990; Baade & Sanderson, 1997; Baim, 1994; Noll & Zimbalist, 1997).

The liberal sport model in the United States also impacts sport studies. Without a sport ministry, the study of sport in the United States lacks the state support enjoyed in countries like Canada (Harris, 2006, p. 83). This has encouraged the growth of a business-oriented version of sport management on university campuses while sport sociology has dwindled (Yiannakis et al., 2015). Further, sport sociology in the United States tends to be fractured and decentered (Donnelly, 2015; Ingham & Donnelly, 1997). There are few programs that offer a doctoral degree in sport sociology. Generally, the socio-cultural study of sport is offered as an option within a kinesiology or sport management department. This means that most sport sociologists fill a sport slot in a department not dedicated to sport studies or they are non-specialists teaching a sociology of sport class (Atkinson, 2011; Donnelly, 2015; Nixon, 2010; Yiannakis et al., 2015). For example, I hold a PhD in sociology and work in a sociology department. To work with other sport scholars, I collaborate with colleagues in psychology, philosophy, and business who are the only dedicated sport scholars in their departments. The lack of institutionalization allows me to pursue inter-disciplinary research outside of the mainstream of my field but I do so largely independently and with little institutional support.

A HISTORY OF SPORT SOCIOLOGY
IN THE UNITED STATES

US sport sociology has long embraced theoretical and methodological diversity rather than a unified field of study (Eizten, 1987). The history of inter-disciplinarity has been both productive and conflictual. Sage (1997) argues that sport sociology and physical education have a tense and inter-twined relationship. Janet Harris locates the origin of this tension in Kenyon and Loy (1965), who called for a split between academic sport sociology and practical physical education. Kenyon wanted to situate sport sociology within the professional sociology approach of his time, structural-functionalism, but this led to divisions between sport sociology and physical education (Harris, 2006, p. 73). This tension still remains and motivates periodic calls for name changes within the sub-discipline (Harris, 1987), which has most recently centered on "physical cultural studies" (discussed below).

The structural-functional stage in the 1960s and 1970s was a strategic movement to establish sport sociology as a recognized sub-discipline in a US academic setting skeptical of sport scholarship. Socialization became a key concept at this time because, among other things, it helped demonstrate positive outcomes of sport participation and the inculcation of values (Ingham & Donnelly, 1997, p. 367). In the 1970s and 1980s, a second generation of sport scholars entered the field and broke from the positivist approach by emphasizing social problems and political economy (Ingham & Donnelly, 1997, pp. 372 and 375). These perspectives were heavily influenced by Mills (1959), who critiqued abstract empiricism. They were also influenced by classical theorists such as Marx, Weber, and the Frankfurt

School. This movement was further influenced by critical sport scholarship in academic (Brohm, 1978; Rigauer, 1981) and popular texts (Gent, 1973; Hoch, 1972; Meggyesy, 1971; Shaw, 1972) as well as "the revolt of the black athlete" (Edwards, 1969). Some of the more impactful work from this movement includes Loy and Elvogue (1970), Stone (1981), Beamish (1982), Ingham (1985), Coakley (1992), Gruneau (1999), and Sage (1990).

The critical move in US sport sociology opened up new lines of analysis but its focus on labor and political economy was not immediately amenable to feminist concerns. This changed significantly with the emergence of Foucauldian-inspired feminist analysis and the broad embrace of British cultural studies that leaned on Antonio Gramsci (Ingham & Donnelly, 1997). It would be a mistake, however, to suggest that feminist sport studies began in the 1980s. In the wake of Title IX (1972), Vivan Acosta and Linda Jean Carpenter began surveying senior women administrators at National Collegiate Athletic Association (NCAA) colleges in 1977 to take a snapshot of the status of women in intercollegiate sport; the most recent report covers 35 years of women's collegiate athletics (Acosta & Carpenter, 2012). Also, M. Ann Hall did pioneering work in feminist sociology in the 1970s (Hall, 1972, 1978). But with more robust theoretical frameworks, feminist sport sociology became increasingly sophisticated and insightful in the 1980s and 1990s (Birrell, 1988; Birrell & Cole, 1994; Birrell & Richter, 1987; Cole, 1993; Cole & Hribar, 1995; Kane, 1995; Kane & Snyder, 1989; McDonald & Birrell, 1999; Messner, 1988; Theberge, 1981, 1985, 1987).

Evidence of the rising importance of feminist theory is visible in the NASSS scholarship awards. Feminist theory guided 6 of the first 10 books (1993–2003) and 12 of the 22 total books that have won the NASSS Outstanding Book Award. Messner's (1992) groundbreaking study of masculinities was the first book to win this award. Messner uses R. W. Connell's hegemonic masculinity and life history interviews of male former athletes to demonstrate how masculine privilege derived from sport also creates cost and consequences for men ill equipped by masculinity to deal with them. Curry (1991), who also draws upon Connell, won the first *Sociology of Sport Journal* (*SSJ*) Outstanding Article Award the same year. In 1999 Heather Sykes won the *SSJ* Award using queer theory to deconstruct the politics of "the closet" in women's sport (Sykes, 1998). These awards not only demonstrate that feminist sport sociology was institutionally central within US sport studies by the early 1990s but also that critical masculinities studies was an important sub-area (see Curry, 1993, 2000; Davis, 1997; Dworkin & Wachs, 1998; McKay, Messner, & Sabo, 2000; Messner, 2002, 2007; Messner, Dunbar, & Hunt, 2000; Messner & Sabo,

1990; Pronger, 1990, 1999; Sabo, 2001; Sabo & Jansen, 1998; Trujillo, 1991, 1995; Whannel, 1993).

The rise of feminist sport sociology coincided with broader developments in US society and sport, namely the rise of neoliberal capitalism, the expansion of media, and the development of sport promotion (Montez de Oca, 2008; Whitson, 1998). The adoption of new theoretical perspectives (especially Michel Foucault and Antonio Gramsci), the importance of feminism, and the new developments in sport and society created a context that made British cultural studies approaches to the study of media, culture, and political economy appear increasingly urgent. This configuration was especially clear in studies of one or both parts of what Kellner (2001) called an "unholy alliance" between Nike and Michael Jordan. Two studies deserve special attention. Cole and Hribar (1995) use the concept "commodity feminism" to show how Nike markets liberal feminist aspirations to women so that they can produce themselves as better consumers without the political transcendence promised by feminist liberation. Andrews (2001) draws upon Franz Fanon to show how commodity relations converted Michael Jordan's blackness from a possible signifier of danger, whether via street crime or political revolt, into a depoliticized sign of consumption. These studies exemplify a body of theoretically sophisticated research that show how gender, race, culture, nation, class, sexuality, and political economy articulate in sport formations (see Carrington, 1998a, 1998b; Cole, 1996, 2001; Crosset, 1995; Martin & Miller, 1999; McDonald & Birrell, 1999; Miller, 2001; Miller, Lawrence, McKay, & Rowe, 2001; Silk, 2002; Sykes, 1998).

CONTEMPORARY US SPORT SOCIOLOGY

Essentially, the critical-cultural turn of the 1980s and 1990s was institutionalized in the leading US sport sociology journals. At the turn of the 21st century, US sport sociology was a critical endeavor heavily influenced by cultural studies, post-structuralism, feminism, queer theory, critical race theory, post-colonial theory, and theories of globalization. Scholars consistently use political economy perspectives to study the articulation of culture, commodities, consumption, and identities. However, the older critical focus on relations of production had faded (Ingham & Donnelly, 1997). The institutionalization of the critical-cultural turn can be seen in a review of keywords in the *Sociology of Sport Journal* (*SSJ*) (2010−2014) and

Journal of Sport and Social Issues (*JSSI*) (2010−2015), which are the two leading sport sociology journals in the United States. While this review of 225 articles is not a comprehensive statement on the state of the field, it provides a snapshot of US sport sociology that is consistent with similar research (Dart, 2014; Harris, 2006). The immediate image that emerges from the review is that sport sociologists in the United States have broad and far-ranging interests within the field of sport studies. At the same time, critical social theories, especially feminist theory, guide much of the research, issues of power and social justice are a broad general concern, and most of the research is qualitative in approach.

Given the theoretical focus of the sub-discipline, it is not unusual for authors to list theoretical perspectives in the keywords. Authors were most likely to list feminist theory (15 times). Critical theory was also cited (4 times). The theorists most commonly cited are Michel Foucault (12) and Pierre Bourdieu (11). Similarly, theoretical terms consistent with their approaches are also common, such as discourse (17), epistemology (6), and cultural capital (4). Gender is regularly cited in keywords, women (33) and men (36). While specific racial groups are not listed often, race and racism are cited 32 times. Other specific systems of oppression cited included sexuality (11), gender (7), ability (2), and class (1).

The vast majority of the articles employ a qualitative methodology. However, ethnography (16) and discourse analysis (8) are the only methodological approaches regularly cited. One of the major areas of research cited in keywords is the media. The bulk of the research focuses on "mass media" (33) including television (14), print media (9), and film (3). New media (20), which includes the Internet, social media, and blogs, is another area of study. Neoliberalism (15) was the most commonly cited economic keyword followed by commodities and consumption (11), while invocations of class (5) were less common. The focus on media, neoliberalism, and commodities and consumption is unsurprising during a highly mediated stage of capitalism (neoliberalism), and at a time when the sport system is more consumer than citizen oriented.

When it comes to geographical sites of study, US sport sociology is global with a decidedly British bias. The United Kingdom (20) or one of its nations (e.g., Wales) are the most common keywords. After the United Kingdom came the United States (17), Canada (13), Asia (11), Europe excluding the United Kingdom (9), Latin America and the Caribbean (7), Australia/New Zealand (7), and Africa (3). If we think of Canada, Australia, New Zealand, and South Africa as former British Commonwealth countries, then we see an even stronger British bias (33); Quebec was only cited once amongst the Canadian keywords. The countries listed appear to reflect a regional bias based on scholars' location or place of origin. It also illustrates the international nature of these journals.

My review of keywords used since 2010 supports what others have said about sport sociology in the United States, but it also has limitations. For instance, a simple review of keywords could give the impression that US sport sociologists are less concerned with the specific sports they study than with "sport" as a general category of study. In total, specific sports were only identified 38 times, which means only 17% of the authors felt a specific sport was a relevant keyword. However, when we look at the titles, about 47% of the 225 titles identify either a specific sport or specific sport league such as the National Football League (NFL). So although we should approach my review of keywords with some caution, what I found is consistent with Dart's (2014) content analysis of the titles, abstracts, and keywords of the same journals over the past 25 years. Differences that did appear can probably be explained by the fact that Dart's study covered a much longer time period in addition to a more extensive methodology.

In a field so clearly unified around qualitative approaches to the study of culture and power, a person should be forgiven for recalling Monty Python's *Life of Brian* (1979) when looking at the level of disunity and discord within US sport sociology. Malcolm (2014) explains that much of the disunity in North American sport sociology has resulted from an ongoing process of professionalization that is characterized by the formation of symbolic boundaries around what constitutes relevant knowledge. This is a social and political process of pulling certain authors, theories, methodologies, and goals into the group while excluding others (see also Dart, 2014). The recent push to change the name "sociology of sport" to "physical cultural studies" is an excellent example of our disunity.

British cultural studies entered sport sociology in the United States in the 1980s and subsequently increased in popularity through the 1990s and 2000s (Ingham & Donnelly, 1997). The editors of our two leading journals provide an indication of the institutional centrality of cultural studies in US sport sociology: Toby Miller (1996−1999) and C. L. Cole (1999−present) at *JSSI* and Nancy Theberge (2002−2004), Pirkko Markula (2009−2011), Michael Atkinson (2012−2014), and Michael D. Giardina (2014−present) at *SSJ* are all important cultural studies scholars. In a context favorable to cultural studies, David L. Andrews began to promote a model for the sociological study of sport at the University of Maryland that blends the terms "physical culture" and "cultural studies" into "physical cultural studies" (PCS). His push for a theoretically sophisticated, empirically rich, and politically engaged study of the social and cultural dimensions of sport and human movement was motivated by a crisis in kinesiology rooted in the embrace of science and sub-disciplinarity. The more expansive term PCS is then presented as a means to help build a comprehensive and integrative kinesiology that includes a humanistic and social scientific dimension (Andrews, 2008). Andrews and Giardina (2008) further add that PCS makes a double movement between (1) the fact that sport is often marginalized in cultural studies despite celebrations of the "popular" and (2) although sport scholars who identify with cultural studies are proliferating, many are ill-informed in cultural studies' basic precepts. They then suggest that the theory and method of articulation as outlined by Hall (1986) should guide the intellectual endeavor of PCS. In a special issue on PCS in *SSJ*, Silk and Andrews (2011) went farther by calling for PCS to replace sociology of sport as the signifier for social and cultural studies of sport in North America (see also Atkinson, 2011; Giardina & Newman, 2011). Michael Friedman organized a session on PCS at the 2012 NASSS meeting in New Orleans, which was followed in 2013 (Quebec) by a feminist response that questioned whether or not PCS offered a new approach to sport sociology. The discussions about PCS have been productive, however, given the historical divide between academics and practitioners as well as inertia, it seems unlikely that "physical cultural studies" will replace "the sociology of sport" as the general term for our scholarly endeavor. Rather, as Malcolm suggests, it marks out a social network among sport sociology scholars who currently hold prominent institutional positions in the field.

CONCLUSION

The sociology of sport in the United States is vibrant, diverse, and contentious. That vibrancy, diversity, and contention is rooted in the field of study, the field's intellectual history, and the larger structural context of the United States. The market approach to both sport and academia, the historical divide between sociological academics and physical education practitioners, and the rise of critical and cultural approaches to sport studies have all impacted the current formation of sport sociology in the United States. Despite jockeying for position within their home institutions and the larger field, sport sociologists continue to produce engaging research on sport and society from a variety of cultural studies perspectives.

Sport sociology in the United States may never hold the prestige of some other areas of research, or at least not enough for many of its practitioners. The sports writer Dave Zirin (2008) suggested that sport sociologists move away from the traditional professional concerns and anxieties of academics in order to become more engaged in public debates about the role of sport in society. Very few US-based sport sociologists would disagree with this suggestion and claim that, in fact, that is what they do. Indeed, it is a central goal of physical cultural studies. However, disagreement arises over what that actually means in practice in terms of placing emphasis on traditional academic publishing or writing more editorials in newspapers. But if history is a predictor for the future, we will continue into the near future in a fashion very similar to what has been described here.

FIVE KEY READINGS

1. **Cole, C. L., & Hribar, A. (1995). Celebrity feminism: Nike style, post-fordism, transcendence, and consumer power.** *Sociology of Sport Journal, 12*, 347–369.

   C. L. Cole and Amy Hribar draw upon Michel Foucault to analyze the cultural dynamics of neoliberal capitalism. They show that Nike's invocation of feminist liberation is a clever marketing ploy that obscures the exploitation inherent to Nike's labor process, and is thus an example of commodity feminism. Ultimately, they show that cultural dynamics are a structural component of political economy.

2. **Hartmann, D. (2003).** *Race, culture, and the revolt of the black athlete: The 1968 Olympic protests and their aftermath.* **Chicago, IL: University of Chicago Press.**

   Doug Hartman provides an excellent example of historical sociology by drawing on archival records and oral histories of the iconic 1968 Olympics in Mexico City. Hartman shows that sport participates in the formation, deformation, and reformation of racial hegemonies. In this sense, sport is both responsive to and constitutive of broader social patterns and power relations.

3. **Ingham, A. G. (1997). Toward a department of physical cultural studies and an end to tribal warfare. In J.-M. Fernandez-Balboa (Ed.),** *Critical*

postmodernism in human movement, physical education, and sport (pp. 157–180). Albany, NY: State University of New York Press.

Alan Ingham provides a broad overview of sport sociology in North America with insight into its history and structural organization. He finds the field to be riven with cleavages and factions. He suggests a physical cultural studies approach as a means to unify a historically disunited field.

4. Messner, M. A. (2002). *Taking the field: Women, men, and sports.* Minneapolis, MN: University of Minnesota Press.

Michael Messner draws upon feminist theory to provide an institutional theory of sport that reveals how gender is a structuring force in contemporary society. He argues that gendered institutions need to be studied at multiple levels: the interactional, the cultural, and the structural. In this way, he reveals power dynamics that operate at both the institutional center and margins of sport.

5. Zimbalist, A. (1999). *Unpaid professionals: Commercialism and conflict in big-time college sports.* Princeton, NJ: Princeton University Press.

Andrew Zimbalist analyzes the political economy of the National Collegiate Athletic Association (NCAA). He shows that the historical development of heavily commercialized collegiate sport ultimately profits off of low-cost, (primarily) working-class, African American labor. The result has been the development of an extremely large, wealthy sport institution that creates market distortions.

REFERENCES

Acosta, R. V., & Carpenter, L. J. (2012). Women in intercollegiate sport: A longitudinal study. Thirty-Five Year Update, 1977–2012. Retrieved from http://webpages.charter.net/womeninsport/AcostaCarpenter2012.pdf

Andrews, D. L. (2001). The fact(s) of Michael Jordan's blackness: Excavating a floating racial signifier. In D. L. Andrews (Ed.), *Michael Jordan, Inc.* (pp. 107–152). Albany, NY: SUNY Press.

Andrews, D. L. (2008). Kinesiology's inconvenient truth and the physical cultural studies imperative. *Quest*, *60*(1), 45–62. doi:10.1080/00336297.2008.10483568

Andrews, D. L., & Giardina, M. D. (2008). Sport without guarantees: Toward a cultural studies that matters. *Cultural Studies < = > Critical Methodologies*, *8*(4), 395–422.

Atkinson, M. (2011). Physical cultural studies [Redux]. *Sociology of Sport Journal*, *28*(1), 135–144.

Baade, R. A., & Dye, R. F. (1990). The impact of stadium and professional sports on metropolitan area development. *Growth and Change*, *21*(2), 1–14.

Baade, R. A., & Sanderson, A. R. (1997). The employment effects of teams and sports facilities. In R. G. Noll & A. Zimbalist (Eds.), *Sports, jobs, and taxes: The economic impact of sports teams and stadiums* (pp. 92–118). Washington, DC: Brookings Institute Press.

Baim, D. V. (1994). *The sports stadium as a municipal investment*. Westport, CT: Greenwood Press.

Beamish, R. (1982). Sport and the logic of capitalism. In H. Cantelon & R. Gruneau (Eds.), *Sport, culture and the modern state* (pp. 141–197). Toronto, ON: University of Toronto Press.

Birrell, S. (1988). Discourses on the gender/sport relationship: From women in sport to gender relations. *Exercise and Sport Sciences Reviews*, *16*, 459–502.

Birrell, S., & Cole, C. L. (1994). *Women, sport, and culture*. Champaign, IL: Human Kinetics.

Birrell, S., & Richter, D. M. (1987). Is a diamond forever?: Feminist transformations of sport. *Women's Studies International Forum*, *10*(4), 395–409.

Brohm, J.-M. (1978). *Sport: A prison of measured time*. London: Ink Links.

Carrington, B. (1998a). Football's coming home, but whose home? And do we want it? Nation, football and the politics of exclusion. In A. Brown (Ed.), *Fanatics! Power, identity and fandom in football* (pp. 101–123). London: Routledge.

Carrington, B. (1998b). Sport, masculinity, and black cultural resistance. *Journal of Sport & Social Issues*, *22*(3), 275–298.

Coakely, J. (1987). Sociology of sport in the United States. *International Review for the Sociology of Sport*, *22*(1), 63–79.

Coakley, J. (1992). Burnout among adolescent athletes: A personal failure or social problem. *Sociology of Sport Journal*, *9*(3), 271–285.

Cole, C. L. (1993). Resisting the canon: Feminist cultural studies, sport, and technologies of the body. *Journal of Sport & Social Issues*, *17*(2), 77–97.

Cole, C. L. (1996). American Jordan: P.L.A.Y., consensus, and punishment. *Sociology of Sport Journal*, *13*(4), 366–397.

Cole, C. L. (2001). Nike's America/America's Michael Jordan. In D. L. Andrews (Ed.), *Michael Jordan, Inc.: Corporate sport, media culture, and late modern America* (pp. 65–103). Albany, NY: SUNY Press.

Cole, C. L., & Hribar, A. (1995). Celebrity feminism: Nike style, post-fordism, transcendence, and consumer power. *Sociology of Sport Journal*, *12*(4), 347–369.

Crosset, T. (1995). *Outsiders in the clubhouse: The world of women's professional golf*. Albany, NY: SUNY Press.

Curry, T. J. (1991). Fraternal bonding in the locker room: A profeminist analysis of talk about competition and women. *Sociology of Sport Journal*, *8*(2), 119–135.

Curry, T. J. (1993). A little pain never hurt anyone: Athletic career socialization and the normalization of sports injury. *Symbolic Interaction*, *16*(3), 273–290.

Curry, T. J. (2000). Booze and bar fights: A journey into the dark side of college athletics. In J. McKay, M. A. Messner, & D. Sabo (Eds.), *Masculinities, gender relations, and sport: Research on men and masculinities* (pp. 162–175). Thousand Oaks, CA: Sage.

Dart, J. (2014). Sports review: A content analysis of the international review for the sociology of sport, the journal of sport and social issues and the sociology of sport journal across 25 years. *International Review for the Sociology of Sport*, *49*(6), 645–668.

Davis, L. R. (1997). *The swimsuit issue and sport: Hegemonic masculinity in sports illustrated.* Albany, NY: State University of New York Press.

Donnelly, P. (2015). Assessing the sociology of sport: On public sociology of sport and research that makes a difference. *International Review for the Sociology of Sport*, *50*(4–5), 419–423.

Dworkin, S. L., & Wachs, F. L. (1998). "Disciplining the body": HIV-positive male athletes, media surveillance, and the policing of sexuality. *Sociology of Sport Journal*, *15*(1), 1–20.

Edwards, H. (1969). *The revolt of the black athlete.* New York, NY: Free Press.

Eizten, S. D. (1987). The sociology of sport: An insider's reaction to an outsider's view. *Sociology of Sport Journal*, *4*(2), 116–119.

Foucault, M. (1984). Nietzsche, genealogy, history (D. F. Bouchard & S. Simon, Trans.). In P. Rabinow (Ed.), *The Foucault reader* (pp. 76–100). New York, NY: Pantheon Books.

Gent, P. (1973). *North Dallas forty.* New York, NY: Morrow.

Giardina, M. D., & Newman, J. I. (2011). What is this "physical" in physical cultural studies? *Sociology of Sport Journal*, *28*(1), 36–63.

Gruneau, R. (1999). *Class, sports, and social development.* Champaign, IL: Human Kinetics.

Hall, M. A. (1972). A 'feminine woman' and an 'athletic woman' as viewed by female participants and non-participants in sport. *British Journal of Physical Education*, *3*(6), xiii–xlvi.

Hall, M. A. (1978). Sport and gender: A feminist perspective on the sociology of sport. Sociology of Sport Monograph Series. Ottawa: CAHPER.

Hall, S. (1986). The problem of ideology-marxism without guarantees. *Journal of Communication Inquiry*, *10*(2), 28–44.

Harris, J. C. (1987). Moving toward sociocultural sport studies. *Sociology of Sport Journal*, *4*(2), 133–136.

Harris, J. C. (2006). Sociology of sport: Expanding horizons in the subdiscipline. *Quest*, *58*(1), 71–91.

Hoch, P. (1972). *Rip off, the big game: The exploitation of sports by the power elite.* Garden City, NY: Doubleday Anchor.

Horne, J., Jary, D., & Tomlinson, A. (Eds.) (1987). *Sport, leisure and social relations.* London: Routledge and Kegan Paul.

Ingham, A. G. (1985). From public issue to personal trouble: Well-being and the fiscal crisis of the state. *Sociology of Sport Journal*, *2*(1), 43–55.

Ingham, A. G., & Donnelly, P. (1997). A sociology of North American sociology of sport: Disunity in unity, 1965 to 1996. *Sociology of Sport Journal*, *14*(4), 362–418.

James, C. L. R. (1983). *Beyond a Boundary.* New York, NY: Pantheon.

Jones, T. (1979). *Life of Brian.* HandMade Films Python (Monty) Pictures, United Kingdom.

Kane, M. J. (1995). Resistance/transformation of the oppositional binary: Exposing sport as a continuum. *Journal of Sport and Social Issues*, *19*, 191–218.

Kane, M. J., & Snyder, E. E. (1989). Sport typing: The social 'containment' of women in sport. *Arena Review*, *13*(2), 77–96.

Kellner, D. (2001). The sports spectacle, Michael Jordan, and Nike: Unholy alliance? In D. L. Andrews (Ed.), *Michael Jordan, Inc.* (pp. 37–63). Albany, NY: SUNY Press.

Kenyon, G. S., & Loy, J. W. (1965). Toward a sociology of sport. *Journal of Health, Physical Education, Recreation*, *36*(5), 24–69.

Loy, J. W., & Elvogue, J. F. (1970). Racial segregation in American sport. *International Review for the Sociology of Sport*, 5(1), 5–24.

Malcolm, D. (2014). The social construction of the sociology of sport: A professional project. *International Review for the Sociology of Sport*, 49(1), 3–21. doi:10.1177/1012690212452362

Martin, R., & Miller, T. (1999). *SportCult*. Minneapolis, MN: University of Minnesota Press.

McDonald, M. G., & Birrell, S. (1999). Reading sport critically: A methodology for interrogating power. *Sociology of Sport Journal*, 16(4), 283–300.

McKay, J., Messner, M. A., & Sabo, D. (2000). *Masculinities, gender relations, and sport*. Thousand Oaks, CA: Sage.

Meggyesy, D. (1971). *Out of their league*. New York, NY: Paperback Library.

Messner, M. A. (1988). Sports and male domination: The female athletic body as contested ideological terrain. *Sociology of Sport Journal*, 5, 197–211.

Messner, M. A. (1992). *Power at play: Sports and the problem of masculinity*. Boston, MA: Beacon Press.

Messner, M. A. (2002). *Taking the field: Women, men, and sports*. Minneapolis, MN: University of Minnesota Press.

Messner, M. A. (2007). Becoming 100 percent straight. In M. S. Kimmel & M. A. Messner (Eds.), *Men's lives* (7th ed., pp. 361–366). Boston, MA: Pearson Allyn and Bacon.

Messner, M. A., Dunbar, M., & Hunt, D. (2000). The televised sports manhood formula. *Journal of Sport & Social Issues*, 24(4), 380–394.

Messner, M. A., & Sabo, D. F. (1990). *Sport, men and the gender order: Critical feminist perspectives*. Champaign, IL: Human Kinetics Publishers.

Miller, T. (2001). *Sportsex*. Philadelphia, PA: Temple University Press.

Miller, T., Lawrence, G. A., McKay, J., & Rowe, D. (2001). *Globalization and sport: Playing the world*. Thousand Oaks, CA: Sage.

Mills, C. W. (1959). *The sociological imagination*. London: Oxford University Press.

Montez de Oca, J. (2008). A cartel in the public interest: NCAA broadcast policy during the early cold war. *American Studies*, 49(3/4), 157–194.

Montez de Oca, J. (2013). *Discipline & indulgence: College football, media, and the American way of life during the cold war*. New Brunswick, NJ: Rutgers University Press.

Nixon, H. L. (2010). Sport sociology, NASSS, and undergraduate education in the United States: A social network perspective for developing the field. *Sociology of Sport Journal*, 27(1), 76–88.

Noll, R. G., & Zimbalist, A. (Eds.). (1997). *Sports, jobs, and taxes: The economic impact of sports teams and stadiums*. Washington, DC: Brookings Institute Press.

Pronger, B. (1990). *The arena of masculinity: Sports, homosexuality, and the meaning of sex* (1st ed.). New York, NY: St. Martin's.

Pronger, B. (1999). Outta my endzone: Sport and the territorial anus. *Journal of Sport and Social Issues*, 23, 373–389.

Rigauer, B. (1981). *Sport and work*. New York, NY: Columbia University Press.

Sabo, D. (2001). Pigskin, patriarchy and pain. In P. S. Rothenberg (Ed.), *Race, class, and gender in the United States: An integrated study* (5th ed., pp. 373–376). New York, NY: W.H. Freeman.

Sabo, D., & Jansen, S. C. (1998). Prometheus unbound: Constructions of masculinity in sports media. In L. A. Wenner (Ed.), *MediaSport: Cultural sensibilities and sport in the media age* (pp. 202–217). New York, NY: Routledge.

Sage, G. H. (1990). *Power and ideology in American sport: A critical perspective*. Champaign, IL: Human Kinetics Publishers.

Sage, G. H. (1997). Physical education, sociology, and sociology of sport: Points of intersection. *Sociology of Sport Journal, 14*(4), 317–339.

Shaw, G. (1972). *Meat on the hoof*. New York, NY: Dell Publishing Co., Inc..

Silk, M. L. (2002). '*Bangsa Malaysia*': Global sport, the city and the mediated refurbishment of local identities. *Media, Culture & Society, 24*(6), 775–794.

Silk, M. L., & Andrews, D. L. (2011). Toward a physical cultural studies. *Sociology of Sport Journal, 28*(1), 4–35.

Stone, G. P. (1981). Sport as a community representation. In G. R. Lüschen, G. H. Sage, & L. Sfeir (Eds.), *Handbook of social science of sport* (pp. 214–245). Champaign, IL: Stipes.

Sykes, H. (1998). Turning the closets inside/out: Towards a queer-feminist theory in women's physical education. *Sociology of Sport Journal, 15*(2), 154–173.

Theberge, N. (1981). A critique of critiques: Radical and feminist writings on sport. *Social Forces, 60*(2), 341–353.

Theberge, N. (1985). Toward a feminist alternative to sport as a male preserve. *Quest, 37*(2), 193–202.

Theberge, N. (1987). Sport and women's empowerment. *Women's Studies International Forum, 10*(4), 387–393.

Trujillo, N. (1991). Hegemonic masculinity on the mound: Media representations of Nolan Ryan and American sports culture. *Critical Studies in Mass Communication, 91*(8), 290–309.

Trujillo, N. (1995). Machines, missiles, and men: Images of the male body on ABC's Monday Night Football. *Sociology of Sport Journal, 12*, 403–423.

United States Education Amendments of 1972. Public Law No. 92-318, 86 Stat. 235 (June 23, 1972). codified at 20 U.S.C. §§ 1681–1688.

Whannel, G. (1993). No room for uncertainty: Gridiron masculinity in North Dallas Forty. In *You Tarzan: Masculinity, movies, men* (pp. 200–211). New York, NY: St Martin's Press.

Whitson, D. (1998). Circuits of promotion: Media, marketing and the globalization of sport. In L. A. Wenner (Ed.), *MediaSport* (pp. 57–72). London: Routledge.

Yiannakis, A., Melnick, M., & Morgan, T. (2015). Sport sociology and the origins of NASSS: The early years, 1955–1980. *NASSS.org*. Retrieved from http://www.nasss.org/wp-content/uploads/2015/07/SportSociology_YiannakisMelnickMorgan.pdf

Zirin, D. (2008). Calling sports sociology off the bench. *Contexts, 7*, 28–31.

SOUTH AMERICA

CHAPTER 21

SOCIOLOGY OF SPORT: ARGENTINA

Raúl Cadaa

ABSTRACT

This chapter analyzes the development of the relationship between the social sciences and sport in Argentina − from its first steps, to the present, and to possible future issues. The description of Arbena (1999) from the last part of twentieth century about the situation of the social sciences and sport in Latin America in general and Argentina in particular could not be more precise:

Latin America has produced little scholarly analysis of sport and society, though information and insights are found in other types of writings, journalistic accounts such as club histories and popular biographies. What has been focused on soccer normally treats only the author's own country, and is rarely available in English. Nowhere does a single author or academic group dominate. (Arbena, 2000, p. 548)

We also make reference to how the anthropologist Eduardo Archetti breaks that mold described by Arbena and how he becomes the undisputed referent in the study of the social sciences and sport in Argentina, and how his immense contribution is recognized in the region. We analyze the present status of this topic, its major changes, the development that the area has undergone so far, and the issues that are being studied today. Moreover, we mention the importance of sociology of sport in the

Sociology of Sport: A Global Subdiscipline in Review
Research in the Sociology of Sport, Volume 9, 379−389
Copyright © 2017 by Emerald Group Publishing Limited
ISSN: 1476-2854/doi:10.1108/S1476-285420160000009027

academic field and its formalization. Finally, this chapter also considers possible future trends in the sociology of sport in Argentina.

Keywords: Latin America; Argentina; Archetti; Arbena; sociology of sport

INTRODUCTION: BREATHING SOCCER
FROM THE BEGINNING

You know that the duty of the conclave was to give a bishop to Rome. It seems that my brother cardinals went almost to the end of the world to get him. But here we are.
Pope Francis (March 13, 2013, First "Urbi et Orbi"
Blessing of the New Holy Father Francis)

The World Cup allowed people from different countries and religions to come together. May sport always promote the culture of encounter.
Pope Francis (July 12, 2014; on Twitter, @Pontifex)

How can we analyze the social sciences and sport from "the end of the world" that the Pope geographically presents? How has this area evolved from that remoteness of the centers of power, of the scientific production, and the predominant linguistics? What is being done today from that geographical, economic remoteness and academic resources? Argentina and the rest of South America breathe soccer. This is observed in any aspect of everyday life in our countries: in the economy, in politics, in society, and of course, in academic matters. On several occasions Pope Francis himself (the first Latin American pope) has referred to sports and soccer, in particular. Before the last football World Cup he met the president of Brazil. Later, Dilma Rousseff, then President of Brazil, told an Argentine reporter covering the Vatican's historic events:

This is a Pope that speaks to the weakest, to the youth, to the elderly and to those who need help. I think he is a pontiff who has the capacity to be moved, that will dedicate (himself) to the poor and he has said that that is his main goal. It is a reason for us Brazilians and for all Latin America to be proud of, but above all it is good for the whole world (*Buenos Aires Herald*, March 20, 2013).

The traditional but friendly rivalry between Argentinians and Brazilians also came to the fore at the Vatican when Dilma Rousseff joked about the nationality of the newly elected Pope.

I consider you (Argentinians) have a lot of luck, you have a great pope. Argentina deserves to be congratulated (for it), but we always say that if the Pope is Argentine, God is Brazilian (*Buenos Aires Herald*, March 20, 2013).

This is also highlighted by Vic Duke and Liz Crolley:

Association football is undoubtedly the leading spectator sport in the world and this role is confirmed throughout most of Latin America. On mainland South America, only in Venezuela is *fútbol* less popular than imported North American sports such as baseball (it is only North American who insist on calling the game soccer in order to distinguish it from their own brand of American football). Notwithstanding the world dominance of the sport, football culture varies markedly according to the economic, social, political and historical characteristics of a society. What is distinctive about Argentina is that sport and politics are inextricably linked. Fútbol is an extension of politics; it is part of the political system and anything that begins as a sports issue rapidly becomes politicised. Historically, there are grounds to claim that *fútbol* is the social model around which the political system has been constructed. (Duke & Crolley, 2002, p. 93, italics in original)

The vision of Joseph Arbena is no different. Arbena has written extensively on social sciences and sport in Latin America, and the same cultural logic can be found here:

Defined as everything in the Western hemisphere south of the United States, Latin America has produced little scholarly analysis of sport and society, though information and insights are found in other types of writings, such as journalistic accounts, club histories and popular biographies. What has been done focused on soccer, normally treats only the author's own country, and is rarely available in English. Nowhere does a single author or academic group dominate. (Arbena, 2000, p. 548)

He also adds the same view from the bibliographic production in Spanish from the mid-twentieth century:

Argentina has contributed several important works to this limited field. Mafud (1967) consider soccer an expression of a people's social character and fears that in modern Argentina the pressure to win is causing soccer to lose its ludic content and popular appeal. Sebreli (1981) finds soccer the product of industrialization and urbanization which create alienated workers who seek identity through sports and are easily manipulated by political leaders. Winning gives way to making money; the game becomes a productive activity, the player a mere factor of production. (Arbena, 2000, p. 548)

Arbena also highlights how dominant topics have been developed in Argentina by Argentinian authors:

Romero (1985) holds that soccer's crisis parallels patterns in the political and economic spheres and regrets the increase in violent fan clubs. Archetti (1985) labels soccer a masculine discourse, carried out in explicitly sexual terms, which moves from verbal to actual violence as insecure groups seek to define and maintain that male identity, and links that image of masculinity to the construction of a national identity (Archetti, 1994). Levinsky (1995) examines the business side of soccer to explain its alleged current crisis, and defends (Levinsky, 1996) the controversial behaviour of soccer star Diego Maradona, both on and off the field, seeing him as a 'rebel with a cause' who fights to correct injustice, and who has been abused and misrepresented for threatening the world's soccer power structure. (Arbena, 2000, p. 548)

Arbena brings what he considers the beginning of the groups formed for the study of social sciences and sport in Argentina:

> Levinsky is also founder of the Argentine Institute of Sport Sociology and director of a university sport sociology program, both too new to allow evaluation of their labors. Also, Alabarces, on the faculty of the University of Buenos Aires, and some colleagues have organized a working group on 'Sport and Society' within the Latin American Council on the Social Science (CLACSO) and are teaching courses and doing research in the sports studies field. In addition, Tulio Guterman has constructed a website for publication of a digital journal, *Lecturas: Educación Física y Deportes* (www.efdeportes. com), dedicated to physical education and sports, mainly but not exclusively in Argentina. Most articles are in Spanish, but most are abstracted in English as well. (Arbena, 2000, p. 548)

FROM THE ORIGINS TO THE PRESENT

While the contributions of Arbena (1989, 1999, 2000) and Duke and Crolley (2002) are important to describe the origins of the study of social sciences and sport in Argentina, we should explore deeply the role of Eduardo Archetti in that period. Archetti breaks that mold described by Arbena and becomes the undisputed referent in the study of social sciences and sport in Argentina. Even today, he fulfills the ideal of what is not reached by the area of study to which we refer. In an original way, Archetti investigated local issues and he also explored theoretical frameworks internationally. He published in different languages, with internationally relevant authors, and he is until today the most important figure in the social sciences and sport in Argentina. In November 2003, the president of the International Sociology of Sport Association (ISSA), Joseph Maguire, visited Buenos Aires. The visit had to do with the future organization of the third World Congress of Sociology of Sport, which finally took place in Argentina in 2005. For the first time in a Latin American country the most important event in the international sociology of sport calendar took place. The keynote speaker of this important congress and event was going to be Eduardo Archetti. The proposal was made during a meeting held at the University of Buenos Aires organized by the Interdisciplinary Area of Sports Studies, a group of researchers at that university, and sponsored by the local British Council. The professor and researcher Jennifer Hargreaves, who was the pioneer of the studies of gender and sport and author of *Sporting Females, Critical Issues in the History and Sociology of Women's Sports* (1994) also participated in that meeting. Archetti answered affirmatively in front of River Plate Stadium, a couple of minutes before the Argentina−Bolivia match for the 2006 FIFA World Cup qualification. Unfortunately, Eduardo "Lali" Archetti died in June 2005, a few months before the ISSA congress.

MAIN AREAS OF RESEARCH AND PUBLICATIONS

In this section, I mention the different areas of investigation developed in Argentina and the publications produced not only locally. I refer to works that have been translated from different languages, and to works in Spanish that were published in other countries.

Undoubtedly, one of the topics that has been explored and that continues to attract local researchers is soccer, and the various aspects that surround it. Identity, violence, and hooliganism are some related topics. This includes the work of Vinnai (1986), Verdú (1980), Sebreli (1981, 1998), Archetti (1985, 1994, 1999, 2001), Lever (1985), Romero (1985, 1994), Scher and Palomino (1988), Frydenberg (2011), Frydenberg and Daskal (2010), Guterman (1996), Veiga (1998, 2002), Bromberger (2001), Gil (1998, 2007), Alabarces (2012, 2014), Alabarces, Di Giano, and Frydenberg (1998), Grabia (2009), Di Giano (2005, 2006, 2007, 2010), Bertelli (2006), Garriga Zucal (2007, 2013), Roffé and Jozami (2010), Godio and Uliana (2011), and Molinari and Martinez (2013).

Throughout the short history of the social sciences and sport in Argentina, topics such as *Peronism*, human rights, politics, and public policies are always present in publications, including those of Galmarini (1992), Gilbert and Vitagliano (1998), Vicente (2000), Cadaa (2006), Llonto (2005), Di Giano (2005, 2006, 2007, 2010), Tulio Guterman (1996), Veiga (2006), Gotta (2008), Frydenberg and Daskal (2010), Alabarces (2012), and Suarez (2015). Moreover, there are published books that are related to leisure, games, and free time, including Lautwein and Sack (1975), Sebreli (1984), Munné (1992); to indigenous issues, including Castellote (1986), Martínez Crovetto (1987); and to disability, namely Cadaa (2006) and Rocha (2012).

Also in Argentina there are many publications related to sport that extend into popular literature − stories, novels, and other genres. Although they are not within the study that is our primary concern, there are important and popular authors to highlight such as Eduardo Galeano, Osvaldo Soriano, Juan Villoro, Jorge Valdano, Roberto Fontanarrosa,

Mario Benedetti, Roberto Santoro, Juan Sasturain, Eduardo Sacheri, and Ariel Scher.

Physical education and education related to sports also show significant publications in the field with authors such as Saraví Riviere (2012), Tedesco (2003), Aisenstein and Scharagrodsky (2006), Scharagrodsky (2008), and Cabrini and Mateo (2015).

Mass media and journalism studies include those of Ricardo Lorenzo "Borocotó" (1951), Panzeri (1967, 1974), Alcoba (1980), Levinsky (2002), Bauso (2013), Alabarces (2014), and Vázquez and Cayón (2014).

Gender studies related to sport is very important, including the works of Morelli (1990), Janson (2008), Archetti (1985, 1994, 1999, 2001), Cadaa (2006), and Braceli (2009). Marketing, public relations, and economy have been studied by Desbordes, Ohl, and Tribou (2001), and Rodríguez (2009).

History and social history is important too, with the works of Scher (1996), Lupo (2004), Fernández Moores (2010), and Ariel Scher, Guillermo Blanco, and Jorge Búsico (2010). Philosophy of sport is one of the areas of social sciences and sport that best represent Argentina; because of the work they do in the country and internationally, Claudio Tamburrini and Cesar Torres are listed here (see, e.g., Tamburrini, 2001; Tännsjö & Tamburrini, 2000; Torres & Campos, 2008; Torres, 2008).

Publications and authors that are more obviously associated with the sociology of sport and analysis of sport are relevant and influential in Argentina: Brohm (1982), Elias and Dunning (1986), Jeu (1988), Thomas, Haumont, and Levet (1988), Barbero (1993), Huizinga (2008), García Ferrando, Puig, and Lagardera (2009), Torres (2008), Sassatelli (2012), Molina (2013), and Signorini (2014).

Institutionally we can say that there were two publications that accompanied the first steps in the social sciences and sport locally. After the founding days of the area, a selection of presented works was published: *Deporte y Sociedad* (Alabarces, Di Giano, & Frydenberg, 1998) and *Estudios sobre Deporte* (Aisenstein, Di Giano, Frydenberg, & Guterman, 2001). Nowadays, this area of study has approximately 100 scholars working on some sport-related topic in less than a dozen groups. In 2015, the Argentinian Sociology of Sport Association (ASSA) was formally created with legal status and it will organize a twice yearly public congress. Rather than focusing exclusively on sociology of sport, the association extends its research to other disciplines including anthropology, history, politics and public policies, economy, education, and social history.

CONCLUSION

The sociology of sport in Argentina has entered a maturing process, but there is still a lot to do. All works should start to consider the theoretical framework and increase accuracy in methodology. We should work on a handbook of sociology of sport of our own with a theoretical perspective. From this point of view, the exchange with professionals of this area in the region could be very helpful. The creation in 2007 of ALESDE (Latin American Association of Sociocultural Studies of Sport) and congresses will help improve the level of Latin American researchers. It is true that there is still a deficit in terms of translated work into other languages such as English, but this corresponds to the lack of resources in our countries as well as other places.

In Argentina, there is also lack of resources with which to buy books, to attend conferences, to research, or to publish our own books. It is practically impossible to make ends meet with a salary of a university professor or researcher – they generally need to have another job. Nevertheless, we are really hopeful, moving forward, always looking back to see how we have progressed. In the 1981, *Handbook of Social Science of Sport* edited by Günther Lüschen and George Sage and the 2000 *Handbook of Sports Studies* edited by Jay Coakley and Eric Dunning we do not find any Latin American authors. Coakley and Dunning now contemplate at least a possibility of that, facing the 2020 edition of their handbook. As we anticipate that future from our perspective as editors of this volume, we wonder about the connection between this present *Handbook of Sports Studies* and the next similar volume that might be published.

If the editors of the 2020 volume are a Latin American woman and a black man from postcolonial Africa, how might they select authors and chapter topics? Might they look back at this volume and wonder about our naivety as editors and ask why we did not select other authors or foresee issues related to sport and the law, sport and the environment, sport and postcolonial development, and other topics that should have been discussed at the turn of the millennium? We expect so. And for the sake of the vitality of our field, we hope so (Coakley & Dunning, 2000, p. xxxv). As Latin Americans, we expect the same and we will work hard for it.

FIVE KEY READINGS

1. **Elias, N., & Dunning, E. (1986).** *Deporte y Ocio en el Proceso de la Civilización*. **México: Fondo de Cultura Económica.**

It is very difficult to find an Argentinian work that does not quote this book. Although it is true that this translation dates back to the 1980s, it is still relevant in local research.

2. **García Ferrando, M., Puig, N., & Lagardera, F. (Eds.) (2009).** *Sociología del deporte.* **Madrid: Alianza Editorial.**

This book is a main reference book for studies of the sociology of sport in Argentina. From a pedagogical point of view, it is very useful as a handbook for university students. It improves its quality significantly with each new edition.

3. **Huizinga, J. (2008).** *Homo Ludens.* **Madrid: Alianza/Emece.**

This book does not lose effectiveness over time. The Dutch historian describes how the game is an essential human function, and how the genesis and development of culture have a playful character. It introduces us to the study of games as a cultural phenomenon.

4. **Torres, C. (2011).** *Gol de media cancha, Conversaciones para disfrutar el deporte plenamente.* **Buenos Aires: Miño & Davila.**

As the subtitle expresses, conversations appear in order to enjoy the game fully. Torres wonders about the values that come into play constantly in sports. The contributions of journalists Ariel Scher and Ezequiel Fernandez Moores, as well as the contribution of the social psychologist, former player, and current coach Facundo Sava, are outstanding.

5. **Thomas, R., Haumont, A., & Levet, J. L. (1988).** *Sociología del Deporte.* **Barcelona: Bellaterra.**

Although this book was published a long time ago, the unique organization of the book helps students to quickly understand the main guidelines of sociology of sport as a study area.

REFERENCES

Aisenstein, A., Di Giano, R., Frydenberg, J., & Guterman, T. (2001). *Estudios sobre deporte.* Buenos Aires: Libros del Rojas.
Aisenstein, A., & Scharagrodsky, P. (2006). *Tras las huellas de la Educación Física escolar Argentina: Cuerpo, género y pedagogía* (pp. 1880–1950). Buenos Aires: Prometeo.

Alabarces, P. (2012). *Crónicas del aguante: futbol, violencia y política.* Buenos Aires: Capital Intelectual.

Alabarces, P. (2014). *Héroes, machos y patriotas: el futbol entre la violencia y los medios.* Buenos Aires: Aguilar.

Alabarces, P., Di Giano, R., & Frydenberg, J. (1998). *Deporte y Sociedad.* Buenos Aires: Eudeba.

Alcoba, A. (1980). *El periodismo deportivo en la sociedad moderna.* Madrid: Minuesa.

Arbena, J. (1989). *An annotated bibliography of Latin American sport: Pre-conquest to the present.* Westport, CT: Greenwood Press.

Arbena, J. (1999). *Latin American sport: An annotated bibliography* (pp. 1988–1998). Westport, CT: Greenwood Press.

Arbena, J. (2000). Latin America. In J. Coakley & E. Dunning (Eds.), (2000). *Handbook of sports studies.* London: Sage.

Archetti, E. (1999). *Masculinities: Football, polo and the tango in Argentina.* Oxford: Berg.

Archetti, E. (2001). *El potrero, la pista y el ring: las patrias del deporte argentino.* Buenos Aires: Fondo de Cultura Económica.

Archetti, E. P. (1985). Fútbol, violencia y afirmación masculina. *Debates en la Sociedad y la Cultura, 2*(3), 38–44.

Archetti, E. P. (1994). Masculinity and football: The formation of national identity in Argentina. In R. Giulianotti & J. Williams (Eds.), *Game without frontiers: Football, identity and modernity* (pp. 225–243). Aldershot: Arena.

Barbero, J. I. (1993). *Materiales de Sociología del Deporte.* Madrid: La Piqueta.

Bauso, M. (2013). *Dirigentes, decencia y wines: obra periodística de Dante Panzeri.* Buenos Aires: Sudamericana.

Bertelli, C. (2006). *La Violencia en el Futbol.* Buenos Aires: Baobad.

Braceli, R. (2009). *Perfume de gol.* Buenos Aires: Planeta.

Brohm, J. M. (1982). *Sociología Política del Deporte.* México: Fondo de Cultura Económica.

Bromberger, C. (2001). *Significación de la pasión popular por los clubes de fútbol.* Buenos Aires: Libros del Rojas.

Cabrini, M., & Mateo, J. J. (2015). *Prohibido Gritar: el valor del deporte en la educación.* Madrid: Turpial.

Cadaa, R. (2006). *Deporte y Discapacidad: socio-política, deporte y legislación.* Buenos Aires: HCD Provincia de Buenos Aires.

Castellote, R. (1986). *Juegos de los Indios Norteamericanos: para jugar en la naturaleza.* Madrid: Miraguano Ediciones.

Coakley, J., & Dunning, E. (Eds.). (2000). *Handbook of sports studies.* London: Sage.

Desbordes, M., Ohl, F., & Tribou, G. (2001). *Estrategias del Marketing Deportivo: análisis del consumo deportivo.* Barcelona: Paidotribo.

Di Giano, R. (2005). *Futbol y cultura política en la Argentina: identidades en crisis.* Buenos Aires: Leviatan.

Di Giano, R. (2006). *El futbol y las transformaciones del peronismo.* Buenos Aires: Leviatan.

Di Giano, R. (2007). *Futbol y discriminación social.* Buenos Aires: Leviatan.

Di Giano, R. (2010). *Futbol, poder y discriminación social.* Buenos Aires: Leviatan.

Duke, V., & Crolley, L. (2002). Fútbol, politicians and the people: Populism and politics in Argentina. In J. A. Mangan & L. P. DaCosta (Eds.), *Sport in Latin American Society, past and present* (pp. 93–116). Abingdon: Frank Cass.

Elias, N., & Dunning, E. (1986). *Deporte y Ocio en el Proceso de la Civilización.* México: Fondo de Cultura Económica.

Fernández Moores, E. (2010). *Breve historia del deporte argentino.* Buenos Aires: El Ateneo.

Frydenberg, J. (2011). *Historia Social del Futbol: del amateurismo a la profesionalización.* Buenos Aires: Siglo Veintiuno.

Frydenberg, J., & Daskal, R. (2010). *Futbol, Historia y Política.* Buenos Aires: Aurelia Rivera.

Galmarini, F. (1992). *Deporte, política y cambio.* Buenos Aires: Corregidor.

García Ferrando, M., Puig, N., & Lagardera, F. (Eds.). (2009). *Sociología del deporte.* Madrid: Alianza Editorial.

Garriga Zucal, J. (2007). *Haciendo amigos a las piñas: violencia y redes sociales de una hinchada de futbol.* Buenos Aires: Prometeo.

Garriga Zucal, J. (2013). *Violencia en el futbol: investigaciones sociales y fracasos políticos.* Buenos Aires: Godot.

Gil, G. J. (1998). *Futbol e identidades locales: dilemas de fundación y conflictos latentes en una ciudad "feliz".* Buenos Aires: Miño y Dávila.

Gil, G. J. (2007). *Hinchas en tránsito: violencia, memoria e identidad en una hinchada de un club del interior.* Mar del Plata: Eudem.

Gilbert, A., & Vitagliano, M. (1998). *El terror y la gloria: la vida, el futbol y la política en la Argentina del Mundial 78.* Buenos Aires: Norma.

Godio, M., & Uliana, S. (2011). *Futbol y sociedad: políticas locales e imaginarios globales.* Buenos Aires: EDUNTREF.

Gotta, R. (2008). *Fuimos Campeones: la dictadura, el mundial 78 y el misterio del 6 a 0 a Perú.* Buenos Aires: Edhasa.

Grabia, G. (2009). *La Doce; la verdadera historia de la barra brava de Boca.* Buenos Aires: Sudamericana.

Guterman, T. (1996). *Educación Física, Informática e Investigación.* Revista Digital.

Hargreaves, J. (1994). *Sporting females: Critical issues in the history and sociology of women's sport.* London: Routledge.

Huizinga, J. (2008). *Homo Ludens.* Madrid: Alianza/Emecé.

Janson, A. (2008). *Se acabó ese juego que te hacia feliz: nuestro futbol femenino (desde su ingreso a la AFA en 1990, hasta el Mundial de Estados Unidos en 2003).* Buenos Aires: Aurelia Rivera.

Jeu, B. (1988). *Análisis del Deporte.* Barcelona: Bellaterra.

Lautwein, T., & Sack, M. (1975). *Deporte y Ocio; el juego en la educación de los hijos.* Barcelona: Fontanella.

Lever, J. (1985). *La Locura por el Futbol.* México: Fondo de Cultura Económica.

Levinsky, S. (1995). *El negocio del fútbol.* Buenos Aires: Edición Corregidor.

Levinsky, S. (1996). *Maradona: rebelde con causa.* Buenos Aires: Ediciones Corregidor.

Levinsky, S. (2002). *El deporte de informar.* Buenos Aires: Paidos.

Llonto, P. (2005). *La vergüenza de todos.* Buenos Aires: Madres de Plaza de Mayo.

Lorenzo, R. (1951). *30 años en el deporte.* Buenos Aires: Atlántida.

Lupo, V. (2004). *Historia política del deporte argentino (1610–2002).* Buenos Aires: Corregidor.

Mafud, J. (1967). *Sociología del Fútbol.* Buenos Aires: Editorial Américalee.

Martínez Crovetto, R. (1987). *Deportes y juegos de los indios Ona, de Tierra del Fuego.* Ushuaia: Cabo de Hornos Ediciones.

Molina, G. (2013). *Sociología del fenómeno deportivo: claves para prácticas responsables, sociales y educativas.* Madrid: ESM.

Molinari, A., & Martinez, R. (2013). *El Fútbol: la conquista popular de una pasión argentina.* Buenos Aires: Editorial de la Cultura Urbana.

Morelli, L. (1990). *Mujeres Deportistas.* Buenos Aires: Planeta.

Munné, F. (1992). *Psicosociología del tiempo libre: un enfoque crítico.* México: Trilla.

Panzeri, D. (1967). *Futbol: dinámica de lo impensado.* Buenos Aires: Paidos.

Panzeri, D. (1974). *Burguesía y gansterismo en el deporte.* Buenos Aires: Libera.

Rocha, M. (2012). *Discapacidad y Deporte: hacia la construcción de lazos sociales.* Buenos Aires: Lugar Editorial.

Rodríguez, M. (2009). *Introducción al Marketing Deportivo.* Buenos Aires: Medrano.

Roffé, M., & Jozami, J. (2010). *Futbol y violencia; miradas y propuestas.* Buenos Aires: Lugar Editorial.

Romero, A. (1985). *Deporte, Violencia y Política (crónica negra 1958–83).* Buenos Aires: Centro Editor de América Latina.

Romero, A. (1994). *Las barras bravas y la contrasociedad deportiva.* Buenos Aires: Centro Editor de América Latina.

Rousseff, D. (2013, March 20). Buenos Aires Herald.com. Retrieved from http://www.buenosairesherald.com/article/126840/dilma-meets-pope-francis-renews-invitation-of-rios-world-youth-day

Saraví Riviere, J. (2012). *Historia de la Educación Física argentina.* Buenos Aires: Libros del Zorzal.

Sassatelli, R. (2012). *Consumo, cultura y sociedad.* Buenos Aires: Amorrortu.

Scharagrodsky, P. (2008). *Gobernar es ejercitar: Fragmentos históricos de la Educación Física en Iberoamérica.* Buenos Aires: Prometeo.

Scher, A. (1996). *La patria deportista: cien años de política y deporte.* Buenos Aires: Planeta.

Scher, A., Blanco, G., & Búsico, J. (2010). *Deporte Nacional: dos siglos de historia.* Buenos Aires: Emecé.

Scher, A., & Palomino, H. (1988). *Fútbol, pasión de multitudes y de elites: Un estudio institucional de la Asociación de Fútbol Argentino (1934–1986).* Buenos Aires: Centro de Investigaciones Sociales sobre el Estado y la Administración.

Sebreli, J. J. (1981). *Futbol y Masas.* Buenos Aires: Galerna.

Sebreli, J. J. (1984). *Mar del Plata, el ocio represivo.* Buenos Aires: Leonardo Buschi.

Sebreli, J. J. (1998). *La era del futbol.* Buenos Aires: Sudamericana.

Signorini, F. (2014). *Futbol, llamado a la rebelión: la deshumanización del deporte.* Buenos Aires: Corregidor.

Suarez, O. (2015). *Los cuerpos del poder: deporte, política y cultura.* Barcelona: Córner.

Tamburrini, C. (2001). *¿La mano de Dios?: una visión distinta del deporte.* Buenos Aires: Ediciones Continente.

Tännsjö, T., & Tamburrini, C. (2000). *Values in sport: elitism, nationalism, gender and the scientific manufacture of winners.* London: E & FN Spon.

Tedesco, J. C. (2003). *Educación y sociedad en la Argentina (1880–1945).* Buenos Aires: Siglo Veintiuno.

Thomas, R., Haumont, A., & Levet, J. L. (1988). *Sociología del Deporte.* Barcelona: Bellaterra.

Torres, C. (2008). *Niñez, deporte y actividad física: reflexiones filosóficas sobre una relación compleja.* Buenos Aires: Miño y Dávila.

Torres, C., & Campos, D. (2008). *La pelota no dobla: ensayos filosóficos en torno al futbol.* Buenos Aires: Libros del Zorzal.

Vázquez, B., & Cayón, D. (2014). *Futbol para todos: la política de los goles.* Buenos Aires: Sudamericana.

Veiga, G. (1998). *Donde manda la patota; barrabravas, poder y política.* Buenos Aires: Agora.

Veiga, G. (2002). *Futbol limpio, negocios turbios.* Buenos Aires: Astralib.

Veiga, G. (2006). *Deporte, desaparecidos y dictadura.* Buenos Aires: Ediciones Al Arco.

Verdú, V. (1980). *El Futbol: Mitos, Ritos y Símbolos.* Madrid: Alianza.

Vicente, N. (2000). *Puntapié inicial; hacia una política deportiva.* Buenos Aires: Galerna.

Vinnai, G. (1986). *El Futbol como Ideología.* México: Siglo Veintiuno.

CHAPTER 22

SOCIOLOGY OF SPORT: BRAZIL

Wanderley Marchi Júnior

ABSTRACT

In this chapter, I aim to present a review on the constitution of the sociology of sport as a subfield in Brazil. To do so, I start with the debate over its history, the current status of this academic area and the factors that led to its development. Additionally, I present the main organizations, funding institutions, and the events that support this field. I briefly identify the main postgraduate programs in the country that enable sociological research in sport, mapping their distribution geographically. Next, I present some introductory works of reference on the sociology of sport in Brazil, as well as discussing some authors that were and are key to the field. I highlight the main topics of interest in Brazilian sociology of sport as well as their methodological models and the main theoretical bases of analysis used by late and early career researchers. In conclusion, I evaluate the comprehension and the representation of sport in society and in the academy, pointing to some future perspectives of development and consolidation of the sociology of sport in Brazil.

Keywords: Sociology of sport; Brazil; history; evaluation; perspectives

Sociology of Sport: A Global Subdiscipline in Review
Research in the Sociology of Sport, Volume 9, 391−404
Copyright © 2017 by Emerald Group Publishing Limited
All rights of reproduction in any form reserved
ISSN: 1476-2854/doi:10.1108/S1476-285420160000009028

INTRODUCTION

Talking about the sociology of sport in Brazil is, to say the least, an intriguing and necessary task — intriguing in the sense of challenging, to revisit authors, publications, and historical moments (moments that built and keep building this field of knowledge), and necessary because after decades of working in this field, it is an occasion for reflection and evaluation.

Irrespective of the characteristics imposed by this analysis, it is important to identify and locate the author's point of view. In my case, this is a voice that reflects a path initiated in physical education and, due to sport studies and experiences, saw the opportunity to pursue scholarly qualification in sociology. My involvement in sociology of sport is a consequence of the questions, reflections, and research around this field of study. That said, we may start a set of reflections and findings based on a scholarly path I started in 1984, and that continues to this day.

THE HISTORY OF SOCIOLOGY OF SPORT IN BRAZIL

The sociology of sport in Brazil may be currently considered as a field of knowledge that has in some ways overcome its initial status of "secondary" academic discipline and is currently heading to a stage of academic recognition and consolidation (Ferreira, 2009, 2014; Marchi Júnior, 2015a; Marchi Júnior & Cavichiolli, 2008; Souza & Marchi Júnior, 2010). This claim points to the fact that we are talking about an area that has not reached enough maturity and density to become a featured discipline in the academic set in general. Slow development obviously happens for specific reasons. One of them is the limited number of courses and programs that include the sociology of sport in their undergraduate and postgraduate levels, for instance. Nevertheless, one may consider the sociology of sport in Brazil as a field that is in a process of expansion and gradually achieving recognition. It has an insertion in a number of universities and professional formation courses, with more frequency in physical education courses than sociology (Lovisolo, 2006; Marchi Júnior, 2015a).

As an academic discipline, the sociology of sport dates from the 1970s in Brazil (Betti, 2001) when some professors in isolated efforts started to bring questions and reflections from the social and human sciences to the attention of physical education undergraduate students. Nonetheless, this process was slow and faced resistance, particularly because the main paradigms of the Brazilian physical education curriculum have always been centered on biological and health sciences (Alabarces, 2012; Gastáldo, 2010; Lovisolo, 2006; Marchi Júnior, 2013, 2015a).

This gradual development of the subfield can be assigned to a set of factors that do not necessarily follow a chronological order. Among the main factors is the possibility of professors' qualifications in areas that differ from exclusive biophysiological areas of knowledge and are instead focused on comprehension of social relationships in different levels of dependency and reflectivity. In other words, what was important was the qualification of higher education teachers in studies of physical education who had theoretical and analytical sympathies with the social and human sciences (Ferreira, 2014; Lovisolo, 2006; Marchi Júnior, 2015a). As such, the insertion of physical education higher education teachers in postgraduate programs in sociology, history, and education, among others, can also be a significant element to the relative growth and development of the area.

Another relevant point is the observance of research topics that became relevant according to historical contexts to the sociocultural studies in sport. For instance, football (soccer) is a topic that marked and continues to mark the production field of development for the sociology of sport in Brazil (Souza & Marchi Júnior, 2010).

We may not dismiss more recent facts that definitely mark the history of Brazil and, as a consequence, Brazilian sociology of sport studies. We refer to the sports mega-events that have taken place in Brazil, such as the 2014 FIFA World Cup and the 2016 Summer Olympic and Paralympic Games in Rio de Janeiro. These events have dramatically altered how to think about, consume, and study sports events, as well as their relationship with society.

Within this context, professors and researchers of human and social sciences and physical education that were studying and analyzing sport gradually sought to organize themselves into institutional, scientific, and representative groups (Alabarces, 2012; Almeida, Marchi Júnior, & Cornejo, 2012; Gastáldo, 2010; Lovisolo, 2006; Marchi Júnior, Sonoda-Nunes, & Almeida, 2008). In the national sphere, I highlight some of the institutions and forums that are the main places for the gathering and debate of Brazilian researchers. First, these include the Brazilian College of Sports Sciences (*Colégio Brasileiro de Ciências do Esporte* — CBCE) and its congress (*Congresso Brasileiro de Ciências do Esporte* — Conbrace). This event is surely the biggest academic event in the area of physical education and sport in Brazil. It is held biannually and is divided into thematic working groups, where we find presentations of research in the sociocultural area of

sport. Another important event that congregates the scientific and academic community in the sociology of sport is the Brazilian Congress of the
History of Sport, Leisure and Physical Education. This congress is also
held biannually, but differs from Conbrace in that its editions are composed by thematic panels and its oral presentations are restricted to the
human and social sciences. Still on the national scale, we highlight additional events and associations that systematically open spaces for the
debate of sport using a sociological approach: the National Association
of Postgraduation and Research in Social Sciences (*Associação Nacional
de Pós-graduação e Pesquisa em Ciências Sociais* – ANPOCS), the
Brazilian Society of Sociology (*Sociedade Brasileira de Sociologia* – SBS),
and the Brazilian Association of Anthropology (*Associação Brasileira de
Antropologia* – ABA).

Internationally, I highlight the Latin American Association for the
Sociocultural Studies in Sport (*Asociación Latinoamericana de Estudios
Socio-culturales del Deporte* – ALESDE) that has been holding its conferences biannually since 2008. At these events, the Latin-American community that studies sport in sociological and in other "human" ways is finding
and constituting a relevant space of insertion and representation (Almeida
et al., 2012; Marchi Júnior et al., 2008).

APPROXIMATE NUMBER OF SCHOLARS AND
WHERE LOCATED

In a huge country such as Brazil, it is very difficult to concentrate the
main researchers – from the sociology of sport or any other academic
field – into study centers per se. Brazilian education politics for public
institutions of higher education tend to promote a diversity within departments, sectors, faculties, and other organizational clusters (Marchi Júnior &
Cavichiolli, 2008).

Researchers and professors on the sociology of sport usually seek to
work in public universities from different states of the federation due to the
supposed better conditions for teaching, researching, and promoting activities and services for society. Public universities also offer job stability after
reaching a determined level and time within the institution.

Additionally, in Brazil, those responsible for the development of the
sociology of sport work mostly in public institutions and are geographically spread throughout the country, but at the same time are concentrated

in the South and Southeast regions. This situation seems different from countries such as Canada, England, France, and Portugal (Marchi Júnior, 2013).

However, there are research groups in the sociology of sport that have national and international significance and representation. For instance, there is the Research Center in Sport, Leisure and Society, from the Universidade Federal do Paraná (UFPR), in the city of Curitiba, where many researchers were formed. This center has produced many publications in the sociology of sport. Other important groups include the Universidade Federal do Rio Grande do Sul (UFRGS), the Universidade Estadual de Campinas (UNICAMP), and the Universidade Federal de Minas Gerais (UFMG). Other research groups exist in the Universidade de São Paulo (USP), with campuses in the cities of São Paulo and Ribeirão Preto, in the Universidade Federal do Rio de Janeiro (UFRJ), in the Universidade Federal do Espírito Santo (UFES), in the Universidade Federal de Santa Catarina (UFSC), and in the Universidade Federal do Pernambuco (UFPE) (Ferreira, 2009, 2014; Ferreira, Vlastuin, Moreira, Medeiros, & Marchi Júnior, 2013).

It is important to mention the existence of a classification system to evaluate the postgraduate programs in Brazil put in place by the Coordination for the Improvement of Higher Education Personnel (CAPES). This federal public system evaluates a set of variables to appoint a grade from 1 to 7 to the whole postgraduation program, and not according to concentration or research areas, as would be the case for the sociology of sport (Ferreira, 2009; Ferreira et al., 2013).

Nonetheless, it is possible to point to some of the main programs and their universities, considering the professors, the level of the publications, and the structure to develop the studies in the sociology of sport. Then, we highlight the postgraduation programs in physical education of the UFPR, UFRGS, and UNICAMP.

THE ACADEMIC ENVIRONMENT AND BARRIERS TO RESEARCH

Sport as a sociological subject can be considered as a recent concern, mainly if we consider its insertion in the academic field. In the initial years of the 1980s, and significantly in the following decades, sport was a secondary and marginalized topic. It did not have the same importance and visibility as other traditional topics in sociology, such as work, economy, politics, among others (Elias & Dunning, 1992; Ferreira, 2009, 2014; Marchi Júnior, 2015a).

Yet, more recently, sport has become part of the mainstream of scientific inquiry, mostly due to the growing interest in this social phenomenon that has expanded worldwide in terms of production and consumption.

In Brazil, this context is very clear when one evaluates the publication of graduate dissertations, theses, and journal articles (Ferreira et al., 2013; Ferreira, 2009). Another fact that supports this argument is the presence of institutional support to fund the development of research projects. The main institutions for funding at the national level are CAPES and the National Council for Scientific and Technological Development (CNPq). At the state level, there are also public foundations that fund and support the development of science and technology, accepting submissions related to the sociology of sport as well.

In terms of infrastructure to develop research in the sociology of sport in Brazil, we can report a rather precarious level in comparison to research centers in North America and Western Europe. Still, this aspect has not blocked the development and the increasing number of studies in the universities, which are mostly supported by public funding.

It is important to highlight the different approaches and/or visions of sport in society in the academic field. Widely, sport is seen by Brazilians as a manifestation of entertainment, both in its practice and consumption. In the academic and scientific field, sport has these aspects, but also a problematic connotation that embraces the working struggles, practices, and social representations derived from these struggles, together with political analysis and proposals of national systems to develop sports in their various dimensions (Marchi Júnior, 2015b).

MAIN AREAS OF RESEARCH STRENGTH IN BRAZIL

The insertion of the sociology of sport into postgraduate courses is key to understanding what has a greater centrality for discussion and study in this area. After the 1980s, academic programs started to incorporate research areas related to the sociocultural studies in sport. This is when we can identify "driving topics" for the development of the subdiscipline.

The first studies that could be classified as "sport sociological" discussed the sports practices of massive acceptance that assumed a demobilizing and alienating profile. In this context, Brazilian football was the topic that received most of the notoriety among the early researchers of human and social science. We should briefly note that the qualification of professors in physical education happened in postgraduate programs of sociology, history, economy, philosophy, anthropology, policy sciences, and others. This incursion presented the topic of sport to other disciplines (Ferreira, 2014; Marchi Júnior, 2015a). In the following decades, other points of view were directed to the complexity of sport and new inquiries began to arise. This is visible when one examines the topics that dominated the research in the field of the sociology of sport in Brazil. In the last decades of the 20th century, the main topics for research were critical aspects of Brazilian football in its constituent aspects (organized supporters) and its structural aspects (sport managers, media, and idol-athletes). Additionally, another topic was the cultural studies of capoeira and its historical-social development in Brazil. In the 21st century, the widened formation and possibilities of international multicultural and methodological exchanges in the sociology of sport was key to bring other topics to the debate. In any case, football is still one of the flagships for sociological research in Brazil. The debate over the processes of commodification and spectacularization in sport in the context of a globalized world gains pace, as well as the politics of investment, funding, and legacy of mega-events. Specific sports receive an analytic historical and sociological treatment based on Eurocentric theories. The insertion of women in sport and its sociological meanings, and the process of social violence derived and inherent to sport are also topics of relevance in the research.

However, the impression is that some topics have not received enough strength and representation in Brazil, particularly when compared to international research. For instance, we cite doping, martial arts, and sports in contact with nature, among other issues. Brazil has been historically remembered for its victories and main figures in football. For this reason, inevitably this is the topic that has more visibility in terms of recognition and international reputation in the sociology of sport. Nevertheless, in national terms, football shares space with emerging topics that are gaining public interest. Once again, this is related to the hosting of mega-events such as the Olympic Games and the FIFA World Cup.

MAIN APPROACHES TAKEN

During this analysis of the field of the sociology of sport in Brazil, I show theoretical flows that have arisen and the main topics studied (Ferreira, 2014;

Ferreira et al., 2013; Marchi Júnior, 2015a). First, studies in sport with a sociological perspective have received strong influence from varieties of Marxist critical theory. From this point of view, sport has been criticized for its demobilizing and alienating condition (Marchi Júnior, 2015a). Also, the formation of researchers in the human and social sciences have been influenced by the theories of culturalism and structuralism. In Brazil, these theories were incisively studied over the theoretical and methodological works by Norbert Elias and Pierre Bourdieu (Marchi Júnior, 2015a).

Souza and Marchi Júnior (2010) presented three streams that characterized the development of the sociology of sport in Brazil, aiming to identify and systematize the historical and analytical trends, without excluding other possibilities. The first stream aggregates the socioanthropological studies of football, which later was represented as the "sociology of football." The second stream includes the scholarly productions of recognized physical education professors from the 1980s that were characterized by a combative, critical, and revolutionary aspect about sport. Finally, the third stream deals with historical and sociological studies of sports, which allowed the inclusion of various possibilities of analysis in comparison to the previous streams (Souza & Marchi Júnior, 2010).

It is important to highlight that this summary is a perspective and interpretation of just one author regarding the production and history of the sociology of sport in Brazil. It is clearly not the only interpretation of this academic subfield. For this reason, we can argue that the theoretical and methodological treatment of sociological studies in sport has its contours and directions in accordance with the Brazilian researchers' area of formation. Then, it is possible to observe in the Brazilian states and their public universities that sport has been studied within the presented streams and through theories that were not observed in the presented classification. For instance, we cite authors analyzing sport through postmodern theories, symbolic interactionism, feminist theories, etc.

KEY CONTRIBUTORS AND KEY PUBLICATIONS

Considering the early development of the sociology of sport in Brazil, we can infer that the bibliographical production is limited in comparison to countries with more robust traditions in the area. Nevertheless, we may say that we have relevant works and authors of reference that have been helping the development and the boosting of new studies, new topics, new research problems and theoretical analysis, as a consequence. It is possible to indicate some important works, but it should be reiterated that these are not the only ones.

A precursor work for the sociology of sport in Brazil was the book titled *Educação Física e Sociologia: Obra Social da Educação Física* (*Physical Education and Sociology: Social Work of Physical Education*) written by Inezil Penna Marinho, published in 1942. As a founding work for the area in Brazil, this book was a milestone. Another foundational work was *Introdução à Sociologia dos Desportos* (*Introduction to the Sociology of Sport*) by João Lyra Filho, published in 1973. In this work, Lyra Filho examined various topics and questions related to sport based on discussions and analysis of the human and social sciences.

Within this set of founding and introductory works in Brazil, we point to the book of Georges Magnane, *Sociologia do Esporte* (*Sociology of Sport*), translated from Portuguese in 1969. There, sport was analyzed as a dimension of daily life, as a leisure activity and a means to transmit and build culture. The book also highlights aspects of the process of sport popularization. Another book in this set is the popular *Carnavais, Malandros e Heróis: Para uma Sociologia do Dilema Brasileiro* (*Carnivals, Rogues and Heroes: An Interpretation of the Brazilian Dilemma*, as the English version of 1991), written by Roberto DaMatta and originally published in 1979. DaMatta opened the academic field to view sport as a sociocultural topic with which to analyze the society.

In the following decades, other Brazilian authors related sport and sociological issues through a definition of the sociology of sport and its analytical relationships with others' fields of knowledge. For instance, we can identify this intent in the work of Mauro Betti and his published articles between 1980 and 1990, where he intended to define what is the sociology of sport and its responsibilities for treating the value and institutional and functional relationships around the sporting field. In 2001, Betti published *Educação Física e Sociologia: Novas e Velhas Questões no Contexto Brasileiro* (*Physical Education and Sociology: New and Old Issues in the Brazilian Context*). This book is a mandatory reference to comprehend the development of the sociology of sport in Brazil.

Another work that can be considered as a basic reading in the sociology of sport in Brazil is *O Que é Sociologia do Esporte* (*What Is the Sociology of Sport?*), written by Ronaldo Helal and published in 1990. In this book, the author intended to define the concept of sport, relating it to, and differentiating it from, play and games, as well as developing an analysis of the classification proposed by Allen Guttmann. Still within the introductory works of the area, we highlight the book *Sociologia Crítica do Esporte* (*Critical Sociology of Sport*), written by Valter Bracht and published in 1997. Bracht proposed a theoretical examination of sport based on schools and authors such as Adorno, Horkheimer, Benjamin, Foucault, Bourdieu, and Marx.

It is important to address the role of professors teaching and researching in postgraduate courses in Brazil during this period. Due to their formation in human and social sciences, they supervised and taught new researchers, developed new studies, and gave a consistent and promising contribution to the knowledge production in the sociology of sport. Among them, we need to identify Ademir Gebara, Lamartine Pereira da Costa, Hugo Lovisolo, Sebastião Votre, Maurício Murad, Henrique Toledo, Simoni Guedes, and Luís Carlos Ribeiro.

In the 21st century, other authors and their publications became important and are indicated to better comprehend the sociological analysis of sport where, by taking a subject or topic related to sport, sociological questions are raised. We highlight the publications in violence and football by Heloísa B. Reis; the historical-sociological analysis in sport by Victor A. Melo, Antonio J. Soares, and Ricardo Lucena; the interpretations of the process of professionalization and globalization of football by Marcelo W. Proni; the debates on the market development and spectacularization of Brazilian volleyball by Wanderley Marchi Júnior; and the correlations of football clubs done by Arlei Damo, among many other authors that could be cited in this setting.

Following these trends, Marchi Júnior and Cavichiolli (2008) presented a brief diagnosis of research in Brazil that summarizes what is expected in the works of the sociology of sport. To do so, the authors searched for the most frequent study topics, most used theoretical references, and the main methodological structures.

Finally, we present more recent academic publications that analyze and allow a comprehension over the development of the sociology of sport in Brazil. For instance, we mention the MA thesis of Ana Letícia Padeski Ferreira titled *O Estado da Arte da Sociologia do Esporte no Brasil: Um Mapeamento da Produção Bibliográfica de 1997 à 2007* (*The State of the Art of the Sociology of Sport in Brazil: Mapping the Bibliographic Production from 1997 to 2007*) from 2009 and her PhD dissertation titled *O Campo Acadêmico-Científico da Sociologia do Esporte no Brasil (1980–2010): Entre a Institucionalização, os Agentes e Sua Produção* (*The Academic-Scientific Field of the Sociology of Sport in Brazil (1980–2010): Institutionalization, Agents and Their Production*) from 2014. We also mention the PhD Dissertation of Juliano Souza from 2014 entitled *O "Esporte das Multidões" no Brasil: Entre o Contexto de Ação Futebolístico e a Negociação Mimética dos Conflitos Sociais (The "Sport of the Crowds" in Brazil: Between Football's Action Context and the Mimetic Negotiations of Social Conflicts)*.

THE FUTURE OF BRAZILIAN SOCIOLOGY OF SPORT

Discussing the future inevitably involves both looking back to the past as well as to the current status of the area. In this sense, we can say that advances have been made both in building a field of knowledge and in establishing an institutional and international recognition in Brazilian sociology of sport.

In the past, we had an incipient condition in terms of asking thoughtful research questions, having a consistent theoretical analysis and a small number of national and international publications. Nowadays, the Brazilian setting involves articles, theses, dissertations, and book publications that are still dependent on Eurocentric and North American approaches, but which are also pointing to a "Brazilian way" of doing the sociology of sport. We are obviously not a comprehensive school of the sociology of sport yet, but we visualize a scenario where the area is consolidated in terms of research and scientific production.

However, it is necessary to highlight some of the barriers, such as the low level of English comprehension and production by a majority of the Brazilian scientific community; the absence of a "general theory of sport," reticence and resistance are still present in scholars that do not fully comprehend or accept the complexity of sport as a topic of study, better conditions of work for intellectuals who have to overcome or propose alternatives to overcome these obstacles while supervising a new generation of researchers in the meantime.

Regardless of these barriers, we believe that the future of the sociology of sport in Brazil and, in a broader sense, all Latin America, is potentially favorable and exciting. This is the case particularly if we consider the work in most parts of the country to reach consistency and coherence on the articulation of the sociological problems in sport and its theoretical-methodological basis of analysis. By all means, if we go forward in this direction, the sociology of sport in Brazil is going to have a promising future.

ACKNOWLEDGMENT

I would like to register my gratitude to Bárbara Schausteck de Almeida for revising and translating this chapter and thank the Editor, Professor Kevin Young for his help with the final version of this chapter.

FIVE KEY READINGS

1. **Almeida, B. S., Marchi Júnior, W., & Cornejo, M. (2012). La Asociación Latinoamericana de Estudios Socioculturales de Deporte [ALESDE]: su trayectoria inicial. In D. L. Q. Roldán (Ed.), *Estudios Socioculturales de Deporte*: desarollos, trânsitos y miradas. Asociación Colombiana de Investigación y Estudios Socioculturales del Deporte – Asciende (pp. 87–91). Armenia: Editorial Kinesis.**

   In this chapter, Almeida, Marchi Júnior, and Cornejo describe the trajectory of the constitution and consolidation of the main Latin-American association responsible for the development of the sociology of sport in the process of internationalization.

2. **Betti, M. (2001). Educação Física e Sociologia: novas e velhas questões no contexto brasileiro. In Y. M. Carvalho & K. Rubio (orgs.). *Educação Física e Ciências Humanas* (pp. 155–169). São Paulo: Hucitec.**

   This book is a selection of chapters in which several authors of physical education and social and human sciences analyze study possibilities in sport. In Betti's chapter, we find a discussion on the context of development and qualification of professors and researchers in the sociology of sport.

3. **Marchi Júnior, W. (2015a). Assessing the sociology of sport: On Brazil and Latin American perspectives. *International Review for the Sociology of Sport*, *50*(4–5), 530–535.**

   In this article, Marchi Júnior traces a historical evaluation of the sociology of sport in Brazil, highlighting its main topics of study, its methodological and theoretical analytical basis, as well as pointing to future perspectives in the field.

4. **Marchi Júnior, W. (2015b). O esporte em "cena": perspectivas históricas e interpretações conceituais para a construção de um Modelo Analítico.** *The Journal of the Latin American Socio-Cultural Studies of Sport/ ALESDE,* **5(1), 46−67.**

In this article, Marchi Júnior focuses on an international review to comprehend and to try to delimitate the concept of sport. Additionally, he proposes an analytical model for studies in sport, according to its features in the modern world.

5. **Souza, J., & Marchi Júnior, W. (2010). Por uma gênese do Campo da Sociologia do esporte: cenários e perspectivas.** *Movimento, 16(2),* **45−70.**

Souza and Marchi Júnior aim to review the constitution of the sociology of sport field in Brazil in this article. They present and delineate historical contexts, trends, and streams of the area, as well as future scenarios.

REFERENCES

Alabarces, P. (2012). Veinte años de ciencias sociales y deportes, diez años después. In D. L. Q. Roldán (Ed.), Estudios Socioculturales de Deporte: desarollos, trânsitos y miradas. *Asociación Colombiana de Investigación y Estudios Socioculturales del Deporte − Asciende* (pp. 119−127). Armenia: Editorial Kinesis.

Almeida, B. S., Marchi Júnior, W., & Cornejo, M. (2012). La Asociación Latinoamericana de Estudios Socioculturales de Deporte [ALESDE]: su trayectoria inicial. In D. L. Q. Roldán (Ed.), Estudios Socioculturales de Deporte: desarollos, trânsitos y miradas. *Asociación Colombiana de Investigación y Estudios Socioculturales del Deporte − Asciende* (pp. 87−91). Armenia: Editorial Kinesis.

Betti, M. (2001). Educação Física e Sociologia: novas e velhas questões no contexto brasileiro. In Y. M. Carvalho & K. Rubio (orgs.), *Educação Física e Ciências Humanas* (pp. 155−169). São Paulo: Hucitec.

DaMatta, R. (1979). Carnavais, malandros e heróis: *para uma sociologia do dilema brasileiro.* Rio de Janeiro: Zahar.

Elias, N., & Dunning, E. (1992). *A busca da excitação.* Lisboa: Difel.

Ferreira, A. L. P. (2009). *O estado da arte da Sociologia do Esporte no Brasil: um mapeamento da produção bibliográfica de 1997 à 2007.* Master's degree thesis, Department of Sociology, Universidade Federal do Paraná.

Ferreira, A. L. P. (2014). *O campo científico-acadêmico da Sociologia do Esporte no Brasil (1980−2010): entre a institucionalização, os agentes e sua produção.* Doctorate dissertation, Department of Sociology, Universidade Federal do Paraná.

Ferreira, A. L. P., Vlastuin, J., Moreira, T. S., Medeiros, C. C. C., & Marchi Júnior, W. (2013). Notas sobre o campo da sociologia do esporte: o dilema da produção científica brasileira entre as ciências humanas e da saúde. *Movimento, 19,* 251−275.

Gastáldo, É. (2010). Estudos Sociais do Esporte: vicissitudes e possibilidades de um campo em formação. *Logos, 17*(2), 6–15.

Lovisolo, H. (2006). Sociologia do Esporte: do iluminismo ao romantismo. *Revista Brasileira de Educação Física e Esporte, 20,* 194–196.

Lyra Filho, J. (1973). *Introdução à sociologia dos desportos.* Rio de Janeiro: Editora e Edições Bloch.

Magnane, G. (1969). *Sociologia do Esporte.* São Paulo: Perspectiva.

Marchi Júnior, W. (2013). Can the north explain the south? American sport sociology and its influence in Brazil. In *The world congress of sociology of sport.* Vancouver, Canada: ISSA.

Marchi Júnior, W. (2015a). Assessing the sociology of sport: On Brazil and Latin American perspectives. *International Review for the Sociology of Sport, 50*(4–5), 530–535.

Marchi Júnior, W. (2015b). O esporte em "cena": perspectivas históricas e interpretações conceituais para a construção de um Modelo Analítico. *The Journal of the Latin American Socio-Cultural Studies of Sport/ALESDE, 5*(1), 46–67.

Marchi Júnior, W., & Cavichiolli, F. R. (2008). Diagnóstico da Sociologia do Esporte no Brasil: para a consolidação de um campo de conhecimento. In M. A. Cornejo & W. Marchi Júnior (Org.), *Estudios y Proyectos en Sociología del Deporte y la Recreación en América Latina* (pp. 102–112). Concepción: Trama Impresores.

Marchi Júnior, W., Sonoda-Nunes, R. J., & Almeida, B. S. (2008). Encontro da Asociación Latinoamericana de Estudios Socioculturales del Deporte, Esporte na América Latina, 1. In Anais: *atualidades e perspectivas.* Curitiba: UFPR.

Marinho, I. P. (1942). Educação física e sociologia: *obra social da educação física.* Rio de Janeiro: Tipografia Batista Souza.

Souza, J. (2014). *O "Esporte das Multidões" no Brasil: entre o contexto de ação futebolístico e a negociação mimética dos conflitos sociais.* Doctorate dissertation, Department of Physical Education, Universidade Federal do Paraná.

Souza, J., & Marchi Júnior, W. (2010). Por uma gênese do Campo da Sociologia do esporte: cenários e perspectivas. *Movimento, 16*(2), 45–70.

CHAPTER 23

SOCIOLOGY OF SPORT: CHILE

Miguel Cornejo Amestica

ABSTRACT

This chapter analyzes the evolution and impact of the sociology of sport in Chile. From a socio-historical perspective and considering the different sociological perspectives used to study national sport phenomena, the sociology of sport remains a relatively new field of study within general sociology. Chile's recent hosting of international conferences, such as the Latin American Association of Sociology (ALAS) and the Latin American Association of Sociocultural Studies in Sports (ALESDE), has catalyzed the field by bringing together researchers and promoting academic collaboration. To date, most research in Chile has focused on soccer. However, changes in Chilean society demand that other social aspects of sport as a socio-cultural phenomenon be studied. In future years, it is expected that the sociology of sport will assume a level of importance equal to that of other fields of social research.

Keywords: Sociology of sport; society; research; sports clubs; Chile

HISTORY OF SOCIOLOGY OF SPORT IN CHILE

The practice of modern sport in Chile can be traced to the arrival of European, particularly British, immigrants to the country's port cities of

Sociology of Sport: A Global Subdiscipline in Review
Research in the Sociology of Sport, Volume 9, 405–419
Copyright © 2017 by Emerald Group Publishing Limited
All rights of reproduction in any form reserved
ISSN: 1476-2854/doi:10.1108/S1476-285420160000009029

Valparaiso and Viña del Mar and, later. Iquique and Talcahuano in the second half of the 19th century. According to Modiano (1997), early sport in Chile was heavily influenced by the class and gender divisions of the time period and was marked by an emulation of European, especially British, culture. Indeed, the first people to play sports in the country were British immigrants, who played cricket, rugby, and paper chase, a British horsera-cing game. These practices were soon adopted by creole elites.

By the late 1800s, other sports, such as football, tennis, and track and field gained popularity. This first stage of "Europeanized" sport develop-ment took place wholly in the upper classes (Modiano, 1997), characterized by social representations, such as that of the "gentleman" and "sports-man," and amateurism as the sole purpose of competition. This social class dynamic also led to the formation of exclusive clubs and social circles dedi-cated to sport.

The lower and middle classes joined the process of sport development in Chile at the end of the 19th century, promoting the cultural incorporation of sport, especially football, into Chilean popular culture. Middle-class sport clubs, often associated with labor unions, appeared at this time and were forms of representing urban or neighborhood identity (Santa Cruz, 1996). The diffusion of sport into popular culture was also marked by the participation of philanthropists from the Chilean elite, who encouraged sport association as a way to promote morality. This association has been largely lost, representing a crisis for Chilean sport (Matus, 2015).

Though sport in Chile developed through cross-cultural social processes in the early 1900s, to social scientists, sport did not represent a subject of study in and of itself until much later. Indeed, studies conducted by the Latin American Social Sciences Institute (FLASCO) in the 1950s that focused on the Chilean population did so from the perspective of social class and social politics and were strongly influenced by liberalism and Marxism.

The presidency of Salvador Allende from 1970 to 1973 was marked by the view that sport was "for everyone" (Cornejo, Matus, & Vargas, 2011). In 1972, Allende, influenced by developments in other socialist countries, explained this motive clearly to the country's sport leaders and implemen-ted a series of sport programs at the national level.

While Allende considered sport to be a socio-cultural phenomenon with considerable impact on the population, during the Pinochet military dicta-torship from 1973 to 1989, sport was employed as a tool of entertainment to divert public attention from the country's political situation. Paradoxically, large sporting events, particularly soccer games, were even-tually utilized as a form of protest against the dictatorship.

As Dunning (2003) suggests, the study of sport as a social science continues to be a subject of limited interest particularly in Chile, despite the importance sociology has afforded political analysis as a means of understanding societal development. Eduardo Santa Cruz describes the limited value social science professionals have assigned the study of sport in his book *Crónica de un Encuentro Fútbol y Cultura Popular* to bewildered academics who, he explains, "[l]ooked at me with distinct expressions oscillating between thinking that I was joking or more mercifully lamenting that I was wasting my time on such a banal topic. The friendliest of them thought it to be quaint. Only a few understood ..." (1991, p. 9).

Interest in studying sport from a socio-cultural perspective in Latin American has been driven primarily by physical education professionals who studied at universities in Brazil and Europe. These professionals came together to create a sociology of sport and society working group (GT 23) at the 22nd Congress of the Latin America Association of Sociology (ALAS) at the Universidad de Concepción in Concepción, Chile, in 1999. This working group, chaired by this author, included five presentations and can be considered to be the formal commencement of the study of the sociology of sport in Chile.

At subsequent conferences, the group has continued to promote collaboration among Latin American scholars, eventually leading to the creation of the Latin American Association of Sociocultural Studies in Sports (ALESDE) during the 26th ALAS Congress in Guadalajara, Mexico. ALESDE's founders, Miguel Cornejo of the Universidad de Concepción and Wanderley Júnior Marchi of the Universidad Estadual de Paraná in Brazil, along with other Latin American researchers, have organized a series of international events promoting academic studies and research related to sport and identifying areas of common interest across the region (Schausteck de Almeida, Marchi, & Cornejo, 2012).

APPROXIMATE NUMBER OF SCHOLARS AND WHERE LOCATED

Most of the studies on the sociology of sport in Chile, and in Latin America, focus on football. The empirical explanation for this is that football is the most popular sport in the country and across Latin America. As conferences have brought together sociology and anthropology students and professors from universities across the region, the subject has been analyzed from a variety of perspectives, allowing for an understanding of the sport not only as a passion but also as one that plays a key role in societal identity.

The emerging interest in analyzing sport from a sociological perspective has led to the creation of working groups rooted in institutions, such as GEOSDE (Group of Olympic and Social Studies of Sport) at the Universidad de Concepción, that seek to reflect on sport and raise awareness in the academic and political spheres about its importance in the development of democratic society. The Chilean Network of Social Studies of Sport, a multi-disciplinary organization including sociologists, anthropologists, and historians, has as its principle objective the dissemination, analysis, and study of sport in the Chilean social context. This group has promoted collaboration among specialists in the field of identity, history, and culture in sports through seminars, talks, and workshops. In 2014, the Observatory of Sports was created at the Universidad de Los Lagos with the primary objective of developing and sharing information on the factors that influence sport with the goal of promoting successful and sustainable public sport policies.

In this context, it is evident that sport is slowly gaining the attention of social scientists. The presence of organizations based at universities as well as of small groups of academics at Chilean universities has allowed sport to begin to take its place in the social as well as political spheres.

THE ACADEMIC ENVIRONMENT AND BARRIERS TO RESEARCH

How is football like God? In the devotion it receives from its believers and the skepticism it receives from intellectuals. Galeano (1999)

The above quotation represents the importance that sport, particularly football, holds in Latin America. Chile is no stranger to this popularity, though some academics have argued that other sports also play an important role in Chilean society.

Sport can be instrumentalized by economic and political actors both as a means of creating industry and as a social tool. Politicians and government officials frequently tout, for example, that sport promotes quality of life, keeps young people away from drugs, and promotes inclusivity and rights. At the same time, UNESCO in its International Charter of Physical Education, Physical Activity, and Sport (2015) has called for "the promotion of access to sports for all, without discrimination," urging those charged with designing, implementing, and evaluating sport programs and policies to base them in a foundation of ethics and quality.

Despite the instrumentalization of sport, research in the field has promoted the upgrading of sport policy and decision-making. A study financed by the Universidad de Concepción titled "Mega-Sporting Events in Chile: The Legacy of the 2014 South America Games in Santiago; Sporting and Social Impact: The Case of the City of Peñalolén" aimed to show the impact of a newly constructed "multi-sport" center on relations among the community members (neighbors, leaders, athletes) in a city with a high level of social vulnerability. Another study financed by the National Fund for the Development of Sports (Fondeporte) of the National Institute for Sports, titled "Municipal Services and Their Impact on Sport Practices and Physical Activity: The Case of the Bio-Bio Region" (Cornejo, Matus, & Tello, 2015) will allow the Ministry of Sports to observe how sports are organized and developed in municipalities. The Chilean government through its Ministry of Sports has also financed organizations to study the supply and demand of sport services. These studies have evaluated, for example, the sporting and physical activity habits of Chileans, the availability of municipal sport services, and sport services for the handicapped population.

Unlike European and some Latin American countries, such as Brazil, the Chilean government has yet to provide the same level of support to social sport research as it does to other sciences through its Science and Technology Commission (CONICYT), which is charged with funding research in Chile, and the National Fund for the Development of Sports (Fondeporte).

A likely reason for this lack of resources is that the field of sport in Chile is still missing the critical mass of researchers capable of producing studies and publications at the level of other sciences. A study by Oliva, Zavala, Marchant, Jorquera, and Díaz (2009) suggests that this lack of high-quality scientific research in the area of physical activity and sport in Chile is due to the relatively low number of doctorates obtained in the discipline. Furthermore, most of these doctorates have been awarded in Europe, particularly Spain, France, and the United Kingdom, and in Brazil.

Despite the slow growth of the discipline in Chile, the Universidad Católica de Maule in Talca has launched a doctoral program in the area of Science of Physical Activity, the first of its kind in the country. It is expected that in the coming years, the increasing number of researchers capable of completing and publishing high-quality research in the field of sport will prompt CONICYT to devote more attention and resources to the discipline, further promoting its development in Chile.

MAIN AREAS OF RESEARCH STRENGTH IN CHILEAN SOCIOLOGY OF SPORT

Football as a subject of study in sociology or in any other social science should not be isolated from its surroundings, and the relationships it shares with the political, economic, cultural, and social spheres as well as the sport itself should be considered (Bourdieu, 1988).

Currently, football is the most popular sport in the world, even more popular than the Olympics (Antezana, 2003). Despite this, there are no clear theoretical frameworks for studying football or sport in Latin America, though it is generally considered to be a communitarian ritual, like a social drama or public arena (Alabarces, 2003). Pablo Alabarces describes this phenomenon in his aptly titled *Fútbol y Academia: Recorrido de un Desencuentro* (*Football and Academica: A Journey of Misunderstanding*), in which he identifies the disconnect between the two spheres not only at the Latin American level but also globally. The author argues that the perspective that has most closely captured the study of football is that of journalism, which is "almost contemporaneous with the origin of sports ... sports and journalism follow similar chronological paths" (Alabarces, 1998, p. 261). Nevertheless, this perspective is merely descriptive, narrating stories and facts, but lacking the abstraction needed to more fully understand the phenomenon of sport.

Specifically in the case of Chile, the most common and productive forms of analyzing football have been anthropological and ethnographic ones, likely because scholars have considered football a cultural phenomenon. The first Latin Americans to study football did so from this perspective. In the 1980s, Da Matta argued that the style with which Brazilians played football was a reflection of Brazilian identity, and Archetti has studied the *ethos* of the Argentinian fans from an anthropological perspective, focusing on their verbal conduct and the construction of masculine identity within the space of the stadium (Alabarces, 2003). Another similar approach has considered the subculture of soccer fans, with an emphasis on their symbolic behaviors and moral codes as reflected in their conduct inside and outside stadiums (Alabarces, 2003; Santa Cruz, 1996).

To Santa Cruz, the study of football should begin with the recognition that it is a cultural phenomenon characterized by complex and multifaceted practices where "the hybrid appears to characterize processes in both form and content" (1996, p. 35), suggesting that the phenomenon is best understood through the notion of cultural appropriation, an active process through which foreign elements are internalized and appropriated by local means or decoded through a system that is distinct to each culture. In this vein, Ovalle and Vidal (2014) utilized historiographic and anthropological methods to analyze football, considering its importance in the development of sport in the lower and middle classes.

MAIN APPROACHES TAKEN

According to Elias and Dunning, "Sport appears to be a leisure activity that holds decisive importance in the context of controlled urban-industrial societies" (cited in Dunning, 2003). Despite this, sociology's interest in sport is relatively recent, perhaps because traditional sociological methods and theories have viewed it as an unconventional field in need of validation. According to Dunning (2003), sport as an object of sociological study can fall into three categories: "as a field of study in and of itself; as a sub-field under the umbrella of 'sociology of leisure'; and as a field included in the framework of one or more traditional subfields" (Dunning, 2003).

Nevertheless, in the Chilean context, research on sport from a sociological perspective is scarce and lacks a clear theoretical framework. Bourdieu (1993) has suggested that there is no way to study sport because it was not considered a serious social problem by the founders of sociology. Despite this, the traditional theoretical approaches used in sociology have also been applied to the study of sport.

Under the structural functionalist perspective, sport is considered an institutionalized game characteristic of a social structure comprised of values, norms, penalties, knowledge, practices, roles, and statuses. Therefore, sport is a reflection of society and its principal function is to socialize individuals. Furthermore, sport is viewed as an open social system to which new practices and meanings can be incorporated.

Centered in cultural and social class, the structuralist perspective maintains that one's disposition toward or choice to participate in sport is molded by the interests of the class to which that person belongs. In this context, sport is stratified socio-economically. For example, the cost and availability of equipment and location limit the accessibility of certain sports, such as snowboarding (Bourdieu, 1993). Through this theoretical perspective, it is possible to analyze the role of social class in the development and current state of Chilean sport.

Bourdieu (1993) reinforces this perspective in his suggestion that modern sport originated in the English public schools where the elite appropriated games from the lower and middle classes but changed their form and meaning. In this vein, other theoretical approaches can be found, including the theory of fields of production, in which sport can be viewed as a field that possesses values and capital (García & Lagardera, 1998). Under this perspective, the practice of sport is not equally distributed by class, and the decision to participate in sport is not only a personal one but also one influenced by structural variables, such as ethnic group, family, cultural capital, ethics, aesthetics, and obviously economic capital (Bourdieu, 1993).

Another perspective, symbolic interactionism, has approached the analysis of sport through a methodological vein that is more than interpretive and that aims to study the meanings and values of sport for different social groups. In other words, this approach aims to elucidate the subjective meaning of social action in the field of sport (García & Lagardera, 1998). Another distinct view is that of the figurational perspective, which emphasizes the civilizing process of sport and its role in reducing violence.

As shown by this variety of perspectives, sport is an area of study of sociology that is still nebulous and diverse. Accordingly, it is impossible for theorists and institutions to accept a single definition of sport. The examination of sport is a "no man's land," a multi-dimensional and multi-disciplinary phenomenon in which sociology, psychology, medicine, history, and a number of other disciplines each leave a distinct imprint. Though not encompassing a single approach, sociology has nevertheless been forced to define and delve into the role that sport plays in society.

From a figurationalist perspective, it seems obvious to consider the role that fun plays in sports, but it allows for flexibility in norms, as individuals, by letting go of emotional controls, experience intense emotional experiences that are safe or relatively safe (Dunning, 2003). Brohm (1993) more specifically identified certain ideological functions of sport, such as legitimizing social order, as sport is generally not anti-establishment. On the other hand, sport also tends to integrate people. This function is supported by an ideology that emphasizes uninterrupted linear progress. Sport also reinforces the system of idol creation, providing an illusion of social mobility, and can be seen as a form of preparation for industrial work, as it promotes the principles of performance and productivity and implants a logic of effort and specialization, all of which is presented in a form that is politically neutral.

KEY CONTRIBUTORS AND KEY PUBLICATIONS

Continuing analysis of the sociology of sport centers around, on the one hand, the early studies of the sociology of sport completed in Chile and, on the other hand, two issues that have raised interest: the level of research and the structure and functionality of the scientific and academic communities.

Another issue of interest is how the theoretical perspectives and methodologies employed by sociology can be used to delimit the study of sport and establish values regarding the principal approaches to the discipline. For some sociologists, the study of sport from a sociological perspective, like that of other social fields, is characterized by theoretical and methodological pluralism that reflects the dynamic and complex character of sport (Bourdieu & Coleman, 1991; Gines, 2003). The advances achieved in the study of the sociology of sport from the functionalist, Marxist, figurational, structuralist, feminist, and symbolic interactionist perspectives have allowed for diverse sociological perspectives on sport as a social phenomenon.

In this analytical context, the contributions of the functionalist perspective allow us to analyze sport as an organic phenomenon that reproduces and reinforces the current social model (through the norms, values, penalties, stratification, etc., that are characteristic of sport systems) and that promotes social order through integrative and socializing functions. Examples of studies employing this approach include those of Recasens (1999) on the Chilean *barras bravas* (sporting fan clubs), Diego Valdebenito Véliz's work on the critical analysis of the sport model through the lens of comparative rights (2013), and Matus's (2015) thesis, *The State of Chilean Sports Clubs: The Case of the Bio-Bio Region* (University of Barcelona).

The studies from the perspective of institutions (functionalists) have in particular promoted the interpretation of sport as a complex and diverse field of analysis. The work of Recasens, an anthropologist, on *barras bravas*, for example, attempts to identify the factors that lead to violence before, during, and after professional football games in Chile. Recasens' study focuses on two fan clubs in particular: *Los de Abajo* (Those from Below), who support the Universidad de Chile team, and *La Garra Blanca* (The White Claw), who support the Colo-Colo team. These fan clubs represent the two most important professional football teams in Chile. The phenomenon of violence in these clubs was observed *desde dentro* (from within); therefore, the information studied comes from and represents the experiences and perceptions of the members themselves.

These experiences show that violence is legitimized by stories and myths, as well as by a language and dramatization constructed within the club. It is the stadium where the feelings, passions, and loyalties are released; where a cultural identity and brotherhood is constructed; and where the warm embrace of the group is felt. Recasens' study allows us to understand that the actions and feelings of club members extend beyond a simple football game, and represent the sense of social discrimination and vulnerability shared by a young person and their peers in this particular space.

The work of Valdebenito sheds light on the organization of sport at the national level, considering the basic elements and structures that form a model of sport and observing how these elements work together to promote the development of sport in all of its spheres. Focusing on the contributions and roles of the state and public system (through the Ministry of Sport and the National Institute of Sport), and of the private system (through sport federations, associations, and clubs), Valdebenito exposes the difficulties faced by both systems in the development of sport and physical activity at the national level.

The work of Matus focuses on the sport organizations at a more local level, in the context of the voluntary sport "clubs" of the Bio-Bio region of Chile. This research has deepened our knowledge of these types of organizations, which play a key role in supporting sport and physical activity in Chile by channeling the necessities and interests of the population through democratic processes of personal and collective development.

In this theoretical environment, a multi-dimensional model has been developed that considers these clubs from an external-to-internal and general-to-specific perspective, from the perspective of society and its organizations before to the characteristics of each particular club. This model is supported by third sector, institutional choice and stakeholder theories, and it considers the legal and administrative dynamics that define the clubs at a macro level. From the perspective of the sociology of organizations, this analysis suggests that Chilean sport clubs are currently in a stage of emerging associationism or in a stage of development driven by organizational trajectory. Furthermore, it demonstrates the considerable diversity of organizations, making it clear that there is no one type of sport club in Chile.

Disputing the stabilizing force of sport, the Marxist perspective maintains a more critical posture informed by the view that sport maintains the domination of certain classes over others by contributing to the moral acquiescence of the masses.

Another distinct vision is that of the figurational perspective, which emphasizes the civilizing function of sports. According to this view, sport is a mediating element between the individual and society and has contributed to reduced violence. In this context, studies analyzing *barras bravas*, particularly of the Chilean national football clubs of Colo-Colo and Universidad de Chile, expose how the country's socio-economic model (neo-liberalism) has had a large impact on its society (Recasens, 1999; Santa Cruz, 1996).

It is also necessary to consider the contribution of the structuralist perspective, which has brought to light mechanisms that influence the individual choices of people to participate in sports. According to this perspective, social class is decisive, as social and cultural factors make us choose sport practices that match the likes and interests of the groups to which we belong.

Another perspective that differs from the aforementioned is symbolic interactionism, which instead of focusing on the structural relations of individuals, explores the subjective meaning of social action. Some of the principal objectives of studying sports from this perspective are the understanding of social meaning and emotions in sports. In this way, "sports occupy a distinct significance according to different groups of people, particularly if these groups correspond to different cultural patterns" (Cornejo, 2015).

Despite the weight of these theoretical perspectives, it is not possible to carry out a comparable analysis in Chile. Given the state of knowledge creation in Chile in this area, at this time, we should limit our focus to weighing the different approaches, starting with the following topics that have drawn the interest of scholars, such as (1) the meaning of sport, (2) the social structure of sport (habits, behaviors, and attitudes), (3) sport as an element of socialization or in the scope of physical education, (4) the organizing system and marketing of sport, and (5) the sport system from the perspective of sociology of organizations, which was described in Miguel Cornejo's doctoral thesis (1998), shedding light on the Chilean sport system through scientific analysis.

THE FUTURE

The analysis and state of sociology of sport in Chile merits at least a short reflection on what can be expected in the future. As mentioned, sociology of sport has its roots in the sociology of sport and society working group created at the ALAS Congress in Concepción, Chile, in 1999. In its first iteration, there were few studies, and the majority focused on football. Given the conditions under which the sociology of sport has developed and the academic and scientific weaknesses that characterize the study, the most common studies have been those conducted on football from the perspective of sociological theories, including studies by Santa Cruz (1996), Guerrero (1992), Herrera and Varas (2008), and Ovalle and Vidal (2014), and the contributions of the Nucleus of Studies of Football at the Universidad de Valparaiso.

In the future, it is expected that new organizations such as the Social Network of Sports and the Observatory of Chilean Sports along with existing organizations will explore new lines of research on topics such as violence in sports, doping and its social impact, and the impact of urban practices particularly in young people. Sport is a phenomenon that is increasingly complex, particularly in light of changing interests and demands of populations. Therefore, a form of study that is increasingly empirical, that uses advanced methodological approaches, and that innovates on the frameworks of contemporary academic sociology is needed.

Also fundamental to the better positioning the study of sociology of sport in Chile are the following: greater participation in academic congresses organized by the international associations of sociology of sport, an increase in the number of publications in international journals of sociology of sport, and the integration of the sociology of sport and society ALAS working group with the Latin American Association of Social Studies of Sports (ALESDE). Behind this consolidation should be a stage of projection and cooperation in the academic community, signaling that sport represents an object of study as important as other social fields.

FIVE KEY READINGS

1. **Cornejo, M. (2015). On Alesde and research development in Latin America,** *International Review for the Sociology of Sport*, **Vol. 50 (4–5), pp. 407–412.**

This article offers an analysis of the sociology of sport in Latin America, the evolution of research, and the creation of the Latin American Association of Sociocultural Studies in Sport (ASLESDE). The objective is to create a space for the study of sociology of sport in Latin America.

2. **Recasens, A. (1999).** *Diagnóstico Antropológico de las Barras Bravas y de la Violencia Ligada al Fútbol.* **Facultad de Ciencias Sociales Universidad de Chile. Electronic Books.**

Recasens' book is the result of an anthropological investigation aimed at detecting the factors that incite the violence before, during, and after professional football games in Chile. The study focuses primarily on two *barras bravas* (fan clubs): *Los de Abajo* (those from below), who support the Universidad de Chile team, and *La Garra Blanca*, who support the Colo-Colo team. This work allows for an observation of the characteristics and actors involved, their problems, and how they contribute to violence. These questions reveal the issue to be a latent one.

3. **Olivos, F. (2009).** **"América Latina en juego una aproximación a la sociología del deporte."** *Revista doble Vincula Pensar Latinoamericano,* **No. 1, Year 1.**

This article by Olivas offers an approximation of the sociology of sport as a tool of intellectual analysis that allows social science researchers to consider sport as a field of study. Furthermore, this study explains three of the principle theoretical approaches utilized in the field: figurational, Bourdieusian, and Marxist. Finally, it argues that Chile can be considered a "footballized" country and explores the importance that football plays in the construction of a continent-level identity.

4. **Ovalle, A., & Vidal, J. (2014).** *Pelota de Trapo, Fútbol y deporte en la historia popular,* **Editorial Quimantú Santiago**

This book by Ovalle and Vidal presents an excellent relational analysis between sport, particularly football, and civil society, as well as the relation between the history of football and politics and the role of the neighborhood sport club as an actor in the creation of social and popular spaces. This book also demonstrates how football has been transformed into a social and cultural phenomenon in Chilean society. Interestingly, it was published by the Quimantú Press, which was established by Salvador Allende's government with the goal of promoting public literacy. During the military dictatorship, this press was eliminated, but it has since been revived and has published this interesting book.

5. **Sandoval, P., & García, I. (2014). Cultura deportiva en Chile: desarrollo histórico, institucionalidad actual e implicancias para la política pública, Polis,** *Revista Latinoamericana,* *13*(39), 441−462.

This article by Sandoval and Garcia analyzes the culture of sport in Chile, which despite being discussed in academic circles continues to lack conceptual concordance. This discussion begins with the citizenry's participation in the practice of physical activity and the recreational concept of sport in the national culture, and concludes that the institutional expression of the national culture of sport reproduces a conception of sport as a phenomenon with a logical order, which helps explain the existence of high rates of sedentary lifestyle in the country and other related problems.

REFERENCES

Alabarces, P. (1998). ¿De qué hablamos cuando hablamos de deporte? *Nueva Sociedad*, *154*, 74−86.

Alabarces, P. (2003). *Futbologías. Fútbol, identidad y violencia en América Latina*. Buenos Aires: CLACSO.

Antezana, L. (2003). Fútbol: Espectáculo e identidad. In E. P. Alabarces (Ed.), *Futbologías. Fútbol, identidad y violencia en América Latina* (pp. 85−98). Buenos Aires: CLACSO.

Bourdieu, P. (1988). Programa para una sociología del deporte. In *En pierre bourdieu cosas dichas* (pp. 173−184, Trad. Margarita Mizraji). Barcelona: Gedisa.

Bourdieu, P. (1993). Deporte y clase social. In E. J. Barbero (Ed.), *Materiales sociología del deporte*. Madrid: La Piqueta.

Bourdieu, P., & Coleman, J. S. (Eds.). (Coord.) (1991). *Social theory for a changing society, boulder*. New York, NY: Westview Press Russel Sage Foundation.

Brohm, J. M. (1993). Tesis sobre el deporte. In E. J. Barbero (Ed.), *Materiales sociología del deporte*. Madrid: La Piqueta.

Cornejo, M. (1998). Les acteurs institutionnels du sport a CONCEPCION (CHILI). Thèse Doctorat, Université Joseph Fourier Grenoble France.

Cornejo, M. (2015). On alesde and research development in Latin America. *International Review for the Sociology of Sport*, *50*(4−5), 407−412.

Cornejo, M., Matus, C., & Tello, D. (2015). *Los servicios deportivos municipales y su impacto en las prácticas deportivas y de actividad Física*. El Caso de la Región del Biobío. Proyecto n° 1500120009, Financiado por el Fondo Nacional del Deporte. Cs. Del Deporte. Chile.

Cornejo, M., Matus, C., & Vargas, C. (2011). La educación física en chile una aproximación histórica, *revista digital EF*. Deportes.com Bs. Aires Argentina, n° 161 año 16.

Dunning, E. (2003). *El Fenómeno deportivo, estudios sociológicos en torno al deporte, la violencia y la civilización*. Editorial Paidotribo.

Galeano, E. (1999). *El fútbol a sol y sombra* (3ª reimp). Santiago: Editorial Pehúen.

García, M., & Lagardera, F. (1998). *Sociología del Deporte*. Ciencias Sociales Editorial Alianza.

Gines, S. (2003). *Teoría Sociológica Moderna*, Barcelona Ariel.

Guerrero, E. (1992). *El Libro de los campeones*. Iquique Ediciones el Jote Errante.

Herrera, R., & Varas, J. (2008). *Fútbol, cultura y sociedad*. Santiago: Universidad Academia de Humanismo Cristiano.

Matus, C. (2015). *La situación de los clubes deportivos chilenos. El caso de la región del Biobío.* Doctoral Thesis, Universidad de Barcelona.

Modiano, P. (1997). *Historia del deporte en chileno, orígenes y transformaciones 1850−1950.* Ediciones Digeder.

Oliva, C., Zavala, M., Marchant, F., Jorquera, P., & Díaz, C. (2009). El estado del arte en educación física: Un análisis epistemológico de la investigación en Chile. *Revista Ciencias de la Actividad Física, 17*(34), 57−70.

Ovalle, A., & Vidal, J. (2014). *Pelota de trapo, fútbol y deporte en la historia popular.* Santiago: Editorial Quimantú.

Recasens, A. (1999). *Diagnóstico antropológico de las barras bravas y de la violencia ligada al fútbol.* Facultad de Ciencias Sociales Universidad de Chile.

Santa Cruz, E. (1991). *Crónica de un encuentro fútbol y cultura popular.* Ediciones Instituto Profesional Arcos.

Santa Cruz, E. (1996). *Origen y futuro de una pasión.* Editorial LOM.

Schausteck de Almeida, B., Marchi, W., & Cornejo, M. (2012). *La asociación latinoamericana de estudios socioculturales del deporte ALESDE: Su trayectoria inicial, in estudios socioculturales del deporte.* Compilador David Quitían, Editorial Kinesis.

UNESCO. (2015). *Carta Internacional de la Educación Física y el Deporte.* Conferencia Paris, Francia, Noviembre 11.

Valdebenito, D. (2013). *Análisis crítico del modelo deportivo nacional (chileno) a la luz del derecho comparado,* licenciado en Ciencias Jurídicas y Sociales. Universidad de Chile.